Richard Glazebrook

Heat and Light

An elementary text-book theoretical and practical for schools and colleges

Richard Glazebrook

Heat and Light

An elementary text-book theoretical and practical for schools and colleges

ISBN/EAN: 9783337105723

Printed in Europe, USA, Canada, Australia, Japan

Cover: Foto ©Paul-Georg Meister /pixelio.de

More available books at **www.hansebooks.com**

CAMBRIDGE NATURAL SCIENCE MANUALS
Physical Series.

HEAT AND LIGHT

AN ELEMENTARY TEXT-BOOK
THEORETICAL AND PRACTICAL

FOR COLLEGES AND SCHOOLS

BY

R. T. GLAZEBROOK, M.A., F.R.S.
ASSISTANT DIRECTOR OF THE CAVENDISH LABORATORY,
FELLOW OF TRINITY COLLEGE, CAMBRIDGE.

STEREOTYPED EDITION.

CAMBRIDGE:
AT THE UNIVERSITY PRESS.
1897

[*All Rights reserved.*]

Cambridge:
PRINTED BY J. & C. F. CLAY,
AT THE UNIVERSITY PRESS.

PREFACE.

IT has now come to be generally recognised that the most satisfactory method of teaching the Natural Sciences is by experiments which can be performed by the learners themselves. In consequence many teachers have arranged for their pupils courses of practical instruction designed to illustrate the fundamental principles of the subject they teach. The portions of the following book designated EXPERIMENTS have for the most part been in use for some time as a Practical Course for Medical Students at the Cavendish Laboratory.

The rest of the book contains the explanation of the theory of those experiments, and an account of the deductions from them; these have formed my lectures to the same class. It has been my object in the lectures to avoid elaborate apparatus and to make the whole as simple as possible. Most of the lecture experiments are performed with the apparatus which is afterwards used by the class, and whenever it can be done the theoretical consequences are deduced from the results of these experiments.

In order to deal with classes of considerable size it is necessary to multiply the apparatus to a large extent. The students usually work in pairs and each pair has a separate table. On this table are placed all the apparatus for the experiments which are to be performed. Thus for a class of 20 there would be 10 tables and 10 specimens of each of the pieces of apparatus. With some of the more elaborate experiments this plan is not possible. For them the class is taken in groups of five or six, the demonstrator in charge performs the necessary operations and makes the observations, the class work out the results for themselves.

It is with the hope of extending some such system as this in Colleges and Schools that I have undertaken the publication of the present book and others which are to follow. My own experience has shewn the advantages of such a plan, and I know that that experience is shared by other teachers. The practical work interests the student. The apparatus required is simple; much of it might be made with a little assistance by the pupils themselves. Any good-sized room will serve as the Laboratory. Gas should be laid on to each table, and there should be a convenient water supply accessible; no other special preparation is necessary.

The plan of the book will, I hope, be sufficiently clear; the subject-matter of the various Sections is indicated by the headings in Clarendon type; the Experiments to be performed by the pupils are shewn thus:

EXPERIMENT (1). *To illustrate the Rectilinear Propagation of Light by the pinhole Camera.*

These are numbered consecutively. Occasionally an account of additional experiments, to be performed with the same apparatus, is added in small type. Besides this the small-type articles contain some numerical examples worked out, and, in many cases, a notice of the principal sources of error in the experiments, with indications of the method of making the necessary corrections. These latter portions may often with advantage be omitted on first reading. A few articles of a more advanced character, which may also at first be omitted, are marked with an asterisk.

A book which has grown out of the notes in general use in a laboratory is necessarily a composite production. I have specially to thank Mr Wilberforce and Mr Fitzpatrick for their help in arranging many of the experiments. Mr Fitzpatrick has also given me very valuable assistance by reading the proofs and suggesting numerous improvements. The illustrations have for the most part been drawn from the apparatus used in the class by Mr Hayles, the Lecture Room Assistant, and Mr E. Wilson.

R. T. GLAZEBROOK.

CAVENDISH LABORATORY,
January 1, 1894.

CONTENTS.

HEAT.

CHAP.   PAGE

I. HEAT AND ENERGY 1
    Nature of Heat, Relation between Heat and Energy, Conservation of Energy.

II. TEMPERATURE AND ITS MEASUREMENT . . . 7
    Effects of Heat on Bodies, Temperature, Thermometers, Scales of Temperature, Sources of Heat.

III. THERMOMETERS 17
    Construction of a Thermometer. The fixed points. Air Thermometers, Maximum and Minimum Thermometers.

IV. CALORIMETRY. THE MEASUREMENT OF A QUANTITY OF HEAT 29
    Heat a Quantity, Specific Heat, Capacity for Heat, Latent Heat, Ice Calorimeters, Special Forms of Calorimeters.

V. EXPANSION OF SOLIDS 53
    Coefficients of Expansion, Measurement of Expansion, Practical consequences of Expansion.

VI. DILATATION OF LIQUIDS 74
    Absolute and Relative Dilatation, Measurement of Coefficient of Dilatation, Weight Thermometer, Absolute Dilatation of Mercury, Dilatation of Water.

CHAP.		PAGE
VII.	DILATATION OF GASES	96

Boyle's Law, Charles' Law, Air Thermometer, Absolute Temperature.

VIII.	CHANGE OF STATE, SOLID TO LIQUID	116

Fusion of a Solid, Melting point, Change of Volume, Freezing Mixtures, Laws of Fusion.

IX.	CHANGE OF STATE, LIQUID TO VAPOUR	123

Evaporation, Vapour-pressure, Dalton's Laws, Vapours and Gases, Critical Temperature, Boiling, Connection between Boiling-point and Pressure, Hypsometry, Heat needed for Evaporation, Cryophorus, Freezing Machines, Hygrometry, Dew-point, Hygrometers.

X.	THE TRANSMISSION OF HEAT BY CONDUCTION	160

Conduction, Convection and Radiation, Experiments on Conduction, Thermal Conductivity, Practical Effects of Conduction.

XI.	THE TRANSMISSION OF HEAT BY CONVECTION	173

Convection Currents, Hot-water heating Apparatus, Ventilation, Trade-Winds, Ocean Currents.

XII.	THE TRANSMISSION OF HEAT BY RADIATION	178

Radiant Energy, The Thermopile, Transmission, Reflection and Refraction of Radiation, Diathermanous and Adiathermanous Substances, Intensity of Radiation, Radiating Power, Rectilinear Propagation, Law of the Inverse Square, Absorption, Emission and Reflection of Radiation, Law of Cooling, Prevost's Theory of Exchanges.

XIII.	THE MECHANICAL EQUIVALENT OF HEAT	211

Joule's Experiments, Work done during Expansion of a Gas, Mayer's Experiments.

CONTENTS.

LIGHT.

CHAP.   PAGE

I. VISIBLE RADIANT ENERGY—LIGHT 3
   Nature of Light, Luminous Bodies, Rays of Light, Rectilinear Propagation, Shadows, Intensity of Illumination, Law of Inverse Square, Photometry.

II. VELOCITY OF LIGHT 21
    Römer's observations, Aberration, Fizeau's method, Foucault's method.

III. REFLEXION OF LIGHT 30
     Laws of Reflexion, Images, Reflexion at a plane mirror, Multiple Reflexions, The Kaleidoscope.

IV. REFRACTION AT PLANE SURFACES 49
    Simple Experiments on Refraction, Laws of Refraction, Refractive Index, Total Reflexion, Critical Angle, Refraction through a plate, Refraction through a prism, Measurement of Refractive Index, Images formed by Refraction.

V. REFLEXION AT SPHERICAL SURFACES . . . 84
   Experiments with Mirrors, Principal Focus, Focal Length, Geometrical Foci, Formulae connected with Mirrors, Magnifying Power, Methods of Calculation, Images seen by reflexion in a Mirror.

CONTENTS.

CHAP.		PAGE
VI.	LENSES	109

Refraction at Spherical Surfaces, Experiments with Lenses, Forms of Lenses, Images formed by a lens, Formulae connected with Lenses, Vision through a Lens.

VII. OPTICAL INSTRUMENTS. THE EYE; VISION . . 139

The Optical Lantern, The Camera, The Eye, Experiments on Vision, Defects of Vision, Spectacles.

VIII. AIDS TO VISION 156

Simple Microscopes, Telescopes, The Compound Microscope, The Sextant, The Spectrometer, The Ophthalmoscope, Experiments on Vision through Lenses.

IX. THE SPECTRUM. COLOUR 178

Experiments with a Prism, Dispersion, The pure Spectrum, Dispersion in Lenses, Spectrum Analysis, Absorption Spectra, The Solar Spectrum, Colours of bodies, Colour Sensation, Colour Blindness.

HEAT.

CHAPTER I.

HEAT AND ENERGY.

1. The Nature of Heat. When we stand in the sunshine or in front of the fire it feels hot. If we take hold of some ice or snow it feels cold. Heat is the name given to the cause of these and the like sensations. In the first case heat enters our body, in the second it leaves it and our sensations make us aware of its transference. What then is the Nature of Heat?

This question can be more fully answered when we have studied some of the effects which Heat causes and some of the methods by which Heat can be produced. We shall then be able to appreciate the meaning of the statement that,

Heat is one of the forms in which Energy becomes known to us.

We will however at once consider this statement a little more in detail.

2. Work and Energy. If a body, under the action of a force, moves in the direction in which the force acts, work is done on the body.

Thus, when a man lifts a weight, he applies force to it and does work; when a cannon ball penetrates a target it exerts force on the target, and does work, being itself stopped in the process.

The capacity that a body or system of bodies has for doing work is called Energy.

Thus the statement that heat is one of the forms of energy implies that heat is one form which the capacity of a body for doing work may take.

Now a body may have Energy because of its position relative to other bodies and of the forces which act on it. Energy in this form is called Potential; a stone at the top of a cliff, the weight of a clock which has just been wound up, or the coiled mainspring of a watch, all possess potential energy.

Again a moving body possesses energy; a falling stone can do work. Energy in this form is called Kinetic.

*3. Transformation of Energy. Energy can change from kinetic to potential or vice versa.

A stone at the top of a cliff has no kinetic energy; relative to the cliff its energy is all potential. As the stone falls it loses potential energy, for this is proportional to its height above the earth, being measured by mgz where m is the mass of the stone, z its height and g the acceleration due to gravity; at the same time it gains kinetic energy, for this is measured by $\frac{1}{2}mv^2$, where v is the velocity, and this increases till the stone reaches the ground. Moreover, we can shew that, for a falling body, the gain in kinetic energy is equal to the loss of potential energy, for if z be the height when the velocity is v and h the height from which the stone started we have from Dynamics

$$\tfrac{1}{2}mv^2 = mg(h-z),$$

since $h-z$ is the space in which a body moving with uniform acceleration g has acquired a velocity v; now $\frac{1}{2}mv^2$ is the gain of kinetic energy, while $mg(h-z)$ is the loss of potential energy; thus these are equal.

In this case and in many others we meet with in Mechanics, there is neither gain nor loss of energy, it is simply changed from the potential to the kinetic form.

4. Apparent loss of Energy. When the stone has reached the ground it has apparently lost its energy, it has no potential energy, for it can fall no further; it has no kinetic energy, for it is at rest. Careful observation would shew however that another change has taken place; the stone has been heated.

Or again, a railway train in motion even after the steam has been shut off has a large store of kinetic energy. When the brakes are put on and the train brought to rest this kinetic energy disappears as such, but here again heat has been produced, in this case, by the friction.

5. Heat and Work. Various experiments shew us that there is some connection between heat and work. Thus, take a strip of lead and bend it backwards and forwards or hammer it; in both cases work is done and it will be found that the lead is warmed. Or again attach a brass tube AB fig. (1) to a whirling table so that it can be made to rotate rapidly round a vertical axis by turning the flywheel C. Fill

Fig. 1.

the tube with water and close it with a cork; on turning the wheel the tube can be easily made to rotate rapidly. DD are two pieces of wood in each of which there is a semicircular groove; these are united by means of a hinge and can be made to clip the tube tightly. On doing this there is considerable friction produced; more energy is needed to turn the wheel; the water becomes heated, and finally boils. Work has been transformed into Heat.

Now though in the experiments just described, it would be impossible to measure with accuracy the work done and the heat produced, we can in various ways arrange experiments in which these measures can be made.

6. Joule's Experiments. This was first done satisfactorily by Dr Joule of Manchester in 1843, and it is to his experiments, which lasted over many years, that most of our knowledge of the connection between heat and work is due.

In one investigation he employed the following arrangement. A known mass of water is contained in a vertical brass cylinder. Within this a shaft carrying paddles revolves. Vanes are secured to the sides of the cylinder and the moving paddles whirl between them. The friction between the paddles and the water produced heat. By observing with a thermometer the temperature of the water, the heat produced can be calculated (see Section 176).

A wooden cylinder is attached to the shaft and two thin strings are coiled in the same direction round the cylinder. The strings pass over two pulleys and carry known weights. On releasing the shaft the weights fall, turning the paddles and stirring the water. The energy lost by the weights in the fall can be calculated and thus the amount of energy required to produce a given quantity of heat can be determined.

Joule found as the result of these and similar experiments that the amount of energy required to produce a definite quantity of heat is itself a definite quantity; in order to produce the unit quantity of heat that is to raise 1 gramme of water 1° Centigrade, 41·9 million ergs of work are needed.

7. The Conservation of Energy. Thus in the case just described, the potential energy of the weights is not lost, it is transformed into heat; the weights, the water and other substances which have been heated, possess the same amount of energy at the end as at the beginning; only the distribution of the energy has been changed; the weights have less, the water more.

The same is true of the falling stone; the potential energy it possessed on the cliff, has been changed, firstly into the form of the kinetic energy of the visible mass and then into heat in the stone itself and in the ground where it struck; some has been used to produce the noise of the blow, some in heating slightly the air through which the stone has fallen; the sum total of all these different forms remains the same.

Again conversely, Energy in the Heat form can be transformed into Mechanical Work. The steam engine is a familiar instance of a machine for this purpose. Part of the heat produced by the combustion of the fuel in the furnace passes into the boiler and thence with the steam into the cylinder; as the steam expands in the cylinder it loses heat, and work is done by the engine.

In this case the practical difficulties in the way of measuring the exact amount of heat which is used in doing the external work are very great. Still when heat is turned into work and due allowance is made for all the losses which take place it is found that the work produced is always proportional to the heat producing it—one unit of heat, if it can be converted entirely into work, will produce 41·9 million ergs. It is true that in order to convert the heat entirely into work certain other conditions have to be fulfilled, but we need not attempt to discuss these at present. We are thus justified in stating that Heat is a form of Energy.

*8. The Nature of Heat-energy. It is a further question, and one we can go but a little way towards answering if we ask, What is the nature of heat-energy? Let us consider it briefly.

We know that all bodies are made up of a large number of particles called molecules. These molecules are extremely small, still we have now a fairly accurate idea of their size. In all substances they are in a state of rapid agitation, vibrating backwards and forwards, colliding with each other and with the sides of the vessel containing the substance.

In a gas the molecules are much less closely packed than in a liquid or a solid. It is only when they come very close together that they exert any force on each other; for the greater part of their existence they are free from each other's action; in consequence of their motion they possess kinetic energy and it is practically certain that the heat of the gas is almost entirely the kinetic energy of agitation of its molecules. When the gas is heated the molecules are made to vibrate more rapidly, they gain kinetic energy and the gain is a measure of the heat supplied.

To some extent a similar statement is true also of a solid, the molecules are in a state of vibration and heat increases the energy of this vibration, but the molecules are also on the average much closer together than in a gas. Each molecule is acted on by forces due to its neighbours and thus possesses potential energy; the action of heat may modify these forces and so alter the potential, as well as the kinetic, energy of the molecules. Thus we can say very little about the form in which heat-energy exists in a solid or a liquid; in a gas we know that it is in the main the kinetic energy of agitation of the molecules, in a solid it is in all probability in part the kinetic energy of the molecules, in part their potential energy arising from the forces they exert upon each other.

*9. Historical Account of the principle of the Conservation of Energy. As we have said our knowledge of the true nature of heat dates from the experiments of Joule in 1843, still it had been foreshadowed at a much earlier time. Lord Bacon in the *Novum Organon* states his belief that Heat consists in a kind of motion or "brisk agitation" of the parts of a body. Robert Boyle one of the original members of the Royal Society expressed the same opinion, so also did John Locke; but the first experiments from which the truth might have been deduced were those of Benjamin Thompson, Count Rumford, who in 1799 produced sufficient heat by friction to raise about 27 lbs. of water from the freezing to the boiling point, and of Sir Humphrey Davy who in the previous year had shewn that ice could be melted by friction only. Rumford's experiments give us enough data to calculate the mechanical equivalent of heat; he omitted however one experiment which was necessary to make his reasoning conclusive. Davy failed to draw correct conclusions from his work.

Séguin in 1837 and Mayer in 1842 calculated the equivalent; they both however made assumptions which though true needed experiment for their justification. This experiment was performed by Joule in 1845.

CHAPTER II.

TEMPERATURE AND ITS MEASUREMENT.

10. Effects of Heat. When heat is applied to bodies it produces the following among other effects :

(1) Change of dimensions or of volume.
(2) Change of internal stress.
(3) Change of state.
(4) Change of temperature.
(5) Electrical and chemical effects.

We will briefly consider each of these in turn.

(1) *Change of dimensions.*

Most bodies expand or increase in volume on being heated. In laying down the rails on a line of railway an interval is left between consecutive rails to allow for this. The tyre of a wheel is put on red hot, as it cools it contracts and binds the wheel tightly together. Boiler plates are riveted with red-hot rivets for the same reason. The pendulums or balance wheels of clocks and watches require compensation, otherwise each change of temperature would cause a variation in the clock's rate. The ocean currents and the trade winds are due to the change in volume, and therefore of density, of the water or air produced by heat.

(2) *Change of internal stress.*

Many of these changes of volume are accompanied by changes in the stresses or internal forces between the molecules of the body. As the wheel tyre contracts it is subject to great force. Walls of buildings have been drawn together by passing iron bars through them, heating the bars and screwing on nuts to the projecting ends; as the bars contract they draw the walls together. An air balloon placed in front of a fire expands, the pressure which the contained air exerts on the india-rubber covering increases and bursts the covering.

(3) *Change of state.*

Many substances can exist in the three states of bodies—solid, liquid, or gaseous,—changing from one to the other on the application or withdrawal of heat. A lump of ice melts when sufficient heat is applied and becomes water; apply more heat, the water becomes warmer, and after a time it boils, being converted into steam. Ice, water, steam, are all different forms of the same chemical compound of oxygen and hydrogen; the application of heat, among other effects, may change the arrangement of the molecules of the substance and the forces between them and thus convert ice into water or water into steam.

(4) *Change of temperature.*

Place the hand in a basin of cold water. It feels cold: apply heat to the water, it gradually becomes warmer; in scientific language its "temperature" is said to rise. Or again, put a red-hot poker into a vessel of water, the poker is cooled, the water heated, heat passes from the poker to the water, the temperature of the poker is lowered, that of the water increased. In both these cases there is a transference of heat from one body to the other, the body from which the heat passes is said to have the higher temperature.

11. Definition of Temperature. *Temperature is the condition of a body on which its power of communicating heat to or receiving heat from other bodies depends.*

If when two bodies A and B are put into thermal communication, heat passes from A to B, then A is said to be at a higher temperature than B.

Two bodies A and B have the same temperature, if when they are put into thermal communication there is no transference of heat between them.

The flow of heat from one body to a second depends on the difference between the temperatures of the two; the body at the lower temperature may originally possess more heat than the other, but heat will pass into it raising its temperature and reducing that of the hotter body. The total amount of heat in a bucket of water may very likely be greater than that in a red-hot poker; still the poker is at the higher temperature and is thereby able to communicate some of its heat-energy to the water at a lower temperature. The temperature determines the direction of the flow.

Temperature is analogous to level or pressure in hydrostatics. Consider two reservoirs A, B connected by a pipe with a tap. On opening the tap, water may flow from A to B or vice versa, or there may be no flow at all. The condition which determines which of these alternatives takes place is the difference of level between the surfaces of the water in A and B. If the level in A is above that in B water flows from A to B and vice versa. Water from a reservoir on a hill side, even though it be small in quantity, runs down to the sea because the reservoir is above the level of the sea.

Or again, take a vessel containing compressed air and open the stop-cock; the air rushes out into the atmosphere, where the pressure is less, until the pressures within and without the vessel are equalized. The temperature of the hot body corresponds to the pressure of the air, the air flows from places of high to places of low pressure. Heat passes from a body at a high temperature to one at a lower temperature.

Temperature is also analogous to potential in the science of electricity. Positive electricity flows from places of high potential to places of low potential.

12. Comparison of Temperatures. Experience shews us that while our ideas of temperature and of the difference between two temperatures may in the first instance be derived from our sense of touch, no accurate knowledge can be obtained from that source alone.

If a piece of metal and a piece of flannel which are lying

side by side in front of the fire be touched, the metal will appear hotter than the flannel though the two may be shewn by a suitable experiment to be at the same temperature; if on the other hand the two be very cold the metal will appear the colder; the sensation does not depend only on the temperature but also on the rate at which heat is transferred through the metal or the flannel.

We require some other method of measuring temperatures. We must for this purpose employ one of the other effects produced by heat on matter; the effect usually chosen is the dilatation or increase of volume of a liquid. Suppose we have two bodies A and B and we wish to determine which of the two is at the higher temperature. We take a third body C the change in volume of which we can easily measure; the mercury or alcohol in an ordinary thermometer is such a body[1]. When heat passes into the thermometer, raising its temperature, the liquid expands. Place it in contact with A. Heat passes into it and the column of mercury rises until the temperature of the thermometer is the same as that of A. Note the height of the column. Now place the thermometer in contact with B. If B is at a higher temperature than A more heat will pass into the thermometer and the column will rise still further, if B is at a lower temperature the column will fall.

We can thus determine which of the two A or B is at the higher temperature.

We cannot however yet say whether this difference is greater or less than that between two other bodies D and E, neither can we compare a temperature observed in one place with another observation of temperature made elsewhere unless we can transport the same thermometer. For such purposes we need a scale of temperature.

13. The fixed points on a thermometer. The

---

[1] This thermometer consists of a glass tube of fine bore terminating in a bulb. The tube and part of the bulb are filled with mercury (or alcohol) the rest of the tube being empty. Small changes in the volume of the mercury in the bulb shew themselves by a considerable motion of the end of the column in the narrow tube. We shall explain later the mode of filling and testing a thermometer.

temperature at which ice melts is found to be always the same at ordinary pressure[1].

The temperature of steam issuing from boiling water is also constant when the pressure is constant.

These two facts are verified by experiments which we shall describe later, for the present we are considering how we may use them to construct a scale of temperature. They give us two fixed points which can be marked on the stem of a thermometer; when the mercury stands at the lower of the points the thermometer is at the temperature of melting ice, when the mercury is at the upper mark the temperature is that of steam at a certain standard pressure.

14. Scales of Temperature. The difference in temperature between these two fixed points is very considerable; we need some means of subdividing it so that we may compare any two temperatures more closely than would be possible if we only had the two fixed points of reference. As the temperature rises from the freezing point to the boiling point the mercury in a glass thermometer expands by a certain definite amount.

Definition. *A rise of temperature of one degree is that rise of temperature which causes the mercury to expand by some definite fraction of the total expansion between the freezing and the boiling points.*

There are three scales of temperature in more or less common use.

(1) The Fahrenheit Scale. The number of degrees between the two fixed points is 180. Thus the temperature changes by 1° Fahr. when the volume of the mercury of a mercurial thermometer alters by $\frac{1}{180}$th part of the total increase between freezing point and boiling point. On Fahrenheit's Scale the freezing point is marked 32°; the boiling point is thus 32° + 180° or 212°.

---

[1] A small change is produced by variation of pressure but it is too small to affect the determination of the lower fixed point.

(2) The Centigrade Scale. The number of degrees between the two fixed points is 100. Thus the temperature changes by 1° C. where the volume of the mercury in a mercurial thermometer alters by $\frac{1}{100}$th part of the total increase between the freezing point and the boiling point. On the Centigrade Scale freezing point is marked 0°, boiling point 100°.

(3) Réaumur's Scale. The number of degrees between the two fixed points is 80. Thus the temperature changes by 1° Réaumur where the volume of the mercury in a mercurial thermometer alters by $\frac{1}{80}$th part of the total increase between the freezing and the boiling point. On Réaumur's Scale, freezing point is marked 0°, boiling point 80°.

Fahrenheit's Scale is in common use in this country for ordinary purposes while Réaumur's is still similarly employed on the continent. The Centigrade Scale has now been very generally adopted for scientific work.

15. Comparison of Scales of Temperature. To compare the three scales consider a thermometer to which all three are fitted, fig. 2. Let A be the freezing point, B the boiling point, P the position of the end of the mercury column, and let F, C, R be the readings on the three scales respectively corresponding to the point P.

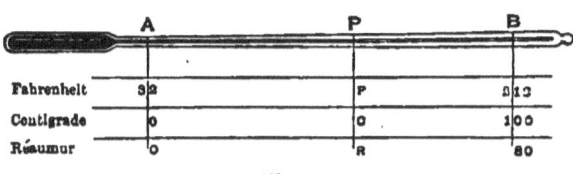

Fig. 2.

Now on the three scales respectively the distance AP represents $F-32$, C, and R degrees, while AB represents 180 $(212-32)$, 100, and 80 degrees. But AP is the same fraction of AB, whichever scale be employed.

Thus the fractions[1] $\dfrac{F-32}{180}$, $\dfrac{C}{100}$ and $\dfrac{R}{80}$ are all equal;

$$\therefore \dfrac{F-32}{180} = \dfrac{C}{100} = \dfrac{R}{80}.$$

and from these expressions the relations between the scales can be found.

It must be noticed that for Fahrenheit readings below zero Fahrenheit, we must treat F as negative, and, in order to find the number of degrees between freezing point and the reading, we must add 32 to the reading instead of subtracting as explained above. The corresponding Centigrade reading will of course be negative.

Examples. (1) *Find the Centigrade and Reaumur readings corresponding to* 60° *Fah.*

60° Fah. is 60 − 32 or 28° above freezing point.

1° Fah. = 5/9 of 1° C.

$\therefore$ 28° Fah. = 28 × 5/9 C. = 15°·55 C.

1° Fah. = 4/9 of 1° R.

$\therefore$ 28° Fah. = 28 × 4/9 R. = 12°·4 R.

Or, using the formula, and denoting by C. and R. the Centigrade and Reaumur readings corresponding to 60° Fah. we have

C. = 5/9 (60 − 32) = 15°·55.

R. = 4/9 (60 − 32) = 12°·4.

(2) *Find the Fahrenheit reading corresponding to* 18° *C.*

The number of Fah. degrees in 18 degrees C. is 9/5 of 18, or 32·4.

$\therefore$ the Fahrenheit reading is 32°·4 + 32° or 64°·4.

Or, from the formula,

F. = 32° + 9/5 C. = 32° + 32°·4 = 64°·4.

(3) *The freezing point of mercury is given by the same numbers on the Centigrade and Fahrenheit scale, find this temperature.*

If C. and F. are corresponding readings on the two scales, then

F. = 9/5 C. + 32.

But by the question, F. and C. are to be represented by the same number, X suppose, then

$X = \tfrac{9}{5} X + 32$.

$\therefore \tfrac{4}{5} X = -32$.

$\therefore X = -40$.

---

[1] It must be noted that F is the Fahrenheit reading corresponding to a Centigrade reading C, not the number of degrees Fahrenheit which are equal to C degrees Centigrade, this last number is $F - 32$.

16. Electrical and chemical effects due to heat. For our purpose the most important electrical effect due to heat is that discovered by Seebeck who found that if a circuit be composed of different materials, two wires say of iron and copper joined together at each end, and if the temperature of the two junctions be different then an electric current is produced round the circuit. Since a very small electric current can be measured easily this fact is made use of in the Thermopile to measure small differences of temperature.

Heat also produces an important effect in changing the electrical resistance of bodies. This has been made the basis of a method of measuring high temperatures.

Certain crystals also shew electrical effects when heated.

Many chemical effects require heat for their production. Thus the combustion of coal is due to the combination of the carbon of the coal with the oxygen of the air. This combination only takes place at a high temperature. Heat is therefore required to raise the temperature and start the action which, when once started, produces sufficient heat for its continuance.

17. Sources of Heat. Among the sources of heat available for our use we may reckon

1. The Sun.
2. Chemical action.
3. Mechanical action.
4. Electric currents.
5. Change of physical state.
6. The internal heat of the earth.

(1) *The Sun.* Of the above the Sun is by far the most important. We shall have to study at a later stage how the Sun's heat reaches us in the form of radiant energy as it is called.

Directly or indirectly the sun is the source of nearly all the available energy we possess. For our food we are indebted to the sun. Vegetable life depends on sunshine. Our fuel

—coal—is due to the sun's action which in past time enabled plants to decompose the carbonic acid of the air and store up the carbon which we use. The winds and tides, the rainfall which feeds our rivers and is the source of our waterpower, all depend on solar action. Life as we know it would be impossible without the sun.

(2) *Chemical action.* Many chemical actions are accompanied by the production of heat. First among these we may place combustion. When carbon and oxygen unite, a great amount of heat is evolved. Still more is produced by the combination of hydrogen with oxygen as in the oxyhydrogen flame. The heat of our bodies is due to the combination of our food with the oxygen of the air.

(3) *Mechanical sources.* Of these friction is the chief; we have already considered the connection between heat and mechanical work which is transformed into heat by friction.

(4) *Electricity.* When an electric current passes through a conductor it heats it. If the current be sufficiently large and the resistance of the conductor considerable, the rise of temperature may be great. The filaments of incandescent lamps are made to glow by the passage of a current. Water can be boiled and food cooked by heat thus produced.

(5) *Change of physical state.* Just as it requires heat to melt ice, so heat can be obtained by freezing water. The molecules of the substance in the liquid form possess more energy than in the solid; absorb this energy and the liquid becomes a solid. When steam condenses to water, heat is given out. It is possible to cool down various solutions, of which sulphate of sodium is one, below the temperature at which they would normally solidify. If this be done and a small bit of the solid be then dropped into the solution, solidification at once takes place, and is accompanied by a considerable production of heat, and a corresponding rise of temperature.

(6) *The internal heat of the earth.* A large store of heat exists in the interior of the earth but not in a very available form.

18. Historical. The suggestion to use the temperatures of melting ice for the fixed point is due to Newton (1701). He used the temperature of the human body which he marked 12 as his upper fixed point. The thermometer was originally invented by Galileo, who employed an air thermometer (Section 23) to determine the temperature of the human body. Soon after his time thermometers containing a liquid in a sealed glass tube were made in Florence for Rinieri, who recorded a number of observations on temperature. These thermometers were lost on the suppression of the Accademia del Cimento, but discovered in 1829. Their scale was then compared with that of Réaumur, and Rinieri's old observations regained their scientific value. One of these thermometers was given by the Grand Duke of Tuscany to the late Prof. Babbage. On his death it was presented by his son to the University of Cambridge, and is now in the Cavendish Laboratory.

It appears from the investigations of Dr Gamgee that Fahrenheit in 1714 used as his two fixed points the temperature of a mixture of ice and salt, in definite proportions, which he called 0°, and the temperature of the human body. This he originally marked 24°. In later thermometers he introduced four times as many divisions, marking the temperature of the human body 96°. Having obtained this scale he continued it up the tube, and found that water boiled at 212° and froze at 32°. These then were taken as more convenient fixed points and more accurate observation has proved that if boiling point is called 212°, the normal temperature of the body is 98°·4, instead of 96°, as taken by Fahrenheit.

CHAPTER III.

THERMOMETRY.

19. Construction of a Mercury Thermometer.
A bulb A is blown at one end of a glass tube of narrow uniform bore. A cup or funnel B is formed at the other end[1]. At C a short distance below the funnel the tube is drawn out by heating it in a blowpipe flame so as to form a narrow neck. This is for the purpose of sealing off the thermometer when made.

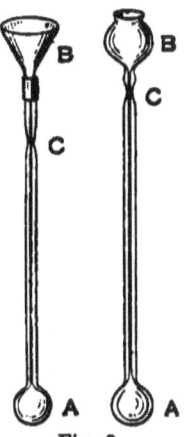

Fig. 3.

If mercury be poured into B it will not run down the tube to fill the bulb, the bore is too narrow; the following method is therefore adopted. A small quantity of mercury is placed in B and the bulb is gently heated; the air expands and some of it bubbles out through the mercury in B. The bulb is then allowed to cool and the pressure of the enclosed air falls. The atmospheric pressure forces some of the mercury down the tube and, if sufficient air has been expelled, into the bulb. When this takes place the mercury in the bulb is boiled, the vapour of mercury forces most of the air out of the upper part of the bulb and tube. When the bulb is again cooled the mercury vapour condenses and more mercury flows in from the reservoir. By repeating the process once or twice the last traces of air may be removed, and the bulb and tube filled with mercury.

[1] In the Laboratory a small funnel may be attached by a piece of india-rubber tubing to the open end, as in the left-hand figure.

Now place the bulb and tube in a bath at a rather higher temperature than the highest at which the thermometer is to be used. Some of the mercury expands into the funnel; remove this and allow the thermometer to cool slowly; the mercury contracts; have a blow-pipe with a small intense flame ready, and as the end of the column is just passing the narrow neck C, heat the tube at that point in the flame and draw off the funnel end. By this process the tube is sealed at C. The mercury, as it cools, contracts, leaving a space filled only with mercury vapour.

Certain precautions are needed before the thermometer can be used. It is found that glass which has been strongly heated continues to change in shape and volume for some time after it has cooled. In consequence of this the mercury rises up the tube, even though the temperature does not change. This process continues for some time; moreover a similar change though smaller in amount takes place whenever the thermometer is heated to a high temperature. By a proper choice of glass for the thermometer tube and by special treatment of the instrument when filled, these defects can be very considerably reduced.

Again, the distance between the fixed marks is usually divided into equal parts. The corresponding portions of the tube will not be equal in volume unless the bore is uniform, and, unless they are equal, the degrees of temperature as given by the thermometer will not really coincide with our definition, for the increase in volume of the mercury for each degree will not be the same. If the tube were as in the figure (fig. 4)—where the want of uniformity is purposely much exaggerated—and if the distances AB, BC, CD etc. be equal, it is clear that the volume between A and B is larger than that between C and D; the amount of expansion required to bring the mercury from A to B is greater than that which will bring it from C to D, so that the rise of temperature indicated by AB is really greater than the rise indicated by CD, though nominally the two are the

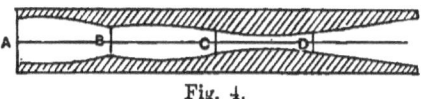

Fig. 4.

same. To avoid this error the tubes of standard thermometers are calibrated. This is done by breaking off from the column a small thread of mercury, placing it by varying the temperature in different parts of the tube and measuring its length. From this measurement the want of uniformity in the tube can be corrected (see Glazebrook and Shaw, *Practical Physics*, p. 89).

Good thermometers for use in scientific work are compared with a standard which has thus been calibrated, and a Table of corrections to the apparent readings is formed.

20. The fixed points.
EXPERIMENT (1). *To determine the fixed points of a thermometer.*

(*a*) The Freezing Point. Wash some ice[1], break it small and pack it round the bulb of the thermometer in a glass or metal funnel (fig. 5), so that the water which forms as the ice melts may drain away into a vessel placed below to receive it. The mercury sinks; heap the ice up round the tube until only the top of the column is visible, and leave it thus for about a quarter of an hour; then with a fine file make a scratch on the glass opposite to the top of the column. This marks the freezing point.

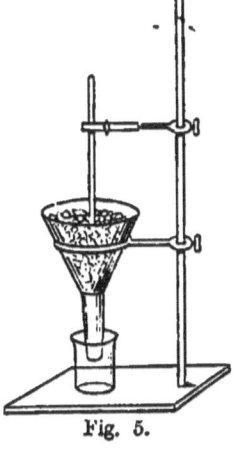

Fig. 5.

(*b*) The Boiling Point. Place the thermometer in the steam issuing from boiling water. The temperature of the water, if it contain soluble impurities, may differ from that of the steam. In order to secure that the thermometer may be surrounded with steam, a piece of apparatus called an hypsometer is used; a simple form of hypsometer is shewn in fig. 6. A conical tin or copper cover, BC, with an inner tube fits loosely on to a glass flask. A cork passes through the top of the tube and the thermometer is inserted through a hole in the cork, its bulb being well above the surface of the water in the flask. As the water boils steam passes round the thermometer bulb and issues between the flask and the loose cover, flowing down on the outside of the flask between it and

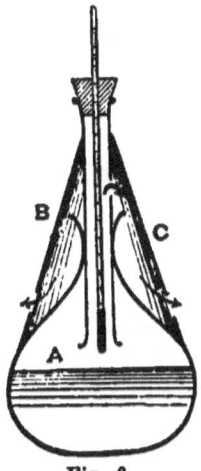

Fig. 6.

---

[1] The ice obtained in the usual way from a dealer has very often some traces of salt about it, this affects the freezing point.

the cover. The thermometer is thus in a current of steam which is protected from the cooling action of the air by the outer downward current. After a time the mercury becomes steady. Adjust the thermometer until the top of the column is just visible above the cork, leave it in that position for a few moments to make sure that the bulb and tube have reached a steady temperature, and then mark the level of the column. Read the height of the barometer; the mark gives the boiling point of water for the pressure at the time of observation. If this be not the standard pressure 760 mm., a correction is required, and this may be obtained as follows.

It has been found that near the standard pressure an increase in pressure due to 26·8 mm. raises the boiling point by 1° C., and also that for small differences of pressure the change of the boiling point is proportional to the difference in pressure (see § 121). Thus suppose the observed pressure is 752 mm. we have the proportion

$$\frac{\text{required correction}}{1°} = \frac{760-752}{26\cdot 8},$$

$$\therefore \text{required correction} = \frac{8°}{26\cdot 8} = 0°\cdot 3.$$

Hence the observed boiling point is 0°·3 too low.

Since 1° Fah. is ⅝ of 1° C. a change of boiling point of 1° Fah. will be produced by a change of pressure of ⅝ of 26·8 or 14·9 mm. Thus the change in boiling point measured in degrees Fahrenheit due to a given change in pressure can be found by dividing the pressure difference by 14·9.

Experiments with Thermometers.

(1) Test the fixed points of the given thermometer. The thermometer has been already graduated; determine by the above methods whether the fixed points are correct.

Suppose that in the steam the thermometer reads 99°·5, the height of the barometer being 752 mm. The correction for pressure is, we have seen, +0°·3. Thus the corrected boiling point is 99°·5 + 0°·3 or 99°·8. The upper fixed point therefore has been placed too high by 0°·2.

(2) Mix a little salt with the ice and notice the fall in temperature, then place some salt in the boiling water and observe the boiling point,

immersing the thermometer bulb in the salt and water. It will be too high.

(3) Compare the readings of the two given thermometers. Place the two thermometers (a Fahrenheit and a Centigrade) close together in a water bath, taking care that their bulbs are as near together as possible, and read the two; while taking the readings, stir the water gently and thus secure uniformity of temperature. Let the Centigrade thermometer read 15°. Now since 100 degrees Centigrade are equivalent to 180 degrees Fahrenheit each degree Centigrade is 9/5 of a degree Fahrenheit. Thus 15° C. are equivalent to $9/5 \times 15°$ Fah. or 27° Fah. Thus the reading is 27° above freezing point on the Fahrenheit scale, and since freezing point reads 32° Fah. the Fahrenheit reading corresponding to 15° C. is 27° + 32° or 59° Fah.

Assuming the Centigrade thermometer to be correct, determine thus the error of the Fahrenheit instrument.

21. Graduation of a Mercury Thermometer. When the fixed points are determined the thermometer is graduated by dividing the distance between them into equal parts 180, 100 or 80 according to the scale used. These divisions are continued above the boiling point, and below the freezing point; on the Centigrade and Réaumur scale temperatures below the freezing point are marked as negative. The zero of the Fahrenheit scale is 32° Fah. below freezing point; temperatures below zero are negative.

22. Comparison of the Mercury and other Thermometers. Mercury is not the only liquid used in filling thermometers. Mercury freezes at about $-40°$ C. Alcohol does not freeze till a much lower temperature has been reached, about $-130°$ C., and therefore for very low temperatures alcohol is employed. In some thermometers sulphuric acid is the liquid used.

Such thermometers are graduated by comparison with a mercury thermometer.

The following experiment will explain the reason for this. Suppose we have two thermometers each of uniform bore: the one containing mercury, the other some other liquid, say sulphuric acid. Let the freezing and boiling points of each of the two be determined and marked, and divide the distance between these on each thermometer into 100 parts. Place the two thermometers side by side in a bath at say 45° C. The column in the mercury thermometer stands at 45° on the scale, that in the sulphuric acid thermometer is not at 45° but at 41°; if we were to suppose the second thermometer graduated by dividing the distance between the fixed points into equal parts, the temperature as given by it would not be 45° but 41°.

A rise of temperature, which produces in mercury an expansion of 45/100 of that which occurs between the fixed points, does not produce 45/100 of the expansion occurring in sulphuric acid between the same fixed points. We might have defined the temperature with reference to the expansion of sulphuric acid; the scale so obtained would differ from that which we have adopted, and therefore the alcohol or sulphuric acid thermometers are graduated by comparison with a standard mercury thermometer. If we experimented with other liquids we should find similar results. Water would give the most anomalous result, for when the mercury thermometer was at 4° the water thermometer would be below zero.

23. The Air Thermometer. For some purposes temperature is measured by the expansion of air or some other gas.

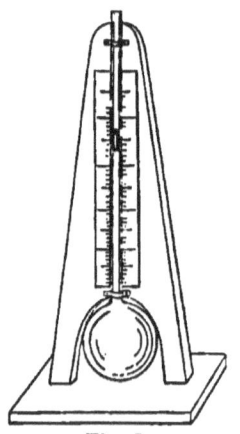

Fig. 7.

The simplest form of air thermometer would consist of a bulb, fig. 7, with tube attached filled with dry air. The end of the tube is open and a small pellet of mercury or sulphuric acid separates the air in the bulb from the external atmosphere. As the temperature rises the air in the bulb expands, driving the pellet of acid before it; as it falls the air contracts; the position of the pellet indicates the volume of the enclosed air. Now this volume depends in part on the temperature and in part on the pressure of the surrounding air. If the pressure varies, the temperature remaining the same, the pellet will move. In using such an air thermometer therefore it is necessary to know the pressure of the air, which is given by the height of the barometer, and to make an allowance if this pressure varies during an experiment.

An air thermometer is very much more sensitive than a mercury instrument for, for a given rise of temperature, a volume of air expands by about twenty times as much as the same volume of mercury. Thus if we had an air thermometer and a mercury thermometer with the same sized bulb and tube, the tube of the air thermometer would need to be about twenty times as long as that of the mercury thermometer in order that the two fixed points might be engraved on both. If however this were done and the two tubes divided each into 100 equal parts, as in the experiment with the sulphuric acid thermometer, we should find in this case that the two scales agreed throughout almost exactly. If the two be put into a bath in which the mercury thermometer read 15°, the air thermometer reads 15° also. The scale of the mercury thermometer is practically the same as that of the air thermometer. This will be seen to be of great importance, and we shall recur to the point again when discussing problems connected with the expansion of gases.

The form of air thermometer just described was used by Boyle in his experiments "On Cold" which were made about 1665.

Another form used by Boyle in the same experiments and called by him the open weather-glass is shewn in fig. 8.

A glass tube A passes through an air-tight cork into a bottle B, reaching nearly to the bottom of the bottle. The lower part of the bottle and part of the tube are filled with some coloured liquid. Above the liquid is the air or other gas, the expansion of which measures the temperature. As the temperature rises the pressure of the enclosed air increases and the liquid rises in the tube.

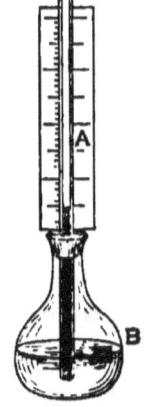

Fig. 8.

A third form of air thermometer was that used originally

in 1597 by Galileo, the inventor of the thermometer. This is shewn in fig. 9.

The air is contained in a bulb from the bottom of which a tube descends into an open beaker or bottle containing coloured liquid. By heating the bulb some of the air is forced out through the liquid. As the air cools the liquid rises in the tube, becoming stationary when the temperature has become constant. If the temperature changes slightly, the liquid moves. These instruments are all useful as delicate thermoscopes, they enable us to *detect* slight changes of temperature; they are difficult to use as thermometers or temperature measurers.

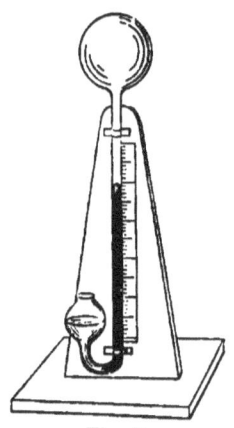

Fig. 9.

24. The differential Air Thermometer. In one of its forms this instrument consists of two bulbs with a tube joining them, bent as $ABCDE$ in fig. 10. The portion BCD contains coloured liquid which, so long as the two bulbs are at the same temperature, stands at the same level within the tubes. If the temperature of one of them, A say, rises more than that in E, the pressure in A is increased, the end B of the liquid is depressed while D rises. Thus small differences of temperature between A and E are easily detected.

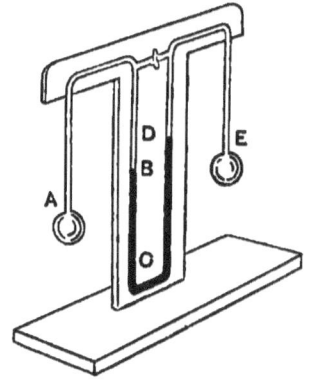

Fig. 10.

Reasons for the use of mercury in thermometers.

(1) The scale of a mercury thermometer agrees very closely with that of the air thermometer.

(2) Mercury readily transmits heat through its substance, so that the whole of the mercury in the thermometer very rapidly comes to the same temperature.

(3) It requires less heat to raise the temperature of a given mass of mercury than is required for an equal mass of most other liquids. This is of great importance, for when a thermometer is used to measure the temperature of a hot body it absorbs heat from that body until the temperatures of the two become equal. By this process the temperature of the hot body is reduced; if it requires much heat to raise the temperature of the thermometer the hot body might be appreciably cooled in the process and its temperature as measured by the thermometer might differ appreciably from its temperature before it was brought into contact with the thermometer.

(4) Other advantages are: mercury can readily be obtained pure; it does not wet glass and therefore does not stick so much to the tube. It is opaque and can be easily seen; it remains liquid over a considerable range of temperature, viz. from about $-40°$ C. to $350°$ C.

25. Special forms of Thermometers. Rutherford's Maximum and Minimum Thermometers.

Rutherford's maximum thermometer is an ordinary mercurial thermometer usually mounted with the tube nearly horizontal. A small glass or enamel index (AB, fig. 11) in shape like a pin

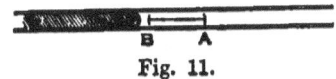

Fig. 11.

with a head at each end fits loosely into the tube above the mercury. As the temperature rises the convex surface of the mercury pushes the index forwards. As the temperature falls the mercury column retreats, leaving the index behind. The end B of the index indicates the highest temperature which the instrument has reached.

In Rutherford's minimum thermometer the same principle is applied. Alcohol is employed and the index is in the liquid. The surface is concave and as the column contracts it draws down the index, as it expands the alcohol passes by the index leaving it in the lowest position it has reached. Thus the end A of the index registers the minimum temperature to which the instrument has been exposed. Both instruments

Fig. 12.

are set by bringing the indices in contact with the end of the column of mercury or alcohol respectively.

26. The Clinical Thermometer. This is a sensitive maximum thermometer having only a short range, being usually graduated from about 95° Fah. to 110° Fah. A constriction is formed in the tube just above the bulb (fig. 13). As the

Fig. 13.

mercury rises it passes this constriction; as the temperature falls the thread breaks at the narrow part of the tube, the lower portion contracting into the bulb while the upper portion remains unchanged; in position the upper end of this portion registers the highest temperature to which the thermometer has been subject. By gently tapping or shaking the thermometer with the bulb downwards, the mercury can be forced past the constriction and the instrument set.

27. Six's Thermometer. This is a maximum and minimum instrument combined. The tube is bent as shewn in fig. 14. The bulb A and the tube AC are filled with alcohol, the expansion of which measures the temperature. The tube BD also contains alcohol, but the bulb B is only partly filled with it. The lower portion of the tube CED is filled with mercury separating the two columns of alcohol. The alcohol in BD merely serves the purpose of maintaining both ends of the mercury column under the same conditions. A small iron index is placed at each end of the mercury column, and a small spring attached to each index presses it against the side of the tube; the friction is sufficient to hold the index supported in any position. As the temperature rises, the alcohol in A expands; it pushes the end C of the mercury down and the end D up, raising the index at D. When the temperature falls again, the column at D falls and the index remains behind; the lower end of the index at D measures the maximum temperature. As

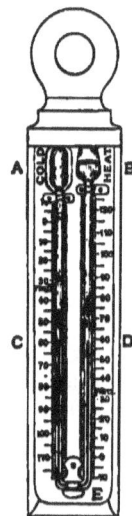

Fig. 14.

the temperature falls C rises, carrying with it the index, which in its turn remains suspended at the highest point it reaches. The lower end of this index then registers the minimum temperature.

The temperature is read on two vertical scales attached to the two tubes.

The instrument is set by bringing the indices into contact with the ends of the mercury column. This is done by the aid of a magnet.

EXAMPLES.

TEMPERATURE AND THERMOMETRY.

1. How is temperature measured by a mercury thermometer, and how are the fixed points of such a thermometer determined? Why is mercury selected for use in a thermometer?

2. What is an air thermometer? How is it constructed, and how is it used? What means have we, besides the air thermometer, of measuring temperatures between 400° and 800° C.?

3. Describe experiments illustrating the difference between temperature and heat.

4. A thermometer is graduated so that it reads 15 in melting ice and 60 in normal steam; convert into Centigrade degrees the readings 20 and 90 taken on that thermometer.

5. Describe some form of maximum and of minimum thermometer, explaining how they act.

6. Calculate the temperatures Centigrade corresponding to 100° F., —40° F., 0° F., 98° F.

7. Distinguish clearly between heat and temperature. Describe some form of a maximum and minimum thermometer.

8. Temperature may be defined as "The quality of a body in virtue of which it seems hot or cold;" and qualities are not capable of being *directly* measured: explain then the principle on which a thermometer is ordinarily used to measure temperatures.

Is it strictly correct to say that the temperature of one body is twice as great as that of another?

HEAT.

9. Convert the following readings of a thermometer graduated according to the Fahrenheit scale into degrees of the Centigrade scale: 86°, 0°, −22°; also the following readings of a Centigrade thermometer into degrees of the Fahrenheit scale: 100°, −10°, −30°. What is the temperature at which the reading of a Fahrenheit thermometer is a number twice as large as that observed simultaneously on a Centigrade thermometer?

10. Describe the mode of determining the fixed points on a thermometer, and explain the nature of the correction necessary when the barometer stands higher than the normal height.

11. The latent heat of fusion of ice on the Centigrade scale is 80: find its value on the Fahrenheit scale.

12. How would you test the readings of an ordinary clinical thermometer?

CHAPTER IV.

CALORIMETRY. THE MEASUREMENT OF A QUANTITY OF HEAT.

28. Heat a Quantity. Heat is a Physical Quantity; if it requires a definite amount of heat to raise the temperature of a kilogramme of water from 15° to 16°, it will require the same quantity to raise a second kilogramme through the same range of temperature. If the two kilogrammes be mixed they require twice the amount of heat to raise their temperature which was required by each kilogramme separately; we can add together the two amounts of heat just as we can add together the two kilogrammes of water; we are justified in speaking of an amount or quantity of heat.

29. The Unit Quantity of Heat. We must measure a quantity of heat by some one of the effects it produces. In practice the effect chosen is the change it causes in the temperature of a definite mass of water. We state then as a **Definition,** *The unit quantity of heat is the amount of heat required to raise the temperature of* 1 *gramme of water from* 4° C. *to* 5° C.[1]

To raise 2 grammes through this range will require 2 units of heat, and so on, so that m heat units is the quantity of heat required to raise m grammes of water from 4° to 5°.

It does not necessarily follow that 1 heat unit will raise a gramme of water 1 degree at any other part of the scale, say

[1] The reason for selecting this temperature will appear afterwards.

from 20° to 21°. Experiment shews however that this is very nearly the case, and so for most purposes we may take as a Heat Unit the quantity of heat required to raise 1 gramme of water 1° C. This same amount of heat is given out by 1 gramme of water in cooling 1° C.

30. Experiment (2). *To shew that the quantity of heat required to raise the temperature of a given mass of water 1° is very approximately the same at all parts of the scale.*

For this and many of the following experiments some kind of calorimeter is required. A cylindrical vessel, fig. 15, made of thin copper about 10 cm. in diameter and 10 cm. high will serve the purpose. It may be mounted on three cork feet to prevent loss or gain of heat from direct contact with the table on which it rests. If greater accuracy is needed it should be suspended inside a second larger copper vessel. This larger vessel may be enclosed in a wooden box and protected from external changes of temperature by cotton wool or other non-conducting packing. A definite quantity of water is placed in this calorimeter and quantities of heat are measured by the changes which take place in the temperature of this water. For accurate work and indeed for some of the experiments described below the water must be *weighed*; for most of the experiments it will be sufficient to *measure* it, pouring it into the calorimeter out of a measuring flask or a burette.

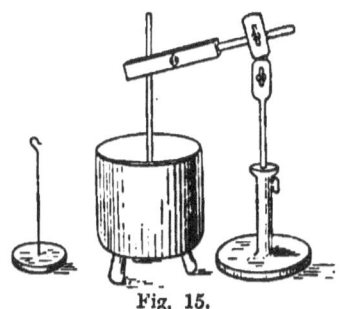

Fig. 15.

Measure out into the copper vessel a quantity, about 250 cubic centimetres, of warm water, at a temperature of about 30° C., and into a second vessel an equal quantity of water at about the temperature of the room, say 15° C. Note the temperatures, and immediately after having read the temperature of the warm water pour the cold into it and take the temperature of the mixture, it will be found to be approximately the mean of the two; thus in the given example it would be about $22°·5$. The heat given out by the 250 grammes of warm water in cooling through $7°·5$, from $30°$ to $22°·5$, is just sufficient to raise the temperature of the same mass of cold water through the same amount, viz. from $15°$ to $22°·5$. Thus it requires the same amount of heat to raise 250 grammes of water through $7°·5$, whether the rise be from $15°$ to $22°·5$ or from $22°·5$ to $30°$.

As we have already stated, the law is not absolutely true, and if the experiments were done with great care, using precautions to prevent loss or gain of heat from external causes, the resulting temperature would not be the mean of the two initial temperatures, but rather higher than the mean.

31. Measurement of a Quantity of Heat. Since then the amounts of heat required to raise a gramme of water through each degree may for our purposes be considered as the same, it follows that $T-t$ heat units are needed to raise one gramme of water from $t°$ to $T°$, i.e. through $(T-t)$ degrees.

Again the number of heat units required to raise m grammes of water $1°$ is m.

Hence the number of heat units required to raise m grammes of water from $t°$ to $T°$ is $m(T-t)$.

We thus see how to calculate either the amount of heat required to change the temperature of a given mass of water by a given number of degrees or the change in temperature produced by a given number of heat units.

Example. *Two quantities of water at different temperatures are mixed together, to find the temperature of the mixture.*

Let the masses of the two quantities be m_1, m_2 grammes and their temperatures $t_1°$, $t_2°$ respectively.

Let the temperature of the mixture be $t°$. Then the quantity of heat absorbed by the mass m_1 in rising from $t_1°$ to $t°$ is $m_1(t-t_1)$ heat units, while the quantity given out by m_2 in cooling from $t_2°$ to $t°$ is $m_2(t_2-t)$ heat units; if the experiment could be conducted so that there was neither loss nor gain of heat from other sources, these two quantities would be equal, the heat given by the hot body passes into the cold body and

$$m_1(t-t_1) = m_2(t_2-t).$$

Thus
$$t = \frac{m_1 t_1 + m_2 t_2}{m_1 + m_2}.$$

This result may be verified by an experiment such as is described in § 30.

32. Specific Heat. The unit quantity of heat raises the temperature of 1 gramme of water 1° C. Experiment shews that this same quantity of heat will raise the temperature of a gramme of most other substances more than 1° C. Thus a gramme of Lead or Mercury would be raised about 30° C. by one heat unit, a gramme of Silver or Tin about 20° C., a gramme of Copper 10° C. Conversely equal masses of different bodies in cooling through the same range of temperature give out different quantities of heat.

This is shewn by the following experiment. A number of balls of different materials, lead, tin, copper, zinc, iron, etc. and of about the same mass are placed in a vessel of boiling oil or water. By means of a string or fine wire attached to each ball it can be readily removed from the bath. Remove the balls simultaneously and place them on a cake of paraffin or beeswax supported on the ring of a retort stand. This cake is prepared by melting the paraffin and allowing it to run out into a flat circular vessel. The balls will melt the paraffin, but the amount melted by each ball will be different.

If the wax be not too thick the iron, zinc and copper balls may melt through it, but the time taken in so doing will be different, the tin ball will not penetrate so deeply while the lead ball will melt less wax than any of the others. It is clear then that the different balls give out different quantities of heat; the experiment however could not be used to measure the amount of heat given out, for much of the heat will escape into the air, and the rate at which the melting takes place depends on the rate at which heat can pass through the substance of the balls as well as on the amount of heat given out by the balls.

The following experiment however will give more measurable results.

33. EXPERIMENT (3). *To compare the amounts of heat given out by different bodies in cooling through the same range of temperature.*

CALORIMETRY.

Take a number of bodies, lead, tin, copper, etc. having small wire handles attached, of equal mass, M grammes; M should be about 400 grammes; and place them in a vessel of boiling water.

Measure out into the copper calorimeter (Exp. 2) m cubic centimetres of water; the mass of this is m grammes—m may conveniently be about 250. Take its temperature with a sensitive thermometer. The thermometer should read to fifths of a degree Centigrade—let it be $t°$. Now take one of the bodies, say the copper, out of the bath of boiling water and place it rapidly in the calorimeter; in doing this care must be taken to carry as little of the hot water as possible with the copper. Observe the temperature of the water, keeping it stirred by moving the copper about; the temperature rises for a time and then becomes stationary. Note this temperature, let it be $T°$. Then, if for the present we suppose that no heat was lost in transferring the copper to the calorimeter, and that all the heat given out by the copper has passed into the water, since the copper has fallen in temperature from 100° to $T°$ and the water has risen from $t°$ to $T°$, we find that M grammes of copper in falling through $(100 - T)$ degrees can raise m grammes of water through $(T - t)$ degrees; that is the copper gives out $m(T - t)$ heat units.

Thus M grammes of copper in falling 1° give out

$$m(T - t)/(100 - T) \text{ heat units.}$$

Repeat the experiment with the lead and tin, the resulting temperature T' in each case will be different. Thus the quantities of heat given out by equal masses of copper, tin, and lead in cooling 1° C., are different. With the numbers given if t the original temperature be 15° the values of the final temperature for copper, tin and lead respectively, will be about 26°·2, 21°·6 and 18°·8.

Thus while the copper raises the temperature of the water 11°·2, the tin only raises it 6°·6 and the lead 3°·8. The fall of temperature of the copper moreover is less than that of the tin or lead; thus we see that the amount of heat given out by 1 gramme of copper in cooling 1° is greater than that given out by 1 gramme of tin or lead under similar circumstances.

34. Definition of Specific Heat. *The ratio of the quantity of heat required to raise the temperature of a given mass of any substance 1° to the quantity of heat required to raise the temperature of an equal mass of water 1° is called the specific heat of the substance.*

35. Definition of Capacity for Heat of a Body. *The Capacity for heat of a body is the quantity of heat required to raise the temperature of the body 1°.*

36. Relation between Specific Heat and Capacity for Heat. Let there be m grammes of the substance and let C be its specific heat. Then by the definition

$$C = \frac{\text{No. of units of heat required to raise } m \text{ grms. of substance } 1°}{\text{No. of units of heat required to raise } m \text{ grms. of water } 1°}$$

But (§ 31) the number of units of heat required to raise m grammes of water 1° C. is m.

$$C = \frac{\text{No. of units of heat required to raise } m \text{ grms. of substance } 1°}{m}.$$

Therefore the number of units of heat required to raise m grammes of a substance $1° = mC$. But this quantity is the capacity for heat of the body.

Thus mC is the capacity for heat of a body containing m grammes of a substance of specific heat C.

Again mC heat units will raise mC grammes of water 1°. Hence mC is also the number of grammes of water which will be raised 1° by the heat required to raise the body 1°. This mass of water is called the water equivalent of the body.

37. Definition of water equivalent of a body. *The water equivalent of a body is the number of grammes of water which will be raised 1° by the heat required to raise the temperature of the body 1°.*

Thus in the units we have taken, the capacity for heat of a body and its water equivalent are numerically the same.

38. EXPERIMENT (4). *To find by the method of mixture the specific heat of a given substance.*

Proceed as in Experiment (3) and from the data there given calculate the specific heat thus. Let C be the specific heat of the substance, M its mass, T the final temperature; let m be the mass of the water, t its initial temperature. The substance has fallen in temperature $(100 - T)$ degrees; the heat emitted in falling $1°$ is MC.

Hence the heat emitted is

$$MC(100 - T) \text{ units of heat}$$

The heat absorbed by the water is

$$m(T - t) \text{ units,}$$

for its mass is m grammes and it has risen through $(T - t)$ degrees.

If for the present we assume that all the heat emitted by the substance goes into the water we have

$$MC(100 - T) = m(T - t),$$

$$\therefore C = \frac{m(T - t)}{M(100 - T)}.$$

If we take the numbers found in Experiment (3) for copper, we have

$$m = 250, \quad M = 400, \quad T = 26°\cdot 2, \quad t = 15°,$$

and from this we have

$$C = \frac{250}{400} \cdot \frac{11\cdot 2}{73\cdot 8} = \cdot 095.$$

39. The following table gives the values of the specific heat of a few substances.

Iron	·1138	Mercury	·0333
Copper	·0951	Carbon disulphide	·221
Zinc	·0955	Turpentine	·467
Tin	·0562	Glass	·1877
Silver	·0570	Ice	·5
Lead	·0315	Ether	·517
Gold	·0324	Alcohol	·615
Platinum	·0324	Paraffin	·683

40. Defects of the experiment.

Several sources of error affect the experiment as just described.

(1) Heat is used in raising the temperature of the calorimeter and thermometer as well as that of the water; hence the heat emitted by the hot body does not all pass into the water, some goes into the calorimeter. In consequence the specific heat found will be too low.

(2) The hot body cools very rapidly in being transferred from the bath of boiling water to the calorimeter; its temperature will be less than 100° when it is dropped into the water. This again will make the observed specific heat too low.

(3) Heat is lost by radiation or conduction from the calorimeter to surrounding bodies assuming the calorimeter at a higher temperature than the room, or gained by the calorimeter from those bodies if the calorimeter be cooler than they are.

(4) In transferring the hot body from the bath to the calorimeter some hot water is transferred also. This will make the observed value too high.

(5) The temperature of the boiling water is probably not accurately 100° C.

The errors which would arise from these are corrected partly by calculation, partly by modifying the arrangement of the apparatus.

(1) We can allow for this if we know the amount of heat required to raise the calorimeter, stirrer and thermometer 1°. Let this be m_1 heat units. Now the calorimeter etc. are initially and finally at the same temperature as the water. They are raised therefore through $T-t$ degrees, and the heat required for this will be $m_1(T-t)$.

Thus the total heat absorbed is

$$m(T-t) + m_1(T-t)$$

and we have

$$MC(100-T) = m(T-t) + m_1(T-t)$$
$$= (m+m_1)(T-t).$$

Thus the correction shews itself as an addition to the mass of water in the calorimeter; this is increased by the water equivalent of the calorimeter, stirrer etc. This correction which explains the name "water equivalent" is what we should expect. So far as our problem is concerned we may clearly suppose that the calorimeter absorbs no heat, but that it contains such an additional quantity of water as requires, to produce a rise of temperature of 1°, the same amount of heat as is required by the calorimeter. This quantity of water we have defined to be the water equivalent of the calorimeter.

We can determine the water equivalent of the calorimeter experimentally; in practice it is best found from the fact that it is numerically equal to the capacity for heat of the calorimeter. Thus if m_o be the mass of the calorimeter, c its specific heat, we have for its water equivalent the value $m_e \times c$. The water equivalent of the thermometer is included in the term m_1 but it is very small. In the apparatus described the value of m_e may be about 100 grammes, the value of c for copper is approximately ·1, so that the value of $m_e \times c$ is about 10. The calorimeter for this purpose is equivalent to 10 grammes of water. We ought therefore to suppose that the calorimeter contains $500+10$ grammes instead of the 500, and the value of the specific heat will be about ·095.

(2) and (4). These are guarded against by a suitable arrangement of apparatus. This as usually employed consists of a steam heater, an outer cylinder of thin copper A, fig. 16, closed at both ends but with

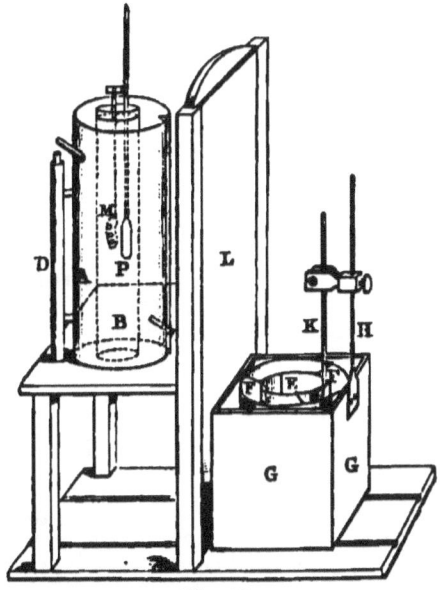

Fig. 16.

a tube B passing through it. The body to be heated hangs by a thread in this inner tube. A thermometer P gives its temperature. The upper end of B is closed by a cork through which the thread and thermometer pass. Steam can be passed through the outer cylinder A from a boiler to a condenser, thus heating M without bringing it in contact either with the steam or the water.

The cylinder turns round a vertical axis D above a horizontal board. A circular hole is cut in the board, which in one position of the cylinder comes directly under the tube B, for other positions of the cylinder the end of the tube is closed by the board. The calorimeter E is contained in a wooden box G to the bottom of which slides are fixed. These run in grooves in the base of the apparatus, and the box can be readily shot under the board to which the heater is fixed. When this is done, the calorimeter is directly under the hole in this board, and when the heater is turned so that the tube B may come vertically over this hole the substance M can be dropped gently into the calorimeter, which is then withdrawn and the rise of temperature measured. To prevent heat reaching the calorimeter by radiation from the heater, a board L sliding in vertical grooves is interposed. When the calorimeter is to be placed beneath the heater this board is raised, when the calorimeter is withdrawn it is again lowered. The hot body is thus raised to a known temperature without becoming wet and can be dropped into the water of the calorimeter without much loss of heat. Its exact temperature is given by the thermometer and thus the error referred to in (5) is avoided.

(3) To avoid loss or gain of heat from external causes, the calorimeter E is polished brightly on the outside (see § 167), and suspended by three strings within a second copper vessel polished on the inside; this second vessel is placed in the wooden box with a packing of wool or felt between it and the box. There is also a lid to the box not shewn in the figure, with a hole through which the thermometer passes. The lid is removed while the hot body is being placed in the calorimeter. (Glazebrook and Shaw, *Practical Physics*, p. 274.)

41. Latent Heat. Heat is required to melt a solid. Thus ice melts at a temperature of $0°$ C. if heat be applied to it. Lead melts at $327°$ C. approximately, sulphur at $113°$ C., silver at $1000°$ C.

Moreover we can shew that a definite quantity of heat is required to melt a given mass—say 1 gramme—of each of these substances, and further that the temperature of the mass remains constant while the melting is in progress.

Definition of Latent Heat of Fusion. *The quantity of heat required to change 1 gramme of a substance from a solid to a liquid form without change of temperature is called the latent heat of fusion of the substance.*

Hence if L be the latent heat of fusion of any substance, the quantity of heat required to melt m grammes of that substance without changing its temperature is mL heat units. Now suppose that m grammes of ice are put into a calorimeter containing M grammes of water at a temperature $T°$ C. The ice, if there be not too much of it, melts and the temperature of the water falls. Let it fall to $t°$ C. The heat emitted by the

M grammes of water as it cools from $T°$ C. to $t°$ C. is used in melting the m grammes of ice and in raising the temperature of the m grammes of water formed from $0°$ C. to $t°$ C.[1].

The heat required for this is $Lm + mt$ units. The heat emitted by the water is $M(T-t)$: if we omit the small corrections these two quantities of heat are to be taken as equal and thus

$$Lm + mt = M(T-t),$$

$$\therefore L = \frac{M}{m}(T-t) - t.$$

Now experiment shews that we may vary the mass of ice or of water or the initial temperature of the water and still always get the same value for L. This value is about 79·2 heat units. We are therefore justified in saying that the amount of heat required to melt 1 gramme of ice is constant and in speaking of "the latent heat of fusion of ice."

42. EXPERIMENT (5). *To find the latent heat of fusion of ice.*

Weigh the calorimeter empty; pour water into it and weigh again. The difference between the two weights gives the mass M of the water[2].

Break up some ice into small pieces. Take the temperature of the water, let it be $T°$ (T should be about 20° C.). Dry each piece of ice on some flannel or cloth and drop it into the water. A stirrer of wire gauze fits the inside of the calorimeter and by placing this above the ice it can be kept below the surface of the water; introduce thus about 50 grammes of ice[3]. As the ice melts the temperature falls; note the lowest

---

[1] If the temperatures be Fahrenheit, since freezing point is 32° Fahr., the melted ice is raised from 32° to $t°$; hence in this case

$$Lm + m(t-32) = M(T-t),$$

or $$L = \frac{M}{m}(T-t) - (t-32).$$

[2] It is necessary to *weigh* the calorimeter and water in this experiment and not merely to *measure* the water put in as in § 33, for the mass of ice introduced can only be obtained by weighing the calorimeter and its contents when the ice is melted; we must therefore know the mass of the calorimeter and water before introducing the ice.

[3] Ice should be added until the fall in temperature is about 10°.

temperature, let it be $t°$. To find the mass of ice added weigh the calorimeter and its contents again. The increase in mass gives m the mass of ice added, and we thus determine experimentally all the quantities but L in the formula above.

Let us suppose we find

Mass of Calorimeter	= 110 grammes.
Mass of Calorimeter and Water	= 630 grammes.
Mass of Water = M	= 520 grammes.
Mass of Calorimeter, Water and Melted Ice	= 685 grammes.
Mass of Ice = m	= 55 grammes.

Observed temperatures $T = 19°·8$, $t = 10°·5$.

Then from the formula $L = \dfrac{M(T-t)}{m} - t$ we obtain as the latent heat of fusion of ice 77·5.

43. Sources of error in this experiment.

(1) The heat given up by the calorimeter in cooling from T to t has been neglected. In consequence the value of L is too small.

(2) There may be a transference of heat between the calorimeter and surrounding bodies.

(3) Some water has been carried into the water with the ice. This again makes L too small.

To correct for (1) the water equivalent of the calorimeter must be known and added to M as described in § 40. The equivalent of the given calorimeter if of copper is about 11, and the number 520 will in consequence become 531.

(2) The correction for this is most easily effected by arranging that the temperature t shall be as much below the temperature of the room as T is above it. For half of the experiment the calorimeter is losing heat, for the other half it is gaining it, and the loss and gain about balance. If the temperature of the room be about 15° C. this is secured in the given experiment.

(3) The only way to avoid this is to dry each piece of ice with care before it is inserted. Its effect is clearly to make L too low, for the mass m as found by the experiment is too high, being that of the ice and the water which adhered to it.

44. Latent heat of Vaporization.
Just as heat is required to change a given mass of solid into liquid without

change of temperature, so heat is required to change a given mass of liquid into vapour.

45. Definition of Latent heat of Vaporization.
The Latent heat of Vaporization of a liquid is the amount of heat required to convert 1 *gramme of the liquid into vapour without change of temperature.*

Thus if L be the latent heat of vaporization of water, at any given temperature, the quantity of heat required to convert m grammes of water into steam at that temperature is mL.

This quantity is also given out when m grammes of steam are condensed to water. Suppose now that m grammes of steam are passed into a calorimeter containing M grammes of water at $T°$ C. The temperature rises; let it become $t°$ C. and let the steam be at $100°$ C. Then m grammes of steam are condensed to water at $100°$ and then cooled from $100°$ to $t°$. Heat is given out in both these processes and the total amount thus evolved is

$$mL + m(100 - t).$$

This amount of heat raises M grammes of water from $T°$ to $t°$ and the heat required for this is

$$M(t - T).$$

If as before we suppose that the heat emitted by the steam passes into the water, we have

$$mL + m(100 - t) = M(t - T),$$

$$\therefore L = \frac{M}{m}(t - T) - (100 - t).$$

If we perform the experiment varying the masses M and m and the temperatures T and t, we find that we obtain the same number for L.

This value is 536 heat units, and when we state that the latent heat of vaporization of water is 536 we mean that 536 heat units are required to convert 1 gramme of water at $100°$ C. into steam at $100°$ C. This is sometimes called the latent heat of steam.

46. EXPERIMENT (6). *To find the latent heat of vaporization of water.*

Weigh the calorimeter empty; pour into it about 500 c.c. of water, at the temperature of the room, say 15°, or if it can conveniently be obtained, at some lower temperature, say 5°, and weigh again. The difference gives the mass M of water in the calorimeter. Boil some water either in a metal boiler or in a glass flask. The mouth of the flask is closed with a cork through which a glass tube passes. To this about a foot of india-rubber tubing is attached, and at the end of the rubber tubing a glass nozzle is fitted. As the water boils the steam issues from the nozzle. The steam will usually carry with it a certain amount of condensed water. This may be reduced in quantity by wrapping wool or felt round the india-rubber tube; most of the water left may be caught by a suitable trap shewn in fig. 17. This consists of a wide glass tube closed with corks through each of which a glass tube passes. To one of these, passing through the top of the wide tube, the india-rubber tube is fitted; the other which passes through the bottom of the wide tube, but reaches inside it nearly to the top, is connected with the nozzle; the whole is covered with wool; the greater portion of the water conveyed by the steam is deposited in the lower part of the wide tube, the steam which issues from the nozzle is nearly dry. The calorimeter is placed in a convenient position near the boiler and protected from direct radiation from the boiler by a screen. When the steam is issuing freely from the nozzle, take the temperature of the water in the calorimeter, let it be $T°$ C. Bring the nozzle quickly below the surface of the water in the calorimeter, the issuing steam is condensed by the cold water and the temperature given by the thermometer rises somewhat rapidly; when it has risen about 20° C. withdraw the nozzle, taking care to carry off as little water as possible. Stir the water and note the highest temperature which the thermometer reaches, let it be $t°$; weigh the calorimeter again, the increase in mass gives the mass m of steam condensed. Then we have sufficient data to find L.

Fig. 17.

Thus suppose we find

Mass of Calorimeter	$= 110$ grammes.
Mass of Calorimeter and Water	$= 605$ grammes.
Mass of Water $= M$	$= 495$ grammes.
Mass of Calorimeter, Water and Condensed Steam	$= 622$ grammes.

$$m = 17 \text{ grammes.}$$
$$T = 15°\cdot2 \text{ C.} \qquad t = 35°\cdot4 \text{ C.}$$

Hence the condensed steam is cooled from 100° to 35°·4 or through 64°·6 C., and the heat given out by the 17 grammes is

$$17L + 17 \times 64\cdot6.$$

This heat raised 495 grammes of water from 15°·2 to 35°·4 or through 20°·2 C. For this $495 \times 20\cdot2$ units are needed;

$$\therefore L + 64\cdot6 = \frac{495 \times 20\cdot2}{17} = 588\cdot2,$$
$$\therefore L = 523\cdot6.$$

47. Sources of Error. These are much the same as in the last experiment.

(1) Some of the heat given up by the steam has been used in raising the temperature of the calorimeter. In consequence the value of L found is too low.

(2) There has been loss of heat by radiation, from this cause also L is too low.

(3) Some hot water has been carried over, thus m is too big and therefore L is too low.

(1) To correct for this, the water equivalent of the calorimeter must be added to M.

(2) An estimate of the rate of cooling can be made by a suitable experiment (see § 170), and the error allowed for. Its magnitude would be reduced by starting at a low temperature, say 5°, and raising the water finally as much above the temperature of the room as it was initially below it.

(3) Care must be taken to dry the steam.

48. Ice Calorimeters. The facts that a definite quantity of heat is required to melt a given quantity of ice or to vaporize a given quantity of water have both been used as a means of measuring quantities of heat.

Thus various forms of ice calorimeters have been devised.

In the simplest form as used by Black, fig. 18, a hole is cut or bored into a block of ice. This can be covered by a slab of ice. The hot body of known mass M is raised to a known temperature T and dropped into the cavity, the cover is put on and after a short time it is removed. The water formed from the melted ice is sucked up into a pipette and its mass deter- mined by weighing or measuring its volume; let it be m grammes and let L be the latent heat of fusion of the ice, C the specific heat of the substance. Then M grammes in cooling through T degrees from $T°$ to $0°$ give out MCT heat units, and this heat melts m grammes of ice for which mL heat units are required,

Fig. 18.

$$\therefore MCT = mL,$$

and $C = \dfrac{mL}{MT}$.

In this form however the measurement will not give accurate results, for (1) it is impossible to prevent some heat from getting into the cavity from sources other than the hot body and (2) it is impossible to get all the water out of the cavity and measure its mass accurately. These difficulties are to some extent overcome in Lavoisier and Laplace's Calorimeter, though by no means completely.

*49. Ice Calorimeter of Lavoisier and Laplace. The instrument, fig. 19, consists of three copper vessels. The inner one A is to contain the hot body. It is fitted with a lid and placed inside a second copper vessel B, the space between the two is filled with ice broken into small pieces. A tube passes through the outermost vessel C into B. The vessel B also has a lid and is surrounded by the third vessel C, the space between B and C is filled with ice and a tube passes into C. Thus the ice in B is entirely surrounded by the ice in C, and so heat from outside cannot pass into B. So long as C is fairly filled with ice, the heat from outside melts ice in C and the temperature remains at zero; no ice is melted in B. If the lids be now removed and a hot body be placed in A, the lids being quickly replaced, some of the ice in B is melted by the heat emitted by the hot body in cooling down to zero, and the water formed from the melting ice runs out through the tube into a vessel placed to receive it. The mass of water thus produced can be weighed. And the specific heat of the solid can be found from the same equation as in § 48 above. For if M, T and C be the mass, temperature and specific heat of the substance, m the mass of the water formed, we have $MCT =$ heat given out by substance in cooling from T to zero $=$ heat used in melting m grammes of ice $= mL$,

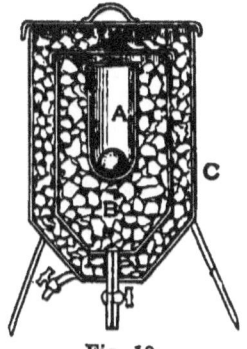

Fig. 19.

$$\therefore C = \frac{mL}{MT}.$$

Even in this form however the instrument is not accurate, for a considerable portion of the water formed in B sticks to the ice, thus m and therefore C are too small.

*50. Bunsen's Ice Calorimeter. The action of this instrument depends on the fact that ice on melting diminishes in volume by a known amount, so that if the change of volume be measured the amount melted and hence the quantity of heat employed in melting the ice can be measured.

This calorimeter consists of a glass tube A, fig. 20, like a large test tube which is sealed inside a larger glass vessel B. At the bottom of this there is attached a small tube CDE bent as shewn in the figure. The bore of the horizontal portion of this should be fairly uniform and the area of its cross section should be known. This tube and the lower part of the vessel B are filled with mercury. The upper part of A is filled with water from which the air has been removed by long-continued boiling.

To use the instrument it is packed in ice inside another vessel, leaving only the horizontal tube DE projecting; some of the water in A is then frozen.

This is done by passing through B, by means of a pump, alcohol which has been cooled below 0° C. by exposure to a freezing mixture. As the ice is formed the combined volume of the water and ice in A increases and some of the mercury is forced out of the tube DE. When the freezing has been sufficient the alcohol is removed and a quantity of water which has been cooled down to 0° C. is placed in B. If the calorimeter is completely packed in ice no heat can now reach the ice in A from outside and the combined volume of the water and ice in B remains constant, the end of the mercury column takes up a definite position in the tube DE,—a scale of millimetres is attached to this tube and thus the position of the end of the column can be noted. Let us suppose this steady state has been attained, and that the mercury in DE stands at a point P_1.

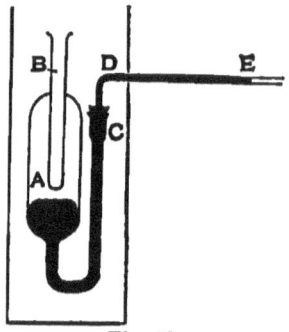

Fig. 20.

Place a hot body in the water in B, let M, C, T be its mass, specific heat and temperature. The heat given up by this body in cooling to 0° C. melts some of the ice in A. The combined volume of ice and water is reduced and the mercury recedes in the tube, becoming steady again finally at a second point P_2; when this is reached the body has been cooled down to 0° and all the heat given up by it has been employed in melting the ice[1]. Measure the distance P_1P_2 in cm., and by

---

[1] Very little heat escapes from the top of the water in B, for as the temperature of the water begins to rise above 0° its density increases slightly (see § 90) and the warmed water remains at the bottom and melts the ice.

multiplying it by the area of the cross-section of the tube in square cm., find the change in the combined volume of water and ice in A, let it be v c.c. Now the volume of 1 gramme of ice 0° is 1·091 c.c., while that of 1 gramme of water is 1 c.c. Thus when 1 gramme of ice becomes water there will be a diminution of volume of ·091 c.c., so that to produce contraction of v c.c. the number of grammes of ice melted will be

$v/\cdot 091$, and this comes to be $v \times 10\cdot 99$ grammes.

To melt this $L \times v \times 10\cdot 99$ heat units are required.

Hence $MCT = L \times v \times 10\cdot 99$,

and
$$C = \frac{10\cdot 99\, Lv}{MT}.$$

*51. The Steam Calorimeter. In the steam calorimeter recently devised by Mr Joly, a body of mass M whose specific heat is to be found is suspended by a fine platinum wire inside a calorimeter. The wire passes through a small hole in the calorimeter and is suspended from one arm of a delicate balance. The body is weighed and its temperature is observed. Let it be $T°$.

Steam is then let into the calorimeter. Some of the steam is condensed on the body, raising its temperature until it reaches 100°. The mass of steam so condensed can be found by again weighing the body in the steam; let this mass be m grammes. Then m grammes of steam in condensing to water at 100° C. have raised the temperature of M grammes of the body from $T°$ to 100°. Hence if C be the specific heat of the body, L the latent heat of steam,

$$MC(100 - T) = mL,$$
$$C = \frac{mL}{M(100 - T)}.$$

*52. Other forms of Calorimeters. Various other forms of calorimeters have been devised for special purposes. Thus in Regnault's experiments on the specific heat of gases he employed two long coils of thin copper tubing through which the gas was passed; there were arrangements for measuring the amount of gas which passed through and for regulating its pressure which was kept constant. One of these coils was immersed in a vessel of boiling oil at a known high temperature, the other was in the water of the calorimeter. As the gas passed slowly through, it acquired the temperature of the oil bath in the first coil, in traversing the second coil it parted with its heat to the water in the calorimeter which in consequence rose in temperature. From this rise in temperature, combined with a knowledge of the mass of water in the calorimeter, the water equivalent of the coil and calorimeter and the temperature of the oil bath, the specific heat of the gas can be found.

The specific heat of a liquid can be found by the method of mixture in various ways. One is to enclose the liquid in a thin copper vessel, to heat this in the same manner as a solid either in hot water or in the steam heater and then immerse it in the water in the calorimeter. In making calculations the heat contributed by the copper vessel must be taken into account.

The following **Example** will shew how this is done. 250 grammes of turpentine enclosed in a copper vessel whose mass is 25 grammes are heated to 100° C. and immersed in 589 grammes of water at 13° C. in a copper calorimeter of which the mass is 110 grammes. The temperature rises to 27°·5. Assuming the specific heat of copper to be ·1 find that of turpentine.

Let C be the specific heat of turpentine.

Then heat given out by turpentine in falling from 100° to 27°·5

$$= 250 \times C \times 72\cdot 5.$$

Heat given out by copper vessel in falling from 100° to 27°·5

$$= 25 \times \cdot 1 \times 72\cdot 5.$$

∴ Total heat given out $= (250\, C + 2\cdot 5) 72\cdot 5.$

Heat absorbed by water rising from 13° to 27°·5

$$= 589 \times 14\cdot 5.$$

Heat absorbed by calorimeter in rising from 13° to 27°·5

$$= 110 \times \cdot 1 \times 14\cdot 5.$$

∴ Total heat absorbed $= (589 + 11)\, 14\cdot 5.$

∴ $(250\, C + 2\cdot 5)\, 72\cdot 5 = 600 \times 14\cdot 5.$

And from this we find $C = \cdot 470.$

Or again, we may determine the specific heat of a liquid by raising some solid of known specific heat to a given temperature, immersing it in a known mass of the liquid and measuring the rise of temperature.

Thus 50 grammes of glass are heated to 100° and immersed in 250 grammes of alcohol at 15°. The temperature rises to 20°. The specific heat of glass is ·198, find that of alcohol.

Let $c=$ specific heat of alcohol.

The heat given out by the glass in cooling from 100° to 20°
$$= 50 \times \cdot 198 \times 80.$$
The heat absorbed by the alcohol in rising from 15° to 20°
$$= 250 \times c \times 5.$$
$$\therefore c \times 250 \times 5 = 50 \times 80 \times \cdot 198.$$
Whence $c = \cdot 63.$

Another form of Calorimeter is Favre and Silbermann's. This consists of a large iron sphere which is filled with mercury; a glass tube of narrow bore is fitted to this, and the mercury is visible in the tube. The instrument is thus like a large thermometer. A tube of thin iron in shape like a test tube penetrates to the centre of the sphere. If a hot body is placed in this tube it communicates its heat to the mercury through the thin iron; the mercury rises in the glass tube. The whole apparatus is packed in some non-conducting material so that all the heat communicated to the mercury is retained by it and the expansion of the mercury is thus proportional to the amount of heat communicated to it. If then we know the temperature of the hot body when it was inserted in the tube and the temperature to which it falls, we can determine the amount of heat it has given out in falling through a known range of temperature and thus find its specific heat.

EXAMPLES.

CALORIMETRY. (SPECIFIC HEAT AND LATENT HEAT.)

1. Describe any good method of determining the specific heat of a solid substance.

The latent heat of tin is 14·25, its specific heat ·064, and its melting point 232° on the Centigrade scale. What will be the corresponding numbers on the Fahrenheit scale?

2. What is meant by a *unit of heat*? Taking the specific heat of lead as ·031, and its latent heat as 5·07, find the amount of heat necessary to raise 15 lbs. of lead from a temperature of 115° C. to its melting point, 320° C., and to melt it.

G. H.

HEAT.

✓ 3. Define the boiling point and the latent heat of vaporization of a liquid. Why is it necessary to note the height of the barometer when determining the upper fixed point of a thermometer? How is this determination made? An alteration of pressure of 26 mm. alters the boiling point of water 1°. Find the boiling point when the height of the barometer is 745 mm.

4. Define latent heat, specific heat, capacity for heat. The specific heat of copper is ·095; calculate the capacity for heat of a kilogramme of copper. A kilogramme of copper is raised to a temperature of 100° C. and placed in an ice calorimeter. How much ice will be melted assuming the latent heat of fusion of ice to be 80?

5. What do you understand by the latent heat of fusion and the latent heat of evaporation of a substance? Explain a method for determining the latent heat of evaporation of water.

6. Explain the statement that the latent heat of water is 80. To a pound of ice at 0° are communicated 100 units of heat (pound-degrees Centigrade). What change of temperature does the ice undergo, and in what way is its volume altered?

7. 2½ kilogrammes of iron (specific heat ·112) at 95° C. are put into 3 litres of water at 15° C. Find the rise of temperature of the water.

8. A mass of 200 grammes of copper, whose specific heat is ·095, is heated to 100° C. and placed in 100 grammes of alcohol at 8° C., contained in a copper calorimeter, whose mass is 25 grammes: the temperature rises to 28°·5 C. Find the specific heat of alcohol.

9. If 25 grammes of steam at 100° C. be passed into 300 grammes of ice-cold water, what will be the temperature of the mixture, the latent heat of steam being taken equal to 536?

10. In 100 grammes of boiling water ($t=100$) there are placed 20 grammes of ice, and the temperature falls to 70° when the ice is just melted. Determine the latent heat of fusion of ice, assuming no heat to be lost.

11. What is meant by the statement that the "latent heat of steam is 536"?

Steam is passed into 100 grammes of water at 15° in a calorimeter. If the mass of water in the calorimeter be by this means increased by 10 grammes, find the final temperature, supposing no heat to have been lost and that the heat absorbed by the calorimeter may be neglected.

✓ 12. Five grammes of a substance at 100° C. are placed in a Bunsen's Calorimeter and the volume of the ice and water is found to decrease by ·05 cubic centimetres. Assuming that water expands by one eleventh of its volume on freezing and that the latent heat of fusion is 79, find the specific heat of the substance.

CALORIMETRY.

13. What is the water equivalent of a vessel, and how may it be determined?

14. A glass beaker contains 1 lb. of water and some ice. When 1 oz. of steam at 100° C. has been supplied to the vessel the contents are at a temperature of 3° C.; how much ice was there to begin with?

(Latent heat of ice = 79, of steam = 537.)

15. Find the specific heat of a substance of which 375 grammes at 100° C., when immersed in 280 grammes of water at 15° C., raise the temperature of the water to 25° C.

16. Into a mass of water at 0° C. 100 grammes of ice at −12° C. are introduced, 7·2 grammes of the water are frozen and the temperature of the ice rises to 0° C.; if the specific heat of ice be ·5, find its latent heat of fusion.

17. Three liquids A, B, C, are given. Four grammes of A at 60°, and one gramme of C at 50°, have, after mixing, a temperature of 55°. A mixture of one gramme of A at 60° and one gramme of B at 50° shews a temperature of 55°. What would be the temperature of a mixture of one gramme of B at 60°, and one gramme of C at 50°? Would the result be different according as the thermometer readings given are those of the Fahrenheit or the Centigrade scale?

18. What are the "latent heat" and the "total heat" of steam? Describe the effect of compressing saturated steam and of allowing it to expand "without loss or gain of heat."

19. Explain why in a Bunsen's Calorimeter there is no need to determine the temperature of the liquid kept in the test tube of the calorimeter when the capacity for heat of a solid is determined.

20. A quantity of turpentine, 250 grammes in mass, is enclosed in a copper vessel whose mass is 25 grammes and is heated to 100° C. On immersing the whole in 535 grammes of water at 13° C. in a copper calorimeter 110 grammes in mass the temperature rises to 27·5° C. Assuming the specific heat of copper to be ·1 find that of turpentine.

21. What will be the result of placing (a) 5 lbs. of copper at 100° C., (b) 30 lbs. of copper at 80° C., in contact with 1½ lbs. of ice at 0° C.?

(Specific heat of copper = ·092, latent heat of fusion of ice = 79.)

22. A ball of copper (Sp. heat = 0·092), whose mass is 5 lbs. is heated in a furnace, and allowed to drop into a gallon of water at 10° C.; the temperature of the water rises to 50° C.; find the temperature of the furnace. What are the objections to this method of measuring high temperatures?

23. A calorimeter of copper weighs 80 grammes and the specific heat of the copper is ·092. It contains 100 grammes of water at 10° C. Steam at 100° C. is passed into it until the temperature rises to 80° C. when the total weight of water is found to be 113·42 grammes. What value does this give for the Latent Heat of Steam?

52   HEAT.

24. The specific heat of copper is ·095; calculate the capacity for heat of a kilogramme of copper. A kilogramme of copper is raised to a temperature of 100° C. and placed in an ice calorimeter. If 118 grammes of ice are melted find the latent heat of fusion of ice.

25. 20 grammes of a substance, at a temperature of 10° C., whose specific heat is ·09515 are mixed with an unknown weight of another substance, at a temperature of 20° C., whose specific heat is ·615. The resulting temperature is 18° C. What was the weight of the second substance used in the experiment?

26. An observer on immersing his thermometer into a mass of water, finds that the mercury in the tube sinks down into the bulb: how could he determine the temperature of the water without the use of another thermometer? Illustrate your answer by an example.

27. A mass of 5 lbs. of metal at 460° C. is placed in 12 lbs. of water at 10° C.; the resulting temperature is observed to be 60°. Find the specific heat of the metal.

28. A mass of 125 grammes of tin at 100° C. is placed in 63 grammes of water at 0° C. The temperature rises to 10° C. Find the specific heat of tin.

29. A pound of platinum is placed in a furnace and having acquired the temperature of the furnace it is immersed in a vessel containing 10 lbs. of water at 10° C. The water rises to 14°·3 C. Find the temperature of the furnace.

30. A vessel contains 850 grammes of water at 8° C. A kilogramme of iron at 100° C. is placed in the water and the temperature rises to 18° C. Shew that the capacity for heat of the vessel is 84·8.

31. If 20 lbs. of water at 44° C. are mixed with 8 lbs. at 100° C., find the temperature of the mixture.

32. A bar of copper whose mass is 80 grammes and temperature 80° C. is immersed in 127 grammes of water at 27° C. The temperature rises 3° C. Find the specific heat of copper.

33. If the heat obtained from the combustion of 1 lb. of coal raise the temperature of 1000 lbs. of iron 50° C., find the number of heat units given out.

CHAPTER V.

EXPANSION OF SOLIDS.

53. Experiments on Expansion. We have already said that most bodies expand as their temperature rises, we proceed to examine in more detail the expansion of solid bodies. The following experiments illustrate this.

EXPERIMENT (7). Take a short rod of metal about 10 cm. in length with flat ends, and make a gauge out of thin sheet brass or some other material to fit the rod exactly. In fig. 21 AB is the rod, CD the gauge; heat the rod in a Bunsen flame. The gauge will no longer fit it but is too short.

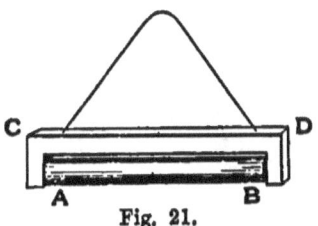

Fig. 21.

The same experiment may be performed with a sphere which has been turned so as just to pass when cold through a metal ring. On heating the sphere it will no longer pass through the ring.

EXPERIMENT (8). Take a rod of metal from 30 to 50 cm. in length. Let one end B rest on a horizontal glass plate while the other is fixed in some suitable manner as by the weight at A in fig. 22. Place a fine needle between the rod and the glass plate in such a way that if the rod moves it will cause the needle to roll on the plate.

Pass the point of the needle through a straw or a strip of thin aluminium foil to serve as a pointer. A small motion of the needle causes the end of the pointer to move over a considerable distance. Arrange under the rod a Bunsen gas-burner. On lighting this the rod is heated and expands. The end A

being fixed, the motion of the end B causes the needle to roll

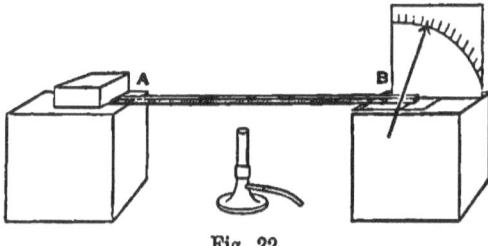

Fig. 22.

on the plate and moves the pointer. On removing the gas-burner the rod cools and the pointer comes back to its original position.

EXPERIMENT (9). *To shew that different bodies expand differently when raised to the same temperature.*

Let a gauge such as that described in Experiment 7 above be made of brass and an iron rod filed so as just to fit it when cold, then if the two be heated by passing them a few times through the flame of a Bunsen burner it will be found that the iron rod will drop out; the brass expands more than the iron.

Or again, take two bars, one of iron, the other of brass, of the same size, about 20 cm. long, 2 cm. broad and ·1 cm. thick, and rivet them together with a number of rivets. Place them over the Bunsen gas-burner: they become curved, the iron being on the inside of the curve, the brass outside: brass expands more than iron.

54. Linear Expansion. The amount by which a rod of metal increases in length for a moderate rise of temperature, say 100° C., differs as we have just said for different metals, but is in all cases very small. A rod of iron 1 metre long would increase in length, if raised through 100° C. in temperature, by about ·12 cm.; the increase in length of a rod of brass of the same length would be about ·18 cm.

Now experiment shews that the increase in length is

proportional to the original length and to the change in temperature. Thus for the same change of temperature 100° C. an iron rod 200 cm. long would increase by $2 \times \cdot 12$ or ·24 cm., while a rod 50 cm. long would increase by $\frac{1}{2} \times \cdot 12$ or ·06 cm.; again if the rod were raised through 200° C. the increase would be ·24 cm., if through 1000° C. it would be 1·2 cm. We are thus led to the following definition.

55. Definition of Coefficient of Linear Expansion.
The ratio of the increase in length produced by a rise of temperature of 1° to the original length is called the coefficient of linear expansion of a rod.

Suppose a rod l_0 cm. in length is heated through $t°$ and let its length become l cm., let a be the coefficient of linear expansion. Then the increase of length for $t°$ is $l - l_0$, thus the increase for 1° is $(l - l_0)/t$ and the ratio of this to the original length is $(l - l_0)/l_0 t$,

$$\therefore a = \frac{l - l_0}{l_0 t}.$$

Hence
$$l - l_0 = l_0 a t,$$
$$\therefore l = l_0 + l_0 a t = l_0 (1 + a t).$$

Thus if we know the original length l_0, the rise[1] of temperature t and the coefficient of linear expansion a, we can find the new length l.

We may put the definition in another form thus; let us suppose that $l_0 = 1$ cm. and that $t = 1°$, then

$$a = \frac{l - l_0}{l_0 t} = l - 1.$$

Now $l - 1$ is the increase in length of unit length, produced by a rise of 1°.

Hence we may say that the coefficient of linear expansion is the increase produced by a rise of temperature of 1° in a length of 1 centimetre.

[1] It must be noted that t is the rise of temperature: if T_0 is the initial temperature, T the final, then $t = T - T_0$, so that we may write
$$l = l_0 \{1 + a (T - T_0)\}.$$

We may obtain the above formula from this definition thus:

the increase of 1 cm. for 1° is a,

∴ the increase of l_0 cm. for 1° is al_0;

and the increase of l_0 cm. for $t°$ is $al_0 t$.

Thus since the new length is the original length together with the increase for $t°$ we have

$$l = l_0 + l_0 at = l_0 (1 + at).$$

Example. The coefficient of expansion of brass is ·0000189. A metre scale is correct at 0° C. What error will be committed in measuring a length of 1 metre with it at 20° C.?

A length of 1 cm. expands by ·0000189 cm. for 1°.

Thus the increase of 100 cm. for 1° is

100 × ·0000189 or ·00189 cm.,

and for 20° it is ·0378 cm.

Hence the error is ·0378 cm.

56. Measurement of Expansion. In order then to measure a coefficient of linear expansion we must measure both the small increase of length produced in a rod of measured length by a rise of temperature and the rise of temperature. Now the increase in length is very small; if it be measured directly very delicate instruments are required; we can however magnify the apparent increase in a known proportion as in the following experiment.

57. EXPERIMENT (10). *To measure the coefficient of linear expansion of a metal.*

AB, fig. 23, is a stout wire of the metal about 1 metre long hanging vertically from a firm support A. A long horizontal lever CBD is attached to the other end of the wire, C is the fulcrum and is secured to the same support as the upper end of the wire; this is shewn to a larger scale in fig. 23 (a). The distance CB is about ·5 cm. and the length CD about 50 cm.

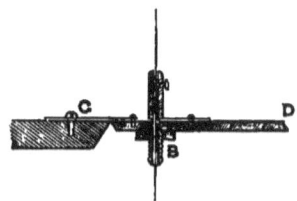

Fig. 23 (a).

These distances must be measured with care.

If the wire expands B moves down and the end D of the lever moves, but the motion of D with the numbers given is one hundred times that of B. By means of a scale the motion of D is measured.

A vertical jacket tube EF of glass or brass closed with corks at the top and bottom surrounds the wire which passes freely through short lengths of glass tubing inserted in the corks at E and F. Two other tubes are inserted into the jacket and by their aid steam can be passed through the jacket raising the temperature of the wire to $100°$.

To make an experiment the temperature of the wire t is read by a thermometer, and its length l_0 measured with an ordinary metre scale. The position of D on the scale is read. Steam is then allowed to pass through the jacket; the wire expands and in consequence D comes to D': measure the distance DD', let it be d; the temperature is now $100°$, so that the rise in temperature is $(100-t)$. The increase in length is BB'. Now from the similar triangles CBB', CDD', fig. 24, we have

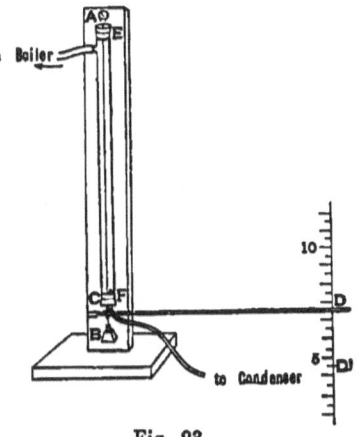

Fig. 23.

$$\frac{BB'}{CB} = \frac{DD'}{CD},$$

$$\therefore BB' = DD' \times \frac{CB}{CD} = d \times \frac{CB}{CD}.$$

Fig. 24.

The lengths CB and CD are determined by measurement of the lever, in the instrument described we have

$$CB/CD = 1/100.$$

$$\therefore BB' = \frac{d}{100}.$$

Now to find a the coefficient of expansion we have to divide the increase in length by the original length and by the rise in temperature: we thus get

$$a = \frac{d}{100 \times l_0 (100 - t)}.$$

If the wire be of copper, 120 cm. long and t be 15° C., we should find $d = 18$ cm. approximately.

Thus
$$a = \frac{18}{100 \times 120 \times 85}$$
$$= \cdot 0000176.$$

58. Lavoisier's Method. In the apparatus used by Lavoisier and Laplace the rod of metal is placed in a horizontal position and rests on rollers in a trough containing oil or water which can be heated.
The lever BD, fig. 25, is vertical; one end rests against the rod at B. A telescope DE is fixed to the lever at D with its axis horizontal; and a mark S on distant scale is viewed through the telescope. As the rod expands DB is turned into the position DB', and a different mark S' on the scale is brought into view.

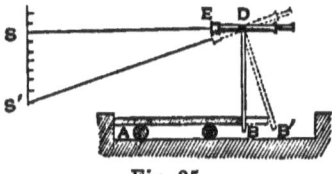

Fig. 25.

If the distances BD and DS be known, we can find BB' the extension, for we have

$$BB' = SS' \cdot \frac{BD}{DS},$$

and from this the coefficient of expansion can be found[1].

---

[1] In fig. 25 the expansion BB' is for the sake of clearness enormously exaggerated.

The measurement can also be made by fixing a mirror M on an axis which can be made to turn by a piece of fine silk attached to the lever at D, fig. 26, and passing over a pulley.

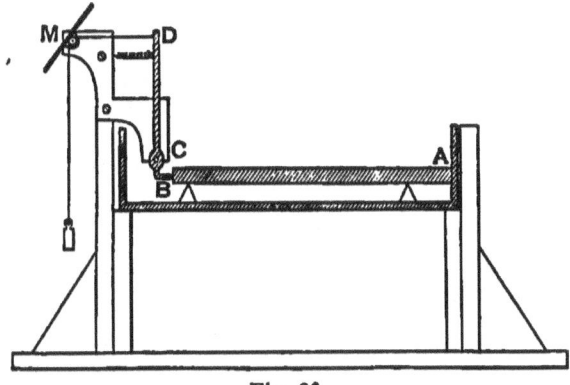

Fig. 26.

Light from a distant lamp falls on the mirror and is reflected on to a vertical scale. As the bar expands the mirror rotates and the reflected beam moves over the scale, the angle through which the beam turns being twice that described by the mirror[1].

In order to keep the end B of the lever pressed up against the bar, a stiff spring is attached to the end D and to the frame of the apparatus. The calculation of the actual expansion from measurements with this apparatus would be difficult and would not lead to accurate results; we should require to know the ratio of the lengths of the arms of the lever BCD, the diameter of the pulley and the distance between the mirror and the scale; it would be necessary also to suppose that the silk did not slip on the pulley.

Example. In the apparatus shewn in fig. 25 in which the arm BD of the lever is 20 cm., and the distance between the telescope and scale 80 metres, when a rod of copper 50 cm. long is put in and heated from 15° to 100° the spot moves through 29 cm.: find the coefficient of linear expansion of copper.

[1] See *Light*, § 24.

In this case the ratio of the arm of the lever to the distance between the mirror and scale, or BD/DS, is $\frac{1}{100}$.

∴ Increase in length $= \frac{1}{100} \times 29$ cm.
$= \cdot 0725$ cm.

∴ $a = \dfrac{\cdot 0725}{50 \times 85} = \cdot 000017$.

59. Micrometer Method of measuring Expansion. Various methods have been devised for the direct measurement of the small increase in length produced by expansion. The following is one which may be employed.

EXPERIMENT. (11). *To measure the coefficient of linear expansion of a rod with a micrometer.*

A micrometer scale is fitted in the eye-piece of a microscope. This consists of a very fine scale engraved on glass; each division of the scale being perhaps ¼ of a millimetre. The microscope is then focussed on a similar scale and the magnified image of this scale is seen in coincidence with the micrometer. The number of divisions of the micrometer which coincide with one division of the magnified scale are then counted. This determines the magnifying power of the object glass of the microscope; let us suppose this is found to be 25. Thus a distance which we know to be ¼ mm. appears to cover 25 divisions when viewed through the microscope, so that 1 division of the eye-piece scale corresponds to $\frac{1}{100}$ mm. in the object viewed.

Suppose then we are looking through the microscope at some fine mark which we see coincident with a division in the eye-piece scale and that this mark is moved so that its image appears to cross a number of divisions n, which we can count, of the eye-piece scale. We know that the mark has moved through $n/100$ mm. We are thus able to measure easily a very small displacement of the mark and can apply this to measure the expansion of a rod. For this purpose take a rod about 1 metre long with a fine mark engraved on it near each end. Measure with a scale the distance between the marks, let it be l_0 cm. Place it in a steam jacket through which steam can be passed, allowing the ends to project through corks in such a way that the marks are just visible outside the tube, and arrange a microscope with a micrometer scale in the eye-piece to view each mark. Place a thermometer in the tube alongside the rod and take the temperature, let it be $t°$; note the position of the mark on each of the micrometer scales. Pass steam from a boiler through the jacket. The marks will appear to move across the scales and after a time will take up a stationary position again when the rod has come to the temperature of the steam; let a and b be the number of divisions of the scales through which the marks have moved. Then, if the divisions of the scales be $\frac{1}{4}$ mm. and the magnifying power of the object glass 25, as described above, the increase in the length of the rod will be

$$\frac{a+b}{100} \text{ millimetres or } \frac{a+b}{1000} \text{ cm.}$$

The original length is l_0 cm., thus the increase in length of unit length is $(a+b)/1000 l_0$, and this is for a rise of temperature of $100-t$. Hence the coefficient of expansion is

$$a = \frac{(a+b)}{1000 l_0 (100-t)}.$$

60. Sources of error in the experiments.

Besides those we have noted there are other sources of error common to the experiments described in Sections 56 to 59.

(1) We suppose that the distance between the microscopes in Section 59 and the distance between the point of suspension and the fulcrum in Section 56 are not altered by the change of temperature. Neither of these statements is strictly accurate, but if the microscopes are fastened down to a stout wooden or stone table, the error will be very small, and the same will apply to Experiment 10 if the support and fulcrum are properly secured.

(2) A portion of the wire in Experiment 10, and of the rod in Experiment 11, is outside the steam jacket, so that the temperature of the whole is not accurately 100°. This can be made small by making the exposed parts as short as possible.

The method of Lavoisier and Laplace described in Section 58 is free from both objections.

The experiment described in Section 59 is a modification of the method employed by Roy and Ramsden. In their apparatus the whole of the bar whose expansion was to be measured was in an oil bath, while the bar to which their reading microscopes were secured was kept in ice. The errors we have just been describing were thus avoided.

61. Coefficients of Expansion.

The approximate values of the coefficient of linear expansion of various substances are given in the following table.

Aluminium	·0000222	Platinum	·0000089
Brass	·0000189	Silver	·0000194
Copper	·0000167	Steel	·0000110
Gold	·0000142	Zinc	·0000298
Iron	·0000117	Ebonite	·0000770
Lead	·0000280	Glass	·0000089

These values are only approximate, for the coefficients depend on the state of the material, and, in the case of a composite substance such as glass or ebonite, on the exact composition of the specimen.

It will be noticed that the coefficient for platinum is the same as for glass. This is very important, for in consequence platinum wire can be hermetically sealed into glass. It would be impossible to do this with copper wire, for the glass and the copper must be heated red hot; in cooling down the glass becomes fairly rigid at about 400° C., but the copper contracts for a given change of temperature nearly twice as much as the glass and so becomes smaller than the hole in the glass through which it passes and cracks the glass.

It will also be observed that the coefficients of expansion are all very small and in consequence their exact determination is a matter of some difficulty.

62. Superficial and Cubical Expansion.

Up to the present we have been dealing with expansion in one direction only, but if a body be heated it expands in all directions, it increases—with some few exceptions—in surface and in volume.

We have therefore to consider the surface or superficial expansion and the volume or cubical expansion of a body.

Now it is found that the increase in surface or in volume is proportional to the original surface or volume respectively and to the change in temperature.

We may thus define the coefficients of superficial and of cubical expansion.

63. Definition. *The Coefficient of $\begin{Bmatrix}superficial\\cubical\end{Bmatrix}$ expansion is the ratio of the increase in $\begin{Bmatrix}surface\\volume\end{Bmatrix}$ produced by a rise of temperature of 1° to the original $\begin{Bmatrix}surface\\volume\end{Bmatrix}$.*

From the definition we may obtain formulae similar to that found in § 55 for the coefficient of linear expansion. For if S_0 be the original area, S the area when the temperature has been raised $t°$, and β the coefficient of expansion, the increase in area for 1° is $(S - S_0)/t$, and β the ratio of this to the original area is given by the equation

$$\beta = \frac{S - S_0}{S_0 t},$$

$$\therefore S = S_0 (1 + \beta t).$$

Similarly if γ be the coefficient of cubical expansion, V_0 and V the volume and t the rise of temperature,

$$\gamma = \frac{V - V_0}{V_0 t},$$

$$V = V_0 (1 + \gamma t).$$

We may also as in Section 55 state that

The Coefficient of $\begin{Bmatrix}superficial\\cubical\end{Bmatrix}$ expansion is the increase in $\begin{Bmatrix}area\\volume\end{Bmatrix}$ of unit $\begin{Bmatrix}area\\volume\end{Bmatrix}$ produced by a rise of temperature of 1°.

64. Relation between Coefficients of Expansion. We may shew in the following way that there is a relation between these coefficients of expansion. Consider a square each side of which is 1 cm. Its area is 1 square cm. Let its temperature be raised $t°$. The area increases to $1 + \beta t$, but each side increases to $1 + at$. Thus the new area is $(1 + at)^2$,

$$\therefore 1 + \beta t = (1 + at)^2 = 1 + 2at + a^2 t^2.$$

Now since a is very small for most materials, $a^2 t^2$ is very small compared with at unless t is very large; for example if $t = 100°$ and the square be made of copper for which

$$a = \cdot 000016,$$

we have $\qquad at = \cdot 0016,$

$$a^2 t^2 = \cdot 00000256,$$

and $a^2 t^2$ is so small that we may omit it: we have then

$$1 + \beta t = 1 + 2at.$$

Thus $\beta = 2a.$

Again consider a cube each side of which is 1 cm. Its volume is 1 c.c. On heating it $t°$ its volume becomes $1 + \gamma t$ cubic centimetres; but each edge becomes $1 + at$ cm. in length.

Thus the new volume is $(1 + at)^3$ c.cm.

Hence $\qquad 1 + \gamma t = (1 + at)^3 = 1 + 3at + 3a^2 t^2 + a^3 t^3.$

Now we have seen that we may neglect $a^2 t^2$ and *a fortiori* $a^3 t^3$ compared with at. Thus we have

$$1 + \gamma t = 1 + 3at,$$
$$\therefore \gamma = 3a = \tfrac{3}{2}\beta.$$

If then the coefficient of linear expansion be known, the coefficients of superficial and of cubical expansion can be found from the above.

The exact meaning of the neglect of the terms involving a^2 and a^3 may be made more clear by the following.

Let $ABCD$ be a square each side of which is 1 cm. and let $A'B'C'D$ be the same square when its temperature has been raised $1°$. Produce AB and CB to meet $C'B'$ and $A'B'$ in F and E respectively.

Then the side DA, 1 cm. in length, has increased by an amount AA', thus AA' is equal to a. DC also 1 cm. has increased by CC', hence CC' is equal to a.

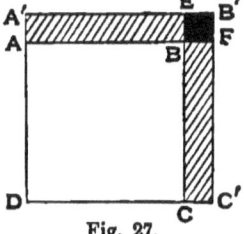

Fig. 27.

Hence also $\qquad BE = BF = a.$

Hence area of parallelogram $AE = a.$
area of parallelogram $CF = a.$
area of square $EF \quad = a^2.$

And the increase of area of the square centimetre $ABCD$ is rectangle AE + square EF + rectangle CF or $2a + a^2$.

In neglecting a^2 compared with a we are neglecting the square EF compared with the rectangle AE; if we remember that AB is 1 cm. while BE or EF for copper is less than two hundred thousandths of a centimetre, it is clear that we may do this and say that the increase in area is the sum of the rectangles AE and CF or $2a$. But β is the increase in area of 1 square cm.

$$\therefore \beta = 2a.$$

65. Linear and Cubical Expansion. Again consider a cube (shewn in fig. 28 with dark lines) each edge of which is 1 cm.; let its temperature be raised 1°, the figure will become a cube having each edge equal to $(1 + a)$ cm. This cube is made up of the original cube together with three square slabs each of which is 1 square cm. in area and a cm. thick, three rectangular strips each 1 cm. high on a base of a^2 square cm. and a small cube whose edge is a cm.

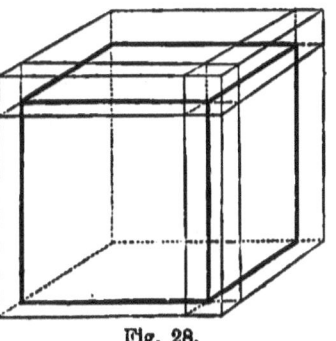

Fig. 28.

Thus the new volume is

$$1 + 3a + 3a^2 + a^3.$$

In neglecting the terms in a^2 and a^3, we are neglecting the volumes of the small cube and of the rectangular strips compared with that of the slabs.

Now by definition the new volume is

$$(1 + \gamma) \text{ c.cm.}$$

Hence we have $1 + \gamma = 1 + 3a$.

$\gamma = 3a$.

The coefficient of cubical expansion is very often called the coefficient of dilatation.

The coefficient of superficial expansion is usually found by determining the coefficient of linear expansion and multiplying by 2.

Methods have been devised for finding the coefficient of cubical expansion directly; one of these is given in § 80. The values so found agree with the number obtained by multiplying the coefficient of linear expansion by 3.

66. Examples on Expansion.

A difficulty is sometimes met with in calculating the change in volume of the interior of a hollow vessel, the bulb of a thermometer for example, which expands by heat. Let us suppose that the bulb is filled with the same material as the walls are composed of. When it is heated the whole expands together; the interior of the bulb will still clearly remain full; the new volume will be found from the old volume by the use of the coefficient of cubical expansion of the material of the walls.

Example. A glass bottle holds when full at a temperature of 0° C. 500 c.cm. of water; how many c.cm. will it hold when heated to 100° C. ?

The coefficient of linear expansion of glass is ·0000089, therefore the coefficient of cubical expansion is 3 × ·0000089 or ·0000267.

Thus the increase in volume of 500 c.c. for a rise of 1° is

500 × ·0000267 or ·01335 c.cm.

Hence the increase for 100° is 100 × ·01335 c.c. or 1·335 c.c.

Thus the new volume is 501·335 c.cm.

67. Relation between Density and Coefficients of Expansion.
We have already seen that the density of a homogeneous body is measured by the ratio of its mass to its volume. Now when a body is heated its mass is not altered but in general its volume is increased, its density therefore is diminished in exactly the same proportion as its volume is increased. Thus if V_0, V be the volumes, ρ_0, ρ the corresponding densities, since the mass is constant we have $V\rho = V_0\rho_0$,

$$\therefore \frac{\rho_0}{\rho} = \frac{V}{V_0}.$$

EXPANSION OF SOLIDS.

Again if γ be the coefficient of cubical expansion and t the rise of temperature

$$\gamma t = \frac{V}{V_0} - 1 = \frac{\rho_0}{\rho} - 1,$$

$$\therefore \gamma = \frac{\rho_0 - \rho}{\rho t}.$$

Now $\frac{\rho_0 - \rho}{t}$ will be the change of density produced by a rise of temperature of 1°. We may therefore say that the coefficient of cubical expansion is the ratio of the decrease of density produced by a rise of 1° to the final density.

Again from the above we have

$$\rho_0 = \rho (1 + \gamma t).$$

Thus $$\rho = \rho_0 \frac{1}{1 + \gamma t}.$$

Now on dividing 1 by $1 + \gamma t$ we get

$$1 - \gamma t + \gamma^2 t^2 - \gamma^3 t^3 + \dots$$

and we have already seen that for most solid substances γ is so small that we may neglect γ^2, γ^3 etc.

Hence we have $\quad \rho = \rho_0 (1 - \gamma t),$

and this form is more readily employed in numerical calculation.

Example. The density of silver at 0° is 10·32 gramme per c.cm., find its density at 800°.

The value of γ for silver is $3 \times \cdot 0000194$ or $\cdot 0000582$.

Hence the value of γt is $\quad \cdot 0456$.

$$\therefore \rho = 10\cdot 32 (1 - \cdot 0456)$$
$$= 10\cdot 32 - \cdot 47$$
$$= 9\cdot 85 \text{ gramme per c.cm.}$$

In what precedes, the coefficients of expansion have been defined as the change per 1° C. in some quantity such as a length.

Since 1° Fah. is $\frac{5}{9}$ of 1° C. the change per 1° Fah. will be $\frac{5}{9}$ of the change per 1° C., that is, coefficients of expansion per 1° Fah. will be found by multiplying the values given in the Table by $\frac{5}{9}$.

68. Practical consequences of Expansion. These are very varied, some of them have already been alluded to, others may be mentioned here. The standards of length are bars of brass or bronze on which certain fine marks have been engraved. The standard yard for example is the distance between two such marks on platinum plugs let into a bronze bar, but this distance depends on the temperature and hence the temperature at which the distance is one yard needs to be defined. The English standard temperature is 62° Fah. or 16$\frac{2}{3}$° C. The standard metre again is correct at 0° C. While making accurate measurements of length, great precautions have to be taken to secure uniformity of temperature.

The rate of a clock depends on the length of the pendulum between the point of suspension and a point called the centre of oscillation; if the pendulum consist merely of a metal rod with a bob at the end, as the temperature rises the rod gets longer and the clock loses and *vice versa*. The period of oscillation is proportional to the square root of the length.

69. Graham's Mercurial Pendulum. This instrument has usually an iron rod, but the bob consists of a glass vessel containing mercury. The coefficient of dilatation of mercury is much greater than that of iron. As the temperature rises the iron expands and this lowers the centre of oscillation, but the mercury expands more, thus raising the centre, and the pendulum is constructed so that the drop from the one cause just balances the rise due to the other.

70. Harrison's Gridiron Pendulum. Let AB, CD be two parallel rods of different material fastened together at the ends B and C and suppose A is fixed. If the temperature rises the end B is lowered, but owing to the expansion of CD, D is raised, and if CD be of more expansible material than AB the rise of D may be just equal to the fall of B, so that the distance AD may remain unchanged; let the lengths of AB and CD be l and l' and let a, a' be the coefficients of expansion.

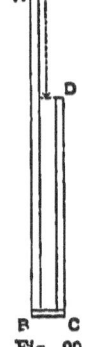

Fig. 29.

Then if the temperature is raised 1° B moves down a distance la, but D moves up, relative to C, a distance $l'a'$. Thus if $la = l'a'$ the distance AD will not change. The necessary condition therefore is that the lengths of the rods should be inversely proportional to their coefficients of expansion.

If now we take an arrangement such as that shewn in
fig. 30, the rods[1] a, a, b being of one material and
the rods c, c of another; the expansion of the
rods a, a, b will lower the bob G, while that of $c,
c$ will raise it. The distance it will be lowered
for a rise of $1°$ will be $(a+b)a$ while the distance it is raised will be ca'; if it be possible
to make these equal the distance OG will not
change and the pendulum will be compensating.
With five rods as shewn and the materials
ordinarily used, iron and brass, this is not
possible, for we should require to have

$$\frac{a+b}{c} = \frac{a'}{a} = \frac{189}{117} = \frac{3}{2} \text{ approximately};$$

and since $a+b$ is necessarily greater than twice
c this is impossible, but by increasing the number of rods the result can be secured.

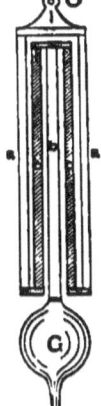

Fig. 30.

With the two materials iron and brass, it will need four brass rods and five iron rods.

71. Balance Wheel of a Watch. The rate of a watch depends mainly on the balance wheel, as the temperature rises this expands unless it is compensated and the watch loses time, for a large wheel will oscillate under a given force, which is supplied by the elasticity of the hair spring, more slowly than a smaller wheel.

Compensation is secured by making the rim in three sections, each section is carried by a single arm and is made of two materials; as the temperature rises the arms expand and their extremities move outwards, but the arcs become more curved, for the more expansible metal is on the outside, so that their free ends move inwards. By properly adjusting the mass of the rim, and this is done by attaching a number of small screws to it, its time of oscillation can be made constant in

---

[1] The rods c and a are duplicated to secure symmetry, the theory so far as the expansion is concerned would be the same if they were single.

spite of variations of temperature. The elasticity of the hair spring diminishes slightly as the temperature rises, in consequence the force acting on the wheel gets less and so the wheel has to be overcompensated to make up for this.

72. Metallic Thermometers. The unequal expansibility of different metals is made use of to measure temperature in Breguet's metallic thermometer. The instrument consists of very thin strips of silver, gold and platinum, which are rolled together so as to form a narrow ribbon. This is then wound into a spiral, the silver being inside, and the platinum outside. The upper end of the spiral is fixed, and the lower end is attached to a pointer which moves over a horizontal scale as the spiral unwinds. If the temperature rises, the silver expands more than the platinum, the spiral unwinds, and a very small change of temperature is sufficient to produce considerable motion of the pointer.

The instrument may be made more sensitive by substituting a mirror for the pointer and reflecting a beam of light from it on to a distant scale.

73. Effects of Expansion. In all engineering work in which metal is employed, special precautions have to be taken to meet difficulties arising from expansion. Thus long iron girders such as are used in bridges or roofs are not rigidly secured to the masonry on which they rest, but are free to move slightly with changes of temperature. An iron girder 50 ft. in length will increase about ·12 of an inch for a rise of temperature of 20° C.

The rails on a railway line are placed at some little distance apart, the holes in the fish-plates being slotted, to allow for expansion; iron gas and water pipes have telescopic joints; furnace bars are made with bevelled ends, and fit loosely into the brickwork of the furnace for the same reason.

Very considerable force may be exerted by a hot body in cooling. This may be shewn by the following experiment.

EXPERIMENT (12). *To shew the stress due to change in temperature.*

Take a bar of iron about 30 cm. long of square section, each side of the square being from 2 to 3 cm.

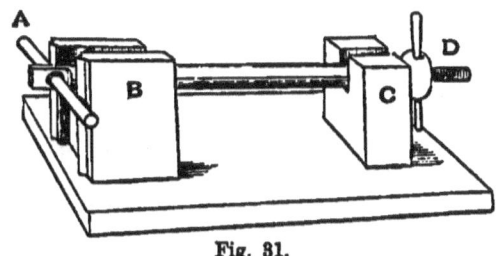

Fig. 31.

One end D of the bar is turned down and a strong screw cut on it. A nut works on this screw. The other end of the bar is forged to the shape shewn at A, and through this a hole about 1 cm. in diameter is drilled; the edges of this hole are V shaped, the bar can fit tightly between two stout vertical supports B, C. Two V shaped projections some 3 or 4 cm. apart are attached to B and a short piece of cast-iron rod passes loosely through the hole in the bar and is pressed up against these V's by the nut working against the support C. The arrangement is shewn fully in fig. 31 (a). Heat the bar red hot. Pass one of the short iron rods through the hole, and place the bar on the supports screwing the nut up tight. As the bar cools it contracts, and the force due to the contraction is sufficient to break the short piece of cast iron which is pressed up against the V's.

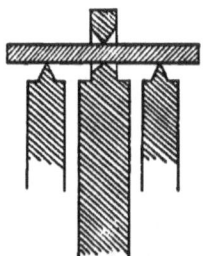

Fig. 31 (a).

We may calculate the force exerted by the bar in cooling through 100° C. thus. Each centimetre would contract on cooling by ·0011 cm.; if then it is prevented from contracting by the application of force, the force must be sufficient to produce an extension of ·0011 cm. in a length of 1 cm. This force has been measured, if the area of the cross section of the bar be 1 sq. cm. the force necessary is found to be about 2,000,000 grammes' weight.

If each side of the bar be 2·5 cm. in length, we must multiply this by 6·25, the area of the bar in sq. cm., and find thus as the force exerted, 12,500 kilograms' weight.

The shrinking of a body in cooling is made use of in various ways. Thus the tyre is put on to a wheel red hot, in cooling it contracts and holds the wooden rim together. Large guns are made by coiling a bar of iron into a close spiral, the turns of the spiral are welded together and a cylinder is thus formed. A number of such cylinders are placed over an inner tube when red hot, each cylinder, as it contracts, compresses those below it, and the stress produced in the breech by the combustion of the powder is thus distributed throughout the material of the gun more evenly than would be possible if the gun were turned out of a single piece of the metal.

EXAMPLES.

EXPANSION OF SOLIDS.

1. The volume of a mass of copper at 50° F. is 1 c. ft.; find its volume at 0° C. and at 100° C.

2. A glass vessel holds 2 litres at 15° C. How much will it hold at 25° C.?

3. The specific gravity of iron at 0° C. is 7·76; find its value at 100° C. referred to water at 0° C.

4. A copper rod 125 cm. long at 0° C. expands by ·209 cm. when raised to 100° C. Find the coefficient of expansion of copper.

5. An iron bridge is 250 feet long. Find its variation of length between the temperatures of—20° C. and 50° C.

6. A copper rod is 150 cm. long at 0°; at what temperature will it have increased by 2 mm.?

7. A rod of iron and a rod of zinc are each 2 metres long at 0° C. How much longer is the zinc than the iron at 50° C.?

8. A gridiron pendulum has 5 iron rods each 1 metre in length and 4 brass rods. Find the length of each brass rod.

EXPANSION OF SOLIDS.

9. An iron clock pendulum makes 86,405 oscillations one day; at the end of the next day the clock has lost 10 seconds; find the change in temperature.

10. The iron rails on a railway line are each 6 feet long. What space must be left between two consecutive rails to allow space for expansion if the temperature may range over 50° C.?

11. The area of an iron plate at 0° C. is 50 sq. cm., find its area at 50° C.

12. What is meant by the statement: The coefficient of linear-expansion of copper is ·000017? If a copper rod is 20 yards long at 0° C., how much longer will it be at 90° C.?

13. If the mean coefficient of expansion of water between 0° and 50° be ·000236, find the weight of water displaced by a brass cube whose side at 0° is 1 centimetre in length when the water and the cube are both at 50° C.

14. A cylinder of iron, 20 inches long, floats vertically in mercury, both being at the temperature 0° C. If the common temperature rises to 100° C., prove that the cylinder will sink ·163 inches.

[Specific gravity of iron at 0° C. = 7·6,
    ,,   ,, mercury ,, = 13·6,
cubical expansion of mercury between 0° and 100° C. = ·018153,
linear ,, iron ,, ,, = ·001182.]

15. The correct length of a steel chain at 0° C. is 66 feet; express as a decimal of an inch the change in its length produced by its temperature being raised to 20° C. The coefficient of linear expansion of steel is ·0000116.

16. A brass pendulum which keeps correct time at 0° C. loses 16 seconds a day at 20° C.; find the coefficient of expansion of brass.

17. An iron rod is 2 metres long at 0° C.; find its length at 15° C., at 100° C. and at 500° C.

18. An iron tube is 1512·45 feet long at 10° C. and 1513 feet at 40° C.; find the linear coefficient of expansion of iron.

19. The rails of a railway are 5 yards long at 0° C. Shew that to allow for a rise of temperature of 55° C. the distance between two consecutive rails must not be less than $\tfrac{1}{\text{A}}$ths of an inch.

20. A mass of silver at 0° occupies 12 cubic inches; determine its volume at 500° C.

21. The area of a tubular iron bridge is 200,000 square feet at 0° C.; find its area at 25° C.

CHAPTER VI.

DILATATION OF LIQUIDS.

74. Definition of Coefficient of Dilatation. Most liquids, like most solids, expand when the temperature is raised and the coefficient of cubical expansion or of dilatation of a liquid is defined thus:

Definition. *The coefficient of dilatation is the ratio of the increase in volume, for a rise of temperature of* $1°$, *to the volume at* $0°$ C.

It may also be defined, as in § 67 with reference to the density, as the ratio of the decrease in density due to a rise in temperature of $1°$ to the final density.

In dealing with solids the coefficient of dilatation has been defined as the ratio of the increase in volume per degree rise of temperature to the volume at the lower temperature; it would have been more accurate to have used throughout the volume at $0°$ C. In the case of solids however the increase in volume is so small that this difference is inappreciable in the result. Thus 10 c.cm. of iron at $0°$ become 10·0037 c.cm. at $15°$; if we suppose this heated still further the increase of volume per $1°$ will be ·000355 c.cm. According to the definition the coefficient of expansion is ·000355/10·004; more strictly it is ·000355/10, for the volume at $0°$ is 10 c.cm. The two differ inappreciably.

In liquids however the dilatation is greater, and the error made in dividing by the volume at the lower temperature instead of the volume at $0°$ may be appreciable.

Thus 10 c.cm. of alcohol at 0° is 10·16 c.cm. in volume at 15° C. The increase in volume per 1° of temperature is ·011 c.cm.; if we divide by 10 we get as the coefficient of expansion the value ·00110, while if we use 10·16—the volume at the lower temperature—as the divisor we find for the coefficient ·00108; and the difference between these numbers is sufficient to be considered.

The coefficient of dilatation of a gas again is much greater than that of a liquid, and in dealing with the expansion of gases it becomes necessary to define the coefficient strictly with reference to the volume at 0°.

75. Dilatation or Cubical Expansion of a Liquid.

In considering a liquid we have only to deal with dilatation or cubical expansion, linear expansion does not concern us. Thus, if we have a solid rod such as $ABCD$ fig. 32, and heat it, the rod increases in length, breadth and thickness to $A'B'C'D$, being equally free to expand in all directions; we can distinguish between the increase in length CC' and the increase in diameter AA'. If we now take a liquid it must be contained in some vessel; let us suppose for the present that the vessel does not expand[1]. The column cannot increase in thickness, and the whole increase in volume shews itself as an increase in the length of the column, the transverse expansion is prevented from taking place, and the liquid which would, if it were free to do so, fill the space corresponding to $AA'B'B$ in fig. 32 is pushed to the end of the

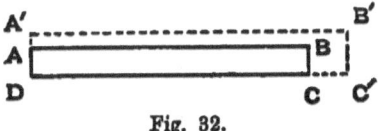

Fig. 32.

column increasing its length still further; the increase in length is proportional to the increase in volume, and from it the coefficient of dilatation may be found by dividing by the original length and by the change of temperature.

---

[1] We consider the effects due to the expansion of the vessel shortly.

76. Absolute and Relative Dilatation. In the above we have assumed that the containing vessel does not expand, and this is practically impossible.

In reality of course the tube or vessel in which the liquid is contained becomes larger when heated, there is some space corresponding to $AA'B'B$ in fig. 32, into which the liquid can expand, and the final length of the column depends in part on the expansion of the liquid and in part on that of the vessel.

To see how the two are connected consider the following argument; let us suppose it possible to heat the vessel without heating the liquid, and then to heat the liquid.

Take a bulb, fig. 33, with a long tube attached to it filled with liquid, and let the liquid stand at a height A in the tube. Suppose the temperature of the bulb raised without heating the liquid. The bulb increases in volume, the liquid remains unchanged; thus the level of the column sinks from A to B, and the volume of the tube between A and B measures the increase in volume of the bulb for the given rise of temperature; it is therefore proportional to the coefficient of cubical expansion of the bulb.

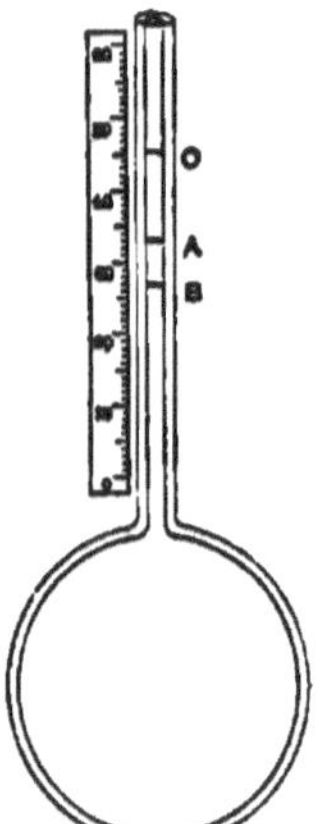

Now let the liquid be heated to the same temperature as the bulb, it increases in volume, the column rises in the tube and finally comes to C. The volume between B and C is proportional to the coefficient of expansion of the liquid. Hence the volume between A and C is proportional to the difference between the coefficients of expansion of the liquid and vessel.

Fig. 33.

But the change in volume AC is what we should actually observe if we raised the temperature of the liquid and vessel together, it is the change in volume which is apparent to us and is thus proportional to the *apparent coefficient of* expansion of the liquid.

We thus get the result that

Apparent coefficient of dilatation of a liquid = coefficient of dilatation of the liquid − coefficient of dilatation of the containing vessel.

The apparent expansion is the expansion which we observe directly without taking account of the changes in the containing vessel; it is often spoken of as the *relative expansion or dilatation*.

Definition. *The coefficient of dilatation of a liquid relative to its containing vessel is the ratio of the observed change in volume when both the liquid and the vessel are heated 1° C. to the original volume at 0° C.*

In determining the observed change in volume the expansion of the vessel is neglected.

Most methods of determining the coefficient of expansion of a liquid give us the relative or apparent expansion only.

To find the coefficient of dilatation we must add to the apparent coefficient the coefficient of expansion of the vessel.

It must be noticed that the change in density produced by a rise in temperature depends on the true coefficient of expansion, for the density is the mass of a unit volume of the liquid, and a change in density involves a change in the actual volume of the liquid not merely a change in its apparent volume relative to some vessel.

Thus by measuring the density of a liquid at different temperatures, we can find its coefficient of dilatation.

77. EXPERIMENT (13). *Absolute and apparent expansion of a liquid.*

Take a glass bulb some 5 or 6 cm. in diameter with a tube 2 or 3 mm. in diameter attached as in fig. 33. Fill it with water[1]. Attach a paper scale to the tube and fix it in a clip. When the temperature has become steady, note on the scale the height of the liquid in the tube. Take a beaker of warm water and suddenly immerse the bulb in the warm water, watching at the same time the level of the liquid in the tube. It will be found that the liquid at first sinks a few divisions on the scale and then rises, finally becoming steady some distance above its former position. The glass bulb acquires the temperature of this warm water some time before the liquid which it contains. The bulb therefore expands and the fall observed at first is due to this expansion. The liquid itself soon becomes heated, and the rise is due to its expansion. Since the liquid expands considerably more than the glass, the final rise is greater than the initial fall and the level of the liquid in the tube at the end is above its original position.

78. Different liquids expand by different amounts for the same rise of temperature. This is shewn by the following experiment.

EXPERIMENT (14). *To compare the apparent expansions of two liquids—such as water and alcohol—for a given rise of temperature.*

Take two thermometer tubes of equal bore terminating in bulbs of the same size. The diameters of the bulbs may conveniently be about 5 cm. and those of the tubes 3 or 4 mm. Fill one bulb and a portion of the tube with water, and the other with an equal volume of alcohol. Attach millimetre scales to both tubes. Place the two bulbs side by side in a vessel of cold water and note the levels at which the liquids stand. Transfer them to a vessel of warm water (the temperature of this water should not be above 55° C.), and note the new levels of the liquids. It will be found that the alcohol has risen through a greater distance than the water; determine the ratio of the distances through which the two

---

[1] To do this, warm the bulb gently, holding the open end of the tube under the water, then allow the bulb to cool. The atmospheric pressure forces some of the water into the bulb. Heat the bulb gradually, until this water boils, still keeping the end of the tube under the water; the steam escapes, carrying with it most of the air in the bulb, and the bulb is filled with boiling water and steam. Now allow the bulb to cool; the steam condenses and water is forced up the tube to fill the bulb.

columns have risen, since the volumes of the two fluids and the bores of the two tubes are respectively the same; this ratio will be the ratio of the mean coefficients of dilatation of the liquids between the given limits of temperature.

79. EXPERIMENT (15). *To determine the coefficient of apparent dilatation of alcohol in a glass vessel by means of an alcohol thermometer.*

Repeat carefully the Experiment of Section 77 with a bulb and tube containing alcohol, but in addition observe with a thermometer the temperatures of the two baths in which the bulb is placed; let them be $t_1°$ and $t_2°$. Let l cm. be the distance the column rises for this rise of temperature, let the volume of the alcohol in the bulb at 0° C. be given as V c.cm. and let the area of the cross section of the tube be a sq. cm. Then the increase in volume for a rise of temperature of $t_2 - t_1$ is la c.cm.

Thus the increase of volume for 1° is $la/(t_2 - t_1)$, and dividing this by V the volume at 0° we find for the coefficient of apparent dilatation the value

$$\frac{la}{V(t_2 - t_1)}.$$

If the coefficient of expansion of the glass be known, by adding it to the apparent coefficient determined as above the true coefficient of dilatation of alcohol can be found.

The volume of the bulb and tube may be found thus. Warm the bulb gently and then allow it to cool with the open end of the tube under mercury. A thread of mercury will be drawn up into the tube; with care a thread some 6 or 8 cm. in length can be obtained without allowing any of the mercury to enter the bulb. Measure the length of this thread, let it be l cm. Warm the air in the bulb again and expel the mercury into a small weighed cup. Weigh the mercury, let its mass be m grammes. Since the density of mercury is 13·59 grs. per c.cm. the volume of the mercury is $m/13·59$ c.cm. and the area of the cross section of the tube, assuming it uniform, is $m/l \times 13·59$ sq. cm.

To find the volume of the bulb. Weigh the bulb and tube empty, then fill it with a liquid of known density, water will usually do, and weigh it again; let the mass of water contained be M grammes. Then taking the density of the water as 1 gr. per c.cm. the volume is M c.cm. Measure the length of tube occupied by water, multiply this length by the area of the tube and subtract the product from M. The result will be the number of cubic centimetres in the bulb.

80. EXPERIMENT (16). *To find the coefficient of dilatation of a liquid relative to glass by the weight thermometer.*

The weight thermometer consists of a glass tube (fig. 34) some 5 or 6 cm. long by about 1 cm. in diameter closed at one end. The other end is drawn out to a fine point and left open. Weigh the tube empty, fill it with the liquid whose coefficient of expansion is required. This is done as in § 77 by repeated heatings and coolings. When it is full leave it for a short time in a beaker of water, with its open end dipping into a small cup of the liquid, until it acquires the temperature of the water[1]; let this be $t_1°$.

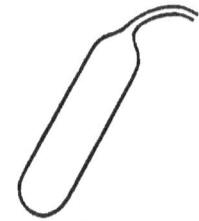

Fig. 84.

Dry the thermometer and weigh it again. The difference between these weighings gives the mass of liquid which fills the tube at $t_1°$; let it be m_1 grammes.

Heat the thermometer to a higher temperature $t_2°$ by putting it in hot water, or better, by suspending it in steam issuing from boiling water; some of the liquid is forced out; wipe this off with a piece of blotting paper, allow the whole to cool, the liquid contracts in the tube; when cold weigh it again, and by subtracting the mass of the empty tube find the mass of liquid which fills the bulb at $t_2°$; let it be m_2 grammes.

Then, neglecting the expansion of the glass, we see that m_2 grammes at $t_2°$ occupy the same volume as m_1 grammes at $t_1°$.

Hence at $t_2°$ a given mass of liquid occupies m_1/m_2 of its volume at $t_1°$.

Subtracting from this the original volume at $t_1°$, we find that the increase of volume for a rise (t_2-t_1) is (m_1/m_2-1) of the original volume.

Hence the coefficient of dilatation, being the ratio of the

---

[1] For very accurate work the beaker should contain ice not water, so that t_1 may be zero.

increase in volume per degree rise of temperature to the original volume, is

$$\frac{m_1 - m_2}{m_2 (t_2 - t_1)}.$$

This is of course the coefficient of dilatation relative to glass. If the coefficient of dilatation of the glass be known, we can get the true coefficient for the liquid. It is not easy however to determine the coefficient of the glass accurately, and the method of § 83 is used to find the true coefficient.

Example. In an experiment with a weight thermometer, 11·222 grammes of glycerine filled the thermometer at 15°; when the thermometer was raised to 100° C. it contained 10·765 grammes; find the coefficient of expansion of glycerine.

11·222 grammes at 15° occupy the same volume as 10·765 grammes at 100° C. Thus the volume of 1 gramme at 100° C. is 11222/10765 (or 1·0425) of its volume at 15°. Thus the increase for 85° is ·0425 of the original volume. Hence the coefficient of dilatation is ·0425/85 or ·00050.

81. Experiments with the weight Thermometer.

The weight thermometer may also be used to find the coefficient of dilatation of a solid in the following way. Take a piece of solid of such a form that it can be inserted into a weight thermometer before its end is drawn out. Determine the mass and volume of the solid. The volume is given by dividing the mass by the density, let it be 10 c.cm. Place the solid in the thermometer and draw out the neck to a fine point. Weigh the tube and solid. Fill the tube with liquid of known density and coefficient of dilatation; let it be glycerine, the density of which is 1·3 grammes per c.cm. and the coefficient of dilatation ·00050. Determine the mass of liquid in the tube; suppose it to be 11·22 grammes and the temperature 0° C.

Raise the temperature to 100°; glycerine is expelled, partly because of the expansion of the liquid, partly because of that of the solid. Weigh the tube and liquid again and find the mass expelled, let it be ·673 gramme; since the coefficient of dilatation of the glycerine is ·0005 the mass expelled in consequence of the expansion of the glycerine will be approximately

·0005 × 100 × 11·22 or ·561 gramme.

The difference of ·112 gramme is due to the expansion of 10 c.cm. of the metal.

Now the volume of ·112 gramme glycerine is very nearly ·112/1·30 or ·086 c.cm.

Thus the increase in volume of 10 c.cm. of metal for a rise of 100° C. is ·086 c.c. The coefficient of dilatation therefore is

·086/10 × 100 or ·000086.

82. Absolute Dilatation of a Liquid. To determine the true coefficient of dilatation of a liquid, we require to compare the densities of the liquid at two different temperatures. This can be done by the following method.

Take a tube of glass some 2 metres long and ·5 cm. in diameter and bend it into the shape shewn in fig. 35. Place it with the two limbs AB, CD vertical, the arm BC being horizontal. Suppose that one limb AB and a portion of the arm BC is filled with one liquid and the other limb DC with a portion of the horizontal arm with a second. Let E be the junction of the two and let A and D be the tops of the columns of liquid in the two arms, let h, h' be the heights AB, DC of the two columns, ρ, ρ' the densities of the two liquids. Then, in the one liquid, the pressure at E is the same as the pressure at B and this is the atmospheric pressure at A together with the weight of a column of liquid of unit cross section and height AB or h.

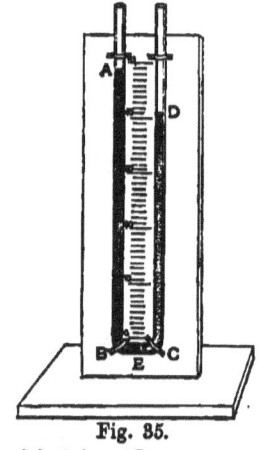

Fig. 35.

Since the cross section of the column is unity its volume is h c.cm.; its mass is $h\rho$ grammes and its weight in dynes is $h\rho g$, where g is the acceleration due to gravity.

In the second liquid the pressure at E is equal to that at C, which is equal to the atmospheric pressure at D together with the weight of a column of the second liquid of unit cross section and height h'. This weight is $h'\rho'g$ dynes.

Hence since the pressure at E is the same in the two liquids we have

$$h\rho g = h'\rho' g$$

or
$$\frac{\rho}{\rho'} = \frac{h'}{h}.$$

We have thus a method of comparing the densities of two different liquids. But the liquids in the two tubes need not be different; the same liquid at two different temperatures may be employed, and we can thus compare its densities at two different temperatures, and so find its coefficient of dilatation.

We notice that the method just described does not depend at all on the diameter of the tubes; these may be the same—as drawn in fig. (35) or they may be different, the result will be unaffected.

83. EXPERIMENT (17). *To determine the true coefficient of dilatation of a liquid.*

Take a tube $ABCD$, bent as in fig. 36. Surround the two vertical limbs AB, CD with wide jacket tubes as shewn in the figure. The ends of the tubes are closed with corks through which the vertical tubes pass. Short pieces of glass tubing are inserted in the corks, and by means of these steam or water can be passed through the jackets. Thermometers can also be inserted if necessary through the upper corks. The apparatus is held in a suitable stand with the long tubes vertical. Insert a plug of cotton wool in the horizontal tube BC and fill the two tubes with the liquid to be experimented on, say turpentine; the plug checks currents which may be set up in

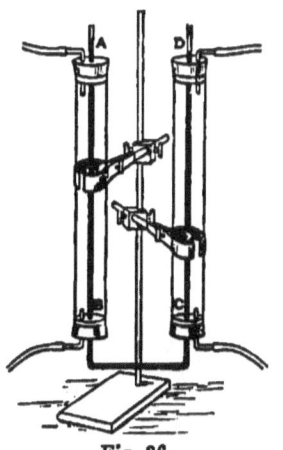

Fig. 36.

the tube. Fill the jacket tube surrounding CD with cold water, or better, pack it with small pieces of ice. The temperature of the liquid in CD will then be zero. Pass steam from a boiler through the jacket surrounding AB, allowing the steam to enter gradually, so as to avoid cracking the glass, at the upper end A of the jacket. The temperature of the liquid in this tube rises to $100°$. When the whole has become steady it will be found that the liquid in AB stands at a considerably greater height than that in CD. Measure by means of a vertical scale—or, if very accurate results are required, by the kathetometer—the heights AB and CD, let them be h and h_0 and let ρ and ρ_0 be the corresponding densities.

Then, since the weight of a column of unit area, height h and density ρ, is equal to the weight of a second column of the same area but of height h_0 and density ρ_0, we have

$$h_0 \rho_0 g = h\rho g,$$

or
$$\frac{\rho_0}{\rho} = \frac{h}{h_0}.$$

But, since ρ_0 and ρ are the densities at 0° and 100° respectively, we have from the second definition of the coefficient of dilatation γ, the value

$$\gamma = \frac{\rho_0 - \rho}{100\rho} = \frac{1}{100}\left\{\frac{\rho_0}{\rho} - 1\right\}$$
$$= \frac{1}{100}\left(\frac{h}{h_0} - 1\right) = \frac{h - h_0}{100 h_0}.$$

Thus observations of the height h_0, and of the difference in heights $h - h_0$, give us the true coefficient of dilatation of the liquid.

If we had filled one jacket tube with water at some temperature t_0, say, not zero, we should have proceeded in the same way, but the divisor in our result would be the difference of temperature $100 - t_0$ instead of 100°. For rough work the jacket round the cold tube may be dispensed with, and the tube assumed to be at the temperature of the air.

When the tubes were filled with turpentine the height of the column h_0 was 95·6 cm. and the difference in height was 9·8 cm.

The coefficient of expansion is thus

$$9·8/100 \times 95·6 \text{ or } ·00102.$$

84. Sources of error.

(1) For a liquid with a small coefficient of expansion, such as mercury for which the value is ·00018, the difference in height will not be large, and with the apparatus as described it will not be easy to measure it accurately.

(2) Some parts of both columns are outside the jackets, the temperatures of these parts are not known with any great accuracy.

(3) Heat may pass both by convection and conduction along the tube BC and the hot and cold liquids will to some extent get mixed. The plug of cotton wool serves to check the convection currents but fails to do so completely.

*85. The absolute dilatation of mercury. The method was devised by Dulong and Petit; and the form of apparatus, used by Regnault, in which the difficulties just mentioned are overcome is shewn in fig. 37. The two tubes are connected at the top by a horizontal tube AD of narrow bore, the ends of which pass into the steam and ice jackets respectively. This tube is kept filled so that the pressures at A and D in the two columns are the same, but by making it long and narrow the transference of heat is very small. The lower connecting tube has the form shewn, the parts at F and G being vertical and close together. Thus the tubes AB and CD are completely jacketed.

The portion FG is in communication with a reservoir of compressed air in which the pressure can be varied by means of a pump.

When the two columns are at different temperatures the levels at F and G are different. The height of the hot column is very approximately the height between F and the horizontal arm AD; that of the cold column is the height between G and the same arm. The difference in height is therefore the difference in level between F and G which can be easily measured accurately.

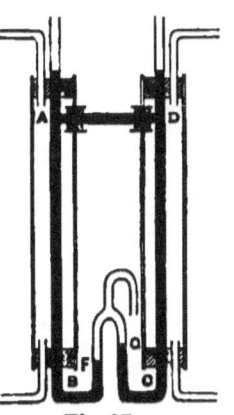

Fig. 37.

A correction is required in consequence of the difference in temperature between the mercury in the vertical limbs FE, HG and that in AB and CD. These tubes are surrounded by a water jacket (not shewn) so that the temperature can be found accurately and the correction made.

86. Measurement of the coefficient of dilatation of a solid. The coefficient of dilatation of a solid, such as the glass of a weight thermometer, may be found by a combination of the two methods of Sections 80 and 83.

For, find by means of the weight thermometer the apparent coefficient of dilatation of some liquid, say mercury, then find by the method of Section 83 its true coefficient of dilatation, the difference is the coefficient of dilatation of the glass. When once this has been found the same weight thermometer may be used to find the true coefficient of any other liquid.

*87. Dilatation at different Temperatures. Since a degree Centigrade is defined in terms of the expansion of mercury in glass, the increase in volume of mercury in a glass tube is the same for each degree Centigrade. This however is not the case with many other liquids. Thus, for example, water increases in volume when raised from 60° to 70° by about four times the increase which takes place between 10° and 20°. The same is true though to a less extent of other liquids. Hence an alcohol thermometer is not graduated by determining two fixed points and then dividing the distance on the tube between these points into a number of equal parts. If this were done, since the increase in volume of alcohol per degree of temperature at high temperatures is greater than at low, then, on putting an alcohol and a mercury thermometer into a bath and gradually raising the temperature, the alcohol thermometer, at the lower fixed point, reads the same as the mercury instrument, but, as the temperature rises, the alcohol instrument lags behind, the reading is lower than that of the mercury thermometer, and the two agree again only when the upper fixed point is reached. For this reason an alcohol thermometer is graduated by comparison with a mercury thermometer at a large number of temperatures.

88. EXPERIMENT (18). *To observe the expansion of various liquids for a given rise of temperature at various temperatures.*

Take a thermometer tube and bulb[1] fitted with a scale of

---

[1] The bulb should contain from 15 to 20 c.cm. and the tube should be 25 to 30 cm. long and about 1 mm. in diameter.

DILATATION OF LIQUIDS.

millimetres such as is described in § 79 and fill it with the liquid, water suppose. Place the bulb in a bath of water with a thermometer, let the temperature be about 10°. Read the thermometer and the height of the water. Raise the bath to about 20°, by pouring in some hot water or otherwise, keep it near this temperature for some little time, until the liquid in the tube has got steady. Read again the temperature and the height of the liquid. Raise the temperature through another 10° to 30°, and so on, then, waiting in each case for the liquid in the bulb to come to the temperature of the bath; thus take a series of simultaneous readings of temperature and height of water column. It will be found that the differences between two consecutive readings get greater as the temperature rises. Enter the results in a table thus:

Temperature.	Reading.	Temperature.	Reading.
10	11	60	94·5
20	18·5	70	122·5
30	31	80	154·5
40	48·5	90	188
50	69·5	100	225·5

Thus, while the rise for the 10° from 10° to 20° is 7·5 mm., that for 10° from 60° to 70° is 28 mm. or nearly four times as much.

The results of an experiment such as this may very conveniently be shewn on a diagram by drawing two lines, OA, OB at right angles, setting off distances ON_1, ON_2, etc. along OA to represent temperatures, and drawing lines N_1P_1, N_2P_2, etc., parallel to OB to represent the height of the liquid in the tube at these temperatures. If the points P_1, P_2, etc. be joined by a curve-line, the expansion of the liquid at various temperatures can be graphically represented.

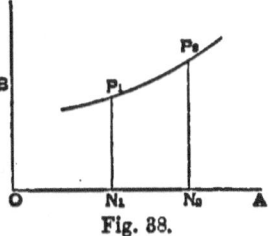

Fig. 88.

89. Dilatation of Water. In consequence of this irregularity in the expansion of water and other liquids when compared with mercury, it is not strictly accurate to speak of the coefficient of dilatation of water as the ratio of the change of volume for a rise of 1° to the original volume, without mentioning the temperature at which the change takes place. If we determine the coefficient of expansion by observing the volume at two different temperatures some way apart the result will be the average coefficient between those temperatures.

The density of water at different temperatures is most accurately determined by weighing a body, such as a piece of glass, in the water at various temperatures. If the coefficient of dilatation of the glass be known its volume at the temperatures of each of the observations is known, and since its loss of weight in water is the weight of water displaced, the weights of a known volume of water at various temperatures can be obtained.

90. Maximum Density of Water. If in the experiment described in § 88 we had started with the temperature at 0° and gradually raised it we should have found, after some calculations explained below, that water at first contracts in volume until a temperature of about 4° is reached, after which it begins to expand. Thus, a given mass of water occupies a less volume at about 4° C. than at any other temperature; its density is greatest at that temperature. A given volume of water, 1 c.cm. say, has a greater mass at 4° C. than at any other temperature; if a vessel such as a weight thermometer be completely filled with water at 4° C. and then be cooled, some of the water will overflow. We may shew this by the aid of the thermometer bulb and tube described in § 80. The following form of apparatus, in which the bulb is replaced by a coil of thin metal tubing is better, for the water will come more quickly to the temperature of the bath than is possible when a bulb is employed; besides either a narrower tube, or a larger bulb, than is required for that experiment is desirable.

EXPERIMENT (19). *To shew that water has a maximum density at about 4° C.*

DILATATION OF LIQUIDS.

Take a piece of lead tubing about 1 metre long and 1 cm. in diameter, close one end, and bend the tube into a flat spiral, turning the open end up so as to be vertical when the spiral rests on the table. Fill the tube with water, and then close the open end with an india rubber cork through which a long glass tube about 1 mm. in internal diameter passes. The water will be forced up this tube and will stand in it as at A. Fit a millimeter scale to the tube.

Place the flat spiral in a suitable vessel and cover it with small pieces of ice; when the column of water in the tube has become steady, note its position on the scale. Pour into the vessel containing the spiral some water which has been cooled down to freezing point, and then gradually raise the temperature of the water. It will be found that as the temperature rises the water column sinks in the tube.

Fig. 39.

As the temperature is still further raised the column ceases to fall and finally at a temperature of about 10° begins to rise.

As the temperature is increased the lead tube expands, and, in consequence of this, even if the water expanded, provided its expansion were less than that of the tube, the water would sink; since however on raising the temperature to 10° the water rises, we see that its coefficient of dilatation is greater than that of lead at 10°, and we have seen that the coefficient increases with the temperature above 10°.

We may infer then from the experiment directly that, at low temperatures, water expands less than lead; while at a temperature of about 10° its coefficient of dilatation has become greater than that of lead. But careful measurement will permit us to deduce more exact results from the experiment. The coefficient of dilatation of lead is known, and therefore the fall which should take place in the water column owing to the expansion of the lead can be calculated. When this is done it is found that, as the temperature rises from 0° to about 4°, the fall per degree is greater than it should be were it due to the expansion of the lead only: the water has contracted in volume from 0° to 4°; at about 4° the fall observed is just that which would be due to the lead; while, from 4° upwards, the observed fall is not so great as it should be if the water still remained unaltered in volume. The water is expanding, but not so fast as the lead; at about 10° the water begins to rise in the tube because at that temperature its coefficient is greater than that of the lead.

If we suppose the tube to contain 100 c.cm. at 0° we shall find the following values for the apparent increase in volume at the various temperatures.

Temperature.	Observed increase in Vol.	Decrease due to Lead.	Increase of Water.
4	− ·0465	·0336	− ·0129
8	− ·0687	·0672	− ·0015
10	− ·0716	·0840	·0124
15	− ·0548	·1260	·0712
20	− ·0065	·1680	·1615
30	+ ·1604	·2520	·4124

The third column gives the decrease due to the expansion of the lead, the coefficient of dilatation of which is ·000084; while the fourth column gives the increase for the water, obtained by adding together the observed increase and the decrease due to the lead. The greatest decrease in the volume of the water is reached at 4°; the volume at 8° is slightly less than at 0°, while at 10° the volume of the water has distinctly risen above its value at 0°.

91. Maximum density of Water. Hope's Experiment. The changes that take place in the density of water when near the freezing-point are shewn in the following manner by Hope's experiment.

EXPERIMENT (20). *To shew that the density of water has a maximum value at about* 4°.

DILATATION OF LIQUIDS.

In fig. 40 *ABC* is a tall metal cylinder about 30 cm. high and 10 cm. in diameter. Near the middle a circular trough some 15 cm. wide and about 10 cm. in height surrounds the cylinder. At *A* and *C* are holes closed by corks through which two delicate thermometers can be inserted into the water, which the cylinder contains; this water should be cooled down to 10° or 12° before the experiment commences. The two thermometers will then read alike. Fill the central trough *B* with a freezing mixture[1].

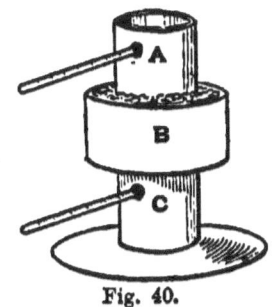

Fig. 40.

The water in the central part of the tall cylinder is thus cooled down; while this is in progress observe the thermometers. It will be found that the lower thermometer sinks gradually to about 4°. The upper thermometer remains nearly stationary at 10° or 12°, if the room is warm it may rise slightly. The water in the central part of the cylinder, as it cools, becomes denser and sinks to the bottom, lowering the temperature there; the warmer water in the upper part of the cylinder being lighter than that below remains unchanged. This continues until all the water near and below the middle has been cooled to about 4°; as the cooling continues below this temperature the water expands, its density becomes less, and the cold water now rises instead of sinking. It will not rise to the top for the water at 10° is less dense than water at 0°. Ice however begins to be formed near the middle, and small crystals of ice rise to the surface and melting there cool the water. The lower thermometer remains at 4° and the upper thermometer falls to the same temperature. The cooling still continues, and the cooled water being now less dense than that at the top rises to the surface; hence the upper thermometer falls to 0° C. the lower one still remaining at 4°.

Thus we see that water at 4° C. is denser than at any other temperature.

---

[1] This, see § 110, is made by mixing well broken ice with salt.

92. Consequences of Expansion of Water. Density of Ice. The fact that water expands on becoming ice has already been alluded to, and the existence of this expansion is readily shewn in many ways. Thus ice floats on the surface of water. In cold weather pipes burst when the water they contain is frozen. We shall explain later a method of measuring this expansion and shall describe some of the consequences to which it gives rise.

The peculiar behaviour of water in expanding between the temperatures of 0° C. and 4° C. is of great importance in the economy of nature. If it were otherwise, if water steadily became denser down to freezing-point, the upper layers of water in a pond or lake would sink as they cooled, freezing would not take place till the whole mass was cooled down to 0° and then would go on rapidly through the mass. As it is the mass is cooled down rapidly by convection currents to 4°. Below that temperature the cooled water above is less dense than the warmer water below; it therefore remains at the top, the cooling below 4°C. takes place by conduction only, and this is a much slower process than the transference of heat by the actual currents of the water. Thus the greater part of the water in the pond remains at 4° while a coat of ice is formed on the surface.

93. Corrections to a barometer reading for expansion. Some of the practical results of the expansion of solids have already been noticed; one other important measurement in which corrections have to be made for expansion should be mentioned. The pressure of a gas is often measured in terms of the height of a column of some liquid; thus the height of the barometer measures the pressure of the atmosphere, but the height of a column of liquid required to balance a given pressure will vary with the temperature of the liquid; while the length of the scale used to measure the height will also change. For both these reasons we need to know the temperature at which the height is measured. In considering the correction required in consequence of the expansion of the liquid—mercury suppose,—we must remember that the pressure is measured by the weight of a column of mercury of unit area and of the given height. The weight of such a column is proportional to the density of the mercury, and the density of the mercury depends on its absolute coefficient of dilatation.

Now h, the observed height, needs correction because the scale is not accurate at the temperature of the observation but at some other; let us suppose it correct at freezing-point, and let H be the real height of the column at the temperature of the observation; let a be the coefficient of linear expansion of the material of the scale. Then since the scale is at $t°$ each centimetre is really $1 + at$ cm. in length. The length of the column is apparently h cm., hence its real length is

$$h(1+at) \text{ cm.,}$$
or
$$H = h(1+at).$$

This height H now requires correcting because the mercury is at $t°$ instead of at the standard temperature zero. Let H_0 be the corrected height, ρ the density of the mercury at $t°$, ρ_0 at zero, γ the coefficient of dilatation of the mercury. We know that

$$\rho_0 = \rho(1 + \gamma t).$$

Now the column of height H_0 is to have the same weight per unit area as the column of height H.

Thus we must have
$$\rho H = \rho_0 H_0 = \rho H_0 (1 + \gamma t).$$
Therefore
$$H_0 = \frac{H}{1+\gamma t} = H(1 - \gamma t),$$

if we neglect terms in $\gamma^2 t^2$ [1], etc.

Hence finally introducing the value of H in terms of h the observed height,
$$H_0 = h(1 + at)(1 - \gamma t).$$

Thus we find the corrected height H_0 at freezing-point in terms of the observed height h.

[1] See § 64, p. 64.

The value thus found may be simplified; thus on multiplying out we have,

$$H_0 = h(1 + at - \gamma t - a\gamma t^2).$$

Now $a\gamma t^2$ is very small compared with at and γt; hence

$$H_0 = h\{1 - (\gamma - a)t\}.$$

The above argument has made it clear that in this problem we are concerned with the absolute dilatation of the mercury, not with its coefficient relative to glass. We may see in another way that this is so, if we remember that the size of a barometer tube does not affect the height of the column; if the temperature of the glass tube could be raised without heating the mercury the height of the column would not change: more mercury would rise from the cistern to fill the additional space caused by the expansion of the tube; if now the temperature of the mercury be raised, the whole of the contents of the tube expand, and the amount of expansion depends on the absolute dilatation of the mercury.

94. Values of coefficients of dilatation. We will close this account of the dilatation of liquids with a table of approximate coefficients of dilatation.

	Mean coefficient of dilatation.	Between
Alcohol	·00109	0— 50
Benzine	·00138	11— 80
Ether	·00210	0— 33
Mercury	·00018	0—100
Turpentine	·00105	−9—106

EXAMPLES.

EXPANSION OF LIQUIDS.

1. A glass bulb with a uniform fine stem weighs 10 grms. when empty, 117·3 grms. when the bulb only is full of mercury, and 119·7 grms. when a length of 10·4 cms. of the stem is also filled with mercury: calculate the relative coefficient of expansion of a liquid which, when placed in the same bulb, and warmed from 0° C. to 28° C., expands through the length from 10·4 to 12·9 cm. of the stem. The density of mercury is 13·6 grammes per c.cm.

DILATATION OF LIQUIDS.

2. What is meant by the coefficient of expansion of a liquid?

If the coefficient of expansion of mercury in glass be $\frac{1}{5550}$, what mass of mercury will overflow from a weight thermometer containing 360 grammes of mercury at 0° C. when the temperature is raised to 98° C.?

3. Describe the process of determining the coefficient of expansion of a liquid like alcohol or paraffin, remembering the necessary preliminary determination of the expansibility of the glass vessel employed.

4. Distinguish between the coefficient of apparent expansion and the coefficient of absolute expansion of a liquid. By what method has the coefficient of absolute expansion of mercury been determined?

5. The weight of mercury in a weight thermometer at 0° C. is found to be 25 grammes, and at 100° C. 24·630 grammes; find the coefficient of expansion of mercury in glass. If the absolute coefficient of expansion of mercury be ·000189 per 1° C., find the coefficient of linear expansion of glass.

6. Explain why in reading a barometer it is necessary to correct the reading for the temperature of the mercury. A barometer with a glass scale reads 755 mm. at 18° C.; find the reading at 0° C. The apparent coefficient of expansion of mercury in glass is ·000155, and the coefficient of linear expansion of glass is ·0000089.

7. A barometer has a brass scale which is correct at 60° Fahr.: the barometer reads 754 at 40° Fahr.; correct the reading of the barometer to 32° Fahr.

[The coefficient of linear expansion of brass is ·00001: the coefficient of cubical expansion of mercury is ·0001 per 1° Fah.]

8. The coefficient of absolute expansion of mercury is ·000182. A weight thermometer of glass contains 10 grammes of mercury at 0° and 9·843 grammes at 100°; find the coefficient of expansion of the glass.

9. A glass bulb contains 800 gms. of mercury at 0° C. It is heated to 99°·5 C., and 12 gms. of mercury are expelled. Assuming the mean coefficient of expansion of mercury between 0° and 100° C. to be ·0001816, find that of the glass.

10. The coefficient of cubical expansion of mercury is ·000180, and of brass ·000060, per 1° C. Find the atmospheric pressure in inches of mercury at 0° C., when a barometer with a brass scale (correct at 62° F.) reads 30 in. at a temp. of 50° F.

11. A mass of mercury occupies 10 cubic inches at 0° C. Find its volume at 15° C. at 100° C. and at 500° C.

12. A mass of mercury occupies 8 cubic inches at 0° C. What rise of temperature will produce an increase of volume of ·0432 cubic inches?

CHAPTER VII.

DILATATION OF GASES.

95. Boyle's Law. The volumes of most bodies can be changed by change of pressure. For solids and liquids however this change is extremely small, and, therefore, in dealing with the dilatation of such bodies due to rise of temperature it has not been necessary to notice those changes in volume which may be produced by variation of pressure.

A gas, on the other hand, alters in volume considerably for small changes of pressure, even though the temperature remain constant, and we require to investigate first the law which regulates this change. This law, called Boyle's Law, was first enunciated by the Hon. Robert Boyle in 1662.

Boyle's Law. *The pressure of a given mass of gas at constant temperature is inversely proportional to its volume.*

EXPERIMENT (21). *To verify Boyle's Law.*

In fig. 41 AB, CD are two glass tubes connected by stout india-rubber tubing and fixed to a vertical stand. AB is closed at its upper end and may be 50 cm. long and ·5 cm. in diameter; CD is a wider tube and is open at the top. A vertical scale parallel to the tubes is

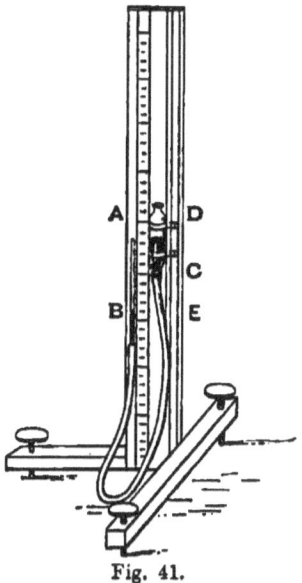

Fig. 41.

attached to the stand, and CD can slide up and down this scale. The india-rubber tubing and the lower parts of the glass tube contain mercury. The upper part of the tube AB is filled with dry air, which constitutes the given mass of air on which the experiment is to be made. The volume of this air is proportional to the length, AB, of the tube which it occupies, and this length can be read off directly on the scale. To find the pressure of the air, let the horizontal line through B meet the mercury in the moveable tube at E, and let D be the top of this mercury column.

Then the pressure at B is equal to the pressure at E, and this is equal to the pressure of the atmosphere at D together with the weight of a column of mercury of unit area and height DE. Thus, if b cm. be the height of the barometer, the pressure at B is measured by a column of mercury of height $b + DE$.

Now, according to Boyle's Law, if the temperature is constant the pressure is inversely proportional to the volume. Hence if the pressure and the volume of the gas in AB be multiplied together the product obtained will be always the same.

Raise or lower the sliding tube until the mercury stands at the same level in the two tubes.

Read on the scale the level of the top of the tube AB and the position of the mercury in the tube; the difference will be proportional to the volume of the air. Since the mercury in the two tubes is at the same level the pressure of the enclosed air is the atmospheric pressure. Observe the height of the barometer, let it be b cm.; the pressure of the enclosed air is measured by a mercury column b cm. in height. Raise the sliding tube. The mercury in the closed column also rises but not so fast; the volume of the enclosed air is reduced, but its pressure is increased, being now measured by the height of the barometer together with the column of mercury between the two levels. Continue to raise the sliding tube until the mercury in the closed tube reaches a point B', half-way between A and B; let the level of the mercury in the open tube when this is the case be at D'. The volume of the enclosed air is now half what it was. Its pressure is measured by $b + D'B'$. Read the levels at D' and B', it will be found that $D'B'$ is equal to b, the height of the barometer; hence the pressure of the enclosed air is now measured by $2b$; that is, it is twice what it was originally. The volume has been halved, the pressure has been doubled. Thus Boyle's Law has been verified for this case.

The verification may be made more complete by taking readings of the volume and of the pressure in a number of other positions of the sliding tube.

If B_1, D_1 be corresponding levels of the two mercury columns, the volume of air is proportional to AB_1, the pressure to $b + B_1D_1$. Set down in two parallel columns the values of AB_1, and of $b + B_1D_1$, and in a third column the numbers obtained by multiplying the corresponding values together. It will be found that these products are constant within the limits of experimental error.

The results of the experiments may be entered in a table thus:

Volume.	Pressure.	PV.
50	76	3800
40	76+18·8	3792
30	76+50·5	3795
20	76+113	3780

The same apparatus may be used for pressures less than that due to the atmosphere by lowering the position of the sliding tube until D is below B; in this case the pressure is given by $b - BD$.

96. Deductions from Boyle's Law. Boyle's Law may be expressed in symbols in various ways. Thus if p be the pressure, v the volume of a given mass of gas; then, since the pressure is inversely proportional to the volume, we have the result that the ratio of p to $1/v$ is constant; denoting this constant by k we find

$$\frac{p}{\frac{1}{v}} = k.$$

Therefore $$p = \frac{k}{v},$$

or $$pv = k;$$

when we say that k is a constant we mean that it does not change when the pressure and volume are changed, if the temperature and mass of the gas are not varied. When a gas is allowed to expand under the condition that the temperature does not alter the expansion is said to be isothermal. If corresponding values of the pressure and volume are plotted the curve formed is said to be an isothermal curve.

Or again, if the volume v becomes v', and in consequence the pressure p is changed to p', since the product of the pressure and volume does not alter we have $pv = p'v'$.

Again, the volume of a given mass of gas is inversely proportional to its density; since, therefore, the volume is inversely proportional to the pressure, we see that the pressure of a gas is proportional to its density; or if ρ be the density, the ratio of p to ρ is a constant. We may write this $p = k\rho$, where k is a constant.

Examples involving Boyle's Law may be worked in various ways. Thus we may use the formula directly as in the following.

(1) *The volume of a mass of gas at 740 mm. pressure is 1250 c.cm., find its volume at 760 mm.*

Let v be the new volume, then from the formula $pv = p'v'$
$$v \times 760 = 1250 \times 740,$$
$$v = 1250 \times 74/76 = 1217 \cdot 1 \text{ c.cm.}$$

Or we may preferably put the argument in full thus:

Volume at pressure 740 is 1250 c.cm.

Volume at pressure 1 is 1250×740 c.cm.

Volume at pressure 760 is $\dfrac{1250 \times 740}{760}$ c.cm.

It is of course by no means necessary to measure the pressure in terms of the height of a column of mercury. Thus,

(2) A bubble of gas 100 c.mm. in volume is formed at a depth of 100 metres in water, find its volume when it reaches the surface, the height of the barometer being 76 cm.

Since the density of mercury is 13·59 grammes per c.cm., the height of the water barometer is $76 \times 13·59$ cm., and this is very approximately 10·34 metres.

100 HEAT. [CH. VII

Thus the pressure at the surface is measured by a column of water 10·34 metres high, that at 100 metres by a column 110·34 metres.

Hence the new volume $= \dfrac{100 \times 110\cdot34}{10\cdot34}$ or 1067 c.mm. approximately.

(3) The mass of a litre of air at 760 mm. pressure is 1290 grammes. Find the mass of 1 cubic metre of air at a pressure of 1·9 mm.

The volume of the given mass of air at a pressure of 1·9 mm. is 1000000 c.cm.

Therefore the volume at pressure of 76 cm. is

$$\frac{10000 \times 19}{76} \text{ or } 2500 \text{ c.cm.}$$

The mass of 1 c.cm. air is ·001293 grammes.

Therefore the mass of 2500 c.cm. is 2500 × ·001293 grammes, and this is 3·24 grammes.

97. Variations from Boyle's Law. More exact experiments have shewn that Boyle's Law is not absolutely true, though for the so-called permanent gases, oxygen, hydrogen, nitrogen and others, it holds very nearly; other gases, such as carbonic acid, which can be condensed to a liquid at ordinary temperatures by the application of a not very large pressure (see § 119), deviate more from the law.

98. Dilatation of gases by heat. The law of the dilatation of gases for rise of temperature was first stated by Charles.

Charles' Law. *The volume of a given mass of any gas, at constant pressure, increases for each rise of temperature of* 1° *C. by a constant fraction (about* 1/273) *of its volume at* 0° *C.*

Thus if the volume at 0° be v_0 c.cm. the increase for each rise of 1° is $v_0/273$, therefore for t° the increase in volume is $v_0 t/273$, hence if v c.cm. be the volume at t°

$$v = v_0 + \frac{v_0 t}{273} = v_0 \left(1 + \frac{t}{273}\right).$$

The formula resembles those we have already arrived at for solids and liquids; some important points of difference should be noted.

(1) It is stated definitely that the pressure is to be kept constant; the formula is not true unless this is the case.

(2) The increase of volume is defined as a fraction (1/273 or ·00366) *of the volume at 0° C.* This point has been already noticed; we have seen that the dilatation of most solids is so small that we may measure the increase in volume at any temperature as a fraction of the volume at that temperature without error; and also that if we adopt the same method for most liquids, the error will not be large. For gases however the dilatation per degree rise of temperature is greater, and the results will not be correct unless it be defined as a fraction of the volume at 0°.

(3) The coefficient of dilatation (1/273 or ·00366) is very approximately the same for all gases; this approximation is more close the more nearly the gases obey Boyle's law.

Thus we have the following values of the coefficients.

Gas.	Coefficient.	Gas.	Coefficient.
Hydrogen	·00366	Carbonic Acid	·00371
Air	·00367	Nitrous Oxide	·00372
Nitrogen	·00367	Sulphurous Acid	·00390
Carbonic Oxide	·00367	Cyanogen	·00388

99. EXPERIMENT (22). *To shew that equal volumes of different gases expand by the same amount for a given rise of temperature.*

Take a flask containing say 50 c.cm., close it with a cork through which passes a glass tube bent twice at right angles as BC in fig. 42, let the end C of the tube pass through a cork into a test tube about 20 c.cm. in volume. Pass a second tube DE through the cork; let one end, D, reach to the bottom of the test tube, while the other is bent over as at E.

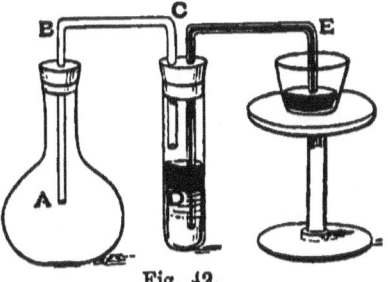

Fig. 42.

Fill the test tube with dry mercury. Prepare two of these pieces of apparatus. Fill one of the 50 c.cm. flasks with air, the other with some other gas, coal-gas, hydrogen or oxygen. Place the two flasks and test tubes side by side in a water bath, in such a way that the end E of the second tube projects out over the edge, and place a weighed beaker to catch the mercury which will be expelled from the test tubes as the temperature rises. Take the temperature of the bath, let it be $t_0°$. We have then in the two flasks equal volumes (50 c.cm.) of air and hydrogen or coal-gas respectively. Now raise the temperature of the bath by pouring in hot water or passing steam through. In each apparatus the gas expands into the test tube, expelling some of the mercury into the beaker; let the new temperature be $t_2°$. Weigh the mercury collected in each of the two beakers; it will be found that the weights are the same. The volume of this mercury measures the increase in volume of the 50 c.cm. of air or hydrogen. Thus for a given rise of temperature[1] equal volumes of these two gases have expanded by equal amounts.

100. EXPERIMENT (23). *To determine the coefficient of dilatation of a gas at constant pressure.*

Take a piece of glass tubing AB, fig. 43, about 1 mm. in bore and not less than 20 cm. long. Pass dry air through it by means of an aspirator or pump, and then close one end with

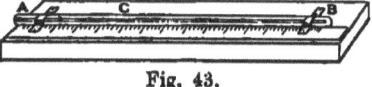

Fig. 43.

a blowpipe flame. Warm the tube so as to expel some of the air, then dip the open end under dry mercury, and so suck up, as the air cools, a small pellet of mercury. Place the tube vertically with its open end upwards and leave it to cool.

---

[1] In this experiment the pressure has not been kept quite constant, the change in pressure however has been the same in the two and affects them equally. By determining the volume of mercury expelled and allowing for the change in pressure we may calculate the coefficient of dilatation.

The amount of air expelled should be such that when the tube comes to the temperature of the room the pellet C may stand at a height of some 14 or 15 cm. above the bottom. Attach to the tube[1] a millimetre scale graduated from the bottom.

The tube is thus an air thermometer such as is described in § 23 but without a bulb.

Place it in melting ice with the open end upwards; the enclosed air contracts and the mercury pellet sinks in the tube; when it has become steady read on the scale the position of its lower end; let the reading be a mm. If the bore of the tube be uniform, the volume of the enclosed air at 0° is proportional to a.

Remove the tube from the ice and place it in boiling water; the enclosed air expands: when the pellet has become steady read its position on the scale; let it be b mm. from the bottom, the volume of the air at 100° is proportional to b. Thus the ratio of the increase of volume for 100° to the volume at 0° is $(b-a)/a$. Dividing this by 100 we get as the mean coefficient of dilatation the value

$$\frac{b-a}{100a}.$$

Example. In an air thermometer as described above the pellet stood at 145 mm. in ice and at 198 mm. in boiling water.

Thus the coefficient of dilatation is

(198 − 145)/145 × 100 or 53/145 × 100,

and this comes to be about 1/274 or ·00365.

101. Graduation of an Air Thermometer. Absolute Temperature. Let us now suppose that we wish to graduate an air thermometer such as that described in Experiment 23. Make a mark on the tube to indicate the positions of the bottom of the pellet in melting ice and in boiling water, or better in the steam issuing from boiling water, respectively. Divide the distance between these graduations into 100 equal parts, and continue the gradua-

---

[1] It is convenient to use for the experiment an old thermometer tube on which the graduations have been engraved.

tions down to the bottom of the tube. It will be found that between the freezing-point and the bottom of the tube there are 273 divisions[1]; so that if we agree to call freezing-point 0° and boiling-point 100°, we must call the bottom of the tube − 273°. Or again if we call the bottom of the tube 0°, freezing-point will be 273° and boiling-point 273° + 100° or 373°.

Now we have seen that the air expands through 100 of these divisions for the rise of temperature from freezing to boiling point or through 100° C.

If now we compare our air thermometer with a Centigrade thermometer by placing them in a bath and raising the temperature, we find that, practically, they agree all the way up the scale. When the air column has expanded through ten divisions the mercury thermometer reads 10° and so on.

The expansion of air at constant pressure—and unless the barometer varies during the experiment the pressure is constant—is regular when measured in terms of the mercury thermometer; each of the divisions on the air thermometer corresponds to the increase or decrease of volume produced by a change of temperature of 1° Centigrade. The scale of the mercury thermometer agrees very closely with that of the air thermometer[2].

If now the temperature be lowered below freezing-point, the mercury pellet sinks through 1 division for each fall of temperature of 1°, and, if we could suppose the gas to continue to contract according to the same law for any fall of temperature however great, on reducing the temperature to − 273° C. below freezing-point the mercury pellet would have reached the bottom of the tube and the volume of the air would have become zero.

This temperature is called the absolute zero of the air thermometer, and the temperature measured from absolute

[1] This is clear from the formula
 $(b - a)/100a =$ coefficient of dilatation $= 1/273$.
Hence if $b - a = 100$ we have $a = 273$.

[2] Careful research has shewn that this agreement is not absolute and depends greatly on the glass used in the mercury thermometer.

zero is called **absolute temperature**. Each degree on the air thermometer is equal to one degree Centigrade, and we may say that absolute zero is $-273°$ C. below freezing-point, or that freezing-point is $273°$ Absolute above zero.

Again, since $t°$ C. means $t°$ above freezing-point, and freezing-point is $273°$ above absolute zero, we see that $t°$ C. corresponds to $273 + t°$ absolute; that is, to find the measure of a temperature on the absolute scale, we have to add $273°$ C. to the Centigrade temperature.

Again, temperature on the absolute scale is measured by the height of the mercury pellet above the bottom of the thermometer tube, but the volume of the air column is also proportional to this same height; thus we get the result that *The volume of a given mass of gas at constant pressure is proportional to its absolute temperature.*

This is the form of the law connecting the volume and temperature of a gas which is most useful for numerical calculations.

We can obtain the above results more rapidly from the formula thus:

We have $\qquad v = v_0 \left(1 + \dfrac{t}{273}\right).$

Let t be the temperature in Centigrade degrees at which the volume is zero.

Then $\qquad 0 = v_0 \left(1 + \dfrac{t}{273}\right).$

$$\therefore t = -273°.$$

We call this the absolute zero of the air thermometer, and say that absolute temperature is temperature reckoned from absolute zero.

Let T be the absolute temperature corresponding to $t°$ C. and put $T_0 =$ absolute temperature of freezing-point $= 273°$.

Then $\qquad T = t + 273 = t + T_0.$

Also $\qquad v = v_0 \dfrac{(273 + t)}{273} = \dfrac{v_0 T}{T_0}.$

$$\therefore \dfrac{v}{T} = \dfrac{v_0}{T_0}.$$

That is, the volume of a mass of gas at constant pressure is proportional to its absolute temperature.

We have worked hitherto in degrees Centigrade; but since a degree Fahrenheit is $\frac{5}{9}$ of a degree Centigrade and the dilatation of a gas is $\frac{1}{273}$ per degree Centigrade, its dilatation per degree Fahrenheit is $\frac{5}{9}$ of $\frac{1}{273}$ or about $\frac{1}{491}$. Thus the absolute zero on Fahrenheit's scale is 491° Fahrenheit below freezing-point, and since zero Fahrenheit is 32° Fahrenheit below freezing-point the absolute zero is 491° − 32° or 459° Fahrenheit below zero Fahrenheit.

Again, since the coefficients of dilatation of all permanent gases are nearly the same, the absolute zero of any gas thermometer is approximately the same temperature.

In the above the fraction 1/273 has been used throughout as the coefficient of dilatation of a gas. The results might have been made more general by the employment of a symbol a for this quantity. In this case we should have the equation

$$v = v_0(1+at),$$

and the temperature at which v is zero will be $-1/a$. Thus if a is the coefficient of expansion of any gas the temperature of the absolute zero of that gas is $-1/a$. Let us put

$$T_0 = \frac{1}{a}, \qquad T = T_0 + t = \frac{1}{a} + t.$$

Then
$$v = v_0(1+at) = v_0 a\left(\frac{1}{a} + t\right)$$
$$= \frac{v_0}{T_0} \cdot T.$$

Thus
$$\frac{v}{T} = \frac{v_0}{T_0},$$

or the volume is proportional to the absolute temperature.

Lord Kelvin has shewn how to construct a scale of temperature known as "Thomson's Absolute Scale" which is independent of the substance in the thermometer, be it gas, mercury or anything else. He has further proved by the experiments of Joule and himself that this absolute scale is very nearly identical with that of the air thermometer. Hence the terms "absolute" scale, "absolute" temperature, etc. which apply really in strictness only to Thomson's scale are used in connection with the air thermometer. (See Maxwell's *Heat*, Chapter XIII.)

Examples. (1) *A litre of hydrogen at 15° C. is heated at constant pressure to 100° C., find its volume.*

The absolute temperatures are $15+273$ or $288°$ and $100+273$ or $373°$. Hence if v is volume

$$v = \frac{373}{288} \times 1000 \text{ c.cm.} = 1295 \text{ c.cm.};$$

or we may express the argument in full thus,

Volume at $288°$ absolute is 1000 c.cm.

Volume at $1°$ absolute is $\dfrac{1000}{288}$ c.cm.

Volume at $373°$ absolute is $\dfrac{373}{288} \times 1000$ c.cm.

∴ required volume is 1295 c.cm.

(2) *The temperature of a litre of gas is $27°$ C. At what temperature will the volume have increased by 500 c.cm.?*

$$27° \text{ C.} = 273 + 27 = 300° \text{ Abs.}$$

Hence if T is the required temperature

$$\frac{T}{1500} = \frac{300}{1000},$$

$$T = 450°.$$

∴ the Centigrade temperature is

$$450° - 273° \text{ or } 177° \text{ C.}$$

102. Law connecting Pressure, Volume and Temperature of a Gas. By combining Boyle's Law and Charles' Law we can obtain a relation between the pressure, volume and temperature of a gas when all are allowed to vary in the following way.

Consider a mass of gas; let p, v and T be the pressure, volume and temperature of the gas, the temperature being measured from absolute zero.

Let the pressure be changed to p_1 and the temperature to T_1, and in consequence let the volume become v_1; we require to find v_1. We may suppose the two changes to take place separately and reason thus; during the first change the temperature remains constant and Boyle's Law holds, during the second the pressure is constant and Charles' Law is true.

Thus we get

Volume at pressure p, temperature T, is v.

Volume at pressure 1, temperature T, is pv.

Volume at pressure p_1, temperature T, is $\dfrac{pv}{p_1}$.

Volume at pressure p_1, temperature 1, is $\dfrac{pv}{Tp_1}$.

Volume at pressure p_1, temperature T_1, is $\dfrac{pvT_1}{Tp_1}$.

Therefore $$v_1 = \frac{pvT_1}{Tp_1},$$

or $$\frac{p_1 v_1}{T_1} = \frac{pv}{T}.$$

The reasoning may be made clearer by a diagram in the following way.

Let the air be contained in a cylinder, fig. 44, with a piston, and let A be the position originally. When the pressure is changed to p_1, the temperature remaining constant, let the piston come to A' and let v' be the new volume. And finally, when the temperature is changed to T_1, the pressure remaining p_1, let A_1 be the position of the piston.

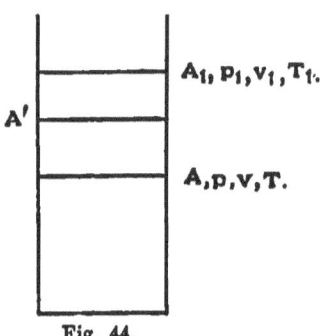

Fig. 44.

Then for the first change from p to p_1, T being constant, Boyle's Law holds and
$$v' = \frac{pv}{p_1}.$$

For the second change from T to T_1, p_1 being constant, Charles' Law holds, and
$$v' = \frac{Tv_1}{T_1}.$$

DILATATION OF GASES.

Therefore
$$\frac{pv}{p_1} = \frac{Tv_1}{T_1},$$

or
$$\frac{pv}{T} = \frac{p_1 v_1}{T_1}.$$

A short algebraic proof can be given thus. Since v varies inversely as p when T is constant and v varies as T when p is constant we know from Algebra that v varies as T and inversely as p when p and T both vary. Hence pv/T is constant.

103. Change of Pressure at Constant Volume. A case of the above law of special importance arises when the changes of pressure and temperature are such that the volume remains constant. We are then to have $v = v_1$; putting this value in the formula

we find
$$\frac{pv}{T} = \frac{p_1 v}{T_1},$$

or
$$\frac{p}{T} = \frac{p_1}{T_1}.$$

In other words, the pressure of a gas when the volume is kept constant, is proportional to its temperature reckoned from the absolute zero of the air thermometer.

Again, let the temperature from which the experiment is started be that of the freezing-point, so that $p_1 = p_0$, the pressure at the freezing-point, and $T_1 = T_0$, the absolute temperature of freezing-point; on turning to Centigrade temperature we have

$$T_0 = 273°, \quad T = 273 + t,$$
$$p = \frac{p_0 T}{T_0} = p_0 \frac{(273 + t)}{273}$$
$$= p_0 \left(1 + \frac{1}{273} t\right).$$

And this is an equation of exactly the same form as that found for the volume of a gas at constant pressure in § 101.

Thus we may say that *The pressure of a gas at constant volume increases by a constant fraction ($\frac{1}{273}$) of the pressure at the freezing-point for each rise of temperature of 1° Centigrade.*

This law has been deduced by an application of Boyle's Law and Charles' Law. Since it has been shewn that gases do not obey Boyle's Law exactly, the result, in the form given, is not absolutely true. Careful experiments shew that the fraction which multiplies t in the two formulæ is slightly different. The difference however is too small to concern us here.

The law which has just been enunciated can be verified by a modification of Balfour Stewart's constant volume air thermometer.

104. EXPERIMENT (24). *To prove that the pressure of a mass of gas at constant volume increases by $\frac{1}{273}$ of the pressure at $0°$ C. for each rise of temperature of $1°$, and to find the coefficient of increase of pressure of a gas at constant volume.*

The apparatus required is similar to that described in § 95 for verifying Boyle's Law. The closed tube AB is removed, and is replaced by a tube shewn in fig. 45 at AB, bent twice at right angles, and terminating in a bulb B, some 5 or 6 cm. in diameter. The horizontal tube and part of the vertical tube near A are of narrow bore; the lower part of the vertical tube where it joins the india-rubber tubing is wider. The bulb is filled with clean dry air, and a mark is made at A, either on the glass, or on the stand behind the glass. In performing the experiment the mercury is always brought up to this mark by raising or lowering the sliding tube CD. The volume of the air in the bulb and tube is thus kept constant.

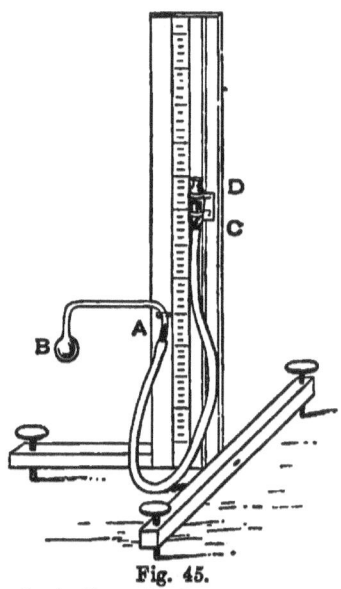

Fig. 45.

Now place the bulb in melting ice; as the air cools its pressure becomes less and the mercury tends to rise above A, but, by adjusting the sliding tube, it can be kept constantly at A. When the column has become steady, read the height of the mercury in the sliding tube CD above A. Add this height to the height of the barometer and thus find the pressure p_0 under which the air at 0° has the given volume. If D be below A the distance AD must be subtracted from the height of the barometer to give the pressure. Remove the bulb from the ice and place it in a vessel of warm water, which can be made to boil, or in steam. The air expands and the mercury is driven down below A, but by raising the sliding tube it can be brought back to A. Do this, and when the temperature has become steady, read the height of the mercury in the sliding tube above A. Add this to the height of the barometer, and so find p the pressure of the air at 100°. Subtract p_0 from p; divide the result by p_0 and by 100, and thus find the mean coefficient of increase of pressure between 0° and 100°.

To prove that the increase of pressure is uniform, let the bath cool slowly, keeping the level of the mercury steady at the mark A, and as it cools past each tenth degree, 90°, 80°, etc. read the pressure; if the cooling take place sufficiently slowly, so that the water of the bath and the air in the bulb may be at the same temperature, the differences between these pressure readings, which give the fall of pressure for each 10°, will be the same. These observations might have been made as the temperature was rising. It may not be possible to take the observations exactly at each tenth degree, in this case take a series of simultaneous readings of pressure and temperature, then form a series of corresponding differences of pressure and of temperature, by subtracting each pressure reading from the previous one, and similarly for the temperatures. Divide the pressure differences by the corresponding differences of temperature, and so find a series of values of the increase of pressure per degree of temperature at different parts of the scale. These values should all be equal. To find the coefficient of increase of pressure they must be divided by the pressure at 0°, the quotient will be approximately $\frac{1}{273}$ or ·00366.

112   HEAT.   [CH. VII

Examples. These may be worked either directly from the formula or by the unitary method already employed in § 96.

Thus 500 c.cm. of air at 22° C. and a pressure of 730 mm. are cooled to the standard temperature 0° C. and a standard pressure 760 mm.; find the volume.

The absolute temperatures are

$$273+22 \text{ or } 295° \text{ and } 273°.$$

Thus
$$v = \frac{730 \times 500}{295} \times \frac{273}{760}$$

$$= 444\cdot 5 \text{ c.cm.},$$

or otherwise

Volume at 295° and 730 is 500 c.cm.

Volume at 295 and 1 is 500×730 c.cm.

Volume at 1 and 1 is $\dfrac{500 \times 730}{295}$ c.cm.

Volume at 273 and 1 is $\dfrac{500 \times 730 \times 273}{295}$ c.cm.

Volume at 273 and 760 is $\dfrac{500 \times 730 \times 273}{295 \times 760}$ c.cm.

Hence new volume $= 444\cdot 5$ c.cm.

*105. Forms of Air Thermometers. The instrument which has just been described is the constant volume air thermometer, in it the temperature is measured by means of the increase in pressure of the air. The instrument described in § 100 is with some small modifications a constant pressure air thermometer, the temperature is there measured by the expansion of the air at constant pressure.

Other forms of air thermometers are sometimes employed; some of these have already been described § 23. The following is one which is useful for high temperatures. A bulb is taken with a narrow tube attached. This is drawn out to a fine point. The bulb is raised to the temperature which we require to measure and the end of the tube sealed off with a blowpipe; the air in the bulb fills the bulb at atmospheric pressure, and at the temperature T to which it was heated: if we can find the volume of the same mass of air at some other temperature, we can find T. Weigh the bulb. Place it with the tube downwards under water and break off the end of the tube with a sharp file. The water enters the bulb. Adjust it till the level of the water in the bulb is the same as that of the water outside. Close the end of the tube with the finger, invert the bulb and lift it out of the water. Dry the outside and weigh it again. The bulb is not filled with the water and the volume occupied by air is the volume, at the temperature of the bath $T_1°$, of the air which at $T°$ filled the bulb.

We wish to find this volume. Fill the bulb with water completely and weigh again. The difference between the last two weighings gives the mass of water which fills the space whose volume we wish to find; if the mass be found in grammes, we obtain at once the volume we require in c.cm.; let this volume be v_1. The difference between the last weighing and the mass of the empty bulb will be the mass of water which fills the bulb, and this gives the volume v of the bulb.

Thus a mass of air which at temperature T fills the volume v has at temperature T_1 the volume v_1.

Therefore $\qquad T = T_1 v/v_1.$

The temperatures are of course absolute temperatures.

Example. The following observations were made in an experiment as just described:

Mass of empty bulb 14·53 gr.

Temperature of bath 17° C.

Mass of partly filled bulb 43·77 gr.

Mass of bulb when full 65·64 gr.

Hence $\qquad T_1 = 273 + 17 = 290°$ absolute.

$\qquad\qquad v_1 = 43\cdot77 - 14\cdot53 = 29\cdot24$ c.cm.

$\qquad\qquad v = 65\cdot64 - 14\cdot53 = 51\cdot11$ c.cm.

Whence $\qquad T = \dfrac{51\cdot11 \times 290}{29\cdot24} = 506°\cdot8.$

Hence the temperature required in Centigrade degrees is

$\qquad\qquad 506°\cdot8 - 273°$ or $233°\cdot8.$

In the above calculations we have neglected the effect of the expansion of the glass bulbs and tubes which contain the gas. Since the coefficient of dilatation of glass is very small compared with that of air, ·000023 as against ·00366, the error is too small to be perceptible without more delicate apparatus.

HEAT.

EXAMPLES.

EXPANSION OF GASES.

1. State Boyle's Law and express the results on a diagram in which the pressure is represented by vertical lines, the volume by horizontal lines. If the gas be more compressible than is given by Boyle's Law, how does the curve differ from the above?

2. Enunciate the laws of Boyle and Charles. If a gas has a volume of 45 litres at a pressure of 760 mm. and temperature 27°C., at what pressure will its volume be 30 litres when the temperature is 77°C.?

3. Explain accurately what is meant by the statement that the coefficient of expansion of air is 1/273. The volume of a certain quantity of air at 50°C. is 500 cubic inches. Assuming no change of pressure to take place, determine its volumes at −50°C. and at 100°C. respectively.

4. State the effect on the volume of a given mass of air, of altering its temperature without altering its pressure; also the effect on its pressure of altering its temperature without altering its volume.

5. A mass of air occupies 25 cubic feet at a temperature of 15°C. and a pressure of 15 lbs. per square inch. What will be its volume at 100°C. and a pressure of 25 lbs.?

6. What will be the volume of a mass of air measuring 10 c. feet at 0°C. if the temperature be raised to 273°C. and the pressure doubled?

7. State the gaseous laws and shew how it follows from them that for a gas at pressure p, volume v, and absolute temperature T, pv is proportional to T. Explain carefully what you mean by absolute temperature.

8. Describe some practical form of constant volume air-thermometer: state clearly what measurements you would make to obtain the coefficient of increase of pressure with rise of temperature: and what precautions should be taken that an accurate result might be obtained.

What is the absolute zero of the air-thermometer?

9. A quantity of gas is collected in a graduated tube over mercury. The volume of the gas at 10°C. is 50 c.c. and the level of the mercury in the tube is 10 cm. above the level outside; the barometer stands at 75 cm. Find the volume which the gas would occupy at 0°C. and 76 cm. barometric pressure.

10. A quantity of air 3 c.c. in volume at atmospheric pressure is introduced into the space above a barometric column which originally stands at 760 mm. The column is depressed by 190 mm.; find the volume occupied by the air.

DILATATION OF GASES.

11. A quantity of dry air occupies 1000 c.c. at 20° C. and under a pressure of 760 mm. of mercury. At what temperature will it occupy 1400 c.c. under a pressure of 750 mm. of mercury?

12. The density of air at 0° C. and 760 mm. pressure is 1·29 grammes per litre. What is its density at 491° F. and 1000 mm. pressure?

13. A mass of gas occupies a volume of 35 c.c. at a pressure due to 75 cm. of mercury and temperature of 15° C., find its volume at a pressure due to 76 cm. of mercury and temperature 0° C.

14. When the height of the barometer is 76 cm. the volume of a given mass of gas is 100 c.c., the temperature being 0° C. When the temperature is raised to 100°, and the pressure increased by that due to 28 cm. of mercury, it is found that the volume is the same; find the coefficient of increase of pressure of the gas.

15. The pressure of a mass of air kept at constant volume increases by that due to 2·78 mm. of mercury for a rise of temperature of 1° C. If the pressure at 0° be that due to 760 mm., find the temperature when the pressure is that due to 899 mm.

16. The volume of a mass of air at standard pressure and temperature is 1 litre. Find the volume (i) when the barometer rises 25 cm., (ii) when the pressure is that due to 600 cm., the temperature remaining in each case unchanged.

17. Find the volume of the mass of air in Question 16 at standard pressure (i) at a temperature of 100° C., (ii) at a temperature of −100° C.

18. Find the volume of a litre of air at 0° C. and 760 mm. (i) at 100° and 785 mm., (ii) at −100° C. and 600 mm.

19. A quantity of gas occupies 150 cubic inches at a temperature of 2° C. when the barometer stands at 29·7 inches, find its volume at 16° C. if the barometer rise to 30·6 inches.

20. A quantity of gas occupies 42·5 cubic inches at a pressure of 30·4 inches of mercury and temperature 33° C., find the pressure if the volume is altered to 40 cubic inches and the temperature to 6° C.

21. If 1000 cubic inches of air at 0° C. occupy 1366 cubic inches when raised to 100° C. at constant pressure, find by how much the temperature of the same mass of air must be raised in order that its pressure may be doubled, its volume remaining constant.

CHAPTER VIII.

CHANGE OF STATE. SOLID TO LIQUID.

106. Fusion of a Solid. Melting-point. If heat be applied to a solid body, its temperature rises, and the body usually expands, until a certain temperature is reached at which the body begins to melt. This temperature is called the fusing-point; the further application of heat produces no rise of temperature, until the body is melted, and the whole has become liquid.

The latent heat of fusion of a solid has already been defined as the quantity of heat required to change 1 gramme of the solid to a liquid without change of temperature, and the method of determining the latent heat of fusion of ice has been explained.

EXPERIMENT (25). *To find the melting-point of paraffin wax.*

Take a piece of glass tubing, draw out one end to a fine point and close it. Place some small fragments of paraffin wax in the tube; melt it by placing it in hot water and then let it solidify so as to fill the tube. Fasten the tube to a thermometer, with an india-rubber band or otherwise, so that the narrow part of the tube may be alongside the bulb. The wax when solid is opaque. Place the tube in a beaker of water, and gradually warm the water, keeping it stirred, noting the temperature. When the temperature of the melting-point is reached, and the wax becomes fluid, it loses its opacity, becoming transparent; observe carefully the reading of the thermometer when this occurs; allow the bath to cool, and note the temperature at which the wax again becomes opaque. If the heating has been sufficiently slow, the two temperatures will differ very slightly; the mean of the two may be taken as the melting-point.

A similar method may be employed to find the melting-point of many other substances.

Many bodies, however, do not change suddenly from the hard solid to the liquid state and vice versa. Thus glass can exist in a soft plastic state over a wide range of temperature and in consequence of this can be worked and moulded.

Iron has a plastic condition, just below the temperature at which it melts, and when in this state can be welded. Plumber's solder remains a viscous substance while cooling through a considerable number of degrees.

The plasticity of ice is much greater just below the melting-point than it is at a lower temperature.

Such bodies become soft or plastic solids before melting; there is however a temperature at which a sudden absorption of heat occurs and the plastic solid becomes a fluid. This temperature is the melting-point.

107. Change of Volume on melting. Some bodies contract on melting, others expand. Ice, iron, brass. all occupy a greater volume in the solid than in the liquid state. It is in consequence of this that sharp castings may be taken of these substances; thus ice floats on water, and solid iron in the liquid metal.

Other bodies, such as wax and bismuth, expand when melted. The contraction of paraffin wax is easily shewn by filling a test tube with melting wax and allowing it to solidify; the solid wax does not nearly fill the tube.

EXPERIMENT (26). *To determine the contraction of ice on melting.*

Take a test tube holding about 20 c.cm. Fit it with a good cork, through which a tube passes; the bore of the tube should be about 5 mm. and its length some 12 or 15 cm. Measure the bore of the tube, and find the area of its cross-section. Determine also the volume of the test tube up to the cork. This may be done by letting water run in from a burette. Fill the test tube with cold water which has been well boiled. Insert the cork and attach a millimetre scale to the tube. Freeze the water in the test tube by putting it in a freezing mixture. This must be done gradually and carefully, so as to freeze the water from the bottom, otherwise the expansion on freezing will burst the test tube. As the freezing proceeds the water which at first was just visible in the glass tube above the cork rises up the tube; note the distance it has risen when the freezing is complete; and, by multiplying this by the area of the tube in square centimetres, find the increase in volume of the contents of the tube on freezing. When all the water in the test tube has become solid repeat the observation in the reverse order by melting the ice and observing the fall of the water.

108. Relation between Melting-point and Pressure. The melting-point of ice and of other bodies which contract on melting is lowered by increasing the pressure to which they are exposed.

Thus at a pressure of about 160 kilogrammes per square cm., or nearly 160 atmospheres, ice will melt at $-1°$ C. instead of at $0°$ C.

This lowering of the freezing-point may be shewn by the following experiments.

(1) An iron cylinder AB, fig. 46, is closed with a strong screw C. It is then filled with water and frozen; a metal ball is placed on the top of the water and the cylinder closed by the screw. The whole is then covered with ice, the ball being at the top of the cylinder; pressure is then applied by means of the screw. On opening the cylinder, the water inside is found to be still frozen, but the ball is at the bottom. The water has become liquid under the pressure and the ball has sunk to the bottom; on removing the pressure the water has again frozen.

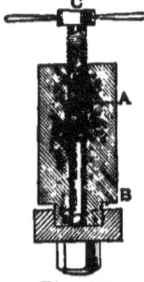

Fig. 46.

107–109] CHANGE OF STATE. SOLID TO LIQUID.

(2) Take a strong wooden mould of any form, such as a hollow cylinder with a wooden piston or plunger, pack it tightly with snow or powdered ice; press the plunger firmly down by means of a small hydraulic press or heavy weights. On again opening the cylinder after removing the pressure it will be found to contain a solid cylinder of clear ice.

109. Regelation. This same process is illustrated every time a snowball is made. When the snow is too cold it will not bind. When it is near its melting-point, comparatively little pressure is needed to make it melt; on removing the pressure the water formed freezes again and the snow binds. This phenomenon is known as regelation.

EXPERIMENT (27). *To observe the effects of regelation.*

(1) Place two pieces of ice in water and press them strongly together; remove the pressure; the two pieces are frozen together.

(2) Support a block of ice on the ring of a retort stand or in any convenient manner. Fasten one end of a stout copper wire to the table; pass the wire over the ice and attach a heavy weight, 10 or 20 kilos, to the other end. It will be found that the wire cuts its way through the ice, but that water formed freezes up again above the wire so that the continuity of the ice remains unbroken, though the wire passes through.

Underneath the wire the ice is subject to considerable pressure; it therefore melts, although at the temperature of the freezing-point or even a little below it. The water formed flows round the wire to the upper surface where it is free from pressure. But heat is required to melt the ice and the copper wire is a good conductor[1], hence heat is conducted from the water above the wire through the wire to melt the ice. The water is at the temperature of the freezing-point and therefore the abstraction of heat from it causes it again to freeze.

Thus the heat required to melt the ice below the wire is obtained from the freezing of the water above the wire.

[1] See Chapter x., § 145.

In substances such as beeswax or paraffin which expand on melting the opposite effects are produced; the melting-point is raised by pressure.

110. Freezing Mixtures. Heat is required to melt a solid and the action of many freezing mixtures depends on this fact.

EXPERIMENT (28). *To observe the fall of temperature produced by melting.*

(1) Drop a few crystals of ammonium nitrate into a beaker of water in which a thermometer is placed; the temperature will be observed to fall as the crystals melt. The action of the water melts the crystals. Energy is needed to produce the change from solid to liquid and the energy is obtained from some of the heat present in the water, which is thereby lowered in temperature.

(2) Break some pieces of ice up into small fragments and mix them with salt; the ice melts, absorbing the latent heat of fusion from the mixture, and the temperature is reduced to between $-15°$ C. and $-20°$ C. Fahrenheit's zero, $32°$ Fah. below freezing-point, was obtained in this manner.

111. Development of Heat by (1) *Chemical Change.* Heat is developed by many chemical combinations; it may happen that when a body is dissolved in water the product combines with the water and developes heat; if this heat exceeds the heat required for the solution a rise of temperature will be the result. This is the case when caustic potash is dissolved in water.

(2) *Solidification.* Again, heat is developed in the act of solidification. Water was cooled by Despretz in fine tubes some $20°$ below freezing-point. When this cooling has been produced, solidification may be caused by a slight disturbance. Ice is formed and the temperature rises to the freezing-point.

EXPERIMENT (29). *To observe the development of heat produced by solidification.*

Make a very strong solution of acetate of soda by heating it with water in a flask; close the flask with a plug of cotton wool and allow the solution to cool; it can be cooled with care to temperatures very considerably below that at which it would normally become solid. Remove the cotton wool and insert a thermometer, this will very often be sufficient to produce solidification, if not drop in a small crystal. The mass solidifies at once and the temperature rises very considerably.

112. Laws of Fusion. We may thus sum up our results with the following laws of fusion.

(1) *A substance begins to melt at a temperature, which is constant for the same substance, if the pressure be constant, and is called the melting-point.*

(2) *The temperature of the solid remains unchanged while fusion is taking place.*

(3) *If a substance expand on solidifying, like ice, its melting-point is lowered by pressure; if it contract, like wax, its melting-point is raised by pressure.*

(4) *The latent heat of fusion of a substance is the quantity of heat absorbed by unit mass in changing from the solid to the liquid state without change of temperature. This amount of heat is constant for a given body melting at a given temperature.*

It should also be remembered that the effect of pressure in changing the melting-point of a solid body is very small, being in the case of ice about $\frac{1}{150}$ of degree Centigrade for one atmosphere.

EXAMPLES.

FUSION AND SOLIDIFICATION.

1. In what way does pressure alter melting-points? Consider the cases of ice, cast iron, wax, and phosphorus.

2. Explain the way in which two blocks of ice at 0° C. may be made to unite by the application of pressure.

122   HEAT.

3. Give a sketch of the formation and motion of glaciers. Describe any experiments with ice, which illustrate the subject. Account for the fact that a snowball by sufficient pressure may be converted into a ball of clear ice.

4. Describe an experiment to prove that ice contracts on melting. A copper wire is passed round a block of ice and supports a heavy weight. It is found that the wire eats its way through the ice but that the latter freezes up again behind the wire. Explain this.

5. A pound of ice at $-10°$ C. is heated under atmospheric pressure to $200°$ C. Trace the changes of volume and state which it undergoes, and shew how to calculate the amount of heat required to produce them, giving numerical values where you can.

6. Describe in detail the process of freezing of a pond until the ice is strong enough to support heavy loads. What would be the effect on its bearing power of breaking the ice all round the edge?

7. Explain the adhesion of two pieces of melting ice when pressed together and let go. Why is it not readily possible to make snowballs during hard frost?

8. Describe the changes that a pound of ice undergoes in being heated from $-10°$ C. to $60°$ C.: and shew what amount of work would have to be done to supply the heat necessary to raise its temperature through this range.

[The specific heat of ice is ·5, the latent heat of fusion of ice 79.
The mechanical equivalent of heat 1390 foot-pounds.]

9. It is said that the heat received on the earth from the sun would, if uniformly distributed, melt in 2 hrs. 13 minutes a shell of ice over the earth 2·5 cm. in thickness. Supposing all the heat which falls on it to remain in the water thus formed, how long would it take to turn it into steam; the latent heat of fusion of ice being 79, and that of evaporation of water 537? The radius of the earth may be taken as 6440 kilometres and the specific gravity of ice as ·9.

10. What mass of ether at $0°$ C. must be evaporated in order to freeze 5 grammes of water at 0, the latent heat of ether being 95?

11. Find the latent heat of fusion of ice and the latent heat of evaporation of water on the Fahrenheit scale.

12. A cryophorus contains 50 grammes of water at $0°$ C., find what mass of ice is formed when 1 gramme of water is evaporated, assuming the latent heat of evaporation of water at $0°$ C. to be 606.

CHAPTER IX.

CHANGE OF STATE. LIQUID TO VAPOUR.

113. Evaporation. If a small quantity of water be exposed in a flat dish or saucer, in a fairly dry room at ordinary temperatures, the water disappears in a short time and the dish becomes dry. If the experiment be repeated with ether or alcohol the result is the same but the dish dries much more rapidly. The liquid has passed gradually into the gaseous state, and this process when it goes on slowly from the surface of the liquid is called evaporation.

In a similar manner some solids may pass directly into the gaseous state. Thus snow sometimes disappears in dry frosty weather, the water-substance passes from the solid to the gaseous state without becoming liquid between. Camphor behaves like ice; such a change is called volatilization.

A substance which passes readily into the gaseous state is called volatile.

DEFINITION. *Evaporation is a gradual change of a substance from the liquid to the gaseous state which takes place at the surface of the substance at all temperatures.*

The substance when in the gaseous state, produced thus by evaporation, is called a vapour. The distinction between a vapour and a gas will be considered in what follows and a definition of a vapour will be given in § 119.

114. Pressure of Vapours. When a volatile liquid such as water or ether is placed in a closed vessel containing dry air, evaporation takes place and the quantity of vapour in the vessel is increased. The vapour formed exerts pressure like a gas and hence the pressure on the sides of the vessel is increased. The formation of vapour continues until the pressure which it exerts has reached a certain limiting value depending on the nature of the substance which is evaporating and on the temperature. This limiting value does not depend on the size or shape of the vessel which contains the vapour, or upon the nature of the gas, air, hydrogen, or whatever it may be which the vessel contains in addition to the vapour, provided (1) that there is no chemical action between this gas and the vapour, and (2) that some liquid remains in the vessel.

When the pressure exerted by the vapour which a space contains at a given temperature has reached the limiting value for that temperature, the space is said to be *saturated* with the vapour.

When a space is saturated with vapour the pressure exerted by the vapour is known as the saturation pressure of the vapour.

If the volume of a space which is saturated with vapour be reduced, the pressure of the vapour is not altered, some of the vapour is condensed to the liquid state but the pressure remains the same; if the volume of the space be increased, provided that it contains sufficient liquid, more liquid evaporates and the pressure exerted by the vapour soon[1] attains the same value as before the alteration of volume.

If the temperature of a space containing liquid and saturated with its vapour be raised[2], more liquid is evaporated and the saturation pressure of its vapour is increased; if on

---

[1] Since however evaporation takes time the pressure immediately after the increase in volume will be too small, but it will quickly rise to its former value.

[2] If the space also contains air or some other gas it must be remembered that when the temperature is changed the pressure of this gas is altered. The total observed change of pressure is due to the change in the pressure of the gas together with the change in the pressure of the vapour, and in finding the latter change the change in the pressure of the gas must be allowed for.

the other hand the temperature falls, some of the vapour is condensed to liquid and the saturation pressure is less than previously.

*115. Experiments on Vapour Pressure. In making experiments on the pressure of vapours the apparatus shewn in fig. 47 will be found useful.

It is a modification of that used in § 95 for verifying Boyle's Law.

Fig. 47.

The tube AB shewn in fig. 41 is replaced by a tube AB, fig. 47, having two stopcocks S_1 S_2 at the upper end. These are placed one above the other with a short length of glass tubing between them. The volume of the tube between S_1 and S_2 may conveniently be about ·25 c.cm. Above the upper stopcock is a funnel. When the upper stopcock is open the funnel and space between S_1 and S_2 may be filled with water or any other liquid which is to be examined. Close the upper stopcock S_1 and open S_2; the liquid in $S_1 S_2$ runs down into the space AB, and on evaporation exerts pressure on the mercury in AB. This pressure can be measured by the aid of the sliding piece CD, fig. 41. The tube AB can be surrounded by a wider glass tube forming a jacket; by putting warm water into this jacket the temperature of the vapour can be varied and the laws of the variation of its pressure with temperature measured.

With this apparatus the following experiments may be performed.

EXPERIMENT (30). *To measure the pressure of water vapour at a given temperature.*

Adjust the apparatus, which should be absolutely dry, so that, when the taps S_1 S_2 are open, the mercury may stand at the same level in AB and CD of figure 41. The pressure of the air in AB is then the atmospheric pressure. Close S_2, put some water in the funnel above S_1 and so fill the space $S_1 S_2$ with water[1].

[1] The air sticks in the tube between the stopcocks and care is necessary to fill the tube.

126   HEAT.   [CH. IX

Note the level of the mercury in the tube AB. Close S_1 and open S_2.

The water runs down into AB and some of it evaporates; the pressure in AB is increased and the mercury is driven down in AB and rises in CD.

Wait for some little time, to allow the space to become saturated, and make sure that some water is left uncondensed in AB; if no water is visible, introduce some more in the manner just described. The difference in level between the mercury columns in AB and CD does not measure the pressure of the vapour directly, because the air in AB now occupies a greater volume than previously; its pressure is therefore less than it was. Raise CD until the mercury in AB comes back to its original level. The air in AB has now the same volume and pressure as before, the height of the mercury in CD above that in AB measures the pressure due to the vapour.

Thus the saturation pressure of aqueous vapour at the temperature of the experiment and in presence of air at atmospheric pressure is measured.

EXPERIMENT (31). *To observe the effect of change of temperature on the saturation pressure of a vapour.*

Place some warm water at a temperature say of 30° C. in the jacket tube.

More of the water in AB evaporates, the pressure of the vapour is increased, and the column of mercury in CD is forced up. Adjust the height of CD until the level in AB is the same as before, and measure the height of the column in CD above AB. This gives the excess of the pressure in AB over the atmospheric pressure.

Now this excess is due to (1) the increase of the pressure of the air in AB produced by a rise of temperature at constant volume, and (2) the vapour pressure of the liquid. The increase due to the change of temperature can be calculated as described in § 102. It will be $p_0\{T/T_0 - 1\}$, where p_0 is the atmospheric pressure, T_0 the absolute temperature at which the stopcocks were closed, T the absolute temperature at the time of the observation[1]. Subtract this from the total observed increase: the difference gives the vapour pressure of the liquid at the temperature of the observation.

On making the observations it will be found that the vapour pressure increases greatly as the temperature rises.

EXPERIMENT (32). *To shew that the vapour pressure is independent of the pressure of the air present.*

Let the space AB be filled with dry air, the mercury in the tube being also dry. Open the stopcocks and adjust the level of CD, so that the mercury is at the same height in the two tubes. Close the stopcocks and raise CD until the air is compressed to about half its volume. Note the level of the mercury in AB in this case and also the level of that in CD. Fill the funnel and tube with liquid, and proceed with the experiment as before, adjusting CD so that the level in AB remains the same. The increase of the height of the mercury column in CD over its height before the liquid was admitted to AB gives the vapour pressure in the presence of air at twice the atmospheric pressure.

It will be found that the pressure is the same as that observed previously at the same temperature.

By starting in the same way with the level in CD below that in AB we can experiment when the air is at less than atmospheric pressure.

If the slide be sufficiently long we can with the same apparatus examine the effect of vapour pressure in a vacuum. For this purpose it must be possible to lower CD some 80 or 85 cm. below the top of AB.

Open the taps S_1 and S_2 and raise CD until the mercury rises above S_2; close S_2 and lower CD.

If $C1$ be lowered sufficiently so that the difference in level between S_2 and the top of the column in CD may be greater

---

[1] By altering slightly the method of observation, and filling AB first with dry air at atmospheric pressure and at the higher temperature 80° and then admitting the moisture, the necessity for this correction may be avoided.

than the barometric height, the mercury will fall slightly in AB, leaving a vacuum between the top of the column and the stopcock.

Boil some water for some time so as to free it from air; allow it to cool, and introduce it in the manner already described above the mercury in AB. The mercury is depressed; adjust CD so as to bring the column in AB up to the same mark as previously, and then measure the pressure of the vapour at the temperature of the observation. It will be found to be the same as that observed previously at the same temperature when there was some air in AB^1.

EXPERIMENT (33). *To shew that the vapour pressure at a given temperature due to two vapours which do not act chemically on one another is the sum of the vapour pressures due to each liquid separately at the same temperature.*

Observe in the manner described in Experiment 30 the vapour pressures due to each of the two liquids, say benzene and water. Mix the two liquids, introduce the mixture into the space above the mercury, and observe the pressure again. It will be found to be the sum of the pressures previously observed. The temperature must be kept the same throughout the experiment.

116. Pressure of water vapour at various temperatures. For experiments on vapour pressure in a vacuum the following arrangement of apparatus is more convenient. A tube about 80 cm. long and 1 cm. in diameter AB, fig. 48, is cleaned and dried, closed at one end, and then filled with clean dry mercury, and inverted with the open end in a cistern of mercury. A barometer is thus formed and the mercury in the tube sinks to the barometric height, about 76 cm., above that in the cistern.

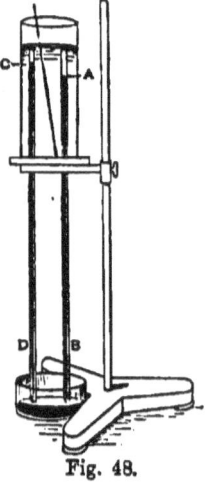

Fig. 48.

[1] For observations on vapour pressure in a vacuum, the form of apparatus described in § 116 is preferable.

CHANGE OF STATE. LIQUID TO VAPOUR.

A small quantity of the liquid is placed in a pipette, the lower end of which is bent upwards, so as to be inserted in the mercury in the cistern with its open end below the barometer tube; by blowing gently into the pipette a small quantity of the liquid can be caused to rise in drops through the column to the surface of the mercury. This liquid evaporates into the vacuum above the column which is depressed, and the depression measures the vapour pressure. By surrounding the tube with a jacket which can hold water and raising the temperature of this water, the vapour pressure at various temperatures given by the thermometer in the jacket can be found.

In order to allow for changes in the height of the barometer during the experiment it is usual to set up two barometer tubes side by side in the same water-jacket, and to introduce the liquid into one only.

The difference in height of the two columns gives the vapour pressure directly. This second tube is shewn at CD in the figure. To measure this difference in height a vertical scale may be set up alongside the tube, or for more accurate work a kathetometer may be used. This was the method employed by Regnault in his researches on the vapour pressure of water at low temperatures.

The scale is necessarily at some little distance from the tubes and it is not easy therefore to read the height exactly. To get over this difficulty it is convenient to fix a piece of card one edge of which can be set horizontally a little way in front of the tubes. The observer then places his eye so that the top of the mercury column is just hidden by the card, and then keeping his eye fixed reads the graduation of the scale which coincides with the card; in applying this method it is necessary that the tube and the scale should be at the same distance from the card. Greater accuracy will be secured if a reading telescope is used to view the scale and column.

EXPERIMENT (34). *To compare the vapour pressure of various liquids at a given temperature.*

Fit up side by side in the same jacket a number of barometer tubes as described above; allow one to remain as a barometer.

Introduce into each of the others respectively small quantities of the liquids to be experimented on, taking care to introduce in each case sufficient to allow some of the liquid to remain unevaporated on the top of the mercury columns.

Measure the differences in height between the barometer column and the columns in the other tubes.

These differences give in each case the pressure, in mm. of mercury, of the vapours in the respective tubes.

EXPERIMENT (35). *To measure the pressure of aqueous vapour at different temperatures.*

Fit up as in the last experiment two barometer tubes in a

PRESSURE OF AQUEOUS VAPOUR IN MM. OF MERCURY.

$t°$ C.	mm.	$t°$ C.	mm.	$t°$ C.	mm.	$t°$ C.	Atmos.
−10	2·08	16	13·54	90	525·39	100	1·0
− 9	2·26	17	14·42	95	633·69	110	1·4
− 8	2·46	18	15·36	99	733·21	120	1·96
− 7	2·67	19	16·35	99·1	735·85	130	2·67
− 6	2·89	20	17·39	99·2	738·50	140	3·57
− 5	3·13	21	18·50	99·3	741·16	150	4·7
− 4	3·39	22	19·66	99·4	743·83	160	6·1
− 3	3·66	23	20·89	99·5	746·50	170	7·8
− 2	3·96	24	22·18	99·6	749·18	180	9·9
− 1	4·27	25	23·55	99·7	751·87	190	12·4
0	4·60	26	24·99	99·8	754·57	200	15·4
1	4·94	27	26·51	99·9	757·28	210	18·8
2	5·30	28	28·10	100	760·00	220	22·9
3	5·69	29	29·78	100·1	762·73	230	27·5
4	6·10	30	31·55	100·2	765·46		
5	6·53	35	41·83	100·3	768·20		
6	7·00	40	54·91	100·4	771·95		
7	7·49	45	71·39	100·5	773·71		
8	8·02	50	91·98	100·6	776·48		
9	8·57	55	117·48	100·7	779·26		
10	9·17	60	148·79	100·8	782·04		
11	9·79	65	186·94	100·9	784·83		
12	10·46	70	233·08	101	787·59		
13	11·16	75	288·50	105	906·41		
14	11·91	80	354·62	110	1075·37		
15	12·70	85	433·00				

water-jacket. Introduce some water above the mercury in one. Place a thermometer and stirrer in the bath. Vary the temperature of the water and take a series of readings of the difference of level of the two columns, and of the corresponding temperatures, keeping the bath well stirred. Enter the results, which give in mm. of mercury the pressure of the aqueous vapour at the different temperatures, in a Table, as shewn on the previous page.

This Table gives the results of Regnault's experiments on the pressure of aqueous vapour at varying temperatures from $-10°$ C. to $230°$ C.

117. Dalton's Laws for vapours. By means of experiments such as those described the laws regulating the pressure of vapours known as Dalton's Laws have been established. They may be stated thus.

(1) *The saturation pressure of a vapour depends only on its temperature.*

(2) *The pressure of a mixture of gases and vapours, which have no chemical action on each other, is the sum of the pressures, which each would separately exert, if it were alone in the space occupied by the mixture.*

Example. *The pressure of a mass of air saturated with aqueous vapour at 15° is observed to be 756 mm.; find the pressure due to the air alone.*

The saturation pressure of aqueous vapour at 15° is 12·7 mm. Hence the pressure due to the dry air is 756 − 12·7 or 743·3 mm.

*118. Unsaturated vapours. The first of the above laws applies only to saturated vapours, the pressure exerted is the maximum pressure which can be exerted at the temperature; some of the liquid must be present, so that if the temperature rise more vapour can be formed.

If the pressure of a vapour at a given temperature is not the maximum which it could exert at that temperature, the vapour is said to be unsaturated.

Thus, if a *small* quantity of water be placed in a *large* space filled with dry air, the whole of the water will evaporate without the pressure reaching the saturation pressure. The vapour is unsaturated. Under these circumstances the vapour obeys approximately the gaseous laws; if the volume of the space increase the vapour pressure decreases approximately according to Boyle's Law; when the volume is doubled the vapour pressure is halved, and so on. If the volume decrease the vapour pressure increases in the inverse ratio, until the maximum or saturation pressure for the temperature is reached. When the pressure has risen to its maximum value no increase of pressure is produced by a further diminution of volume; some of the vapour is condensed, the pressure remaining unchanged.

Similarly, if the temperature be raised, the volume remaining unaltered, the pressure increases in accordance with Charles' Law, being proportional to the absolute temperature. If the temperature be reduced, the pressure falls in accordance with the same law, until, at a certain temperature, it reaches the saturation pressure for that temperature; for a further reduction of temperature the pressure falls more quickly than it would do were it still to follow Charles' Law; some of the vapour is condensed to liquid, and, as the temperature is further reduced, the pressure falls, remaining always at the saturation pressure for the given temperature.

These results may be indicated on a diagram thus:

Take two lines OA, OB, fig. 49, at right angles and let the volume be measured by lines parallel to OA, the pressure by lines parallel to OB.

Let OL represent the saturation pressure at the temperature of the experiment, and draw LK parallel to OA.

Let ON_1 represent the volume of a quantity of unsaturated

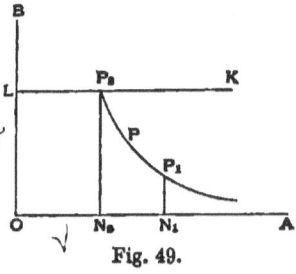

Fig. 49.

vapour, and N_1P_1 its pressure. As the volume of the vapour is reduced, the pressure increases and the relation between the two is shewn by the curve line P_1PP_2, which is approximately the same as that for a gas.

This continues until a volume, ON_2 in the figure, is reached at which the curve line cuts LK. The pressure becomes equal to the saturation pressure at that temperature. As the volume is still further reduced, there is no increase in pressure until the whole is condensed to liquid; the relation between pressure and volume is shewn by part of the horizontal line KL. The line P_1P_2L is called an isothermal line.

Again, in fig. 50, let the horizontal line OA represent temperatures, and the vertical line OB pressures.

Corresponding to each temperature measure off vertical lines to represent the saturation pressure; the ends of these lines will lie on a curve such as LP_2K.

Let N_1P_1 be the pressure of an unsaturated vapour corresponding to a temperature ON_1. The relation between pressure and temperature will be given by a straight line P_1P_2 which would cut AO produced at a point corresponding to the temperature of $-273°$ C.

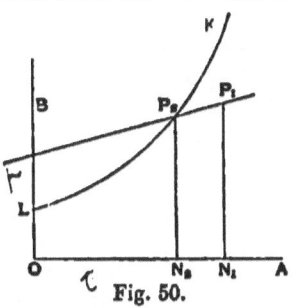

Fig. 50.

Let this line cut LK in P_2, and let ON_2 be the temperature corresponding to P_2. Then, until the temperature falls to ON_2, the relation between pressure and temperature is given by the straight line P_1P_2; if the temperature be still further reduced, the relation will be given by the curve P_2L.

Examples. (1) *The pressure of a mass of aqueous vapour 100 c.cm. in volume is 4·35 mm., the temperature being 20°; find the pressure when the volume is 50 c.cm., and also the volume at which the gas becomes saturated, the maximum pressure being 17·4 cm.*

If the vapour obey Boyle's Law, the pressure when the volume is 50 c.cm. will be double that when the volume is 100 c.cm., or 8·7 mm. This is less than the saturation pressure and therefore is the pressure required. Again, assuming Boyle's Law to hold up to the saturating pressure, the volume when the pressure is 17·4 is

$$100 \times 4·35/17·4 \text{ or } 25 \text{ c.cm.}$$

Thus, when the volume has been reduced to 25 c.cm. the vapour becomes saturated.

(2) *A given space is just saturated with vapour at 15° C., there being no liquid present; find the pressure exerted by the vapour at 30°.*

At 15° C. the pressure is that due to 12·7 mm.; from 15° to 30° the vapour obeys Charles' Law approximately. Thus

$$\text{Pressure at } 30° = \frac{12\cdot 7 \times (273 + 30)}{273 + 15}$$

$$= 13\cdot 36 \text{ mm.}$$

*119. Vapours and Gases. Critical temperature.
So far, the distinction we have drawn between vapours and gases has been that a vapour can be liquefied by reducing its volume, while, for the temperatures at which we have supposed the experiments conducted, a gas continues to obey Boyle's Law for all pressures; this distinction for most practical purposes is sufficient.

But by suitable devices a gas can be liquefied. Thus Faraday liquefied nearly all the gases known to him except oxygen, hydrogen, marsh-gas, and carbonic oxide. One simple arrangement of apparatus used by him is shewn in fig. 51. It consists of a strong bent tube. Some substance from which the gas to be experimented on can be evolved by heating is placed at one end, and the tube is hermetically sealed. The other end is placed in a freezing mixture of ice and salt. On heating the tube the gas is given off, the pressure becomes very great and the gas is condensed to liquid in the cold end.

Fig. 51.

Dr Andrews liquefied carbonic acid gas by filling a strong glass tube with it, and allowing the open end of the tube to communicate with a reservoir of mercury. By means of a screw plunger the mercury was forced up the tube, thus compressing the gas. Carbonic acid gas, at a temperature of about 13° C., can be liquefied at a pressure of about 48 atmospheres.

By the aid of this apparatus Andrews was able to shew that, so long as the temperature of this substance was below 30°·9 C., it could be liquefied by pressure, but if its temperature exceeded this value no pressure however great reduced it to the liquid state. This temperature is called the critical temperature for carbonic acid. Below its critical temperature carbonic acid gas has the properties of a vapour; it can be liquefied by the application of sufficient pressure; above this temperature pressure will not liquefy it. When near its point of condensation, carbonic acid does not obey Boyle's Law at all accurately; at some distance from this point its pressure at a given temperature is, in accordance with the law, very nearly proportional to its density.

Other gaseous substances have their critical temperatures; that of ether is about 187° C. while for water it is over 400° C. These substances in the gaseous form then at ordinary temperatures are vapours. They can be condensed by pressure to liquids, for at ordinary temperatures they are below their critical temperature.

On the other hand, the critical temperatures of the so-called permanent gases are extremely low, that for oxygen may be about $-130°$ C., for nitrogen $-167°$ C., but the values are difficult to determine. These substances at ordinary temperatures are above their critical temperature; they cannot be liquefied by pressure only; to produce liquefaction they must be cooled down to below the critical temperature, and since their vapour pressure is enormously high they require even at the low temperature great pressure to produce liquefaction. The temperature corresponding to the point P_2 in fig. 50 is very low, while the pressure is high.

Definition of critical temperature. *There is for all substances in the gaseous state a temperature such that the substance can be liquefied by pressure only if it be below this temperature, and cannot be liquefied if it be above this temperature. This temperature is called the critical temperature.*

A substance in the gaseous state below its critical temperature is called a vapour, above this temperature it is a gas.

Commonly however the term vapour is used, in a more restricted sense, for a substance in the gaseous state, which, at ordinary temperatures, can be liquefied by moderate pressure. Thus ether vapour is spoken of as a vapour, for it can be liquefied by a pressure of about half an atmosphere at temperatures of from 12° to 15° C.

Carbonic acid gas can be liquefied also at these same temperatures by pressure only, but the pressure required is some 50 atmospheres, about 100 times that needed to liquefy ether. Carbonic acid gas is therefore commonly, though not strictly, spoken of as a gas.

120. Ebullition or Boiling. A reference to the Table on p. 130 shews that at the temperature of 100° C. the pressure of aqueous vapour is 760 mm. of mercury. Now the standard atmospheric pressure is 760 mm., and water is seen *to boil* at this pressure and temperature. Thus in this case water boils at the temperature at which the pressure of its vapour is equal to the pressure to which the liquid is subject.

We proceed after some necessary definitions and explanations to describe some experiments to shew that this rule holds generally.

Definition of Boiling or Ebullition. *Boiling or ebullition is the change of a substance from the liquid to the gaseous state, which takes place throughout the mass of the liquid.*

Thus vapour is formed both by evaporation and by boiling; in the first case however the change takes place at the surface of the liquid only, in the second case it proceeds over the heating surface.

When heat is applied to a mass of liquid, such as a quantity of water in a beaker placed over a Bunsen burner, the lower layers of liquid are first warmed. These expand and rise to the surface, their place is taken by the colder layers from above, and by this process the mass is warmed through; the air which is contained in the water expands, as the temperature is increased, and rises in bubbles to the surface. After a time the temperature of the lower layers is raised up to or slightly above[1] 100° C. Water vapour or steam is formed as bubbles which rise into the colder layers above and are condensed, causing the water to "simmer," whilst the steam

---

[1] "Slightly above" because the pressure at the bottom of the vessel is greater than one atmosphere.

CHANGE OF STATE. LIQUID TO VAPOUR.

parts with its latent heat of evaporation, warming the water, and mixing up the layers until the whole mass reaches 100° C.

When this stage has been reached the steam rises to the surface and escapes into the air, and the simmering noise ceases. The water is boiling; the steam is formed throughout the mass, because water vapour at 100° exerts a pressure just equal to that of the standard atmosphere.

EXPERIMENT (36). *To shew that the pressure of water vapour when boiling is equal to the atmospheric pressure.*

(a) Fill a barometer tube with mercury as described in § 116. Introduce some water above the mercury, and jacket the whole tube as shewn in fig. 52 with a wide glass tube. Connect the upper end of this steam jacket to a boiler and allow the steam to escape from the jacket through a pipe at its lower end. Admit the steam gradually into the jacket: as the temperature rises, the pressure of the water vapour in the tube increases, and the mercury column is depressed, until when the whole has become steady the level of the mercury is the same[1] inside the tube and in the cistern. The pressure exerted by the water vapour is equal to the atmospheric pressure.

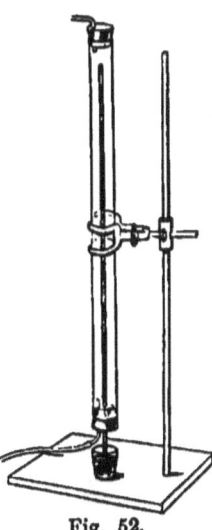

Fig. 52.

(b) The following experiment illustrates the same point.

ABC, fig. 53 and 53 a, is a bent tube closed at C, open at A, the arm AB being the longer. The arm BC contains some water freed from air by boiling; below the water is mercury filling the lower part of the tube and rising in the arm AB.

---

[1] If there is a large quantity of water left in the tube, owing to the weight of this water, the mercury inside the tube will be slightly below that outside.

The level of the mercury in this arm is below that in BC. The water and mercury completely fill BC. The tube AB passes through a cork closing a flask. The flask contains water which can be boiled, and the steam as it rises surrounds the lower part of the tube and escapes through a hole in the cork. The upper part of the neck of the flask can if necessary be jacketed as shewn in fig. 6.

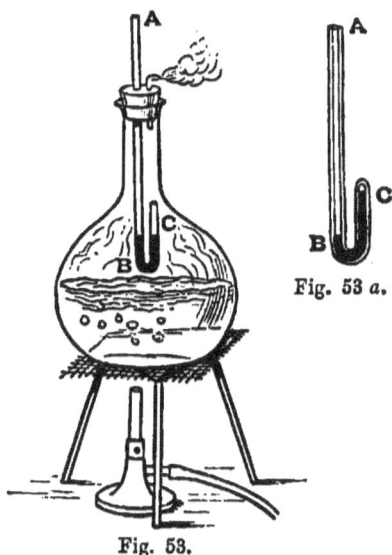

Fig. 53 a.

Fig. 53.

After the water has been boiling for some time the temperature of the water in the tube BC rises to 100° C. and the pressure of the vapour formed there forces the mercury down CB and up BA until it stands at the same level in the two arms. Thus the pressure of the vapour in BC is equal to the pressure on the mercury in AB, that is to the atmospheric pressure.

Thus we see that water boils at a temperature at which the pressure of its vapour is equal to the atmospheric pressure.

121. Boiling under diminished pressure. Assuming the law which has just been enunciated to hold generally we should expect that by reducing the pressure the temperature at which water boils may be reduced also; observation and experiment both shew this to be the case.

Thus on the top of a mountain the temperature of boiling water is much less than 100° C. At the top of Mont Blanc the temperature of the boiling-point is about 85° C. The following experiments illustrate this point.

EXPERIMENT (37). *To shew that the boiling-point of water is reduced by reducing the pressure.*

(1) Boil some water in a beaker or flask, place it under the receiver of an air-pump, wait till the water has ceased to boil and then exhaust rapidly; the boiling recommences.

(2) Boil some water in a strong Florence flask; when the water is boiling freely remove the burner and cork up the flask tightly. Invert it so that the water may cover the cork, as in fig. 54, and wait till the boiling ceases. The space above the water is filled with water vapour at a fairly high temperature, and the water is subject to the pressure of this vapour. Allow some drops of cold water to fall from a sponge on to the flask which is thereby cooled; some of the vapour is condensed, the pressure on the water surface is reduced and the boiling recommences.

Fig. 54.

EXPERIMENT (38). *To measure the temperature of steam issuing from water boiling under various pressures.*

Take a retort flask AB in fig. 55. At B there is an aperture through which a thermometer passing through a tightly fitting cork can be inserted. A is connected by means of a glass tube C and india-rubber tubing to an air-pump. A water suction pump which will work continuously is best. At C a side tube sealed into the glass tube, thus forming a T-piece, passes through a cork into a small flask or beaker. This cork fits tightly and a second tube, bent twice at right angles, passes

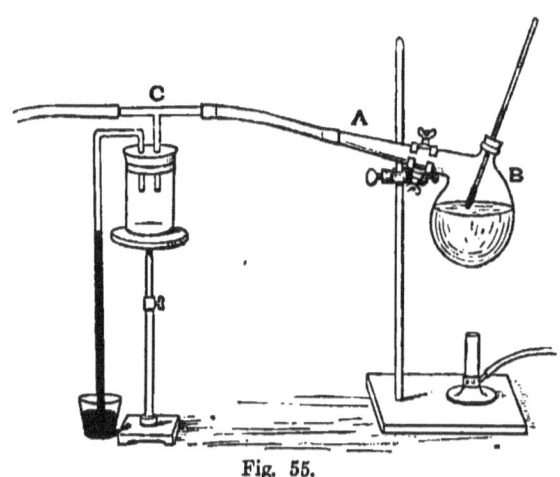

Fig. 55.

through it and has its open end immersed in a vessel of mercury, thus forming a pressure gauge. This tube must be longer than the height of the barometer and should have a scale attached.

Heat the water in the flask AB by a Bunsen burner and start the pump. The pressure of the air above the water is thus reduced, and the mercury rises in the gauge tube; the water begins to boil under the reduced pressure, the vapour formed being carried off by the pump as it is produced. By regulating the supply of heat and the rate of flow of the pump, a steady condition can be obtained, under which the water continues to boil, and the pressure and temperature remain unchanged; the pump removes the vapour as fast as it is formed. Read the temperature and the height of the mercury column in the gauge tube. Subtract this latter from

121–122] CHANGE OF STATE. LIQUID TO VAPOUR. 141

the barometric height and thus obtain the pressure within the apparatus.

Alter the supply of gas and the rate at which the pump is working and thus obtain a series of readings of corresponding pressures and boiling temperatures.

The results may be entered in tabular form thus:

Pressure in mm. of mercury.	Temperature in degrees Centigrade.	Pressure in mm. of mercury.	Temperature in degrees Centigrade.
30	29·3	235	70·1
55	40	350	79·7
100	50	525	90
150	60·2	760	100

The beaker at C is not *necessary* for the experiment; it forms however a convenient addition, for without it water vapour finds its way into the space above the gauge column and condenses there; in measuring the pressure the presence of this water has to be allowed for. Even with the beaker some vapour passes into the gauge and condenses; this may either be allowed for in the calculations or it may be vaporized from time to time by heating the gauge tube gently. If a continuous acting air-pump be not available, an arrangement for condensing the vapour must be used. The glass tube from the retort AB is bent downwards and communicates with a large flask; this flask is in communication with the air-pump. A three-necked bottle is convenient for this, the third opening being connected to the gauge. This bottle also serves the purpose of the beaker at C in fig. 55. The lower part of the tube from the retort AB is surrounded by a condenser jacket through which water at various temperatures can be made to flow. This water condenses the steam in the tube and the liquid formed by the condensation runs down into the bottle. The apparatus is partly exhausted by the air-pump. As the water boils under reduced pressure the vapour formed is condensed and the pressure and temperature can be read as before.

122. Boiling-point of a liquid. A comparison of the Tables on pp. 130 and 141 shews that the pressure under which water can boil at a given temperature is its vapour pressure at that temperature. We thus obtain the following

Definition of the boiling-point of a liquid. *The boiling-point of a liquid is the temperature at which the*

vapour pressure of the liquid is equal to the pressure on the surface of the liquid.

The necessity for the correction to the boiling point of a thermometer described on p. 20 and the method of calculating it can now be explained.

The second fixed point on a thermometer registers the temperature of steam issuing from boiling water at a standard pressure, that due to 760 mm. of mercury; if the pressure be lower than this the temperature of the steam will be less than 100° C. Experiments such as have been described shew that water boils at a temperature of 99° C. if the pressure be 733·2 mm., and further that for small variations the change in boiling-point is very approximately proportional to the change in pressure.

Thus the boiling-point falls by 1° C. for a reduction of pressure of 26·8 mm., and the change in boiling-point caused by any not very large change of pressure is found by dividing that change by 26·8.

123. Boiling under increased pressure. In a similar manner if the pressure be increased the temperature of the boiling-point is raised. This can be shewn by boiling water in a strong metallic vessel fitted with a pressure gauge and a safety-valve. A thermometer is inserted with its bulb in the steam. It is found that at a pressure of about two atmospheres the boiling-point is raised to 120° C.

This fact is made use of in high-pressure engines to raise the temperature of the steam, which in some cases may be as high as 200° C.; the pressure of the steam will then be about 15 atmospheres.

*124. Measurement of heights by Boiling-points —Hypsometry. By means of a Table such as that given on p. 141 two observations of the boiling-point may be used to determine the difference of level between two stations. For, by observing the boiling-point, the atmospheric pressure can be determined from the Table. Thus the difference of pressure between the two stations can be found. But this difference of pressure is the weight of a vertical column of air 1 sq. cm. in all between the two stations. Hence the mass of this column

CHANGE OF STATE. LIQUID TO VAPOUR.

is known; we require to find its height. Now the density of air depends on its pressure and temperature: if the stations are not too far apart, we may assume that the average pressure and temperature are the mean of those observed at the two stations. From this the average density of the air between the two can be obtained, since we know that the density of dry air at 0° C. and 760 mm. is ·001293 gramme per c.cm. Calculate the average density of the air at the pressure and temperature of the observation and divide the mass of the column by this density; the result will give the height of the column, that is the difference in level between the two stations. The result is only approximately correct, for the assumptions made are only approximately true. A more elaborate calculation however can be made, from which a more accurate result can be found.

It can be shewn that the height in centimetres is approximately given by the following rule.

Multiply the difference between the logarithms of the two barometer readings by 2×10^6, the result is the required height in centimetres.

Example. *The boiling-point at the lower station is* $99°·7$ *and at the upper station* $95°$ *C., the temperature of the air at the two stations being* $13°$ *C. and* $7°$ *C. Find the difference in level.*

The pressure at the lower station is that due to 751·9 mm. of mercury and at the upper that due to 633·7 mm. The difference of pressure is 118·2 mm. and the mean pressure 692·8 mm. and the mean temperature 10° C.

The mass of 1 c.cm. of mercury being 13·59 grammes, the mass of the column of air 1 sq. cm. in area between the stations is therefore

$$13·59 \times 11·82 \text{ grammes.}$$

The density of air at 10° C. and 692·8 mm. is

$$\frac{·001293 \times 692·8 \times 273}{760 \times 283} \text{ grammes per c.cm.,}$$

and hence the difference in level is

$$\frac{13·59 \times 11·82 \times 760 \times 283}{·001293 \times 692·8 \times 273} \text{ cm.,}$$

or about 1413 metres.

In obtaining this result no allowance has been made for the aqueous vapour in the air. In consequence of its presence the density should be rather greater than the value used in the calculations, and the height therefore rather less.

125. Heat required for evaporation. We have already seen in the Sections on Calorimetry that heat is needed to produce evaporation, and have explained the method of finding its amount in the case of water boiling at the ordinary pressure; the latent heat of evaporation has been defined as the quantity of heat required to change one gramme of liquid to vapour without change of temperature. It is in consequence of this fact that a body can be cooled by rapid evaporation. Thus drop a few drops of ether on the hand, it immediately feels cooler; or wrap a little muslin round the bulb of a thermometer and sprinkle a little ether over the muslin; the temperature as indicated by the thermometer falls, for the ether evaporates, absorbing heat from the mercury and cooling it. Energy is changed from the form of heat to that of the agitation of the molecules of the vapour.

EXPERIMENT (39). *To freeze water by rapid evaporation.*

Pour a little water on to a block of wood; take a small thin metal capsule and place it in the water. Pour a little ether into the capsule and then cause the ether to evaporate rapidly by blowing at it with a small pair of bellows. Heat is absorbed from the water which is cooled and finally frozen.

126. The Cryophorus. The action of this instrument affords another instance of the production of a low temperature by rapid evaporation. It consists of two glass bulbs A and B, connected by a tube. There is some water in one of the

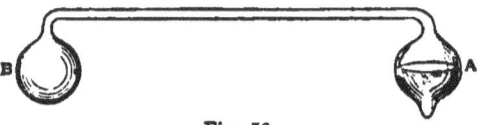

Fig. 56.

bulbs and the whole has been freed from air by boiling before the bulb was finally sealed up; thus the instrument contains nothing but water and the vapour of water. Get all the water into the bulb A and place it inside a beaker, covering it with cotton-wool wadding or some non-conducting material[1].

Now surround the second bulb, B, with a freezing mixture carefully made; the vapour which the bulb contains is condensed and frozen; this reduces the pressure on the water in A, more vapour is given off, absorbing heat from the water, which is thereby cooled, and this process goes on so rapidly that the water in A is cooled down to the freezing-point, and finally frozen. Vapour is produced in A and passes over to B, carrying with it its heat which it gives up to the freezing mixture. Some of this is warmed by the energy abstracted from A and the water in A thereby is frozen.

127. Practical consequences. Freezing Machines. The evaporation of liquids is commonly used as a means of producing very low temperatures; various freezing machines depend on it for their action.

Atmospheric air and oxygen have recently been liquefied in large quantities by Prof. Dewar at the low temperature produced by the evaporation of ethylene, and remain liquid at atmospheric pressure in consequence of the low temperature produced by their own very rapid evaporation.

If a quantity of carbonic acid be liquefied under pressure and then allowed to escape as a fine jet, the evaporation from the outer surface cools the core of the jet so that the liquid is frozen and can be collected as a solid.

To do this the jet of liquid carbonic acid is allowed to escape into a closed wooden box. On opening the box, solid carbonic acid is obtained; the solid melts but slowly, when exposed to the air, for it takes time to absorb the heat necessary to melt it; but, by pouring sulphuric ether on the mass, melting is facilitated and an intense freezing mixture is produced by which mercury can be frozen readily. Pour a little mercury into a hollow in a block of wood and place a

---

[1] If this be not done the water in the bulb when cooled absorbs heat rapidly from the air around, and the experiment may fail in consequence. If the room be very warm, it is sometimes desirable to cool the instrument by putting it in cold water before beginning.

wire in the mercury. Place some solid carbonic acid on the mercury and then pour some ether over the whole. The mercury is frozen solid and can be lifted off the block by the wire. Immerse the solid mercury in water; it melts, and each drop as it falls downwards through the water freezes the water with which it comes in contact, forming tubes of ice through which the liquid mercury pours.

128. Hygrometry. The formation of dew. There is generally some aqueous vapour present in the air. This may be shewn by various experiments. Thus, place a small quantity of calcium chloride in a saucer and leave it in the room. The chloride gradually dissolves in the moisture it absorbs from the air. Or again, dry carefully the outside of a flask or beaker, and then fill it with very cold water, the outside of the flask becomes dimmed with moisture deposited on it from the air.

Fill the lower part of a U tube with fragments of pumice which have been soaked in sulphuric acid, then heated to redness, and finally saturated with the acid. Close each end with a cork, through which a narrow glass tube passes, and weigh the tube and its contents carefully. Attach one end of the tube to an air-pump, and draw the air of the room through it for a time, then weigh again; it will be found that the tube has increased in weight. This increase is due to the aqueous vapour absorbed from the air by the acid. The condition of the atmosphere with regard to the aqueous vapour present in it is spoken of as its hygrometric state, and the part of Physics which deals with this is called Hygrometry.

EXPERIMENT (40). *To measure the mass of aqueous vapour present in a given volume of air and to find the pressure due to the vapour.*

This is done by passing a known volume of air through drying tubes and measuring their increase in mass. Take a large bottle such as a Winchester quart or a small carboy. Find its volume by filling it with water from a measuring flask. Bore three holes in a cork which will close its mouth; fit a thermometer into one, and through the others pass two glass tubes which reach down to the bottom of the vessel. Bend one of these tubes to form a siphon by which the bottle can be emptied. On emptying the bottle by this siphon air is drawn in through the other tube, and, when the bottle is completely emptied, a known volume of air has entered. Fill the bottle and siphon and close the end with an india-rubber tube and a pinchcock. The second tube is connected to a small bottle, B, filled with freshly fused calcium chloride.

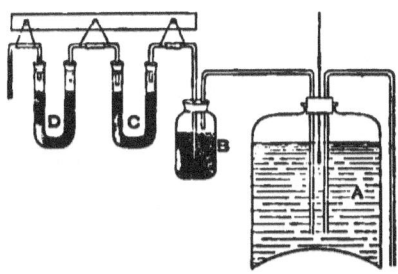

Fig. 57.

Another glass tube passing to the bottom of this bottle is connected with the drying tubes. Two of these, C, D, placed one behind the other, are used. When air passes through, most of its moisture is absorbed by the first drying tube; the increase of weight therefore of the second tube C should be very small. The object of the bottle B is to prevent the moisture from the aspirator A reaching the drying tubes, all that passes along the tube between A and B is absorbed by the calcium chloride in the bottle.

Weigh the drying tubes and connect up the apparatus, using very short pieces of india-rubber tubing to make the connections[1].

Since all the air which enters the aspirator is supposed to pass through the drying tubes, it is necessary that the connections should be air-tight. To test this close the tube at

---

[1] This india-rubber tubing may absorb some moisture. A better way therefore of making the connections is that described in Glazebrook and Shaw's *Practical Physics*, Section 42, but it needs somewhat more elaborate apparatus.

the end of the drying tubes with a pinchcock; on opening the siphon tube no water should run out; if this condition holds, remove the pinchcocks and allow the water to flow from the aspirator. Read the temperature from time to time. When the aspirator is empty disconnect the drying tubes and weigh again; the increase in weight gives the mass of aqueous vapour which was contained in the volume of air, which, at the temperature and pressure of the experiment, fills the aspirator.

The mass of aqueous vapour per c.cm. of air under the conditions of the experiment is thus found.

We can find from this the pressure due to this aqueous vapour thus.

The mass of a cubic centimetre of dry air at freezing-point and at a pressure of 760 mm. is known to be ·001293 gramme. Let e be the pressure of the aqueous vapour, and T the absolute temperature[1] at the time of the experiment. We wish to determine e. Now the mass of air which at pressure e and temperature T would occupy 1 c.cm. is[2]

$$\cdot 001293 \times \frac{e}{760} \times \frac{273}{T}.$$

Moreover it is known that the specific gravity of aqueous vapour referred to air at the same pressure and temperature is ·622. Hence the mass of aqueous vapour which at pressure e and temperature T occupies 1 c.cm. is

$$\cdot 622 \times \cdot 001293 \times \frac{e}{760} \times \frac{273}{T} \text{ grammes,}$$

and it is this mass of aqueous vapour which has been determined by the experiment. Let us suppose the result of the experiment to have shewn that there are w grammes of vapour per c.cm. of air. Then

$$w = \frac{\cdot 622 \times \cdot 001293 \times e \times 273}{760 \times T},$$

and from this on reducing we find

$$e = 3460 \times T \times w \text{ mm.}$$

The quantity w is measured it must be remembered in grammes per c.cm.

In finding w from the observations a correction is required because the air in the aspirator is saturated while that outside is not; the effect of this will however be small. See Glazebrook and Shaw, *Practical Physics*, § 42.

[1] See § 101. $T = 273 + t$, if t is temperature Centigrade.
[2] See § 102.

129. The Dew-point. Under ordinary circumstances, the air is not saturated with aqueous vapour, so that the pressure exerted by the vapour is less than the saturation pressure. If the air in a room or open space be cooled down, the pressure remains constant and equal to the atmospheric pressure; the air contracts in volume and more air enters from outside, but the pressure does not change. For the pressure of the aqueous vapour in the air, this statement again is true, supposing the air not to be saturated. This pressure also remains constant until, as the cooling proceeds, a temperature is reached at which the air becomes saturated; the pressure of the vapour at this temperature is the same as it was originally; but, if the air be cooled below this temperature, some of the vapour is condensed as moisture and the pressure falls. The temperature at which such condensation takes place is called the dew-point, and the saturation pressure of the aqueous vapour at the dew-point is equal to the pressure of the aqueous vapour under the original conditions.

Definition. *The temperature at which a mass of air is saturated with the aqueous vapour it contains is called the dew-point.*

It follows from the above that the pressure of the aqueous vapour in the air, under given conditions, is equal to the saturation pressure at the dew-point. Thus we can find the pressure of the aqueous vapour present by determining the dew-point, and then finding from the Table on p. 130, the saturation pressure at that temperature. There are various methods of finding the dew-point: these will be described shortly.

130. Relative humidity. The feeling of wetness or dampness in the air does not depend mainly on the absolute amount of vapour present but rather on the nearness of that vapour to its point of saturation. Thus, on a warm day in summer, there is probably much more vapour present per cubic centimetre than on a damp winter day. In the latter case, however, the temperature of the air is very little above the dew-point, the air is nearly saturated. A very small fall of temperature will cause the vapour to be deposited as moisture,

On the summer day however, though much more moisture is present, and the dew-point is therefore higher, the temperature is much higher; a greater fall is needed before the dew-point is reached and the air begins to feel damp.

Definition. *The ratio of the pressure of the aqueous vapour present in the air at a given temperature to the saturation pressure at that temperature is called the relative humidity.*

Thus, to determine the relative humidity we require to find the dew-point and to make use of Regnault's Table of saturation pressures.

Example. *The temperature of the air is* 16° *C., the dew-point is* 10° *C.; find the relative humidity.*

The pressure of the aqueous vapour present is equal to the saturation pressure at the dew-point or 10°, and this is 9·17 mm. The saturation pressure at 16° is 13·54 mm.

Thus the relative humidity

$$= \frac{9\cdot17}{13\cdot54} = \cdot677.$$

131. Determination of the Dew-point.

EXPERIMENT (41). *To determine the dew-point and to find the pressure of the aqueous vapour present in the air.*

Take a small beaker or wide test tube, coat the inside with Brunswick black, and allow it to harden. Fit the vessel with a stirrer, a piece of bent copper wire serves for this, and fill it about three-quarters full with water at about the temperature of the room. Add some ice in small pieces, stirring well, and waiting till each piece is melted before adding the next. Keep a thermometer in the water during the process, and watch the blackened surface of the glass carefully. The temperature of the surface falls and, after a time, reaches the temperature of the dew-point. Moisture begins to be deposited from the air on the glass, and this deposit is fairly easily seen on the blackened surface. Read the temperature at which the deposition begins. This temperature is the dew-point. Look up in the Table p. 130 the saturation pressure of aqueous vapour which corresponds to this temperature. This pressure is the pressure of the aqueous vapour present in the air at the time of the experiment.

The results obtained by this rough apparatus are liable to various errors. It is not easy to determine accurately the temperature at which the dew begins to be deposited, and various forms of hygrometers have been devised with a view to its more exact measurement.

132. Daniell's Hygrometer. This consists of two glass bulbs, A and B (fig. 58), connected by a tube. The two bulbs contain ether and ether vapour, the air having been exhausted from them before the apparatus was sealed up. The one bulb, A, is made of blackened glass and inside it there is a thermometer, the bulb of which is in the ether, while the scale is visible above the blackened bulb. The thermometer gives the temperature of the ether. The other bulb B which contains only ether vapour when the experiment begins is covered with some muslin.

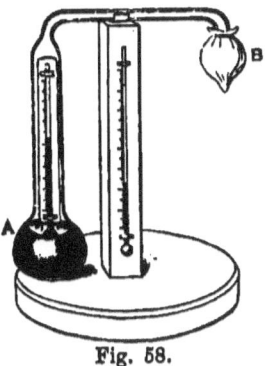

Fig. 58.

A second thermometer mounted outside gives the temperature of the air.

To perform an experiment pour a little ether on the muslin covering of the bulb B. The ether evaporates, absorbing heat in the process and thus cooling down the vapour in the bulb. Some of the vapour is condensed, and in consequence more ether evaporates in A. The bulb A is thereby slowly cooled down, until it reaches the temperature of the dew-point, which is indicated by a deposit of dew on the outside of the bulb. Read the temperature as given by the thermometer in A. This temperature will be the dew-point provided (1) that the first deposit of dew has been observed, and (2) that the temperature of the ether is also the temperature of the outside of the glass bulb. As a matter of

152   HEAT.   [CH. IX

fact it is probable that neither of these conditions has been satisfied: the error introduced may to some extent be compensated for by stopping the experiment as soon as dew is observed, and allowing the apparatus to rise in temperature by absorbing heat from the room. Watch for the disappearance of the dew and note the temperature at which this takes place. This temperature should not differ greatly from that at which the dew appeared; and the mean of the two will give a more accurate value for the dew-point.

133. Regnault's Hygrometer. This consists of a thin silver tube, fig. 59, like a short test tube mounted on a stand. Two small tubes A and B (fig. 59 a) enter the larger tube, one of them B opening near the bottom, the other A near the top. A delicate thermometer passes through a cork which closes the silver tube, the bulb of the thermometer, which should be small, being near the bottom. The test tube

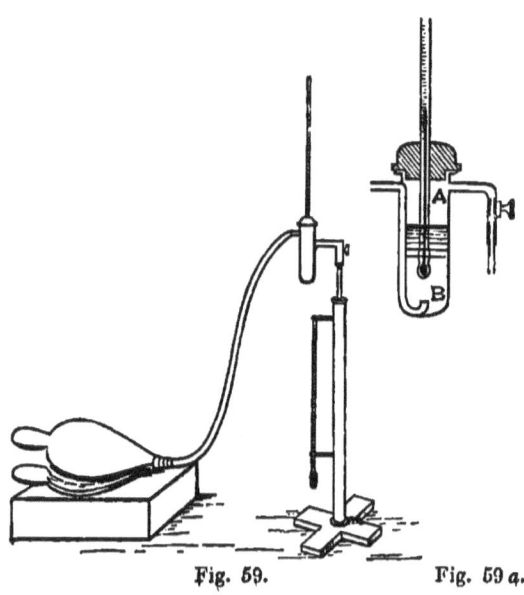

Fig. 59.   Fig. 59 a.

is partly filled with ether, covering the thermometer bulb, and air is caused to bubble through the ether either by blowing it in with a pair of bellows through B, or sucking it out with a pump, through A. This produces evaporation of the ether and a consequent fall of temperature, until, at last, the ether and tube are reduced to the dew-point. This is indicated by the deposit of dew on the silver tube. Observe the temperature at which this deposit takes place. Allow the evaporation to stop and the temperature to rise until the dew disappears. Note the temperature at which this occurs; it should not differ greatly from that first observed, and the mean of the two may be taken as the dew-point.

134. Dines' Hygrometer. In this instrument a delicate thermometer, DE, is fixed in a horizontal position in a groove in a wooden block.

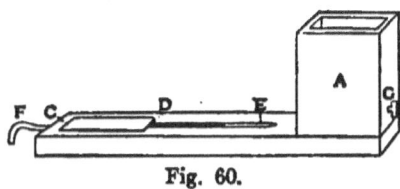

Fig. 60.

The bulb is placed inside a metal box, the upper side of the box being covered by a very thin piece of black glass, and the thermometer bulb being in contact with the glass.

A tube leads from the box, B, to a reservoir, A (fig. 60), and is closed near the reservoir by a tap G. An overflow tube F leads out of the box. The reservoir is filled with water

Fig. 60 a.

cooled by ice. This cooled water is allowed, by adjusting the tap, to pass slowly along the tube through the box. The glass plate is thus cooled down, its temperature being given by the thermometer, until a deposit of dew becomes visible. As soon as this is seen, the temperature is read, and the flow stopped. The temperature at which the dew disappears is also observed, and the mean of the two when they do not differ greatly may be taken as the dew-point.

When the temperature of the dew-point has been determined the pressure of the vapour can be found from the Tables as has been already described. When this pressure e is known the formula proved in § 128 will give w the number of grammes of aqueous vapour iu a cubic centimetre of air; for we have, if T is the absolute temperature,

$$w = \frac{e}{3460 \times T}.$$

135. The wet and dry bulb Thermometers. This instrument, which consists of two thermometers mounted side by side, is often used to determine the pressure of the aqueous vapour in the air. The bulb of one of the two thermometers, A (fig. 61), is kept constantly moist by means of a piece of cotton-wick wrapped round it, and dipping into a small vessel of water at the side. This wick should be thoroughly cleansed from grease by boiling in caustic potash, and then washing with distilled water; this will ensure a flow of water to the bulb.

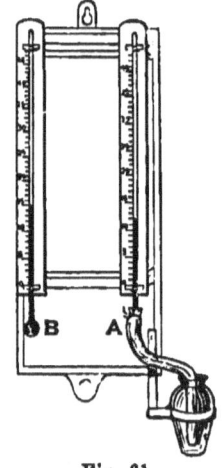

Fig. 61.

The water evaporates, and absorbs heat from the thermometer. Thus the temperature as indicated by this thermometer is lower than that given by the thermometer B. The difference will depend on the rapidity with which the evaporation proceeds, and the rate of evaporation will depend on the temperature and the amount of moisture already present.

If the air is very dry, evaporation will procéed rapidly, heat will be absorbed from the thermometer at a rapid rate and the temperature of A will fall considerably below that of B. If, on the other hand, the air be nearly saturated, evaporation will be slow and the difference of temperature small.

A formula can be obtained, connecting together the pressure of the aqueous vapour, the two temperatures, and some other quantities which can be observed. From this formula, which can be verified by direct experiment, Tables have been constructed giving the pressure of the aqueous vapour, when the temperature of the dry-bulb thermometer is observed, and also the difference of temperature between it and the wet-bulb thermometer.

Such a Table is given below, in it the first vertical column gives the readings of the dry bulb thermometer and the top horizontal column the difference of temperature in degrees centigrade between the dry and the wet bulb thermometers. The Table shews the pressure in mm. of mercury of the vapour present in the air. And from the first two columns of the Table the dew-point can be found.

t°C.	0	1	2	3	4	5	6	7	8	9	10	11
0	4·6	3·7	2·9	2·1	1·3							
1	4·9	4·0	3·2	2·4	1·6	0·8						
2	5·3	4·4	3·4	2·7	1·9	1·0						
3	5·7	4·7	3·7	2·8	2·2	1·3						
4	6·1	5·1	4·1	3·2	2·4	1·6	0·8					
5	6·5	5·5	4·5	3·5	2·6	1·8	1·0					
6	7·0	5·9	4·9	3·9	2·9	2·0	1·1					
7	7·5	6·4	5·3	4·3	3·3	2·3	1·4	0·4				
8	8·0	6·9	5·8	4·7	3·7	2·7	1·7	0·8				
9	8·6	7·4	6·3	5·2	4·1	3·1	2·1	1·1	0·2			
10	9·2	8·0	6·8	5·7	4·6	3·5	2·5	1·5	0·5			
11	9·8	8·6	7·4	6·2	5·1	4·0	2·9	1·9	0·9			
12	10·5	9·2	8·0	6·8	5·6	4·5	3·4	2·3	1·3			
13	11·2	9·8	8·6	7·3	6·2	5·0	3·9	2·8	1·7			
14	11·9	10·6	9·2	8·0	6·7	5·6	4·4	3·3	2·2	1·1		
15	12·7	11·3	9·9	8·6	7·4	6·1	5·0	3·8	2·7	1·6	0·5	
16	13·5	12·1	10·7	9·3	8·0	6·8	5·5	4·3	3·2	2·1	1·0	
17	14·4	13·0	11·5	10·1	8·7	7·4	6·2	4·9	3·7	2·6	1·5	0·4
18	15·4	13·8	12·3	10·9	9·5	8·1	6·8	5·5	4·3	3·1	2·0	0·9
19	16·4	14·7	13·2	11·7	10·3	8·9	7·5	6·2	4·9	3·7	2·5	1·4
20	17·4	15·7	14·1	12·6	11·1	9·7	8·3	6·9	5·6	4·3	3·1	1·9
21	18·5	16·8	15·1	13·5	12·0	10·5	9·0	7·6	6·3	5·0	3·7	2·5
22	19·7	17·9	16·2	14·5	12·9	11·4	9·9	8·4	7·0	5·7	4·4	3·1
23	20·9	19·0	17·3	15·6	13·9	12·3	10·8	9·2	7·8	6·4	5·1	3·8
24	22·2	20·3	18·4	16·6	14·9	13·3	11·7	10·1	8·7	7·2	5·8	4·5
25	23·6	21·6	19·7	17·8	16·0	14·3	12·7	11·1	9·5	8·0	6·6	5·2
26	25·0	22·9	21·0	19·0	17·2	15·4	13·7	12·1	10·5	8·9	7·4	6·0
27	26·5	24·9	22·3	20·3	18·4	16·6	14·8	13·1	11·4	9·8	8·3	6·8
28	28·1	25·9	23·7	21·7	19·7	17·6	16·0	14·2	12·5	10·8	9·2	7·7
29	29·8	27·5	25·3	23·1	21·1	19·1	17·2	15·3	13·6	11·9	10·2	8·6
30	31·6	29·2	26·9	24·6	22·5	20·5	18·5	16·6	14·7	13·0	11·2	9·6

Example. *The temperature of the dry-bulb thermometer is* 15°, *that of the wet-bulb thermometer* 12°; *find the pressure of the vapour and the dew-point.*

The difference between the two is 3°. Now the first column of the Table gives the temperature of the dry-bulb thermometer and the top line the differences. Look down the column headed 3° until you come to the number in the same horizontal line as the 15° in the first column. This is the pressure required; and from the Table it is found to be 8·6 mm. Now the Table on p. 130 shews that the saturation pressure at 9° is 8·57 mm., and the dew-point is the temperature at which the actual pressure is the saturation pressure. The dew-point is thus just over 9°. To find it more exactly observe from the Table that, for 1°, from 9° to 10°, the saturation pressure increases from 8·57 to 9·17 or through ·6 mm. We wish to find the change in dew-point corresponding to an increase in pressure of ·03 mm. (8·6 − 8·57). This change will be ·03/·6 of 1° C. or 0°·05 C.

Thus the dew-point is 9°·05 C.

136. Simple Hygrometers. The action of many simple forms of hygrometers depends on the fact that some substances readily absorb aqueous vapour when it is present in the air, and change their form or appearance in the process.

A substance, which readily absorbs moisture, is said to be hygroscopic.

Thus sea-weed is very hygroscopic; a bunch of sea-weed hung up in the air, in damp weather, when there is plenty of vapour present, absorbs some of it and swells up considerably.

Catgut again is hygroscopic. If a piece of catgut be hung up, supported at one end, and carrying a light weight at the other, it will absorb moisture in damp weather and untwist; if the weather be dry it twists up again.

These changes are made use of in the "old man and his wife" hygroscope, in which one figure comes out in dry weather, the other in wet.

In de Saussure's hygroscope a light weight is hung at the end of a long hair which is hygroscopic. This end of the hair is attached to the short end of a lever. As the hair becomes damp, it contracts in length, and a small elongation or contraction is shewn by a considerable motion of the long end of the lever.

In other hygroscopes some hygroscopic material is coated

with a substance such as a salt of cobalt which changes colour on the absorption of moisture. When there is much aqueous vapour present blue becomes red.

The method of treating numerous problems, involving hygrometry, and the pressure of vapours, may be best illustrated by the following numerical example.

Example. *Ten litres of oxygen are collected over water at a pressure of 750 mm. and a temperature of 15°, being saturated with vapour; find the mass of dry oxygen and of aqueous vapour, having given that the density of hydrogen at 0° and 760 is ·0896 gramme per litre, and that the specific gravities of oxygen and of aqueous vapour, referred to hydrogen, are 16 and 9 respectively.*

It follows from this that the mass of a litre of oxygen under standard conditions is 16 × ·0896 or 1·434 gramme, while that of a litre of aqueous vapour under the same conditions is ·806 gramme. The total pressure of the damp oxygen is the sum of the pressure due to the oxygen and the pressure due to the vapour. This latter, since the space is saturated at 15°, is 12·7 mm. Thus the pressure due to the oxygen is 750 − 12·7, or 737·3 mm. We have thus 10 litres oxygen at 15° and 737·3 mm.

The volume of this at 0° and 760 will be

$$\frac{10 \times 737 \cdot 3 \times 273}{760 \times 288} \text{ litres,}$$

and the mass

$$\frac{10 \times 737 \cdot 3 \times 273 \times 1 \cdot 434}{760 \times 288} \text{ grammes.}$$

This reduces to 13·19 grammes, while since there are 10 litres of vapour at 15° and 12·7 its volume at 0° and 760 will be

$$\frac{10 \times 12 \cdot 7 \times 273}{760 \times 288} \text{ litres,}$$

and its mass

$$\frac{10 \times 12 \cdot 7 \times 273 \times \cdot 806}{760 \times 288} \text{ grammes,}$$

which reduces to ·128 gramme.

EXAMPLES

VAPOURS AND HYGROMETRY.

1. One hundred cubic centimetres of oxygen, saturated with aqueous vapour, are collected at a pressure of 740 mm. and a temperature of 15° C. Find the volume of dry oxygen at 0° and 760 mm., having given that the maximum pressure of aqueous vapour at 15° is 12·7 mm.

158   HEAT.

2. Distinguish between saturated and unsaturated vapours.

What is meant by the statement, that when the dew-point is 20° C., the maximum pressure of aqueous vapour in the air is that due to 17·4 mm. of mercury?

3. Distinguish between a vapour and a gas. The pressure of aqueous vapour at a temperature of 50° C. is ·12 atmospheres; how would you proceed to verify this statement?

4. How would you distinguish between *vaporisation* and *ebullition*? Does the boiling-point of a liquid depend on the pressure on its surface? Illustrate your answer with an experiment.

5. What is Dalton's law as to the pressure of vapours? How is it used in finding, from observations of the dew-point, the pressure of the aqueous vapour in the air?

6. Describe an experiment showing that water can be frozen by its own evaporation. What weight of vapour must evaporate in order to freeze a gramme of water already at freezing-point?

7. Explain how to determine the amount of aqueous vapour present in the air from a knowledge of the dew-point.

8. Define the dew-point. How is dew formed, and why is it more copious on some substances than on others?

9. Calculate the weight of a litre of hydrogen collected over water at 15° when the height of the barometer is 765 mm.; the density of hydrogen at 0° and 760 mm. is ·000089 gramme per c.cm., and of aqueous vapour nine times that of hydrogen, while the maximum pressure of aqueous vapour at 15° is 12·7 mm.

10. In a chemical experiment a certain quantity of oxygen is given off, and this is collected over water in a tube graduated in c.cm.: the volume read off on the tube is 40 c.cm. and the water stands in the tube 50 centimetres above the water outside the tube: it is required to find the mass of the gas.

The water is at a temperature of 20° C. and the barometer reads 755; the density of mercury is 13·96 grammes per c.cm.: the pressure of aqueous vapour at 20° is 17·4 mm. of mercury: and the mass of a cubic centimetre of oxygen at 0° C. and 760 mm. pressure is ·00143 gramme.

11. Explain the following table taken from the weather report of the "Times."

| | Temperature | | Pressure of vapour, Inches | Weight of vapour in 10 cubic feet of air | Drying power of air per 10 c. ft. | Humidity Saturation=100 |
	Air	Dew-point				
Noon	67°	38°	·229	25 grains	48	34
9 p.m.	58°	38°	·229	26 ,,	28	48
2 a.m.	54°	38°	·229	26 ,,	21	55

CHANGE OF STATE. LIQUID TO VAPOUR. 159

12. A closed vessel contains air saturated with water vapour at a temperature of 100° C. When the temperature is raised to 150° C. without alteration of volume the pressure is that due to 2 atmospheres. What would be the pressure of the air alone at 0° C., when occupying the same volume?

13. State and explain the law as to the pressure of a mixture of air and water vapour. What is meant by the hygrometric state of the air? Explain how to determine the pressure of the aqueous vapour in the air from a knowledge of the dew-point and a table of the saturation pressures of aqueous vapour.

14. The temperature of the air in a closed space is observed to be 15° C. and the dew-point 8° C. If the temperature falls to 10° C. how is (1) the dew-point, (2) the pressure of aqueous vapour in the air affected?

15. The dew-point is observed to be 15°, and the temperature of the air is 20°. The saturation pressure of aqueous vapour at 15° is 12·7 mm., find the pressure of the vapour in the air.

16. Find the weight of a litre of hydrogen and water vapour at 15° C. and under a pressure of 750 mm. of mercury. Of this pressure 18 mm. is due to the water vapour, the rest being due to the hydrogen. A litre of hydrogen at 0° C. and at a pressure of 760 mm. weighs $\frac{1}{11}$ of a gramme.

17. Find the weight of a cubic metre of air saturated with moisture, the pressure being 750 mm. of mercury, and the temperature 15° C.

(Pressure of aqueous vapour at 15° C. = 12·7 mm. of mercury, weight of 1 c.cm. of dry air at 0° C. and 760 mm. = ·001293 gr. Specific gravity of aqueous vapour referred to air = ·623.)

18. Why is it necessary to note the height of the barometer when determining the upper fixed point of a thermometer? How is this determination made? An alteration of pressure of 26 mm. alters the boiling-point of water 1°. Find the boiling-point when the height of the barometer is 745 mm.

19. Describe and explain the action of the Cryophorus. Water can be frozen in a dry climate by exposing it in shallow pans under a clear sky even though the temperature of the air be above the freezing-point. Explain this.

For action of barometer and relation of vapor pressure to atmospheric pressure etc., see, Brittanica — "Meteorology."

CHAPTER X.

THE TRANSMISSION OF HEAT. CONDUCTION.

137. Conduction of Heat. If one end of a piece of metal be placed in the fire the other end gradually becomes hot.

Heat-Energy is communicated to the particles of metal in the fire. These communicate some of their energy to the neighbouring particles and thus the energy travels from particle to particle along the bar. This process is called the conduction of heat.

Definition. *Heat is said to be transmitted by conduction when it passes from the hotter to the colder parts of a body or from one body to a colder body in contact with it.*

138. Convection of Heat. The air over any hot surface has its temperature raised and in consequence expands and, becoming less dense than the surrounding air, rises, carrying its heat-energy with it. A process such as this is called convection. The heat is transmitted by the actual motion of the heated particles.

Definition. *Heat is transmitted by convection when material particles conveying the heat are carried from one point to another.*

139. Radiation of Heat. The sun's rays pass through the air without appreciably heating it. If they be allowed to fall on the bulb of a thermometer the temperature as indicated by the thermometer rises; if the bulb be covered with lampblack the rise of temperature is greater than if the bulb be of clear glass. Energy reaching the thermometer from the sun has travelled through the air without greatly raising its temperature, and has been transformed into heat on reaching the thermometer bulb.

Experiment further shews that the energy in this case travels in straight lines or rays. It is known as radiant energy, and the process of its transference is called radiation.

There are some substances through which radiant energy passes unchanged in amount, in the case of other substances some or all of the radiant energy is transformed into heat; such substances are said to absorb the radiation they receive and their temperature is raised by this absorption.

Definition. *Heat-energy is transmitted by radiation when it passes from one point to another without raising the temperature of the medium through which it travels.*

140. Experiments on the Conduction of Heat. If we touch various substances lying side by side in a room some will appear warmer than others even though we may find, on testing them with a thermometer, that their temperatures are the same; if the room be cold any pieces of metal in it will appear very cold to the touch, while the woollen curtains or carpet will seem to be quite warm. On the other hand if the temperature of the various objects be above that of the hand, the metallic bodies will appear distinctly warmer than the woollen.

The sensation of warmth depends not merely on the temperature of the objects touched but on the rate at which heat is transferred through their masses; the metallic bodies appear cold in the first case because heat can pass rapidly from the observer's hand into their interiors; they appear warm in the second case because heat passes rapidly from them to the observer.

In the case of a woollen body heat travels much more slowly and it does not appear so cold when touched, for the parts near the point of contact soon become raised to the temperature of the hand and the gradual diffusion of heat into the interior is a slow process.

Thus these observations shew us that different bodies have different conductivities for heat; we shall define later the exact meaning of the term conductivity. The following experiments will illustrate this difference.

EXPERIMENT (42). *To shew that different materials conduct heat differently.*

(*a*) Take a number of rods of different materials, wood, glass, bone, copper, iron etc.; place one end of each in a beaker of boiling water. The exposed ends of the wood and glass rods are hardly appreciably raised in temperature; while the iron and copper rods become very hot.

(*b*) Take two rods, one of iron the other of copper, each about 30 cm. long and 5 mm. in diameter. Place one end of each rod in a Bunsen flame and, after waiting for some time for the temperature to become steady, find the point on each rod at which a fragment of paraffin wax placed on the rod is just melted. The temperature is the same at these two points; it will be found that the point on the copper rod is much further from the source of heat than that on the iron rod. In a given time more heat is transmitted along the copper than along the iron rod, and so the temperature rises to the melting point of paraffin at a greater distance from the source of heat.

(*c*) In fig. 62 *ABC* is a metal trough through which a

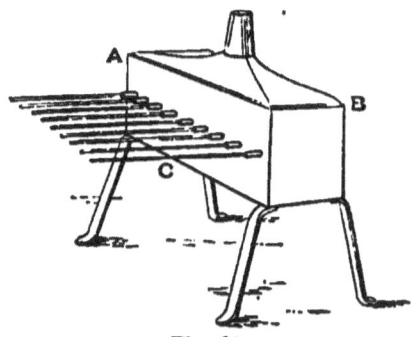

Fig. 62.

number of narrow tubes some 3 mm. in diameter pass. A number of rods of different materials are all covered with a thin coating of paraffin wax and then inserted in the respective tubes. The trough is filled with boiling water so that one end of each of the rods is raised to a high temperature. Heat is conducted down each of the rods, melting the wax as the temperature rises to the melting-point of the paraffin. It will be observed that the melting of the wax proceeds at a very different rate and extends to different distances along the bars. If the temperature of the trough be kept steady at 100° by passing in steam or by some other suitable means, it will be found that after a time the line of separation between the melted and unmelted parts of the wax no longer moves along the bar but remains stationary. This stationary position on each bar marks the points at which the temperatures of the respective bars are all equal to the melting-point of the wax, and it can be shewn that the conductivities of the bars are proportional to the squares of the distances of these points from the trough.

141. Definition of Thermal Conductivity. *Consider a plate of any material* 1 *cm. in thickness. Let one face be kept at a temperature of* $t°$, *the other at a temperature of* $(t-1)°$. *The quantity of heat which passes per second through each unit of area of the plate is called the thermal conductivity of the material of the plate.*

We may calculate the quantity of heat passing through a plate of known thermal conductivity k thus.

Consider a plate of unit thickness: let the temperature of one face be t and of the other t'. Then experiment shews that for moderate differences of temperature the flow of heat per unit area is proportional to $(t-t')$, and is equal to $k(t-t')$ units per second.

Let the thickness of the plate be d cm., the temperature of the faces being t and t', then in the steady state the fall of temperature is uniform through the plate, and since in d cm. the fall is $t-t'$ the fall per cm. is $(t-t')/d$. Hence the flow of heat per second per unit area of the plate is $k(t-t')/d$. If now the plate contains S sq. cm., since the flow for each unit of area is the same, the total quantity of heat crossing is $k(t-t')S/d$ per second; and hence in T seconds the quantity Q which passes is given by

$$Q = \frac{k(t-t')\,S\,.\,T}{d}.$$

Example. *The thermal conductivity of iron is ·2. Find the quantity of heat passing per hour into a boiler the plates of which are 1·2 cm. thick, and the area of the heating surface 50000 sqr. cm., the temperature of the outer surface being 120°, that of the inner 100°; find also the mass of water evaporated.*

The fall of temperature for 1·2 cm. is 20°.

Thus the fall per cm. is $\dfrac{20^c}{1\cdot 2}$.

The flow of heat per cm. per sec. is $\dfrac{20 \times \cdot 2}{1\cdot 2}$.

Hence the total flow per hour is $\dfrac{20 \times 2 \times 50000 \times 3600}{12}$ or 600,000,000 units. Hence taking the latent heat of water as 536 we have as the mass of water vaporised

$$\frac{600{,}000{,}000}{536} \text{ grammes,}$$

and this reduces to 1,119,500 grammes approximately.

142. Difference between thermal conductivity and rate of rise of temperature.

When heat is applied to one end of a rod or bar the rate at which the temperature rises at any point does not depend only on the thermal conductivity, but also on the specific heat. The quantity of heat reaching the portion of the bar about the point in question will depend on the thermal conductivity only.

The rise of temperature produced in a unit of volume is proportional to the quantity of heat reaching the volume divided by the product of the density and the specific heat.

Thus the time which the bar at any given point will take to rise to a given temperature will be approximately proportional to the product of the density and the specific heat divided by the conductivity. Suppose now we take two bars of the same size of lead and iron respectively, the thermal conductivity of iron is about ·16, that of lead ·11, the product of the specific heat and density for iron is 8·7 and for lead 3·6. Hence the times of rising to the same temperature for iron and lead are respectively in the ratio of 87/16 to 36/11 or as 5 to 3.

Thus when the bars are each first heated at one end, a point on the lead close to the source rises in temperature nearly twice as fast as a point at the same distance from the hot end on the iron, and hence a given temperature such as that required to melt wax is attained by a point on the lead bar more quickly than by the corresponding point on the iron bar.

This may be shewn by the following experiments.

EXPERIMENT (43). *To shew the difference in the rate of rise of temperature of lead and iron bars.*

(a) Take two short cylinders of lead and iron some 3 or 4 cm. in length and about 2 cm. in diameter with flat ends. Coat one end of each with wax and place them upright on the flat top of a metal box through which steam[1] is passing from a boiler. The lower ends of the cylinders become raised to 100°. Heat is conducted through the cylinders to the wax and it will be found that the wax begins to melt first on the lead.

(b) Take two rods of the same size, about 1 cm. in diameter and 15 or 20 cm. long, and solder them to opposite faces of a box through which steam can be passed, so that each projects in a horizontal direction as shewn in fig. 63. Coat each rod

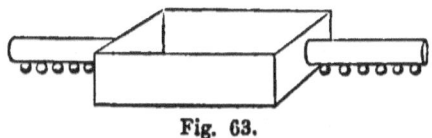

Fig. 63.

with a thin layer of paraffin and fasten, at intervals of about 1 cm., to the under side of each a number of shot about 3 mm. in diameter, securing them by imbedding them slightly in the

[1] A small biscuit box with the lid soldered on having suitable inlet and outlet tubes serves the purpose.

wax. Pass steam through the box allowing it to flow for some time, or if more convenient heat it by pouring in boiling water. The wax begins to melt and the shot to drop off first on the lead bar, but in the end, when the temperatures have become steady, the wax has been melted to a greater distance on the iron bar than on the lead, and more shot have dropped off it. The distance to which the wax is melted depends on the conductivity of the material, and this is greater for iron than for lead.

143. The variable and the steady state in the Conduction of Heat.

Consider any length AB of a bar such as that used in the last experiment. Suppose the temperature is measured at a number of points P_1, P_2 etc. along the bar and at each such point erect perpendiculars to the bar P_1Q_1, P_2Q_2 etc. to represent the observed temperatures.

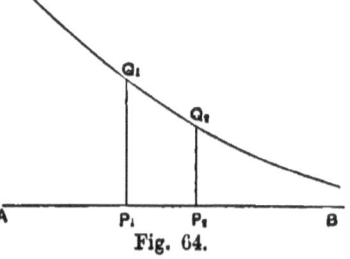

Fig. 64.

The ends of these perpendiculars will lie on a curve such as that shewn in fig. 64, and the temperature at any other point may be found by drawing a line perpendicular to the bar to meet the curve. Thus the change of temperature per centimetre length of the bar can be found at all points. This is called the temperature gradient; the quantity of heat entering any cross section is obtained by multiplying the temperature gradient by the area of the section and by the thermal conductivity. If we take sections at two points P_1 and P_2 the quantity of heat entering per second at P_1 is greater than that leaving at P_2. If the temperature of the bar is changing the difference between the two quantities of heat is used partly in changing the temperature of the portion of the bar between P_1 and P_2, partly in supplying the loss from the surface of this portion to the surrounding air. The conditions of the bar are then variable.

After a time a condition is reached in which the excess of the heat entering at P_1 over that leaving at P_2 is only just sufficient to supply the surface loss. When this state is reached throughout the bar there is no further change of temperature, the state everywhere has become steady.

*144. Comparison of thermal conductivities.

Experiment (44). Take two long bars say of iron and copper from 1 to 2 metres long respectively. Bore a series of small holes in each at distances of 10 cm. apart, each hole being just large enough to contain the bulb of a thermometer; place a little mercury in each hole. Arrange the bars so that one end of each is inside a vessel which can contain melted lead or solder.

Such a vessel can conveniently be made out of a short length of iron pipe, the bars are secured by means of fireclay or some other luting into the opposite ends of the pipe. A large aperture cut in one side of the pipe serves to insert the lead or solder, and the whole is mounted with the bars in a horizontal position as shewn in fig. 65.

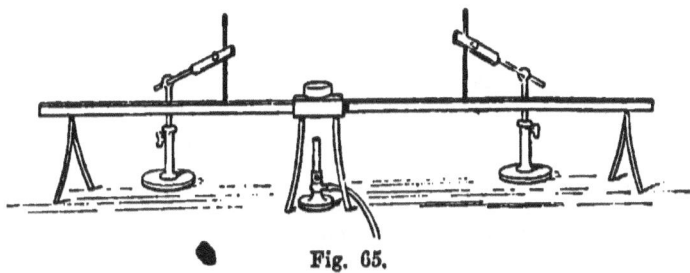

Fig. 65.

Heat the vessel in a Bunsen flame, to which, for accurate work, a gas regulator may be attached to keep the temperature constant.

When a steady condition has been reached place the thermometer in turn in each of the holes in the bars and read the temperatures. It will be found that the temperature falls much more rapidly along the iron, than along the copper bar. Take a number of points on the iron bar at which the temperatures are known, the holes in which the thermometers are inserted will be most convenient, and determine from the observations of the fall of temperature on the other bar the points which have the same temperatures as those selected on the iron bar[1]. Measure the distances of these points from the source of heat. The ratio of the squares of the distances of the respective points of equal temperature from the hot ends will be found to be the same, and this ratio can be shewn to be the ratio of the thermal conductivities.

***145. Measurement of thermal conductivity.** The amount of heat emitted per second from each centimetre of a bar such as one of those used in Experiment (44) when at a given temperature can be found from a separate experiment. This consists in heating the bar or a second similar bar to some uniform high temperature and leaving it to cool. The temperature is observed at equal intervals of time as the bar cools, and thus the rate of loss of temperature per second is found at various temperatures. From this the quantity of heat emitted per second by each centimetre when at a given temperature can be found.

Consider now a portion of the bar such as P_1P_2 in fig. 64: the quantity of heat entering per second at P_1 is kSa if S is the area of the bar and a the temperature gradient; the quantity leaving at P_2 is $kS\beta$, where β is the temperature gradient at P_2, and thus we have when the steady state is reached

$kS(a-\beta)$ = heat emitted per second by the portion of the bar between P_1 and P_2.

But since the temperature of the bar at all points between P_1 and P_2 is known, this quantity of heat emitted per second can be calculated from the results of the preliminary experiment, and then we have

$kS(a-\beta)$ = a known quantity of heat; and since S, a, β can all be observed, k is given by this equation.

This explains the principle of the method by which Forbes and others have measured the thermal conductivity of various substances.

The following is a Table of the values of the conductivities of various substances.

[1] This is best done by drawing a curve in which horizontal lines represent distances along the bar and vertical lines the observed temperatures at certain points, as described in Section 143.

Substance	Conductivity
Copper	·96
Iron	·20
Stone	·0059
Sand	·0026
Water	·0020
Fir-wood, across fibres	·00026
,, along fibres	·00047
Glass	·00050
Wool	·00012
Paraffin wax	·00014
Paper (unsized)	·000094
Air and some other gases	·000049

146. Practical effects of Conduction of Heat. Other experiments have been devised to illustrate the difference in conductivity, and many domestic appliances depend for their action on the good or bad conductivity of various materials. Thus woollen materials such as blankets are used for warmth, for they are bad conductors and the heat of the body escapes slowly through them. For the same reason ice, which it is desired to keep, is wrapped in a blanket or placed in a box packed in sawdust; the heat of the room is conducted slowly through the sawdust.

A Norwegian cooking stove consists of a box packed in felt or some non-conducting material. The food which it is desired to cook is raised to the boiling-point and then the vessel which contains it is enclosed in the stove. The heat escapes so slowly that the contents are kept for some time at a temperature not greatly below boiling-point, and are cooked.

Water can be boiled in a vessel of thin paper without charring it, for the temperature of the water does not rise above 100° and if the paper be thin the heat applied to the outer surface is conducted through so rapidly that the temperature of that surface does not rise very greatly above 100° and so is not charred; if the thin paper be replaced by a vessel of cardboard, owing to the greater thickness of the cardboard the outer surface is raised considerably above the 100° C. and the cardboard is charred.

EXPERIMENT (45). *To illustrate the difference in conductivity between wood and metal.*

Take a cylinder about 3 or 4 cm. in diameter one half of which is wood, the other half metal. A piece of paper is wrapped round the cylinder and held over a Bunsen flame for a short time. The paper in contact with the wood soon becomes scorched and burnt, that in contact with the metal remains uncharred; the metal conducts the heat away so rapidly that the temperature never rises to the point at which the paper would be charred.

147. The Davy safety-lamp. The high conductivity of metals is made use of in the Davy lamp. To illustrate the principle of the lamp, take a piece of copper or brass gauze with a close mesh and lay it on the top of a tripod stand. Place a gas burner underneath in such a position that if the gauze be removed and the burner lighted the top of the flame would be above the former level of the gauze. Light the burner and replace the gauze. The gauze appears to damp out the flame, which only burns below; there is no flame above. Turn the gas off. When the gauze has cooled turn it on again and apply a light above the gauze. The gas now burns above but the light does not penetrate below. In both cases the heat is conducted away so quickly by the metal gauze, that the temperature of the inflammable gas on the side of the gauze remote from the flame is never raised to ignition point. In the first experiment some gas passes through unburnt and will ignite if a flame be applied above the gauze.

In the Davy safety-lamp shewn in fig. 66 the flame is surrounded by a thick wire gauze double in the part directly above the flame. If the lamp is brought into an atmosphere containing a little fire-damp (carburetted hydrogen) a blue cap shews itself above the flame. The temperature within is sufficient to ignite the fire-damp. If the blue cap increases in size, so as to fill or nearly fill the space within the gauze, danger is indicated, for

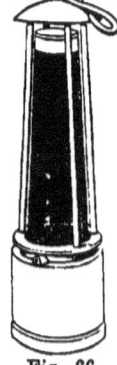

Fig. 66.

the temperature of the gauze may thereby be raised sufficiently to cause ignition outside. In more modern lamps many improvements have been introduced into the original form with a view of increasing the safety and improving the light.

148. Conduction of Heat in Liquids. Observations on the thermal conductivity of liquids are difficult to perform satisfactorily. Change of temperature produces variation in density, and convection currents (see Section 150) are set up which complicate the results. The following experiments however may be performed.

EXPERIMENT (46). *To illustrate the low thermal conductivity of water.*

(a) Arrange an air thermometer as shewn in fig. 67 so that the bulb can be surrounded by water.

This is most easily done by taking a small bell-jar with an open mouth, fitting to the opening a cork with a hole through which the tube of the thermometer can pass, and supporting the whole in a retort stand[1] with the bulb of the thermometer uppermost. Fill the bell-jar with water and arrange across its upper end a small tripod on which a capsule can rest.

Place a small quantity of methylated spirits in the capsule and ignite it; the upper layers of water are heated, but it is some time before any effect is observed on the thermometer, and when a rise of temperature is noticed it will be found to be very slight indeed. In consequence of the low conductivity of the water the heat reaches the thermometer very slowly. On mixing the water in the bell-jar with a stirring rod a considerable rise of temperature is observed, shewing that the temperature of the upper layers can be raised by the heat applied without

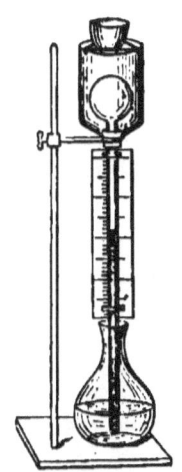

Fig. 67.

---

[1] If a bell-jar is not readily obtainable, a wide-necked bottle from which the bottom has been removed will serve.

much affecting those below. If the water be replaced by mercury and the experiment repeated the rise of temperature will be much more rapid. Mercury is a good conductor of heat.

(b) Take a long narrow test tube and place a small lump of ice at the bottom, either weighting it so as to sink in water by wrapping some wire round it, or securing it at the bottom by a piece of wire gauze fitting the tube tightly.

Fill the tube with water and hold it with its upper part in the flame of a spirit lamp or Bunsen burner. The water becomes heated and may be boiled for some time without melting the ice. The heat is conducted down the tube very slowly.

149. Conduction of Heat in Gases. Air and other gases are very bad conductors of heat. The transference of heat through them takes place almost entirely by convection. The low conducting power of wool, feathers and sand and other porous substances is due in great measure to the air they contain. The material prevents the free circulation of the convection currents, the heat is transmitted in the main by conduction and the process is slow. If the bulb of an air thermometer as used in Experiment 46 be surrounded by a loose pile of powdered gypsum or some other light material and the experiment repeated, heat will reach it very slowly; if the powder be tightly packed round the bulb, the air being thereby expelled from the mass, the transference will be much more rapid.

When a pan or kettle containing water is placed on the fire the temperature of the under side of the pan does not rise much above 100°. At this temperature the gas given off by the coal does not ignite, hence there is under a great part of the pan a layer of comparatively cool gas. Such a layer conducts heat slowly and the process of boiling is thereby delayed. To obviate this the bottoms of some kettles are fitted with a number of small metal feet or legs. These project some way into the furnace, and their lower ends being at a considerable distance from the water can be raised in temperature much above boiling-point. The layer of non-conducting gas therefore is not formed over them and the heat is conducted to the water more rapidly.

CHAPTER XI.

TRANSMISSION OF HEAT BY CONVECTION.

150. Convection currents. When a liquid or gas is heated the density of the heated part becomes less, it therefore rises carrying its heat with it, and currents are set up in the substance by which the tendency toward uniformity of temperature is promoted.

We have had in Hope's experiment § 91 an example of such currents. Heat is transferred by the motion of the heated particles carrying their heat-energy with them. Such a process is called convection.

EXPERIMENT (47). *To illustrate the convection of heat.*

(*a*) Take a large sized flask and fill it with water, drop in some particles of aniline dye and heat it over a Bunsen burner. As the dye dissolves a stream of coloured water will be seen rising up the centre of the flask above the burner and diffusing gradually back down the sides where the water is cooler.

(*b*) Take a wide-mouthed bottle from which the bottom has been removed. Fit a cork to it and pass two glass tubes through the cork, one of these AB being straight, the other CDE bent, as shewn in fig. 68. Fit the other ends of the tubes through a cork in a flask in such a way that AB may just pass through the cork while

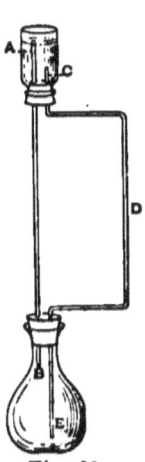

Fig. 68.

DE reaches nearly to the bottom. Secure the apparatus in a stand with AB vertical and fill it with water to above the level of the tube AB, taking care that no air is left in the flask. Place some aniline dye in the upper reservoir AC so as to colour the water. Heat the flask BE from underneath with a Bunsen burner. The water in the flask and the vertical tube AB becomes hotter than that in the reservoir and the longer bent tube. Hence the water rises from the flask along the tube BA and coloured water flows down the bent tube to take its place. A circulation of water round the tubes is thus set up and after a time the plain and coloured waters become mixed.

(c) Repeat Experiment (46) (a), using instead of the capsule of burning spirit a small vessel containing a freezing mixture. The index rises in the air thermometer, shewing that the bulb is cooled. This is due to convection. The water at the top is cooled and becoming denser sinks, thus reducing the temperature of the thermometer.

151. Hot water heating apparatus. The experiment 47 (b) of the last section illustrates the principle of a hot water heating apparatus. A pipe rises from the upper part of a boiler to a tank or reservoir at the top of the building which it is wished to heat. The downward pipe corresponding to CDE passes through a number of metal coils in the various rooms and finally enters the boiler again at the bottom. The water is cooled as it circulates through the pipes and its heat given up to the rooms.

This method of heating illustrates the three processes of conduction, convection and radiation. The heat passes from the furnace to the water by conduction through the plates; it is transferred to the interior of the pipes by convection, the hot water in its flow carries the heat; it passes to the exterior of the pipes by conduction and escapes into the room by radiation from the surface of the pipes and by convection in the currents of air which the warm pipes set up.

152. Convection in air. Light a piece of brown paper or blotting-paper, blow out the light and let the paper smoulder. Hold a glass tube open at both ends over the paper; some of the smoke passes up the tube. Heat the upper part of the tube with a Bunsen flame or spirit lamp; the upward flow is very decidedly increased; a convection current is set up which draws the smoke up the tube.

Light a candle and place it at the bottom of a fairly wide lamp glass. The bottom of the glass may be covered with water as shewn in fig. 69 to prevent the ingress of air from below. The candle can obtain no supply of air and soon goes out. Cut a piece of card about the width of the glass, leaving a wider part at the top so that the card is T-shaped, and insert it at the top so as to divide the upper part of the tube into two portions. The candle will now burn, and, by holding a piece of smoking paper near, it will be seen that there is a draught down one half of the tube supplying fresh air and up the other half carrying off the products of combustion.

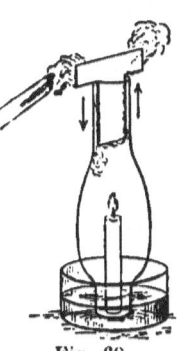

Fig. 69.

153. Ventilation. Convection currents produce an important effect on the ventilation of rooms and buildings. The hot air, heated by the fire, rises up the chimney and cold air enters under the door or round the window to take its place. The hot air in a room in which people are living rises to the top. It is for this reason that in a properly ventilated room the openings for the exit of foul air are at the top, while arrangements are made near the floor to allow the ingress of fresh air. In some cases the entering air is made to pass through a coil of pipes at the back of the fire-place to warm it and thus prevent the chilling effect which might otherwise be produced. In rooms heated by hot water the fresh air should pass over the water-pipes before it is admitted to the room.

154. The Trade Winds. Currents in the atmosphere are to a very considerable extent the result of convection. Thus the air near the equator gets heated and rises and the colder air from the north and south gets drawn towards the equator to take its place. If the earth were at rest this would cause a steady north and south wind on the north and south side of the equator respectively. The earth however is turning round from west to east and a point on the equator is moving faster than one to the north or south of it. The air which is drawn towards the equator from northerly latitudes has a velocity towards the east which corresponds with the velocity of the point from which it was drawn, and this is less than the velocity of the points to which it is coming. It will appear therefore relatively to the earth to be moving from east to west, i.e. the northerly and southerly winds are thereby converted into north-easterly and south-easterly winds. These constitute the trade winds. There is a belt of calm just under the sun where the air is being drawn upwards, and this calm belt lies to the north or south of the equator according to the time of the year. The air which is thus drawn up passes away to the north and south as an upper current, descending again to the surface of the earth about our latitude in the northern hemisphere. This air coming from the equator has a greater velocity towards the east than the earth's surface in this latitude; it therefore appears to come from the south-west and constitutes the south-west wind which blows frequently. The direction and character of the winds at any place are of course much modified by local causes.

Ocean currents are to some extent also produced by convection, but the action of the wind on the surface is in this case the predominating cause.

EXAMPLES.

CONDUCTION AND CONVECTION.

1. A building is heated by hot water pipes; how does the heat get from the furnace of the boiler to a person in the building? What would be the effects on the temperature of the more distant parts of the building of coating the pipes near the boiler, (a) with woollen felt, (b) with dull black lead?

TRANSMISSION OF HEAT BY CONVECTION.

2. What is meant by the thermal conductivity of a substance? An iron boiler 1·25 cm. thick contains water at atmospheric pressure. The heated surface is 2·5 sq. metres in area and the temperature of the under side is 120° C. If the thermal conductivity of iron is ·2 and the latent heat of evaporation of water 536, find the mass of water evaporated per hour.

3. Two equal rods, the one of bismuth, the other of iron, are thinly coated with wax, and one end of each is raised to the same temperature. Describe and account for the phenomena observed in the two rods respectively.

4. Distinguish between the conduction, convection and radiation of heat, and describe experiments by which (a) the conductivity of two metals may be compared, and (b) the conductivity of one metal determined.

5. An iron boiler 1·3 cm. in thickness contains water at the atmospheric pressure. The heated surface is 3 sq. metres in area, and its under side is kept at a temperature of 115° C. Taking the thermal conductivity of iron as ·2, find the quantity of heat entering the boiler in an hour.

6. An iron boiler $\frac{3}{8}$ inch in thickness exposes 60 square feet of surface to the furnace and 600 lbs. of steam at atmospheric pressure are produced per hour. The thermal conductivity of iron in inch lb. sec. units is ·0012 and the latent heat of steam is 536. Find the temperature of the under side of the heating surface. Explain carefully why this is not the temperature of the furnace.

7. Define the thermal conductivity of a substance and describe some way of measuring it.

8. How many units of heat will be conducted in an hour through each square centimetre of an iron plate 0·02 cm. thick, its two sides being kept at the respective temperatures of 0° C. and 50° C., the mean conductivity of iron being 0·12?

9. The opposite sides of a plate are kept at 0° C. and 100° C. by contact with ice and steam. Shew how to deduce the conductivity of the plate by observing the quantities melted and condensed. What are the practical defects of the method?

10. To the two sides of a metal vessel are soldered rods of bismuth and iron; to the rods a number of shot are attached by means of soft wax; the vessel is filled up with boiling water; state and explain what will occur.

11. The inside of the wall of a house is at 15° C., and the outside at 0° C., the wall is of stone, and 50 cm. thick. Find how much heat passes across it per square metre. The conductivity of the stone is ·005 and the unit of heat is the quantity required to raise the temperature of one gramme of water one degree centigrade.

CHAPTER XII.

TRANSMISSION OF HEAT BY RADIATION.

155. Radiation. As has already been explained heat-energy is transmitted by radiation when it passes through a medium without raising its temperature. A medium which permits the passage of radiation is said to be diathermanous; in such a medium the energy does not exist as heat; one which will not permit of such passage is adiathermanous; radiant energy falling on an adiathermanous medium is transformed into heat; it is said to be absorbed by the medium and the temperature in consequence rises.

Radiant energy reaches us from the sun, being transmitted through the 92,000,000 miles between us and the sun in a period of some $8\frac{1}{4}$ minutes, but the space between us and the sun is not thereby warmed. This space is filled with a medium which is known as the ether: the sun has the power of producing motion in the ether, giving to the ether particles kinetic energy and setting up waves which travel outwards with great velocity, about 3×10^{10} cm. or 189,000 miles per second; any diathermanous substance can transmit these waves, though with a reduced velocity. An adiathermanous substance cannot transmit them. When they fall on such a substance the regular vibrations which constitute the waves are quenched, the energy of these vibrations passes into the energy of the irregular motions to which heat is due. Radiation is absorbed and a rise of temperature follows.

When radiation from the sun falls on us it excites two sensations, we feel heat and we see. The vibrations in the ether differ, among other points, in the rapidity with which they are executed. Vibrations of certain degrees of rapidity are capable of exciting the nerves of the eye, to these we give the name of Light. In order to produce the sensation of vision the ether particles must vibrate between 4×10^{14} and 7×10^{14} times per second. These same vibrations falling on other parts of the body excite motion in the nerves there. The energy of the motion is absorbed and heat is produced, but vibrations in which there are considerably less than 4×10^{14} oscillations in a second and which are too slow to affect the eye can produce the sensation of heat; to such vibrations the name of radiant heat is given; for their detection and measurement we use different apparatus to that which we employ in the case of light, and it is these vibrations in the main which we proceed to study experimentally in this chapter. In addition to the sensations of light and heat, radiation falling on a body can produce chemical changes, thus plants require a supply of radiant energy to enable them to assimilate the carbon in the air and grow.

Certain salts of silver are decomposed by the action of radiation and it is in consequence of this fact that photography becomes possible. These chemical changes may be produced by vibrations of the same period as those which affect the eye, i.e. by light. They can also be set up by the less rapid vibrations, or as is specially the case with the silver salts used in photography, they may be caused by vibrations which are too quick to disturb the optic nerve.

Thus radiant energy in the ether may become known to us in different ways, and different names, "thermal," "luminous," or "actinic," have been applied to it; these, however, are all names for the same thing manifesting itself to our sensations in different ways, according to the nature of the recipient on which it falls, and the rapidity with which the vibrations by which it is transmitted are executed. The second part of this book is concerned with the luminous effects of radiation; at present we are dealing with thermal effects, effects that is which shew themselves in a change in temperature of the body receiving the radiation. The laws we are about to enunciate apply in the main equally well to Light and to invisible radiant energy. If however we are dealing with Light the effects are immediately visible, in the case of the invisible radiations we need some apparatus to render their presence sensible; if for example they fall on the bulb of a delicate thermometer the substance it contains expands and we see the motion of the index.

156. Means of measuring radiation. Various forms of apparatus can be used to shew the presence of invisible radiant energy. A sensitive thermometer will often be sufficient, or we may employ the differential air thermometer shewn in figure 10. In any case the bulb on which the radiation is to be received should be coated with lampblack; the reason for this will appear later. The differential ether thermoscope (fig. 70) may also be employed. This consists of two bulbs A and B like the cryophorus (fig. 56) connected by a glass tube and containing only ether and ether vapour. The one bulb A is coated with lampblack. When radiation falls on it, its temperature rises and the vapour pressure of the ether in the bulb A is increased; the consequence is that the ether rises in the tube leading to the bulb B: it may all be forced up into the bulb B, leaving only vapour in A, if the rise of temperature be sufficient.

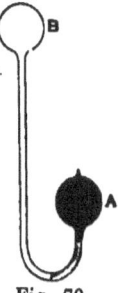

Fig. 70.

Another instrument which is used in radiation experiments is the thermopile.

If the ends of two pieces of wire of different materials, iron and copper say, be connected together, and then one of the junctions be heated, the other being left cold, an electric current is produced; this current can be easily measured by including in the circuit a galvanometer; if the difference of temperature between the junctions be not very great the current is approximately proportional to it. Now a very small current can be measured and hence a very small difference of temperature can be observed.

This is made use of in the thermopile; the metals used are antimony and bismuth, for the current produced by a small difference of temperature is greater for these metals than for others. A number of bars of the metals are arranged alternately as in fig. 71, A 1, 2 3, 4 5 being antimony bars, 1 2, 3 4, 5 B bismuth.

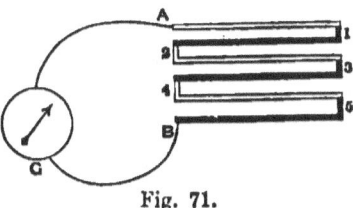

Fig. 71.

The bars are soldered together at 1, 2, 3, 4, 5, and the ends A, B are connected to a galvanometer[1]. If the junctions 1, 3, 5 be heated while 2 and 4 remain cool, a current passes from A to B through the galvanometer, while if the junctions 1, 3, 5 be cold while 2 and 4 are heated, the current through the galvanometer is from B to A. The current always passes from antimony to bismuth across the cold junction. The effect will be produced by a single junction, but by increasing the number the current is usually increased, though this depends on the galvanometer and the connecting wires. In the apparatus as usually made, a large number of junctions are connected up in square order as shewn in fig. 72, the contiguous bars of metal being electrically insulated from each other by strips of mica. In the figure are shewn the connecting screws to which the galvanometer wires are attached. The surfaces on which radiation is to fall are blackened.

Fig. 72.

For some experiments the ends of the thermopile can be fitted with hollow cones. The interiors of these cones may be bright and polished; in this case all the rays which enter the open ends of the cones are reflected from their polished interiors to the face of the thermopile, and since the area

---

[1] A galvanometer is an instrument in which an electric current causes a small delicately suspended magnet to move (see Books on Electricity), and the current can be measured by observing the deflection of the magnet. In Thomson's Mirror Galvanometer a small mirror is attached to the magnet and a spot of light is reflected by the mirror on to a scale. The motion of the magnet is indicated by the motion of this spot.

of the open end of the cone may be considerably greater than that of the face, a much larger amount of radiation is concentrated on the face than otherwise would reach it: in other cases the interior of the cones is covered with a dull black surface; a piece of dead black paper cut into the form of a sector of a circle and fitted inside will form such a surface. In this case the rays which fall on the black surface are absorbed by it. The only rays which can reach the thermopile are those which come from that portion of space which would be visible to an eye situated where the face of the thermopile is and looking out through the cone. There are various other forms of apparatus for measuring radiation. Prof. Boys' radiomicrometer is a very sensitive thermopile and galvanometer combined. It will readily indicate the radiant energy received by it from a candle placed at the far side of a large hall.

In experiments on radiation various sources of radiant energy may be used. For some purposes a Bunsen lamp burning with its usual non-luminous flame will serve. A piece of copper or platinum placed in such a flame becomes red hot and may be used for the source. For other purposes a ball of metal heated red hot in a fire will serve, while for others again a Melloni cube, which is merely a tin or brass box filled with boiling water, is convenient. In the last case it is often desirable to have some means to keep the water boiling, and at the same time to protect the thermopile or thermometer from direct radiation from this source. Screens can generally be arranged to secure this result.

With this apparatus various experiments may be made on radiation.

157. Transmission of Radiant Energy.

EXPERIMENT (48). *To shew that in a uniform medium radiant energy travels in straight lines.*

(a) Take any small source of radiation, a Bunsen burner with a piece of platinum for example, and place a small screen[1]

---

[1] Such a screen may be made by fastening two pieces of tin sheet so that they can stand in a vertical position with their planes parallel and separated by an air-space 1 to 2 cm. in breadth.

opaque to radiation at a distance of 25 or 30 cm. from the source.

Place the thermopile or the blackened bulb of the thermoscope at say 25 cm. behind the screen and within the shadow space formed by drawing lines from the source to points on the edge of the screen. No effect is noticed. A straight line from the source to the thermopile will cut the screen and radiation travelling along such a line is stopped by the screen. Now move the thermopile so that it is just outside this shadow, i.e. so that a line can be drawn from it to the source without cutting the screen. Its temperature immediately rises, radiation travelling in a straight line can now reach the thermopile.

(b) Place a screen with a small hole in it fairly near to the source; place a second screen also with a small hole (say 1 to 2 cm.) in diameter at a little distance away. On placing the thermoscope so that a line can be drawn from it through the two holes to the source, it is affected; in other positions no rise of temperature is indicated.

(c) Place the first screen near the source and in front of it place a metal or card-board tube some 4 or 5 cm. in diameter and some 40 or 50 cm. long in such a position that its axis is directed through the hole towards the source. The inside of the tube should be blackened. The only radiation which can reach the thermopile is that which can travel directly down the tube, and in consequence the thermopile is only affected when directly opposite the end of the tube.

158. Diathermanous and Adiathermanous substances. The percentage of radiant energy, incident on a plate of any material of given thickness, which is transmitted by that plate, is different for different materials and depends also on the nature of the radiations themselves. Thus glass which is transparent to the luminous vibrations is nearly opaque to the invisible vibrations of longer period; the same is true of a solution of alum in water. Rock salt on the other hand allows the passage of radiation of every period to about the same extent, while a solution of iodine in bisulphide of carbon which is opaque to luminous radiation transmits the invisible rays of longer period very freely.

In experiments on radiation we must remember that the visible effect depends on waves whose periods lie within certain definite limits, while the thermopile or thermoscope, covered with lampblack, measures the total quantity of radiant energy which falls on it.

EXPERIMENT (48 A). *To compare the relative diathermancy of plates of various materials.*

Place the thermopile at a convenient distance—say some 50 cm.—from a source of radiant energy. Interpose between the two a screen with a hole in it, which can be covered by the plate whose diathermancy is required, and a stand on which this plate can be supported so as to cover the hole. The numerical results obtained will depend on the nature of the source employed: suppose it to be a spiral of platinum wire or a piece of platinum foil made incandescent by a Bunsen burner or spirit lamp. Have ready a number of plates of the different materials to be examined which can be placed on the stand so as to cover the hole; the plates should all be of the same thickness. Allow the radiation from the source to fall freely on the thermopile, and observe the deflection of the galvanometer when it has become steady. Interpose a plate of some material, say rock salt. The deflection is somewhat reduced; the ratio of the two deflections gives the ratio of the total energy transmitted by the rock salt plate to the total energy falling on it. According to Melloni for a plate ·25 cm. in thickness this is about 92 per cent. Of the remaining 8 per cent. a small part is absorbed by the rock salt, the rest is reflected back to the source from its surfaces. Perform the same experiment for the various other substances; the proportion transmitted varies very greatly, the percentage reflected does not differ greatly for the various plates, hence the percentage absorbed is very different. Thus using as the source the glowing platinum, a plate of glass, which permits the passage of nearly all the luminous vibrations, transmits only about 28 per cent. of the total radiation, while a solution of alum which is transparent to light allows only about 2 per cent. of the whole energy to pass, and this compared with 92 per cent. transmitted by the rock salt. If the source be changed to one which emits a smaller proportion of luminous vibrations, say a sheet of copper heated to 400°, the results are more striking still. The rock salt still transmits 92 per cent. while only 6 per cent. can now pass through the glass; the amount transmitted through the alum is too small to be measured.

Thus in this case nearly all the radiant energy is non-luminous and nearly all can pass the rock salt.

The following experiment illustrates the distinction between the visible and invisible radiations very forcibly. Bisulphide of carbon is fairly transparent to all radiation; by putting a little iodine in the bisulphide it becomes quite opaque to light but still transmits a very large percentage of the total radiation. Thus Tyndall placed a cell containing bisulphide of carbon between an electric lamp and a thermopile, and observed the current produced. He then replaced this cell by a similar one containing the iodine solution, and found in this case that the energy transmitted was $\frac{9}{10}$ths of the previous amount. According then to this observation only $\frac{1}{10}$th of the total energy emitted by the lamp is capable of producing vision, the remaining $\frac{9}{10}$ths cannot affect the eye as light[1].

It has been shewn also by Tyndall that the diathermancy of different gases for radiation from a source such as the glowing platinum spiral is very varied. Thus the absorption of carbonic oxide is about 750 times as great as that of air or oxygen, while that of olefiant gas is more than 10 times as great again, or about 8000 times that of air.

The following table gives some of Melloni's results for different materials and different sources; the numbers given

---

[1] In this and other experiments to be described shortly with the iodine solution, the sides of the cell used to hold the liquid through which the radiant energy has to pass should be of rock salt. If they are of glass, a large proportion of the radiation will be absorbed by the glass.

indicate the total percentage transmission; the plate in each case being ·25 cm. or $\frac{1}{10}$th inch thick.

	Oil Lamp	Incandescent Platinum	Copper at 400°	Copper at 100°
Rock salt	92·3	92·3	92·3	92·3
Fluor spar	72	69	42	33
Iceland spar	39	28	6	0
Glass	39	24	6	0
Quartz	38	28	6	0
Alum	9	2	0	0
Ice	6	0	0	0

Since as measured photometrically nearly all the luminous energy passes the alum, we infer that of the total energy emitted by the Locatelli oil lamp only 9 per cent. is luminous.

These numbers only hold for the thickness given; the amount transmitted decreases rapidly as the thickness increases. We notice also that the percentage transmitted depends on the nature of the source, all the substances except the rock salt exercise a selection in the vibrations they transmit.

159. Reflection of Radiant Energy.

EXPERIMENT (49). *To shew that radiant energy can be reflected.*

(a) Arrange some reflecting surface, a sheet of glass or tin or a thin piece of wood with its plane vertical, in such a way that it can easily be turned about a vertical axis through its centre[1]. Attach a light lath or pointer with its length normal, or perpendicular, to the reflecting surface, in such a way that it moves over the table, tracing out a circle as the reflector is turned round. Adjust two tubes such as that described in Experiment 47 (c) so that their axes may be horizontal and may meet about the middle of the reflecting plate, supporting them in suitable stands, and place a source of

---

[1] This can be done by drilling a hole with a centre-bit into a block which can be clamped on to the table, and fitting a round peg into this hole. The reflecting surface can then be secured to this peg.

radiation, the hot ball suppose, at the end of one tube, the thermopile at the end of the other shading the latter from direct radiation. For most positions of the reflector the effect on the thermopile will be very small, but on turning it round, a position can be found in which the galvanometer needle is considerably deflected; when the deflection is greatest, it will be found that the pointer just bisects the angle between the two tubes. The radiant energy travelling in straight lines down one tube is reflected along the other, and the angle between the normal to the reflecting surface and the incident radiation is equal to that between the normal and the reflected radiation. The experiment can be varied by altering the mutual inclination of the tubes; the pointer always bisects the angle. Fig. 73 shews the arrangement of the apparatus.

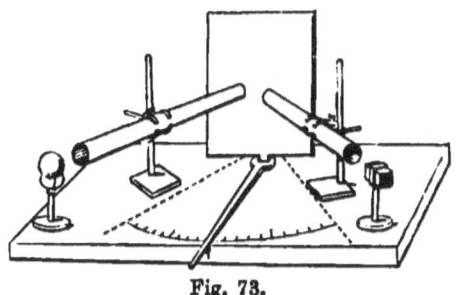

Fig. 73.

(b) Take a source of radiation, such as the ball after it has become non-luminous, but while it is still hot, and place the thermopile at some distance—say a metre—away. The effect will probably be small. Take a long metal tube such as has been already used, but polished brightly inside, and place it between the two, one end of the tube being close to the ball: the galvanometer deflection or the indication of the thermoscope becomes much more marked. A large part of the radiation diverging from the ball enters the tube, and after one

Fig. 74.

or more reflections from the sides as shewn in fig. 74, falls on the thermopile and raises its temperature.

(c) The laws of reflection can be more easily verified in the case of light: we can shew by the following experiment that the invisible radiation follows the same path as the visible.

Take two large concave mirrors[1]. Place a source of light, a small gas flame, at the principal focus of one mirror. Allow the parallel beam which proceeds from the mirror to fall on the second mirror placed as far away as is convenient: the radiation is reflected to the principal focus of this mirror, and on placing at this focus a small piece of paper, an image of the source is formed on the paper. Replace the source of light by the heated ball, and bring the blackened bulb of the thermoscope or the face of the thermopile, near the second mirror. No very large effect will be produced, except when the face of the thermopile is in the position which in the previous experiment was occupied by the sheet of paper. The rays from the ball fall on the first mirror and are there reflected in a parallel beam; after reflection from the second mirror they converge on the thermopile to the same spot as the luminous rays converged when producing the luminous image.

The arrangement is shewn in fig. 75.

Fig. 75.

[1] These are usually made of copper beaten into a spherical form, polished on the inside and coated with silver, and should be some 50 cm. across. A point midway between the centre of the surface and the centre of the sphere is called the principal focus. If a luminous source be placed at this point the rays diverging from it are reflected from the mirror and proceed in a parallel beam parallel to the line joining the centre of the sphere and the principal focus. See *Light* § 50.

If in the above experiment the hot ball be replaced by a piece of ice, or a small beaker or other vessel containing a freezing mixture so as to be at a low temperature, the thermoscope in the focus of the second mirror will shew that the temperature then falls. We shall have to discuss later some of the theoretical consequences of this.

In any of the above experiments a luminous source such as an electric lamp may be employed and the luminous rays cut off by a solution of iodine in bisulphide of carbon.

160. Refraction of Radiant Energy. Light falling obliquely on the surface of glass, water, or any other transparent medium is refracted or bent out of its course according to certain definite laws (see *Light* § 32). The same is true for invisible radiation. Again the amount of refraction depends on the nature of the light; that which consists of the most rapid vibrations is most bent.

EXPERIMENT (50). *To shew that radiant energy can be refracted.*

(a) Allow the rays of light from a bright source to pass through a narrow slit and to fall on a screen, thus producing a white patch on the screen. Interpose in the path of these rays a prism of some transparent material[1]. A coloured patch is now visible on the screen some distance to one side of the original white light. This patch is called a spectrum. It will be found that the bending or deviation of the light has taken place towards the thick end, and away from the edge of the prism, and that the patch is coloured red on the side nearest the original white light, blue or violet on the other side. Now take a linear thermopile, one, that is, which has a single row of junctions arranged in a line one above the other. Since we know that glass absorbs a large fraction of the incident radiation, to get a large effect we use a rock salt prism. Place the thermopile in the spectrum, its length being parallel to the edge of the prism, and move it through the spectrum from the violet toward the red. The galvanometer is deflected, the deflection increasing as the red end is ap-

[1] See *Light* 43.

proached. Continue to move the thermopile beyond the visible red of the spectrum. The needle is still deflected, shewing that the invisible radiation, like the visible, is refracted by the prism but to a less extent. The visible radiation may be cut off by the iodine solution; if the thermopile be left in the invisible part of the spectrum, a deflection is observed of nearly the same extent as before, while if it be placed where the visible part previously was, the effect is much reduced.

(b) It is owing to refraction that an image of a luminous source can be produced by a lens. The simplest observation with a burning glass suffices to shew that the radiant energy from the sun can be concentrated by a lens to the same focus as the light; that the effect is not due to the luminous vibrations can be proved by quenching them with the iodine solution contained in a rock salt cell. Thus if a thermopile or thermoscope be placed at some distance from a source, the effect will be very small, but if a lens of rock salt be inserted so as to focus an image of the source on the pile, a very large effect is produced, and that, even though the luminous energy has been removed by the iodine solution. Hence radiant energy can be both reflected and refracted.

161. Intensity of Radiation at a point. The heating effect produced over a given surface by radiation will be proportional to the quantity of radiant energy which falls on it. It may often happen that this incident radiation is uniformly distributed over the surface, so that if we suppose the surface divided up into any number of equal small portions, the same amount of energy is received by each portion. The total energy received will then be found by multiplying the amount which falls on each small area by the number of such areas in the surface. If we suppose each of the small areas to be one square centimetre, the number of such areas will be the number of square centimetres, and the total amount of radiation received will be obtained by multiplying together the amount received by each square centimetre and the number of square centimetres; or stating it differently, the amount of radiation falling on each square centimetre is obtained by dividing the total amount of energy falling on the surface by the area of the surface in square centimetres.

The amount of radiation received by a surface of given area will depend on the angle between the rays and the surface. More energy will be received by a square centimetre of surface, when it is placed at right angles to the direction in which the rays are travelling, than will reach it when placed obliquely to those rays.

Definition of Intensity of Radiation. *The amount of radiant energy, which falls on each square centimetre of a surface, placed normal to the rays and receiving radiation uniformly distributed, is called the intensity of the radiation at each point of that surface.*

If then we know the intensity of the radiation at each point of a given surface, we find the whole amount of radiation falling on it by multiplying the intensity by the area of the surface; if we know the total amount falling on the surface, we find the intensity, the distribution being uniform, by dividing the total amount by the area of the surface in square centimetres[1].

162. Radiating power of a source of radiant energy. The amount of energy radiated by two different sources in the same time may be very different. Much more energy is emitted per second from a white hot metal ball than from the same ball when nearly cold. Let us take a case in which the radiation is uniformly distributed all round the source. Then if one source is emitting in a given time twice as much energy as a second, twice as much energy will fall in that time on a given area—1 square centimetre say—placed at a given distance from the first source as falls on another square centimetre placed similarly at the same distance from the second source. The amount of energy received by an area in a given position is proportional to the total amount of

[1] If the radiation be not uniformly distributed, the quotient just found will give the average intensity over the surface: the intensity at each point of the surface will vary from point to point, and may be calculated by finding the amount of energy falling on any very small area taken so as to include the point and dividing that amount by the area.

energy radiated from the source. The radiating power of a source may therefore be properly measured by the amount of radiation falling on a definite area placed in a definite position with regard to the source.

Definition of the radiating power of a source. *The radiating power of a source is measured by the amount of radiation which falls on an area of 1 square centimetre placed normal to the rays at a distance of 1 centimetre from the source.*

When then we say that the radiating power of a source is I we mean that I units of radiant energy fall on an area of 1 square centimetre placed normal to the rays at a distance of 1 centimetre from the source.

163. Rectilinear propagation. Law of the inverse square. If we suppose radiation to travel outwards from a source in straight lines, it is clear that a less amount of energy will fall on a given area at a distance from the source than is incident on the same area when moved closer to the source. We can investigate the law of this diminution on the assumption that the energy travels outwards in straight lines.

For let $ABCD$, fig. 76, be a square aperture each edge of which is 1 cm. placed at some little distance from a small source of radiant energy O, so small that we may treat it as a point.

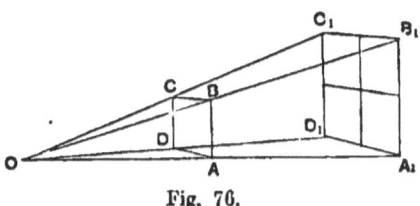

Fig. 76.

Place a second screen behind the first and let the lines OA, OB, OC, OD produced cut this second screen in A_1, B_1, C_1, D_1, respectively. Then the amount of radiation which would fall on $ABCD$ if there were no hole is intercepted by

$A_1B_1C_1D_1$, it is thus distributed over a greater area and the intensity at each point of that area is therefore proportionately less. Now if OA_1 is twice OA, so that the second screen is twice as far from the source as the first, each side of the second square is clearly twice as great as the sides of the first, thus the area of the second square is 2×2 or 2^2 times that of the first. It is therefore 2^2 square centimetres, and the amount of radiation falling on each square centimetre is $1/2^2$ of that which falls, per square cm., on the first. Now suppose the screen moved further away until it is three times as far from O as $ABCD$. Each side of the square formed by producing OA, OB, etc. will now be 3 cm.; the area on which radiation falls still assuming the rectilinear propagation will be 3^2 square cm., and the intensity of radiation will now be $1/3^2$ of its original value; by doubling the distance the intensity of the radiation is reduced in the ratio of 1 to 2^2, by trebling it the reduction is as 1 to 3^2.

Thus the intensity of the radiation at a point due to a given source is inversely proportional to the square of the distance of the point from the source.

This is known as the law of the inverse square for radiant energy and has been deduced from the fact of the rectilinear propagation: we will proceed to give some direct experimental illustrations of its truth.

The following mathematical expression of the law however may be useful. Let I be the radiating power of the source, i.e. the amount of radiation which falls normally on 1 sq. cm. placed at a distance of 1 cm. Thus I the radiating power of a source is also the intensity of radiation at a point 1 cm. distant from the source. Now if the aperture $ABCD$ in fig. 76 above be 1 cm. distant from O the total amount of radiation which passes the aperture is I, and, if the screen be r cm. away from O, each side of the square on which this radiation falls is r cm. The amount of radiation I therefore falls on an area of r^2 sq. cm.; the amount falling on unit area is therefore I/r^2, and this amount measures the intensity of the radiation at each point of that area. Thus the intensity of radiation at a point r cm. distant from a source is found by dividing the radiating power of the source by the square of the distance between the point and the source. Thus we have the formula: Intensity of radiation at a distance r from a source of radiating power I is equal to $\dfrac{I}{r^2}$.

164. Experimental evidence for the law of the inverse square.

EXPERIMENT (51). *To prove that the intensity of the radiation at a point, due to a given source, is inversely proportional to the square of the distance of the point from the source.*

(a) Take a small source of radiation, the platinum spiral heated in the Bunsen burner or the central bright spot of an oxyhydrogen lime light. Place a screen with a small hole in front so as to cut off the radiation from all but a small area of the source; allow this to fall on a thermopile placed at, say, 100 cm. distance from the source. Observe the current through the galvanometer. This is approximately proportional to the rise of temperature of the pile and this again is proportional to the radiant energy falling on it. Thus the energy falling on a given area, the face of the thermopile, can be measured. Let us call the distance d and the current i. Alter the distance to say 80 cm. and again observe the current. Write down in columns the corresponding values of the distance, the current and the squares of the distance. Then form the series of products obtained by multiplying together the corresponding values of the current and of the square of the distance. It will be found that these products are nearly the same, thus the intensity of radiation, measured by the current, multiplied by the square of the distance, is constant, i.e. the intensity is inversely proportional to the square of the distance.

The following table gives Melloni's values, and illustrates how to enter the results.

d	i	d^2	$i \times d^2$
100	10·34	10000	10340
70	21·10	4900	10339
60	28·70	3600	10343

Thus the law is clearly verified.

(b) For this experiment a large radiating surface is required. A tin vessel (fig. 77), whose dimensions are about $75 \times 75 \times 10$ centimetres, may be used. One face is covered with lampblack and the whole filled with boiling water. The hollow cone is fitted to the thermopile and lined with the black paper, the instrument is placed near the heated surface, as at P. If the cone be produced to meet the surface it will cut it in the circle AB. Radiation from points within this circle alone can fall on the pile. Radiation from points outside the circle falls on the blackened paper but is absorbed by it and does not reach the thermopile. Observe the deflection produced.

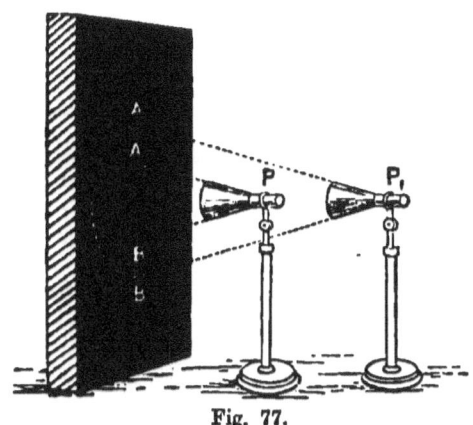

Fig. 77.

Move the thermopile back until it is in a position such as P_1 and observe the deflection; it will be found to be the same as previously, and to remain unaltered whatever be the distance to which the thermopile is withdrawn, provided only that the whole of the circle such as A_1B_1 lies on the blackened surface.

As the thermopile is withdrawn the intensity of the radiation received by it from each point of the source decreases, but the area from which the radiation is received increases. The total amount received depends on the product of these two factors, and this remains constant. Thus the intensity of radiation received from any one point is inversely proportional to the area of the circle, and this area is directly proportional to the square of the distance between P and the surface. Hence the intensity of the radiation received by the thermopile from any one point of the surface is inversely proportional to the square of the distance between that point and the thermopile.

165. The Emission of radiation. We have defined the radiating power of a source as the total amount of radiant energy it emits per second. It is difficult to measure this absolutely as so many ergs or units of work, it is much more easy to compare the amounts of radiation emitted by two or more surfaces and to shew that different surfaces although at the same temperature emit different amounts of radiation.

EXPERIMENT (52). *To compare the amounts of radiant energy emitted by different surfaces.*

(a) Take two small tin canisters with lids to them. Bore two holes in each lid through which a thermometer and stirrer may be inserted. Coat the outside of one with lampblack and leave the second bright. Support each canister on three small cork feet like those employed for the Calorimeter, fig. 15. Fill each with the same mass of hot water at the same temperature, say 60° or 70°, and replace the lids. Take the temperature with a thermometer at intervals of say 5 minutes, stirring the water each time to secure uniformity. It will be found that the blackened canister loses heat much more rapidly than the one with a bright surface.

(b) Place a Leslie's cube on a stand which can turn round a vertical axis as shewn in fig. 78 and place the thermopile with the polished cone near to the cube. One of the faces of the cube—a metal box about 10 cm. in side with a lid—may be coated with lampblack, another painted white or varnished, a third roughened and the fourth polished. Fill the cube with boiling water, replace the lid and turn the polished face to the thermopile, very little effect is produced; note the deflection. Turn the cube so that the radiation from the rough face is received; the deflection is considerably increased. The varnished face produces a greater effect still and the lampblack face the greatest of all. Thus these different faces, though at the same temperature, emit very different amounts of radiation, and these radiating powers can be compared by comparing the respective deflections.

These last two experiments have shewn us that lampblack radiates out more heat at a given temperature than any of the other surfaces with which we have worked. It is convenient therefore to take the radiation of a lampblack surface as a standard with which to compare the radiation from any other

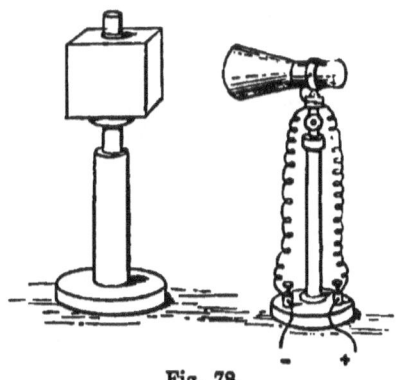

Fig. 78.

surface. The radiation emitted by any surface will be less than that emitted by a lampblack surface at the same temperature; the ratio of the two amounts may be spoken of as the emissive power of the surface.

Definition. *The emissive power of a surface is the ratio of the amount of radiation emitted in a given time by the surface to the amount emitted in the same time by an equal area of a lampblack surface at the same temperature*[1].

166. The absorption of radiation. We have seen that different surfaces at the same temperature emit different amounts of radiation. We shall now shew that they absorb different proportions of the radiation which falls on them.

[1] In the above we have drawn a distinction between the radiating power of a surface, i.e. the actual amount of energy it is emitting per second, and the emissive power, the ratio of the amount emitted by the surface to the amount emitted by lampblack. This distinction is not always observed.

If the substance be partly diathermanous some of the incident energy is absorbed by it, raising its temperature, some is transmitted; if it be adiathermanous the whole incident radiation is absorbed. In what follows, we suppose that the substance is practically adiathermanous, that the amount of energy which can traverse it is negligibly small. The results will to some extent depend on the thickness of the layer of substance, which is emitting or absorbing the radiation.

Definition. *The absorbing power of a surface is measured by the ratio of the amount of radiation absorbed by the surface in a given time to the whole radiation which falls on it in that time.*

A surface which absorbs the whole of the incident radiation is said to be perfectly black. Lampblack is very approximately a perfectly black surface, thus the absorbing power of lampblack may be taken as unity. We may give therefore a second definition of absorbing power identical with the above, but in form resembling more closely the definition of emissive power.

The absorbing power of a surface is the ratio of the amount of radiation absorbed by the surface in a given time to the amount which would be absorbed in the same time by an equal area of a lampblack surface under the same conditions.

EXPERIMENT (53). *To prove that different surfaces have different absorbing powers, and to compare their values.*

(a) Take two air thermometers such as that shewn in fig. 8. Coat the bulb of one with lampblack, that of the other with tinfoil, or better still, with silver. Expose both equally to radiation, e.g. by placing them close together in front of a fire or stove. The temperature of the lampblack instrument rises considerably, that of the silvered instrument is but slightly affected.

(b) Repeat the experiment with the differential air thermometer fig. 10, coating one bulb with lampblack, the other with silver: a similar result is noticed.

(c) In fig. 79, AB, CD are two sheets of tin on suitable stands, one coated with lampblack, the other bright. To the centre of the back of each sheet, a piece of bismuth is soldered as at *K*, and wires are led away to a galvanometer at *G*. The plates are connected by a wire at the top and are placed opposite to each other at some 50 or 60 cm. apart. Between the plates a source of radiation such as the hot copper ball, or a gas jet, is placed. A thermo-electric junction is formed by the contact of the bismuth and the tinned iron, and if the junctions on the two sheets be unequally heated a current is produced, and the galvanometer needle deflected. If the ball be midway between the sheets, the temperature of the blackened sheet is raised very considerably above that of the other; in

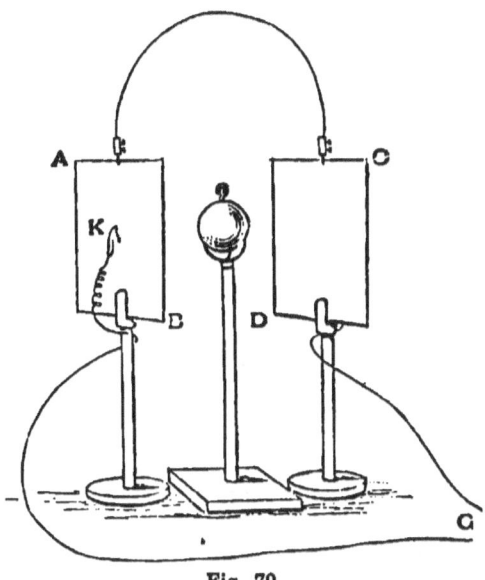

Fig. 79.

order that no current may be produced the source must be very considerably nearer the bright sheet. The blackened surface absorbs a much greater proportion of the incident radiation than the bright, and by measuring the distances of the ball from the surfaces when there is no current, squaring these and taking their ratio, a rough estimate of the absorbing power can be obtained.

(d) More accurate measures of absorbing powers are obtained by coating the thermopile itself with very thin layers of the various substances which are to be examined.

By comparing the results of the experiments described in the last two sections, it is found that good absorbers also emit radiation well. Thus lampblack which absorbs all the incident radiation was found to emit more than any other surface; bright surfaces which emit very little, absorb very little, and in fact, when accurate observations are made it is found that the absorbing and emitting powers of any surface at a given temperature are the same: if a surface emits 20 per cent. of the energy emitted by lampblack it will absorb 20 per cent. of the energy which would under the same circumstances be absorbed by lampblack, i.e. 20 per cent. of the whole incident radiation.

Tyndall made a number of experiments by coating the faces of a Leslie cube with powders of different materials, and obtained numbers which lead to the following results.

Substance.	Absorbing power.	Emissive power.
Rock salt	·319	·307
Fluor spar	·577	·589
Red oxide of Lead	·741	·707
Oxide of Cobalt	·732	·752
Sulphate of Iron	·824	·808

The numbers in the two columns are not greatly different.

The following experiment, a modification of one of Ritchie's, will shew the equality between the absorbing and emissive powers of a surface.

EXPERIMENT (54). *To shew that the absorbing and emissive powers of a surface are equal.*

Take two plates arranged as in fig. 79. Coat one with lampblack and polish the other. Take a Leslie cube of the same material as the plates and treat two opposite faces in the same way as the plates, polish one and blacken the other. Place the cube between the plates, turning the polished face

TRANSMISSION OF HEAT BY RADIATION.

of the cube to the blackened plate and *vice versâ*, and fill the cube with hot water. It will be found that there is no effect on the galvanometer when the cube is midway between the plates.

The blackened face radiates out more than the polished face; but the radiation from the blackened face falls on the polished plate which absorbs only a small fraction of it, while the radiation from the polished face falls on the blackened plate which absorbs nearly all. The total amount of radiation absorbed is the same in the two cases since the temperatures of the two junctions are unchanged, and this can only be the case if this radiation from the polished face bears to the radiation from the blackened face the same ratio as the absorption of the polished face bears to that of the blackened face.

Ritchie in his experiments used, instead of the two plates, two metal vessels, fig. 80, with flat faces. These constitute the bulbs of a differential air thermometer. The Leslie "cube" takes the form of the cylindrical box with flat ends, and is mounted on a stand, which as shewn in the

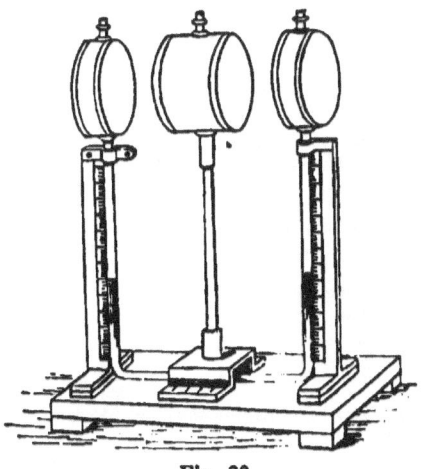

Fig. 80.

figure is fitted with a scale to determine its position between the bulbs.

167. The Reflection of Radiation. We have seen that radiant energy is reflected from a surface on which it is incident. The proportion however which the amount of radiation reflected bears to the incident radiation is different for different surfaces and depends also on the angle of incidence. Moreover, when radiation falls on a surface, that surface becomes heated, and in consequence emits radiation itself; thus the total radiant energy incident on a thermopile placed to receive reflected radiation is made up of the radiation regularly reflected, and the radiation emitted by the surface and diffused in all directions.

Definition. *The reflecting power of a surface is the ratio of the amount of radiation regularly reflected by the surface to the amount of radiation incident on the surface when the incidence is direct*[1].

When radiant energy falls on a surface, part is reflected, and part is refracted into the surface. If the surface is adiathermanous, this refracted portion is absorbed; if it is diathermanous the refracted portion passes through. With most substances the effect is intermediate between these two.

Now for adiathermanous substances the absorbing power is the ratio of the amount entering the surface to the amount incident, the reflecting power is the ratio of the amount reflected to the amount incident, but the amount entering and the amount reflected together make up the whole incident radiation. Hence the sum of the absorbing power and the reflecting power is equal to unity.

Thus we see that substances which absorb radiation readily reflect little and *vice versâ*.

Observation bears out this result; the bright tin surface which absorbs very little radiation is a good reflector, the dull black surface which absorbs nearly all is a very bad reflector.

---

[1] By direct incidence it is meant that the incident rays are at right angles to the surface.

168. Absorption, Emission and Reflection of Radiation.
Accurate experiments shew also that the result just stated is true, numerical measurements of absorbing power have been made and accord with the statement. Now the absorbing power of a perfectly black body is unity. We may therefore state the law thus:

Absorbing power of an adiathermanous substance + reflecting power of the same substance = absorbing power of a lampblack substance; or again, since the absorbing power and the emissive power are the same,

Emissive power of a surface + reflecting power of the same surface = emissive power of a perfectly black surface.

If the substance examined be partly diathermanous, so that an appreciable portion of the incident radiation can pass through, we shall have also to consider the transmitting power of the surface.

Definition. *The transmitting power of a plate is the ratio of the amount of radiation which passes through the plate to the amount which is incident on it.*

The transmitting power was measured in Section 158, Experiment 48 A. It depends on the material and on the thickness of the plate. For such diathermanous substances we have to add the transmitting power to the left-hand side of the equations just given and write emissive power + reflecting power + transmitting power = emissive power of a black body. Exact experiments prove that these laws hold not only for the total radiation emitted and absorbed but for each kind of radiation. Thus some substances exercise a selective absorption, they absorb vibrations of certain periods and transmit those of other periods. These same substances emit readily vibrations of the first set of periods but not those of the other set.

169. Observations on Absorption, Emission and Reflection.
The relation between absorption, emission and reflection can be illustrated by many examples. Thus if a piece of china with a dark pattern on a light ground be heated in a clear fire the dark pattern stands out bright on a

less bright ground. Or again make a cross or mark with ink on a piece of platinum foil or other bright surface and heat the whole over a Bunsen flame; the mark appears much brighter than the rest. Dark clothes are hotter than light, for the dark surface absorbs the radiation, the light surface reflects a large portion of it. The action of a glass fire-screen illustrates the selective absorption of glass, the luminous vibrations are transmitted but these contain only a small portion of the energy radiated from the fire. The same action is shewn in a greenhouse. The luminous vibrations pass through the glass, they are absorbed by the plants and objects inside, much of the energy they convey is radiated out again in invisible radiation of long period; to these the glass is opaque, and the energy is thus kept inside the hothouse and raises its temperature considerably.

Aqueous vapour is opaque also to vibrations of long period; hence it is that a damp cloudy night is apt to be warm, the free radiation of energy from the earth into space is prevented. Clear nights in winter or early spring are often frosty because radiation out into space can continue sufficiently to cool the earth down to the freezing-point.

Again a teapot or pewter hot-water jug is kept bright. Loss of heat by radiation is thus prevented; for the same reason the front part of a copper kettle is polished, the back towards the fire being left dull. The reading of a black bulb thermometer placed in the sun is much higher than that of an ordinary clear glass thermometer lying beside it, whilst on a clear night the black bulb instrument falls below the other.

170. Law of cooling. Common observation tells us that the rate at which a body loses heat by radiation depends upon its temperature and the temperature of the surrounding space. A red-hot ball cools more rapidly through 10° or 20° than the same ball when at a temperature of 40° C. or 50° C. The rate of cooling also depends on the surface. Some experiments led Newton to believe that the quantity of heat emitted per second by a body was proportional to the difference in temperature between the body and the surrounding space. So that if the space be at 15° C. a body at 35° C.—20° C.

above the space—would radiate out twice as much heat in a second as the same body when at 25° or 10° C. above the space. This result is known as Newton's law of cooling— more exact experiment has shewn that it is only true for small differences in temperature between the hot body and the space.

EXPERIMENT (55). *To examine the law of cooling of a hot body.*

The hot body may conveniently be a small flat rectangular copper vessel about 7 × 7 × 1 centimetres fitted with a lid through which pass a thermometer and a stirrer.

The vessel is coated with lampblack and filled with hot water. It is then suspended by silk threads or india-rubber bands inside a larger copper vessel blackened on the inside. This vessel can if desired be placed in a large tub of water and its temperature will thereby be maintained nearly constant; for many experiments it will however remain at a sufficiently constant temperature if exposed to the air of the room.

Keep the water in the inner vessel gently stirred and read the thermometer as the temperature falls from about 70° at intervals of, say, 1 minute; after a time, when the rate of fall has become slower, the intervals may be considerably longer.

Plot the results as a curve representing the times by horizontal lines parallel to OA and the observed temperatures by vertical lines parallel to OB. The curve will have the form shewn in fig. 81.

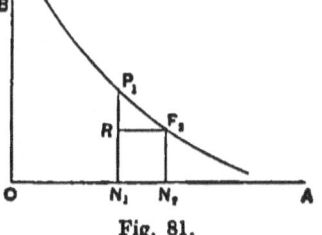

Fig. 81.

Let P_1, P_2 be two points on the curve corresponding to the temperatures P_1N_1, P_2N_2 at times ON_1 and ON_2.

Draw P_2R horizontally. The amount of heat lost in the

interval N_1N_2 is proportional to the fall of temperature, this is measured by P_1R. The average rate at which heat is being lost then, during this time, is proportional to the ratio of the fall in temperature P_1R to the time RP_2 or N_1N_2, and thus can be found from the diagram. If Newton's law held, this rate of fall should always be proportional to the difference between the temperature of the hot body and that of the enclosure; this is not found to be accurately the case.

171. Rate of loss of Heat, Coefficient of Emission.

Experiments on radiation such as the above are complicated by the fact that the greater portion of the loss of heat is due to convection currents in the air round the hot body and not to radiation. Dulong and Petit made observations on the rate of loss in a vacuum; in this case the heat lost is much less than when there is air or any other gas round the hot body. We may use the above experiment in the following way to calculate the loss of heat from the hot body. Let m be the mass of water in the vessel including the water equivalent of the vessel, let the temperature be $t_1°$ C. and after 1 minute let it be $t_2°$ C. Then the heat lost in 1 minute is $m(t_1 - t_2)$, and the heat lost per second or the rate of loss of heat is found by dividing this by 60. If we again divide by the area of the surface we can get what we may call the coefficient of emission of the surface at the given temperature, i.e. the amount of heat lost per second per square centimetre of surface under the given conditions.

Now it is found that this coefficient of emission depends only on the nature of the surface itself and on the temperatures of the surface and of the space into which it is radiating its heat.

We may fill the calorimeter with some other liquid, oil say; at a given temperature it radiates out heat at the same rate at which it radiated when filled with water. The fall in temperature is different in the two cases; the heat emitted, which will depend on the mass and specific heat of the liquid, is the same. Thus, suppose that the mass of the water is m grammes, that of the liquid M grammes, that it takes the water t seconds to cool through 5° C. from 70° C. to 65° C. and

$$S\lambda.H. \times d = K.$$

that it takes the liquid T seconds to cool through the same range: let C be the specific heat of the liquid. The loss of heat from the water is $m \times 5/t$ units per second, that from the liquid when cooling through the same range is $M \times 5 \times C/T$ units per second. It is found that, omitting for the present the small correction due to the capacity for heat of the calorimeter, these two quantities of heat are equal, the heat emitted per second at a given temperature is the same in the two cases.

172. Specific Heat, Method of Cooling. The law just stated which can be verified by using a liquid of known specific heat may be made the basis of a method of determining the specific heat of a liquid. The method is known as the method of cooling.

EXPERIMENT (56). *To determine the specific heat of a liquid by the method of cooling.*

Take the calorimeter described in Section 170. Place in it a certain mass m grammes say of water, heated to about $70°$ C.—m may be about 100. Note the times taken by the water to cool through successive intervals of $5°$—from $70°$ to $65°$, $65°$ to $60°$ and so on down to say $30°$. Empty out the water and place in the calorimeter a mass M of the liquid whose specific heat is required. The mass should be such as to fill the calorimeter to about the same extent as the water. Observe the times taken by the liquid to fall in temperature through the same intervals $70°$ to $65°$ etc. as the water. Let the time taken by the water to fall through some range, $65°$ to $60°$ say, be t seconds, that taken by the liquid over the same range T seconds. Then the amount of heat emitted per second by the water is $5m/t$, that emitted by the liquid is $5M . C/T$, and these two quantities are equal.

Thence
$$\frac{5m}{t} = \frac{5MC}{T},$$

or
$$C = \frac{m}{M} \cdot \frac{T}{t}.$$

*173. **Prevost's theory of exchanges.** We have seen that the amount of heat radiated from a body per second diminishes as the temperature of the body approaches that of its enclosure. Two theories have been propounded to account for this. It may be that the presence of a second body at the same temperature as itself actually stops the radiation from the first body, while the presence of a cold body induces greater radiation; or it may be that the loss of heat is a differential effect, depending upon the difference between the amount of radiant energy emitted by the body and the amount it receives from the other body. This last is Prevost's theory of exchanges. According to it, the radiation emitted from a body depends upon its temperature and the nature of its surface, the radiation which falls on it depends on the temperature and surface of neighbouring bodies: if there is no change of temperature, it is not because the body has ceased to radiate but because the amount radiated is just equal to the amount absorbed from other bodies. Thus when as in Experiment 49 (c) an air thermometer and a hot ball are placed in the foci of two mirrors, the ball radiates to the air thermometer and the thermometer to the ball, the temperature of the thermometer rises because it receives from the ball more radiant energy than it emits; if a piece of ice be substituted for the hot ball, the temperature of the thermometer falls because it now emits more energy than it receives.

Or again, consider an enclosure E, fig. 82, containing a body A; let the temperatures of the body and the enclosure be the same. Suppose also for simplicity that the bodies and the walls of the enclosure absorb all the incident radiation. The body is radiating out energy to the enclosure and receiving radiation from it; these two amounts are equal, hence the temperature is stationary. Now introduce a second body B at a different—say a lower—temperature. B rises in temperature, A and the walls of the enclosure fall. Part of the radiation from A which did fall on the enclosure and was balanced by radiation received from the enclosure now falls on B; B being colder than A is radiating out less energy per

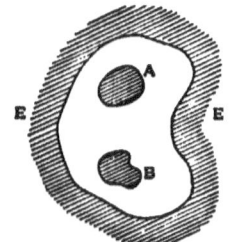

Fig. 82.

unit of area than A, it returns therefore to A less than it receives, it becomes warmer while A is cooled. Similar results follow for the radiation between B and the walls of the enclosure, and this continues until the temperature is equal throughout.

If the surfaces be not perfectly black, the argument will need a little modification to allow for the reflections which take place, but the principles are the same.

*174. Prevost's theory and the relations between the absorbing and emissive powers of a surface. We may shew from Prevost's theory that the absorbing and emissive powers of a body must be equal in the following way.

Consider a black body, such as the blackened bulb of a thermometer, fig. 83, surrounded by a surface which reflects some of the incident radiation and absorbs the rest. Suppose the temperature to remain the same throughout, and let the outer surface reflect, say 30 per cent., of the incident radiation from the black body and absorb the remaining 70 per cent. Then out of every hundred units of energy which leave the black body, 30 are reflected to it from the enclosure; and these 30 are again absorbed by it. Thus out of the original hundred, 70 units leave the black body and enter the enclosure; if this were all the temperature of the enclosure would rise, that of the central body would fall. But the temperatures remain constant; thus the enclosure must in the same time lose 70 units which must enter the black body. These 70 units are radiated by the enclosure to the black body. Thus a surface which absorbs 70 per cent. of the energy absorbed by a black surface at the same temperature, emits 70 per cent. of the energy emitted by that black surface. The emissive and absorbing powers are equal, and the sum of either, together with the reflecting power, is equal to the emissive power of the black surface.

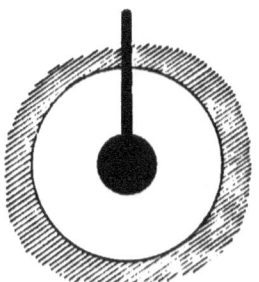

Fig. 83.

EXAMPLES.

RADIATION.

1. How would you shew that radiant heat is refracted similarly to light? Explain the action of a glass fire-screen.

2. A red-hot ball of iron looks equally bright in all its parts and at whatever distance from the eye it be placed. Explain these facts.

3. A vessel containing hot water is placed on a table: explain by what means the vessel and water fall in temperature.

4. Shew that it follows from Prevost's theory of exchanges that the absorbing powers of two surfaces are proportional to their radiating powers; how may this be also verified by experiment?

5. State the difference of behaviour of plates of rock-salt, alum and glass, with respect to the transmission of radiant energy. Describe how the energy radiated from a black body varies as its temperature is continuously raised.

6. What experiments would you undertake to determine (a) the radiating, (b) the absorbing power of a surface? How are they connected?

7. Describe the thermopile. How would you prove experimentally the law connecting the intensity of the radiation at a point with its distance from the source of heat?

8. State Prevost's theory of exchanges and explain the arguments upon which it rests.

A calorimeter is hung up within an outer vessel and it is desired to keep it as far as possible from losing or gaining heat. Explain the advantages, if any, of silver-plating (a) the outside of the calorimeter, (b) the inside of the outer vessel.

9. The bulbs of two identical thermometers are coated, the one with lampblack, the other with silver; compare their readings (1) when in a water bath in a dark room, (2) when in the sun, (3) when exposed on a clear night; explaining why they do not agree on all these occasions.

CHAPTER XIII

THE MECHANICAL EQUIVALENT OF HEAT.

*175. Joule's experiments on the equivalence of heat and energy. These experiments have already been referred to. The arrangement of the apparatus in his last experiments is shewn in figs. 84 and 84 a which are taken from Joule's paper. Fig. 84 a gives the calorimeter and the paddles. The calorimeter is shewn again in fig. 84.

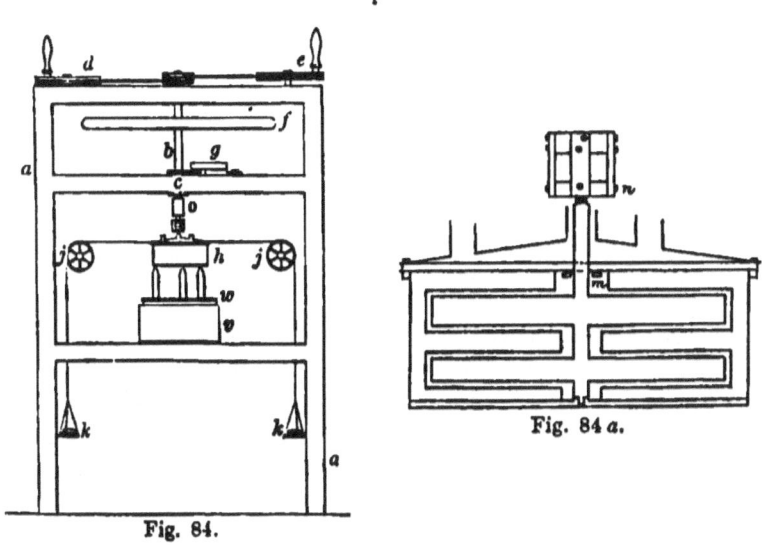

Fig. 84.

Fig. 84 a.

The general plan of the experiment is to heat the water by churning it up with the paddles, to measure the work done in the heating and the heat produced in the water and calorimeter, and to find the ratio of the two. In order to calculate the work done, the following arrangement due to Hirn was employed. The calorimeter is mounted so as to be free to turn round a vertical axis. The paddles are carried on a vertical axis coinciding with that about which the calorimeter can turn. On this axis, bc, are two pieces of box-wood o and n which help to prevent the conduction of heat from the bearing at c down to the water. In the latter experiments the calorimeter was supported on a hollow cylindrical vessel w which floated in water in the vessel v, and thus took the pressure off the bearings. The axle bc carrying the paddles and the horizontal flywheel f can be made to rotate by turning the wheels d and e. At g there is a counter which indicates the number of rotations of the axle. If everything be free the friction between the water and the calorimeter will carry the calorimeter round with the paddles, the water will not be churned and therefore it will not be heated.

By applying force to the calorimeter it can be prevented from rotating; the water will be made to move round inside relatively to the calorimeter and be heated in consequence of the work that is done by the forces between the water and the calorimeter. In Joule's experiments the forces restraining the motion of the calorimeter were the tensions of two thin strings which rested in a horizontal groove round the calorimeter and passing over two light pullies j, j carried weights k, k. These weights could move up and down near two scales by which their positions could be fixed, and were adjusted until they remained stationary, while the shaft and paddles revolved at some suitable uniform speed. If the speed quickened a little the weights rose, if it slowed they sank, and by watching the weights a uniform rate of working could be insured. Thus the tension in the string required to keep the calorimeter at rest is measured. Let us call the tension of each string W, it will be equal to the weight in either scalepan together with the weight of the pan.

Now in the experiment the water is made to rotate by holding the calorimeter fixed and spinning the axle and paddles. We could get the same effect by holding the paddles fixed and allowing the same force W to act on either string and cause the calorimeter to turn, the number of rotations per second and the work done would be the same as in the actual experiment, the weights k, k would move down uniformly and the string unwind off the groove round the calorimeter. Now in this case, if a be the radius of the calorimeter, in a single turn each weight would descend through a distance equal to the circumference or $2\pi a$, and in n turns it would go through n times this distance. The work done therefore by the two weights would be

$$2W \times n \times 2\pi a \text{ or } 4n\pi a W,$$

and the quantities involved in this can be accurately measured. It remains now to determine the heat generated by this work. For this purpose it is necessary to know the mass M of the water in the calorimeter, the water equivalent m of the calorimeter and paddles, and the rise in temperature t of the water. The heat generated then is $(M+m)t$. Thus the ratio of the work done to the heat generated is

$$4n\pi a W / (M+m) t.$$

Corrections will be required for the loss of heat by radiation, the friction at the pullies, the work done in raising the velocity to its steady value and various other points. It follows from Joule's experiments that this ratio which is the amount of work required to produce 1 unit of heat is constant. It is called "Joule's equivalent" and is denoted by J.

In one series of Joule's experiments the average values were

$$M + m = 84280 \text{ grains}$$
$$2W = 18229 \text{ grains}$$
$$2\pi a = 2\cdot 774 \text{ feet}$$
$$n = 4870$$
$$t = 3°\cdot 768 \text{ Fah.}$$

On substituting these numbers in the formula we find for the ratio the value 775. (The actual result given in Joule's

Tables for this series of experiments is 774·57.) This result therefore is the number of foot-grains of work required to raise the temperature of 1 grain of water 1° Fah., or the number of foot-lbs. required to raise the temperature of 1 lb. of water 1° Fah. at 54°·7 Fah. which was the average temperature of this series of experiments. The result given by Joule himself at the conclusion of his last paper as the value for the mechanical equivalent is 772·55 ft. lbs. at 60° Fah. in the latitude of Greenwich.

Now in this result 1 degree of temperature is a degree as reckoned on his mercury-thermometer. This will differ from a degree on the air thermometer by a small amount. Prof. Rowland introduced the correction for this into Joule's work.

The result of introducing these corrections is to make Joule's value come to 776·75 foot-pounds at 15° C., or if we take all Joule's published values instead of the 772·55 of this last series we find as Joule's mean result 779·17.

Expressed in the metric system in terms of the work done in raising 1 gramme through 1 centimetre and the heat necessary to raise 1 gramme 1° C. this number reduces to 427·50.

Prof. Rowland adopts 776·75 as the result of Joule's work, and this in metric units comes to 426·75. Joule's experiments were repeated in 1878 by Rowland who gives as his result 427·52, while Mr Griffiths using a method depending on the heat produced in a wire by an electric current finds 428·4.

Thus we may take the value 778 or 779 foot-pounds of work as representing very approximately the amount of work necessary to raise the temperature of 1 lb. of water 1° Fah. Since a degree centigrade is 9/5 of a degree Fahrenheit the value of J, employing centigrade degrees and pounds, is $779 \times 9/5$ or 1402 foot-pounds. Expressed in ergs the value is $4·194 \times 10^7$.

*176. Determination of J by friction of metal on metal. In some of Joule's experiments the value of J was found by the friction of metal on metal. One experiment by this method can be carried out by means of the apparatus

175-177] THE MECHANICAL EQUIVALENT OF HEAT. 215

shewn in fig. 85 (for practical details see Glazebrook and Shaw, *Practical Physics*, p. 290).

A cast-iron cup C is secured to a vertical axle working in bearings and driven by a band over the horizontal pulley A.

Inside this cup there is a conical brass cup, shewn in section at the side, separated from the iron cup by a layer of cork to which it is firmly secured; a second brass cup fits in this and is carried round by the friction between the two when the axle is rotated. A large wooden pulley D is attached to the upper cup and a string passes round this and over a fixed pulley and carries a weight P. The outer cup is then made to rotate until the friction between the two is just sufficient to begin to

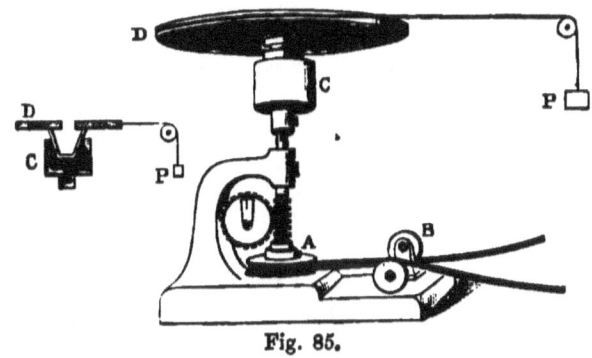

Fig. 85.

cause the inner cup to turn and to raise the weight P; the work spent in overcoming this friction is measured as in the previous experiment. The inner cup contains a known mass of water and the friction heats this water. The heat produced can be calculated in terms of the mass of water, the water equivalent of the calorimeter and the rise in temperature. Knowing the quantity of heat produced and the work expended in its production we can find a value for J.

*177. Work done by the expansion of a gas.
Suppose that a gas is contained in a cylinder with a piston under pressure. Reduce the pressure in some way as by suddenly lifting a weight off the piston. The gas expands and

in expanding does work in overcoming the pressure which remains on the piston. To do this work energy is required, and in consequence the gas is cooled down by the expansion. This may be easily shewn by compressing air into a vessel, leaving it to acquire the temperature of the air, then opening a tap and allowing the air to escape against the face of a thermopile or a delicate thermometer. But now when the expansion has ceased the air occupies a greater volume than before, the average distance between its particles will be greater than previously, and if there are any attractive forces between the air particles work will have been done in overcoming this attraction: part of the cooling effect will be due to this, part only to the external work done in raising the piston. If, on the other hand, there were repulsive forces between the particles, these forces would help to overcome the external force and therefore the cooling would be less than we should calculate from the work done in overcoming the pressure.

Joule shewed that neither of these effects took place in air, or the other permanent gases, to any appreciable extent; there are therefore neither attractive nor repulsive forces acting continuously on the air molecules; when the air is allowed to expand, the cooling produced is wholly accounted for by the external work done.

Joule's apparatus consisted of two copper receivers R and E, fig. 86. These were connected by a tube D with a stopcock, and placed inside a tin vessel which was filled with water; this vessel contained about $16\frac{1}{2}$ lbs. of water and each of the copper receivers would hold about 134 cubic inches. One vessel E was exhausted, the other filled with air at a pressure of about 22 atmospheres, and the temperature of the surrounding water was carefully noted.

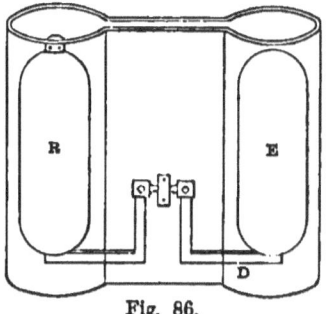

Fig. 86.

The stopcock was then opened and the air allowed to pass into the empty receiver. The water was then stirred and the change in temperature was found to be inappreciable. The vessel from which the gas escapes loses heat, the other vessel gains it, but the loss and the gain are exactly equal, and so, on the whole, after stirring there was no change of temperature. In another experiment the two receivers were put into separate vessels and it was verified directly that the loss of heat in the one was equal to the gain in the other. According to these results then, if a gas expands, all the energy derived from its fall of temperature is used in overcoming the external pressure, none is needed to do internal work[1].

Suppose now that a gas contained in a cylinder with a piston is allowed to expand from a volume v to a volume v', let A be the area of the piston, x the distance it moves and p the pressure, then as the piston moves, the volume increases by Ax, thus $v' - v = Ax$.

The force on the piston is Ap and the piston on which this force acts moves a distance x, hence the work done is

$$Apx \text{ or } p \times Ax.$$

Now $$p \times Ax = p \times (v' - v).$$

Thus in this case when a gas increases from volume v to volume v', at a constant pressure p, the work it does is

$$p(v' - v).$$

It can be shewn that this expression holds generally, and not merely in the case in which the gas is in a cylinder.

*178. Mayer's method of determining J. It has already been pointed out that the specific heat of a gas at constant pressure differs from that at constant volume, and the reason is now clear, if in the first case heat is needed to supply energy sufficient to overcome the external pressure, in addition to raising the temperature, in the second it is only required to raise the temperature; and since by the last experiment the whole difference between these two amounts of heat is used in doing external work, we can get a relation between that heat and the work done. This was Mayer's method of finding J,

---

[1] In more elaborate experiments Joule and Thomson have shewn that this is not absolutely true, but it is a very close approximation.

but he did not shew that his argument was legitimate, because he omitted to prove that none of the energy was used in doing internal work against internal forces. Joule supplied this proof and the argument is now legitimate.

Let v be the volume of a unit of mass of gas, and T the absolute temperature of the same, p its pressure, then in raising its temperature 1° at constant pressure v expands by the amount v/T and the work done is pv/T. Let c_p and c_v be specific heats at constant pressure and constant volume. Since the mass of gas is unity, c_p is the heat which must be applied to raise its temperature 1° C. at constant pressure, c_v at constant volume. Thus the amount used in doing external work is the difference between these or $c_p - c_v$.

The mechanical equivalent of this is found by multiplying by J, it is therefore
$$J(c_p - c_v),$$
and this is equal to the work done; thus
$$J(c_p - c_v) = \frac{pv}{T},$$
hence
$$J = \frac{pv}{T(c_p - c_v)}.$$

Now v is the volume of a unit of mass, it is therefore equal to $1/\rho$ where ρ is the density. Writing this we have
$$J = \frac{p}{\rho T(c_p - c_v)}.$$

The value of c_v is not known with sufficient accuracy to make this a very good method of finding J, we may however if we take air as the gas at the standard pressure one atmosphere and temperature zero, using the ordinary values, put

$p = 1\cdot013{,}000$ dynes per sq. cm.
$\rho = \cdot001276$ grammes per c.cm.
$T = 273$
$c_p = \cdot2375$
$c_v = \cdot1684$.

And from these numbers we find

$J = 4\cdot21 \times 10^7$ ergs per gramme degree centigrade.

*179. Graphical representation of work done by a gas in expanding.

We have just seen that if a gas changes its volume at constant pressure the work done in expansion is measured by the pressure multiplied by the change of volume.

Now let us represent the volume as before in Section 118 by horizontal lines parallel to OA, the pressure by vertical lines parallel to OB. Then, if the pressure remains constant, the curve on the diagram representing the relation between it and the volume is a horizontal straight line such as P_1P_2 fig. 87, in which ON_1, ON_2 represent two volumes v_1, v_2 and N_1P_1, N_2P_2 the corresponding pressures. Then N_1N_2 is the change in volume and the parallelogram $P_1N_1N_2P_2$ measures the work done. A similar construction gives the work done in the more general case when the pressure is not constant, for let PQ, fig. 88, represent the relation between the pressure and the volume, and let the volume change from ON_1 to ON_2 by a very small amount N_1N_2. The change in pressure will be very small and the pressure may be represented as either P_1N_1 or P_2N_2, being something between these values. The work done will lie between the rectangle P_1N_2 and the rectangle P_2N_1; if N_1 and N_2 are very close, it may be represented by the curvilinear area $P_1N_1N_2P_2$. Proceeding thus we see that the work done in any finite change of volume such as LM, is given by the area $PLMQ$, where LP and MQ represent the pressures corresponding to volumes OL and OM.

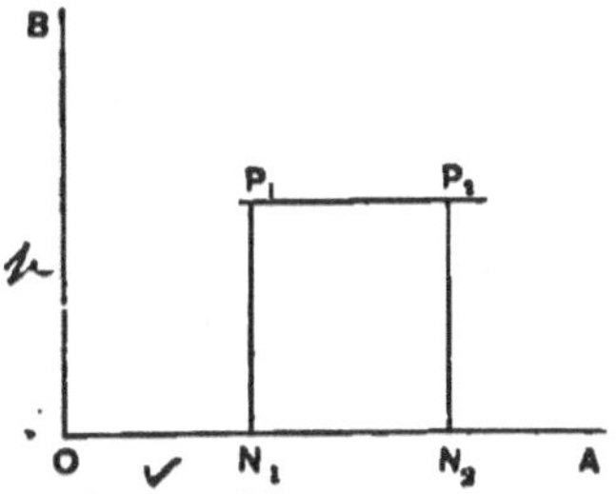

Fig. 87.

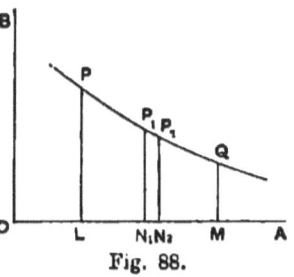

Fig. 88.

This method of measuring work is made use of in the indicator diagrams of steam and other engines.

EXAMPLES.

HEAT AND ENERGY.

1. What do you understand by the statement that Heat is a form of Energy and what are the grounds for this statement?

2. What do you understand by a diagram of energy and by an isothermal line on such a diagram? Shew how to calculate the work done during a series of changes represented on such a diagram.

3. What is meant by the critical temperature, pressure, and volume of a gas? How can these be determined experimentally?

Draw the isothermals of a substance at temperatures above and below the critical temperature.

4. What is meant by the mechanical equivalent of heat, and how has it been determined?

If the work a man does in running upstairs is half spent in producing heat and half in doing mechanical work, by how much will the temperature of a man be raised who runs up a flight of stairs 200 feet high, assuming the specific heat of the man to be the same as that of water, and that no heat is lost by radiation or other causes?

5. The combustion of a gramme of coal produces 8000 units of heat. If an engine employs in pumping water one-tenth of the energy supplied to its boiler by the combustion of coal, find how much coal must be burnt in order to enable it to raise 5000 litres of water to a height of 10 metres.

6. Explain how the mechanical equivalent of heat may be calculated from a knowledge of the specific heats of air at constant pressure and constant volume.

Note any assumptions made in the calculation and state how they may be justified.

7. If the mechanical equivalent of heat be 779 foot-lbs. Fahrenheit, from how high must 10 lbs. of water fall to raise its temperature 1° Centigrade?

8. The Falls of Niagara are 165 feet high. Find by how much the temperature of the water will be increased by the fall, supposing that the whole kinetic energy acquired by the water in its fall is converted into heat.

THE MECHANICAL EQUIVALENT OF HEAT.

9. A meteorite weighing 2000 kilogrammes falls into the sun with velocity of 1000 kilometers per second. How many calories will be produced by the collision?

(Mechanical equivalent of 1 calorie = $4 \cdot 19 \times 10^7$ ergs.)

10. The mechanical equivalent of heat is 1390 foot-pounds, and it is found that a pound of coal produces by its consumption 8000 units of heat. An engine employs 10 per cent. of the heat supplied to its boiler in drawing a weight up a slope of 30°. Find the coal that must be burnt to draw a weight of 100 lbs. for 1 mile along the slope.

11. A quantity of mercury is allowed to fall a distance of 7·79 feet. If all the mechanical energy lost by the fall is converted into heat in the mercury, calculate how much hotter the mercury will be after the fall, taking the specific heat of mercury as $\frac{1}{33}$.

12. In certain experiments on boring cannon it was ascertained that one horse working for 2 hours 30 minutes raised by 180° F. the temperature of a mass equivalent in capacity for heat to 26·58 lbs. of water. Assuming that a horse does 30,000 foot-pounds of work per minute, deduce the value of the mechanical equivalent of heat.

13. Assuming the combustion of a lb. of coal produces 8000 units of heat, how many lbs. of coal must be consumed to produce the equivalent of the work done in raising a weight of 12 stone to a height of 15,000 feet?

14. The combustion of 1 lb. of coal raises the temperature of 100 gallons of water through 4·4 degrees; find the mechanical equivalent of this quantity of heat.

EXAMINATION QUESTIONS.

I.

1. Give an outline of the experiments which led Rumford to believe that Heat was not a material substance.

2. Distinguish between heat and temperature. Define temperature and explain the analogy between it and hydrostatic pressure.

3. Describe the construction and graduation of a mercurial thermometer. What are the fixed points of the thermometer scale?

4. Shew how to reduce the readings of a Fahrenheit thermometer to the Centigrade and Réaumur scales.

5. Describe some forms of maximum and of minimum thermometers.

II.

1. Define the terms unit quantity of heat, capacity for heat, specific heat; and shew from your definition that the quantity of heat required to raise a mass m of specific heat c from $t°$ to $T°$ is $mc(T-t)$.

2. Explain how to determine specific heat by the method of mixture. How would you allow for the heat absorbed by the Calorimeter?

3. Define Latent heat, and explain some method of finding the latent heat of ice.

4. Describe some form of ice Calorimeter.

5. Distinguish between evaporation and boiling, and shew that the boiling point of water depends on the pressure.

III.

1. Define the latent heat of steam.

On passing 10 grammes of steam into 100 grammes of water at 15° the temperature rises to 71°; find the latent heat of steam.

2. Define the coefficients of linear and of cubical expansion of a substance and shew that the latter is three times the former.

Explain some method of measuring the coefficient of linear expansion of a metal.

3. Describe a method of finding the coefficient of expansion of a liquid.

4. Distinguish between the apparent and the real expansion of a fluid and shew that, if a be the real coefficient, and a' the apparent, then $a - a'$ is the coefficient of expansion of the containing vessel.

5. Describe some method of finding the absolute coefficient of expansion of mercury.

In correcting a barometer reading would you use the absolute or the relative coefficient of expansion?

6. State the laws connecting the pressure, volume and temperature of a gas, and describe experiments to prove them.

IV.

1. Explain what is meant by the absolute zero of the air thermometer, and by absolute temperature.

2. Describe an apparatus to prove that air at constant pressure expands in volume for each degree centigrade by 1/273 of its volume at 0° C.

3. How would you prove experimentally that the pressure of a gas at constant volume is proportional to the absolute temperature?

4. Assuming Boyle's Law and Charles' Law prove that the pressure of a gas at constant volume increases by a given fraction of the pressure at 0° for each rise of temperature of 1°.

5. Describe a form of air thermometer suitable for the measurement of a high temperature such as the boiling point of sulphur.

6. Distinguish between a gas and a vapour and state and explain Dalton's Law as to the pressure of mixed vapours.

V.

1. Shew that if a gas expand at constant pressure p from volume v to volume v' then the work done is $p(v'-v)$. Explain why the specific heat of a gas at constant pressure is greater than the specific heat at constant volume.

2. Define the dew-point, and explain some methods of determining it. Shew how to find the pressure of the aqueous vapour present in the air from a knowledge of the dew-point.

3. A quantity of dry air measures 1000 cubic centimetres at 10° C. and 760 mm. pressure. If the same air is heated to 30° and saturated with moisture at that temperature, what must be the pressure in order that the volume may remain unchanged? The saturation pressure of aqueous vapour at 30° is 31·5 mm.

4. Explain what is meant by the critical temperature of a gas. What processes are necessary in order to liquefy oxygen? Distinguish between gases and vapours.

5. Describe the thermopile. How would you prove that if an electric current be produced by applying heat to a junction of two metals, then that junction is cooled if an electric current be made to traverse it?

6. Distinguish between radiation, convection, and conduction of heat; and describe an experiment to compare the conductivities of two bars of metal, explaining carefully why it is necessary to wait till a steady condition is reached before making the measurements.

LIGHT.

!

CHAPTER I.

VISIBLE RADIANT ENERGY—LIGHT.

1. The Nature of Light. Light is the physical cause of our sensation of sight. If we enter a room with closed shutters and which is in darkness, the objects in the room are invisible; if we open the shutters to admit the daylight or strike a match they become visible. The flame of the match is the origin of some stimulus essential to vision to which the name of light is given. Again, the flame of a Bunsen burner, burning in the ordinary way, is practically invisible. It is however as we have seen[1], a source of radiant energy; the temperature of a thermopile or air thermoscope placed near it is raised by the energy absorbed from the flame; if the air supply be cut off, this emission of radiant energy continues, but in addition the flame now becomes visible; some of the energy it emits can affect our eyes and to this we give the name of light.

2. Luminous and Non-Luminous Bodies. A luminous body is one which of itself emits light; the sun, a lamp or candle flame, or a glowing white-hot substance, are examples. Most bodies are non-luminous; they become visible only by means of light which they receive from other bodies and return to our eyes. Thus, when we light a lamp in a dark room and are thus able to see the objects in the room, it is because the light from the luminous flame falls on those objects; part of this incident light is scattered by the objects, and reaching our eye renders them visible; it appears to us to

[1] See *Heat*, p. 182.

come from the objects; they are not luminous but are seen by light emitted originally by the lamp and diffused by them.

3. Terms used in connection with Light. A substance through which light can be transmitted is often spoken of as a *medium* or *optical medium*; thus air, glass, water and many other substances are optical media.

When a substance has identical properties at all points it is said to be *homogeneous*.

Thus water, well-annealed glass, iron, brass, crystals of quartz or other material are examples of homogeneous bodies.

A substance which has different properties at different points is called *heterogeneous*.

A substance which allows the passage of light and through which, if it be of a suitable shape[1], objects can be distinctly seen is called *transparent*; a substance through which light cannot pass is *opaque*: thus glass or water are transparent substances; iron and the other metals, stone, wood etc., are opaque. There are some substances which allow the transmission of light, but through which distinct vision cannot be obtained: these are called *translucent*. Ground glass and oiled paper are such substances.

The terms transparent and opaque are only relative; a thin layer of water is very transparent; as the thickness of the layer increases, the percentage of light which it can transmit becomes less; the amount of light which penetrates to the bottom of the sea is very small indeed. On the other hand by reducing the thickness of a film of metal it can be made transparent. Thin films of iron, gold, silver, platinum and other metals have been made which allow the passage of a very appreciable quantity of light; hence in comparing the transparency and opacity of various media we must have regard to the thickness of the media.

When light enters an opaque medium it is said to be *absorbed* by it.

[1] The bearing of this will be seen later: glass is a transparent substance but distinct vision could not generally be obtained through an irregularly shaped lump of glass, objects seen through it would appear distorted.

For the present we deal only with the transmission of light through homogeneous transparent media.

4. Rays of Light. In any homogeneous transparent medium light travels in straight lines from each point of a luminous object. Any one of these straight lines is called a *Ray of Light*. An assemblage of rays emanating from one point is called a *Pencil of Rays*. When such a pencil falls on the eye of an observer it produces vision of the point from which it emanates. A pencil of rays usually takes the form of a cone. The axis of the cone OA, fig. 1, is called the axis of the pencil. The direction in which the rays travel is shewn by the arrow-heads in the figure[1]. When the light is travelling from the vertex of the cone, as in fig. 1, the pencil is said to be *divergent*.

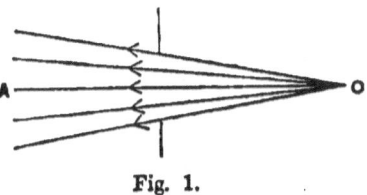

Fig. 1.

In some cases we consider a pencil of rays in which the light is travelling to the vertex of the cone, as in fig. 2. Such a pencil is said to be *convergent*.

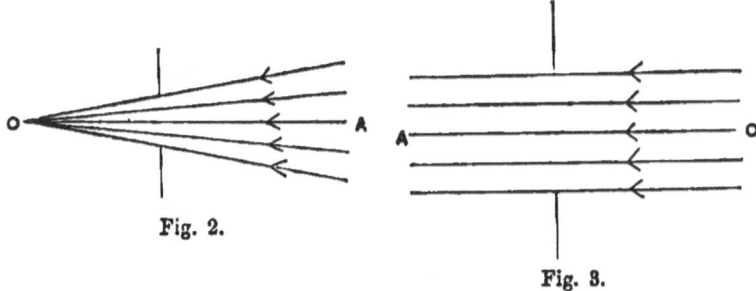

Fig. 2.

Fig. 3.

A *parallel* pencil of rays (fig. 3) is one in which the rays which constitute the pencil are all parallel to one another.

---

[1] It will be found convenient to have an understanding as to the direction in which in the figures light is supposed to be travelling. We shall assume this direction, except where stated to the contrary, to be from right to left.

If the source of light be very distant, such as a point on the sun's surface or a star, the rays reaching the eye from the source will all be practically parallel and the pencil will be a parallel pencil; the rays will really form a cone with a very small vertical angle.

When the vertical angle of the cone formed by the rays is small so that all the rays are close together the pencil is spoken of as a small pencil; this is the case with most of those with which we have to deal, for the aperture of the pupil of the eye is small and the angle it subtends at a luminous point which can be distinctly seen is therefore small.

Though we shall often have to speak of a ray of light, it must be borne in mind that it is not possible physically to isolate a single ray; in reality we always have to deal with a pencil of rays.

A *luminous object* such as the surface of a candle flame consists of a number of luminous points from each of which pencils of rays proceed in all directions. Some of these rays reaching the eye of an observer produce vision.

When rays of light fall on a non-luminous object some of them are *diffused* by it. It is by these diffused rays that the object becomes visible; each point on the object becomes virtually a source from which rays are emitted in straight lines.

5. The Rectilinear Propagation of Light. That light travels in straight lines in a homogeneous transparent medium can be shewn in various ways. For instance, a small object placed between the eye of an observer and a small distant luminous body hides the light when it is directly in the line between the two. The following experiment illustrates the fact.

EXPERIMENT (1). *To illustrate the Rectilinear Propagation of Light by the Pinhole Camera.*

Take a thin sheet of cardboard or metal and make a small hole about a millimetre in diameter through it. Place a lighted candle or other luminous object behind the sheet and a screen of translucent material such as tissue paper in front shading the candle so that light may not fall directly on the screen except through the hole. An inverted picture of the candle is seen on the screen.

Thus let AB (fig. 4) be the candle flame, O the hole in the sheet. Rays of light diverge in all directions from any point, such as A, of the candle flame. Of these a very small pencil passes through the hole O and depicts at A' on the screen a picture of the luminous point A. The same is true for all other points of the flame. A small pencil of rays from each

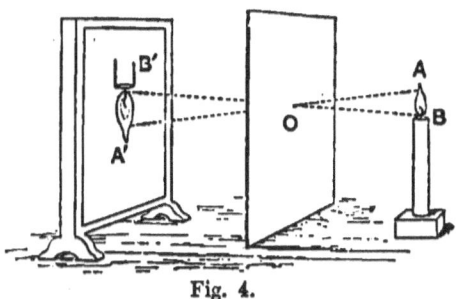

Fig. 4.

point passes through the hole and a picture of the flame is thus produced on the screen. The rays cross at the hole and hence the picture is inverted. By varying the position of the screen it can be shewn from the size and position of the picture formed that the path of each ray is straight.

Suppose now that a second hole is cut in the metal sheet at some little distance from the first, a second picture of the candle flame is formed, and if a number of holes be made there will be a corresponding number of pictures. Moreover, when the holes are close together, the corresponding pictures overlap and the outline becomes blurred; and when the number of holes is sufficient the separate pictures are replaced by a uniform illumination over a portion of the screen. The uniform illumination produced on a screen by light passing through an aperture of considerable size may be looked upon as arising from the innumerable overlapping pictures produced by the small pencils which pass through each elementary portion of the whole aperture.

For some of the experiments to be described below a *small* source of light is required; when such a source is employed it may be treated as a point from which the rays diverge. In many cases it is sufficient to use a gas flame turned down low; in others, when a more brilliant light is required, a small hole some 5 mm. in diameter may be bored in a sheet of metal and placed close in front of a good gas-burner; for demonstrations to a large class the oxyhydrogen lime-light or an arc-lamp may be needed.

In many experiments the filament of an incandescent lamp affords a most satisfactory luminous object; if necessary a shade can be fixed over the globe so as to prevent the passage of light from all except the straight portion of one leg of the filament.

6. The formation of Shadows. Another illustration of the rectilinear propagation of light is afforded by the formation of shadows. Take a *small* source of light O, fig. 5,

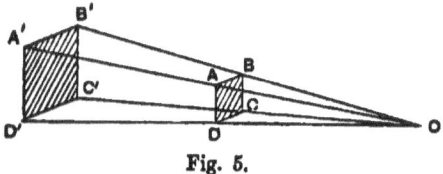

Fig. 5.

and place it at a distance of 2 or 3 metres from a wall. Cut a square or triangular piece of card $ABCD$ and place it in a stand between the light and the wall with its plane parallel to the wall. A shadow $A'B'C'D'$ is cast on the wall. This shadow is of the same shape as the cardboard and is such that, if lines be drawn from O to all points of the boundary of $ABCD$, the points in which these lines cut the wall form the boundary of the shadow; within the area thus traced no light falls, outside it the screen is uniformly illuminated.

If the source of light be not small, it will be found that the shadow is not uniformly dark all over, the central part may be black but it will get brighter as we approach the edges. Thus arrange an ordinary gas flame to cast a shadow of a sheet of card some 10 cm. square on a paper screen at a distance of say two metres, the flat side of the flame being parallel to the card. Prick holes in the screen, (1) near the centre of the shadow, (2) at some point where the darkness is clearly somewhat less than that in the centre, (3) near the edge, and look at the gas flame through these holes. Through (1) no portion of the gas flame is visible, through (2) part of the flame can be seen, while through (3) nearly the whole is visible. The black portion called the *umbra* receives no light from the flame, the lighter part of the shadow called the *penumbra* is illuminated by part of the flame and as the edge of the shadow is approached the portion of the flame from which light is received increases. This is illustrated in fig. 6.

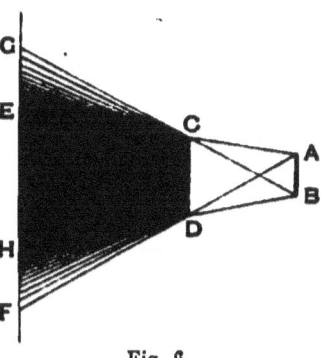

Fig. 6.

Let AB represent a source of light, CD an opaque object somewhat larger than the source, and $GEHF$ a screen on which a shadow is cast. Join AC, AD, BC, BD cutting the screen in E, F, G, H respectively. Then clearly no light can reach the screen between E and H; this part constitutes the umbra. Points between E and G or H and F respectively receive light from a portion of the source, the amount of light increases as the points approach G and F, the outer boundary of the shadow. Consider any point between E and G; join this point to C and produce the line to meet AB, then clearly light from any portion of the source between A and the line so drawn can reach the point on the screen, it will therefore be only partly in shadow.

The conditions are somewhat different if the source of light is larger than the opaque object as in fig. 7. In this case the

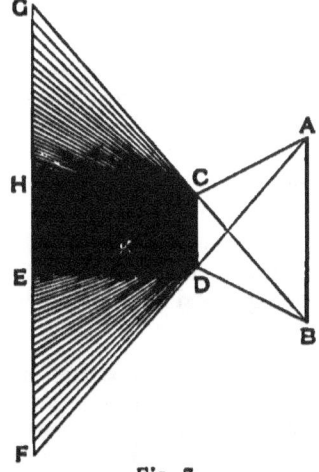

Fig. 7.

lines AC, BD converge and may meet before reaching the screen; suppose they do meet, as at K. Then if the screen were placed between the opaque object and K there would be umbra and penumbra as before; if the screen passed through K the umbra would be reduced to a point, and if the screen be as in the figure beyond K there is no umbra; moreover light can reach a point between H and E from both the bottom and the top of the source. An eye at such a point looking towards CD would see it as a dark object with light above and below.

7. Eclipses. The eclipses of the sun and moon illustrate the formation of shadows. A solar eclipse is caused by the passage of the moon between the sun and the earth. Moreover the sun is much larger than the moon, thus the shadow is formed as in fig. 7, while the distances of the sun and moon from the earth are such that the earth when traversing the shadow is always near the point K. When the earth is nearer to the moon than K, the umbra or region of total eclipse covers a small area of its surface, and, as the moon moves on, this area traces out a narrow band of total darkness; the breadth of the band depends on the distance of the earth from K. If the earth is beyond K there is no umbra, the eclipse is nowhere total, but for an area on the earth corresponding to EH, in fig. 7, it is annular. An eclipse of the moon takes place when the earth passes between the sun and moon. The size of the earth is such that the point K is always well beyond the moon's orbit, thus the eclipse is never annular; the moon may however not pass completely through the umbra of the earth's shadow and in this case the eclipse is partial.

The production of an eclipse may be illustrated experimentally, using a lamp with a ground-glass globe as the source of light and a ball or globe of smaller diameter to represent the moon.

8. Illuminating power of a Source of Light. The amount of light emitted by different sources varies enormously: we shall describe, later, methods by which, for a given source, it may be measured in terms of the light emitted by some standard: we will consider now the meaning of various terms which will be found useful.

When dealing with radiant energy we have already explained how the radiating power of a given source is measured[1]. If we have a source emitting light uniformly in all directions the quantity of light which falls on a given area placed at a given distance from the source will be proportional to the whole amount of light the source emits: now clearly the greater the quantity of light emitted by a source, the brighter will the source be and the greater the illumination it will produce at a given distance. We may thus speak of the illuminating power of a source as measuring the total light energy it emits; this total light energy is proportional to the quantity of light which falls on a given area in any given position with regard to the source. For the sake of definiteness let us consider the light which falls on a unit of area (1 sq. cm.) placed normal to the rays at a unit distance (1 cm.) from the source. This amount of light will be proportional to the total amount of light emitted and will therefore be a measure of the illuminating power of the source.

Definition of Illuminating Power. *The quantity of light which falls on a surface one square centimetre in area at a distance of one centimetre from a source of light, placed so as to be perpendicular to the rays, is called the Illuminating Power of the Source.*

The illuminating power thus defined is proportional to the total quantity of light emitted by the source, when the source is emitting light uniformly in all directions.

9. Intensity of Illumination at a point. Consider now a surface on which light is incident; we may speak of the illumination of that surface, meaning thereby the quantity of light which it receives; this will depend on the illuminating power of the source from which it is receiving light, on its area, and on its position with regard to the source. If the light is uniformly distributed over the area, the total amount received will be proportional to the area. Two square centimetres will receive twice as much light as one, we are thus

---

[1] *Heat*, § 162.

led to consider the amount of light received by each square centimetre of the area; the brightness of the surface when at a given distance from the source will be proportional to this quantity; again the amount of light received by the surface will depend on the direction in which the light falls on it as well as on its distance from the source; if the surface is placed so that the rays strike it at right angles, it will receive more light than if it were inclined to the direction of the rays. The maximum brightness then of a surface uniformly illuminated and placed at a given distance from a source will be proportional to the amount of light which falls normally on a surface one square centimetre in area placed at that distance from the source.

This quantity of light is known as the Intensity of the Illumination *at a point* of the area.

Definition of Intensity of Illumination at a point.

The Intensity of Illumination at a point is measured by the amount of light which falls on a surface one square centimetre in area containing the point, placed so as to be perpendicular to the rays of light.

Suppose now that we have a surface uniformly illuminated and containing a square centimetres in area, and that the intensity of the illumination at each point of the surface is X. An amount of light X falls on each unit of area, thus the quantity which falls on the whole area is Xa, and if Q is the quantity received by the surface, we have $Q = Xa$.

Hence $$X = \frac{Q}{a}.$$

Thus the intensity of the illumination at any point of a uniformly lighted surface is found by dividing the whole quantity of light falling on the surface by its area.

The above applies rigidly only to the case when the surface is uniformly illuminated. By taking however the area a sufficiently small we may treat any case as one of uniform distribution over a very small area, and thus we may say in general that the intensity of the illumination at any point is measured by the ratio of the quantity of light falling on a small area containing the point and placed at right angles to the rays to the area when the area is made very small.

10. Law of the Inverse Square.

It remains now to shew how the intensity of the illumination at a point depends on the distance of the point from the source; the law is of course the same as that proved in *Heat* (§ 163), for the intensity of radiation at a point.

EXPERIMENT (2). *To verify the rectilinear propagation of light and to deduce from it that the intensity of the illumination at a point due to a small source is inversely proportional to the square of the distance of the point from the source.*

Take a small source of light; cut a hole (2·5 cm. in diameter) in a thin piece of wood or metal and place this with its plane vertical and the centre of the hole at the same height as the source at a convenient distance (25 centimetres suppose) from the source. Measure off a series of distances along the table equal to the distance—25 cm.—between the source and the hole. Place a screen at the first of these marks; a circular patch of light is formed on the screen: measure the diameter of the patch, it will be found to be $2 \times 2·5$ or 5 centimetres. Move the screen to the second mark 75 cm. from the source; the patch of light will be found to have increased in area and will now be $3 \times 2·5$ or 7·5 cm. across, thus the diameter of the patch is in all cases proportional to the distance of the screen from the source; the bounding rays of light travel outwards in straight lines; the experiment illustrates the rectilinear propagation.

Suppose now that $ABCD$, fig. 8, is a small aperture, a square centimetres in area, in a screen placed at a distance

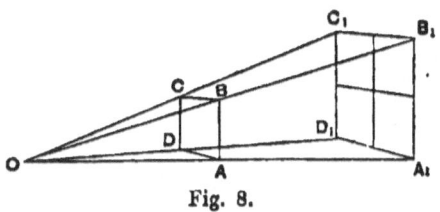

Fig. 8.

of 1 cm. from a source O, the rays from O fall on this aperture very nearly normally and pass through it. Consider a screen 2 cm. from O, the breadth of the patch of light formed on this screen is as we have seen from the above experiment twice that of the aperture; its area therefore since it is proportional to the square of the side is $2^2 a$. Now the same quantity of light which falls on the area a falls also on the patch, and this light is distributed over an area $2^2 a$.

Thus if I is the amount of light falling on unit area at the distance of the aperture—1 cm.—that incident per unit area of the screen at a distance of 2 cm. is $I/2^2$. Now imagine the screen to be removed to a distance of 3 cm., the area of the patch becomes $3^2 a$ and the amount of light per unit area $I/3^2$; when the distance of the screen becomes r centimetres, the amount of light falling on the screen per unit area is I/r^2. But I, which is the quantity of light falling on unit area at unit distance from the source placed normal to the rays, is the illuminating power of the source, while I/r^2, the quantity falling on unit area at a distance of r cm., is the intensity of the illumination at a distance of r centimetres.

Thus *the Intensity of the Illumination at a point at a distance of r centimetres is* $\dfrac{I}{r^2}$, and is found by dividing the illuminating power of the source by the square of the distance of the point from the source.

This result is known as the law of the inverse square; it may be stated thus.

LAW OF THE INVERSE SQUARE. *The intensity of the illumination at a point due to a given source is inversely proportional to the square of the distance of the point from the source.*

The proof may be put rather differently thus. Let O (fig. 9) be a source emitting light uniformly in all directions. With O as centre describe a series of spheres of radii 1, 2...r cm. Light is energy travelling outwards from the source, and the same quantity of energy crosses each sphere per second. Now let $I_1, I_2 ... I_r$ be the amounts of light falling per second on unit area of each sphere respectively. The areas of the spheres are

$$4\pi,\ 4\pi \times 2^2, ... 4\pi \times r^2.$$

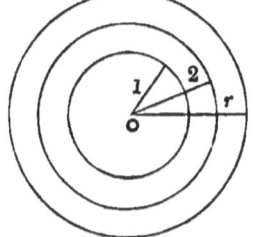

Fig. 9.

Thus the total quantities of light falling per second on each sphere respectively are $4\pi I_1$, $4\pi 2^2 I_2$, ... $4\pi r^2 I_r$, and these are equal, thus

$$4\pi r^2 I_r = 4\pi I_1$$

or
$$I_r = \frac{I_1}{r^2}.$$

But I_1 is the illuminating power of the source, I_r the intensity of the illumination at distance r.

11. Photometry. The various methods of comparing the illuminating powers of two sources of light are based on the law of the inverse square.

By means of suitable apparatus, some forms of which will be described below, the two lights are made to illuminate respectively two neighbouring patches on a screen. The distance of one or other of the lights is adjusted until the two portions of the screen appear of sensibly equal brightness. When this is the case the intensity of illumination at a point on the screen due to each light is the same. Now if I, I' are the illuminating powers of the two lights, a, a' the distance of each from the part of the screen it illuminates, the intensities of illumination due to each are respectively I/a^2 and I'/a'^2.

Thus, when these two intensities are equal, we have

$$\frac{I}{a^2} = \frac{I'}{a'^2},$$

or
$$\frac{I}{I'} = \frac{a^2}{a'^2}.$$

Hence the *Illuminating Powers of two lights are proportional to the squares of the distances at which they produce equal intensities of illumination respectively.*

12. Candle Power. It is necessary of course to have some standard of illuminating power, in terms of which the illuminating powers of other lights may be expressed. The standard ordinarily in use, though it is by no means a satisfactory one, is the illuminating power of the standard candle. Standard candles are sperm candles, six to the pound, burning at the rate of 120 grains per hour. Other sources of light such as a gas flame are compared with one or more such standard candles, and by the candle power of any light is meant the number of standard candles which will have the same illuminating power as the light.

We now proceed to describe one or two forms of photometer.

13. Rumford's Photometer. EXPERIMENT (3). *To determine the candle power of a gas flame.*

Place an upright stick, fig. 10, some 6 or 8 cm., in front of a vertical sheet of white paper; the surface of the paper should be unglazed; arrange a candle A and a gas flame B to

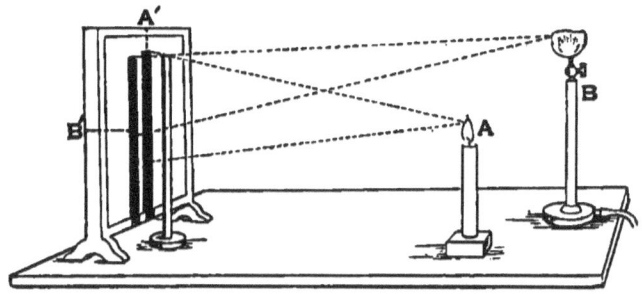

Fig. 10.

cast shadows A', B', respectively, of the stick on the paper, placing the lights so that the two shadows are close together. The shadow A' is illuminated by the gas flame B, while the shadow B' receives light from the candle A. On moving the gas flame away from the paper A' becomes darker, on moving the candle away B' becomes darker. Adjust the distances of the lights from the screen until the two shadows are equally intense. Let a, b be the distances of A and B from the screen, I_a and I_b the illuminating powers of the two lights.

The intensity of the illumination over the screen due to A is I_a/a^2, that due to B is I_b/b^2, and these two are equal. Thus

$$\frac{I_a}{a^2} = \frac{I_b}{b^2},$$

and
$$I_b = \frac{b^2}{a^2} I_a.$$

If the candle A be a standard candle its illuminating power is unity, thus $I_a = 1$ and the candle-power of the gas-flame is b^2/a^2.

14. Bunsen's Photometer. Take a sheet of clean paper with a grease spot on it. This may be made by dropping a spot of grease from a stearine candle on to the paper and removing the wax when hard with a knife.

On placing the paper between your eye and the window or some other source of light, the spot appears brighter than the rest of the paper, it is more translucent and allows more light to pass. Now hold the paper against a dark background. The grease spot looks dark, it allows more of the light, falling on it from the front, to pass through and diffuses less than the rest of the paper.

Consider what happens when the paper is equally illuminated on both sides, the spot allows more light to pass through than the rest of the paper but diffuses less, these two effects just neutralize each other, and the spot and the paper appear of the same brightness. This may be verified as follows. Place two candles as nearly alike as possible on a table in a dark room at a distance of some 2 or 3 metres apart. Mount the paper with the grease spot in a suitable clip or stand which can be moved about between the candles. Place it between the candles, nearer to one than the other; on looking at it from the side of the further candle the spot appears brighter than the rest of the paper, as it is moved towards the observer the spot gets less bright, and a position can be found in which it is hardly distinguishable from the rest of the paper. On moving the paper still nearer the observer the spot becomes darker than the rest.

It will be found that the position in which the spot practically disappears is just halfway between the candles; and in this position the two sides of the paper, being at equal distances from two equal sources, are equally illuminated.

15. The Optical Bench. For the above experiments and many others which will be described later some form of optical bench is desirable. This consists of an arrangement by means of which a series of stands carrying various pieces of optical apparatus, such as a photometer disc, a lens or a mirror, can be made to slide backwards and forwards in a straight line. In most experiments the distances between the various pieces of apparatus are required. These distances are determined by means of a scale attached to the stand on which the uprights slide. A convenient arrangement for a bench is shewn in fig. 11.

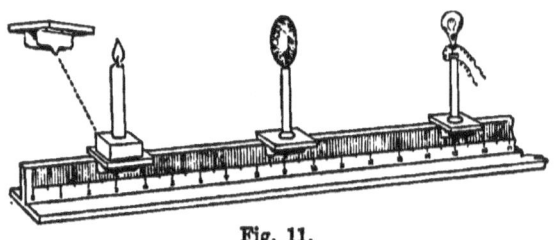

Fig. 11.

A number of rectangular blocks of wood can slide on a wooden bar some 2 or 3 metres in length. The section of the bar is like an inverted T; a scale of centimetres, or if desirable of millimetres, is fitted to the bar. Two pieces of brass plate bent to an Γ shape are screwed on to the under side of the sliding pieces. The vertical parts of these pieces clip the bar fairly tightly but allow the stands to slide. One of the brass pieces carries a pointer by which the position of the slide can be read on the scale.

To the upper side of these sliding pieces various stands are attached. One of these may be arranged to hold a lens, another a Bunsen disc or a cardboard screen, a third an incandescent lamp. Others again may be left flat, so that a piece of apparatus which it is wished to use can be clamped on to them. In any case care must be taken that the apparatus in each stand may be vertically above the pointer attached to the sliding piece; when this is secured the distance between the two pointers gives the distance between the two corresponding pieces of apparatus.

In using the bench as a photometer the Bunsen disc is mounted in the centre upright, and the two lights which are to be compared are secured to two slides. If one of the lights be a candle, a hole may be drilled of the same diameter as the candle in a rectangular block of wood, of such a size that the candle flame is at the same height as the centre of the disc. Set the candle at some convenient position on the bench. Suppose it to be at division 0. Place the gas-flame, if that be the second source, at the other end, suppose at division 300.

Place the disc between the two and slide it about until a position is found at which any difference between the grease spot and the rest of the paper ceases to be visible; let the slider be at division 58. Repeat the observations, looking at the disc alternately from opposite sides. The various positions found for the disc should not differ greatly; let the mean be 60. Then the distance between the disc and the candle is 60 cm., that between the gas-flame and the disc is $300-60$ or 240 cm. Thus the candle-power of the gas-flame is $240^2/60^2$ or 16.

16. Experimental verification of the law of the inverse squares. In the preceding sections on photometry we have assumed the truth of this law. The following experiment may be made to verify it.

EXPERIMENT (4). *To use Bunsen's photometer to verify the law of the inverse squares.*

Obtain five candles as nearly as possible alike. Mount four of these side by side on a block of wood—by drilling in the block four holes into which the candles fit—and the fifth on a separate block. If the candles are exactly alike we have two sources of light, one of which is four times as bright as the other. Place them on opposite sides of the Bunsen disc and adjust it until the grease spot disappears. It will be found that the four candles are about twice as far off from the disc as the one candle. Thus one candle at a certain distance from the disc produces the same illumination over the disc as four candles at twice the distance.

Now if the law of the inverse square does hold, the illumination due to a single candle at a distance $2a$ is $1/2^2$ or

1/4 of that due to a single candle at a distance a. Four candles then at a distance $2a$ should produce the same illumination as one candle at a distance a; the experiment shews that this is the case, thus the result of the experiment is in accordance with the law of the inverse squares.

A similar result may be obtained by using other combinations of candles.

EXAMPLES.

RECTILINEAR PROPAGATION OF LIGHT AND PHOTOMETRY.

1. What do you understand by the intensity of the illumination at a point, and how would you determine experimentally the law connecting the intensity of light with the distance from the source?

2. Describe and explain some way in which the intensities of two sources of light may be compared.

3. The gas supplied for public consumption is supposed to be of 18-candle-power: what does this mean, and how would you determine the candle-power of a particular gas-flame?

4. What is meant by the candle-power of a gas-flame, and how would you proceed to measure it?

5. Explain the action of the grease spot photometer. How would you prove that the illumination on any surface is inversely as the square of its distance from the source of light?

6. A gas-flame, when burning at the rate of 5 cubic feet per hour, placed at a distance of 100 inches from the screen illuminates it equally with a candle placed at 30 inches burning at the rate of 1 oz. in four hours. The gas costs 3s. 6d. per 1000 cubic ft., the candles 1s. per lb. Compare the cost of lighting a room with gas and candles respectively.

CHAPTER II.

THE VELOCITY OF LIGHT.

*17. The Velocity of Light. We have seen that light travels in straight lines. Römer discovered in 1656 that it travels with definite velocity. This velocity is very great, but still it can be measured. Sound also travels with a definite velocity, but its velocity is much less than that of light. The velocity of sound might be found by the following experiment. Two observers provided with good watches are stationed some miles apart. The one observer fires a cannon, noting the time at which the explosion occurs, the second observer notes the time at which he hears the sound. Thus the interval of time taken by the sound to traverse the distance between the two observers is known and hence the velocity of sound can be calculated. By observations similar to this it has been found that sound travels under ordinary conditions of the air at the rate of about 1100 feet per second. The velocity of light however is so great that a method such as the above would entirely fail to give any result. Light we shall shew takes only about 8·25 minutes to reach us from the sun. Hence the interval of time occupied by its passage between two stations on the earth would be practically inappreciable to any but the most refined methods of measurement; an acoustical experiment however will make Römer's method clear.

Let us suppose that a gun is fired from a fixed station at intervals of 15 minutes. An observer at some distance will hear the gun, also at intervals of 15 minutes provided he remains stationary, but suppose that immediately on hearing a report he walks towards the gun and that he has walked a mile when the sound of the second report reaches him. To reach the observer this sound has to travel 1 mile less than the sound of the first; sound takes about 4·8 seconds to travel a mile, hence the interval between the two reports will be only 14 min. 55·2 seconds instead of 15 min. On the other hand, if a second observer walks away from the sound at the same rate, the interval between the consecutive reports will be 15 min. 4·8 seconds, the difference between the two intervals being the time taken by the sound in travelling over the two miles which separate the observers in the two cases. Thus if the observer, from the observations at the first station, were to infer that the interval between the reports was 15 minutes and that, as he walked towards or from the gun, he would hear the consecutive reports at intervals of 15 minutes he would be wrong; in the first case the reports would come before the calculated time, in the second they would be after it. Had he calculated the time at which he would hear the eleventh report he would find himself in the first case $10 \times 4\cdot8$ seconds too late; this 48 seconds being the time which it would take the sound to travel the ten miles between the stations at which the man heard the first and the eleventh report. If now the man walks back, the interval between the calculated and the observed time will get less and less, and when he again reaches the first station the two will exactly agree; he would hear the twenty-first report exactly at the calculated time. If on the other hand the man walks in such a direction that the distance between himself and the gun is not altered the reports are heard throughout at the calculated times.

Now the earth as it moves round the sun is at a varying distance from Jupiter, and Jupiter has satellites or moons which move regularly round him, just as the moon moves round the earth. As one of these moons moves round Jupiter it is eclipsed by him about once every two days and disappears from the view of an observer on the earth. The time of revolution of the moon can be determined; hence the period between two successive eclipses is known and is found to be 48 hours 28 minutes 35 seconds. Now this period can also be directly observed.

Suppose that $ABCD$ (Fig. 12) represents the orbit of the

earth, S the sun, and J Jupiter. Let A be the point on the orbit furthest from Jupiter, C the point which is nearest to him. When the earth is at A or C it is moving at right angles to the line joining it to Jupiter, and the distance between the two does not alter greatly in the interval of two days between two consecutive eclipses, thus in these positions of the earth the observed interval between the eclipses is very nearly the same as the calculated interval of 48 hours 28 minutes 35 seconds.

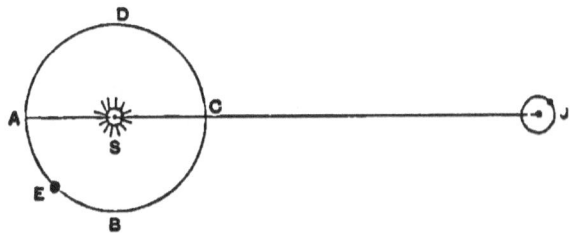

Fig. 12.

Taking then the observations near A the times at which the various eclipses throughout a year should occur can be calculated. But on making observations it was found that, as the earth moved from A through B towards C, the eclipses always happened in advance of the calculated time, and by the time the earth has reached C an eclipse occurred about $16\frac{1}{2}$ minutes before it was expected. As the earth during a second half-year travels back again to A, the observed times of eclipse approach their calculated value and the two agree when the earth is again at A. Compare this now with the illustration of the gun.

The observed effects are similar. The discrepancy between the observed and calculated times will be explained if it takes light $16\frac{1}{2}$ minutes to travel across the earth's orbit from A to C. Now this distance is about 296,000,000 kilometres or 184,000,000 miles, and it is traversed by light in 990 seconds.

Thus the velocity of light is 296000000/990 kilometres, or 184000000/990 miles per second, and this comes to be about 299,000 kilometres or 186,000 miles per second.

***18. Aberration of the Stars.** It was observed soon after the time of Römer that the apparent position of a star depended to a small extent on the position and motion of the earth in its orbit. Bradley shewed that this could be explained when the finite velocity of light was taken into account. The stars are seen in the direction from which the light appears to come. Now the direction in which anything appears to move depends partly upon the motion of the observer; thus if a bird be flying in the same direction as a train but at a less speed the bird will appear to an observer in the train to be going backwards; its apparent motion depends on that of the train.

Drops of rain falling on a still day descend vertically, but a man walking through the rain points his umbrella forwards; to him they appear to come from the front and to fall obliquely. The reason for this will be clear from an illustration. Let A (fig. 13) be a ball falling vertically and suppose an observer wishes to make the ball fall through a tube BC without contact with the sides. If the tube is at rest he must hold it vertically. Suppose however he wishes at the same time to move the lower end of the tube forward at a uniform rate, then it is clear that the tube must be held obliquely with its upper end pointing forward.

For let BC be the axis of the tube when the ball is just entering it at B. Let AA' be the vertical path of the ball, and let BC have come to $B'C'$ when the ball is at A'. $B'C'$ is parallel to BC. Then provided $B'C'$ passes through A' the ball will still be in the tube and would to an observer watching the tube appear to be moving straight down it. But it is clear that if the tube were originally vertical there could not at a future time be

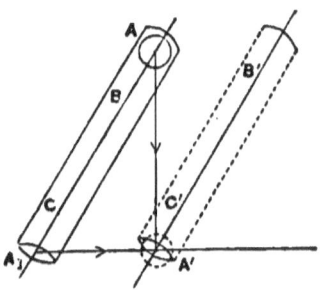

Fig. 13.

a point on its axis such as A' vertically beneath A; in order then that the ball may fall vertically and yet pass through the moving tube this must be held obliquely and to an observer moving with the tube the ball would appear to move obliquely and not vertically. Moreover if a horizontal line $A'A_1$ meet BC in A_1 then since a point on the tube moves through A_1A' while the ball moves over AA' we see that A_1A' is to AA' in the ratio of the velocity of the tube to the velocity of the ball.

Now suppose the tube BC to be the telescope, and A a star from which light is coming in the direction AA', the telescope is being carried forward by the motion of the earth, in order then that the light may travel down its axis it must be pointed not in the direction of the star but at an angle to it, and the inclination will depend on the ratio of the velocity of the earth to that of light. Now we know the velocity of the earth; if then we can observe the inclination between BC and the true direction of the light, the aberration of the star it is called, we can find the velocity of light. The best observations by this method lead to the value 299,300 kilometres per second.

This method as well as that of Römer depends on a knowledge of the dimensions of the earth's orbit; the velocity of the earth is calculated from a knowledge of its distance from the sun, and this distance is not known with very great accuracy. Hence it is desirable to have some means of finding the velocity of light which is independent of astronomical observations. Two such have been devised and will be described in outline.

*19. **Fizeau's Method for finding the Velocity of Light.** Let L (fig. 14) be a source of light and ABC a toothed wheel which can rotate in front of it. Let the light be so placed that the rays travelling to a distant point M have to pass through the intervals between the teeth, so that, as the wheel rotates, the light is alternately cut off by the teeth and allowed to pass through the spaces between them. At M a plane mirror is placed which reflects the light back to the wheel.

Suppose first that the wheel is at rest and in such a position that light can pass through a space and reach the mirror. It is there reflected back and passing through the same space may fall on the eye of an observer placed to receive it. He sees a bright spot in the mirror.

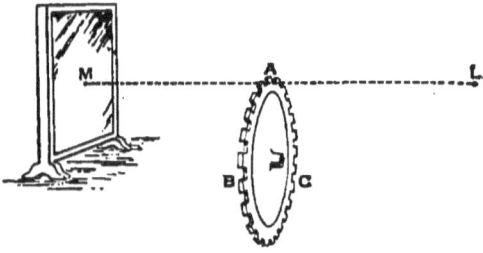

Fig. 14.

Now let the wheel be made to rotate at a uniform rate. It takes the light some time to travel from A to M and back again and it is possible so to adjust the speed of the wheel that by the time the light, which passed through any space, again arrives at the wheel a tooth shall have taken the place of that space; the result will be that the light will no longer pass through to the eye but will be stopped at the wheel, the bright spot seen before will now be eclipsed.

Thus if the wheel be turned so as to eclipse the bright spot we know that the light has travelled from A to M and back in the time taken by the tooth in coming into the position previously occupied by the space. If now the number of turns made by the wheel per second be known and also the number of teeth on the wheel, this time can be found and thus by measuring the distance AM, doubling it, and dividing it by the time the velocity of the light can be obtained. In some of Fizeau's experiments the distance AM was 8663 metres and the wheel had 720 teeth. Thus in 1/720th of a turn each tooth came into the position previously occupied by the tooth in front of it, while in $1/2 \times 720$ of a turn a tooth would come into the position previously occupied by a space. Now Fizeau found that the light was eclipsed when the wheel made 12·6 turns per second. Thus each turn took 1/12·6 seconds and teeth and adjacent spaces interchanged positions in

$$1/12\cdot6 \times 2 \times 720 \text{ second.}$$

This reduces to 1/18144 of a second, and in this time the light had travelled 2 × 8663 or 17326 metres.

Thus the velocity of light is from these experiments 17326 × 18144 or about 314000000 metres per second.

Cornu in 1876 using better apparatus found the value 300,400,000 metres or 300,400 kilometres per second.

The arrangement of apparatus actually employed is shewn in fig. 15.

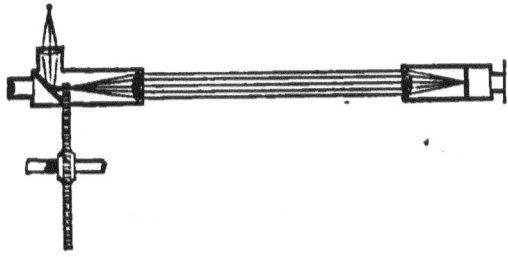

Fig. 15.

*20. **Foucault's Method.** In experiments by this method light from a small source, a narrow slit, S fig. 16, falls on a mirror R, is reflected to another mirror M, reflected back to R, and hence back to S if R remains fixed. The mirror R however can be made to rotate about a vertical axis, so that by the time the light again reaches it it has turned through a small angle into the position R'. The reflected beam therefore does not come back to S but to a neighbouring point S', and the distance SS' can be measured.

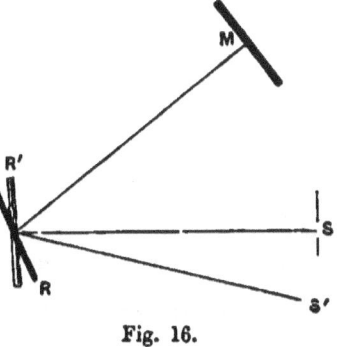

Fig. 16.

From this the angle turned through by the mirror, whilst the light has been travelling from R to M and back, can be found and hence, if the rate of rotation of the mirror be known, the time which it has taken the light to move over twice the distance RM is obtained. Knowing the distance RM we find the velocity of light[1]. By this method Michelson found the value 299,940 kilometres per second.

Summing up the results then we may say that light travels in a vacuum at the rate of about 300,000 kilometres per second.

21. The Nature of Light. Light then in a homogeneous medium travels in straight lines with a definite velocity; from our experiments we can obtain the conception of a ray of light as the straight path along which the light travels. Now other experiments which we are about to consider shew us that when light passes from one medium to a second the rays are bent out of their course at the surface of separation. They continue straight in the second medium, but they are inclined to their former direction; moreover some of the rays do not enter the second medium at all, they are reflected or bent back into the first and continue to pursue a straight path inclined at an angle to that which they previously followed. The laws of this reflexion and refraction have been established by experiment and we can learn much by attempting to develope their consequences. This constitutes the science of geometrical optics, and it is this branch of optics with which we have to deal at present.

We might go further and ask the question, What is light? Physical Optics deals with this, and we are taught by it that Light is radiant energy transmitted by the vibratory motion of the ether. The Science explains how it is that light travels in straight lines and what is meant by a ray; we learn from it that a single isolated ray, such as we sometimes conceive of in our mathematical reasoning, can have no existence by itself. It explains the causes of reflexion and refraction and enables us to deduce from some simple principles the laws which have

---

[1] The above gives merely the outline of the two methods and the figures are only diagrams to shew the path of the light. For further particulars see Glazebrook, *Text-book of Physical Optics*, Chap. XVI.

been discovered by experiment. We proceed therefore to state the laws, leaving for the present their explanation as a consequence of the wave theory of the ether, and merely deducing the geometrical consequences of the facts that light travels in straight lines which are reflected and refracted according to certain laws.

22. Graphical methods of solution. In a large number of the experiments which will be described graphic constructions will be found necessary; much can be learnt with the aid of a rule and a pair of compasses; a small set square is also useful. A large sheet of paper is pinned down to a drawing-board, and the plate or prism at whose surfaces reflexion or refraction is to occur is placed on it. The direction of an incident ray can be fixed by placing two pins upright on the paper and drawing a line through the points in which they stick into the board; the directions of reflected or refracted rays can be fixed in a similar way.

EXAMPLES.

THE VELOCITY OF LIGHT.

1. Explain carefully how it is inferred from observations on Jupiter's satellites that light travels with a finite velocity.

2. Describe the method adopted by Fizeau for determining the velocity of light.

3. How has it been shewn experimentally that the velocity of light is about 3×10^{10} cm. per second?

If the velocity of light were about $\frac{1}{1000}$ of the above value, what changes would take place in the apparent positions of the fixed stars at different times of the year?

CHAPTER III.

THE REFLEXION OF LIGHT.

23. Reflexion of Light. When a ray of light travelling in any medium falls on the polished surface of a second medium, part of the incident light is reflected according to certain laws.

Definition. *A line drawn from any point of a surface so as to be perpendicular to the surface at that point is called a Normal to the Surface.*

LAWS OF REFLEXION. (1) *The incident ray, the normal to the surface at the point of incidence, and the reflected ray lie in one plane.*

(2) *The angle between the reflected ray and the normal is equal to that between the incident ray and the normal.*

The plane which contains the incident and reflected rays and the normal to the surface is called the plane of incidence, the angle between the incident ray and the normal is the angle of incidence, that between the reflected ray and the normal the angle of reflexion; when the incident ray is perpendicular to the surface, thus coinciding with the normal, the incidence is said to be *direct*.

In many optical experiments the arrangements which are best suited for demonstration to a large class are not so well adapted for measurement purposes by the students, we shall generally describe briefly the arrangements for illustrating a demonstration and more fully the practical experiments which should be done by the students individually; the demonstration experiments will usually require a lantern of some form.

24. Verification of the Laws of Reflexion.

Arrange the lantern to give a narrow beam of approximately parallel rays. Fix a plane mirror at the centre of a graduated circle as in fig. 17, with its plane at right angles to that of the circle, and in such a way that it can turn about an axis in its own plane normal to the circle. The stand carrying the mirror should have a pointer attached, and the mirror should be adjusted so that this pointer may be at right angles to its plane. The end of the pointer moves over the graduated circle and the reading of the pointer gives the position of the normal to the mirror. Stretch a piece of oiled paper over a wooden frame which can rest on the plane of the circle and draw a vertical line with a pencil on this paper.

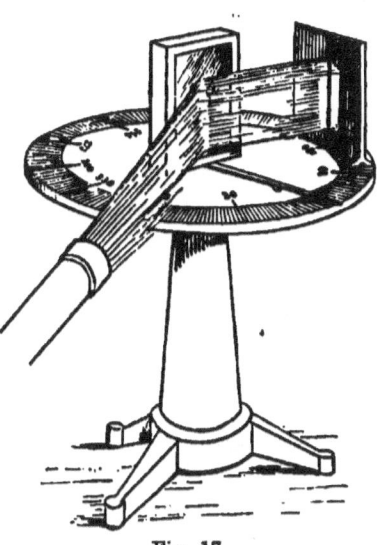

Fig. 17.

Place the paper with the vertical line over the division 0° of the circle and arrange the lantern so that the beam of light may fall centrally on the mirror, while the narrow vertical patch of light produced on the screen is bisected by the pencil line; thus the central ray of the beam passes over the division 0° of the scale and the angle found by reading the position of the pointer gives the angle of incidence. Move the screen about until the reflected beam falls on it and adjust it, keeping the foot of the pencil mark on the circle until the bright patch is again bisected by the pencil line; the position of the line now gives that of the central reflected ray. Read on the scale the position of the foot of the line, the angle between this and the pointer is the angle of reflexion, and will be found to be the same as the angle between the pointer and the incident ray. Thus if the reading of the incident ray be 0° and that of the pointer 30°, the reading for the reflected ray will be 60°.

With this apparatus a series of observations may be made, varying the angle of incidence and observing the corresponding angle of reflexion. The same apparatus can be used to shew that if a mirror on which light is incident in a given direction be turned through any angle the reflected beam is turned through twice the angle. For take a series of readings thus.

Reading of incident light 0°.

Reading of normal.	Reading of reflected light.
15°	30°
20°	40°
30°	60°
40°	80°

Thus while the normal and therefore the mirror turns through 5° from 15° to 20°, the reflected beam turns through 10° from 30° to 40°, or again while the normal and therefore the mirror moves over 25° from 15° to 40°, the reflected beam moves over 50° from 30° to 80°. This law may be shewn to be a simple consequence of the law of reflexion.

In order to verify the first law of reflexion arrange the apparatus so that the incident beam is horizontal and the plane of the circle also horizontal, it will be found that the reflected beam is also horizontal.

EXPERIMENT (5). *To verify the laws of reflexion.*

Fasten a sheet of paper on a horizontal drawing-board and place on this a piece of looking-glass arranged so as to be vertical. This is best done by securing the looking-glass on to one face of a rectangular block of wood. The wood can be laid on the paper and held in position with a weight, the lower edge of the looking-glass should just rest on the paper. Draw a line *ABC*, fig. 18, on the paper coinciding with the edge of the mirror. At *B* draw by aid of the set square a line *BD* at right angles to *AB*, then *BD* is normal to the mirror. Draw a third line *LMB* meeting the mirror obliquely at B making an angle of about 45° with the normal; at two points L, M of this line stick two pins vertically into the paper; look at the mirror obliquely, reflexions of the two pins will be seen; move your head about until when looking with one eye the reflexions of the two pins appear to be in the same straight line, so that the image of one pin is exactly behind that of the other. When this is the case stick a third pin into the board at N so that it may also appear in the same straight line as the two reflexions; join N to B. Then an incident ray falling on the mirror along LMB is reflected along BN.

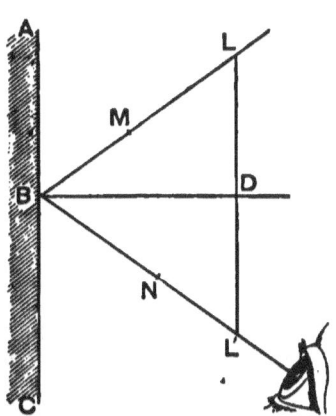

Fig. 18.

To shew that the angles of incidence and reflexion are equal, take a point L' on BN making BL' equal to BL and draw LL' cutting BD in D. Then it will be found by measurement that LD is equal to $L'D$, thus the triangles BLD, $BL'D$ are equal in all respects and the angle LBD is equal to $L'BD$. Moreover if LB be taken as an incident ray it is clear that the incident ray, the normal BD, and the reflected ray lie in one plane.

This may be shewn otherwise thus. Arrange the pins at L and M so that their heads may be at the same height above the board. Arrange the pin at N so that its head just covers the heads of the reflected pins: then the incident ray joining the heads of LM travels parallel to the board and it will be found that the head of the pin at N is at the same height above the board as those of the other two. Thus the reflected ray is also parallel to the board.

25. Images. It may often happen that a pencil of rays diverging from a point is caused by reflexion or refraction either to converge to or to appear to diverge from a second point. In either case the second point is called an *Image* of the first point.

Images may be either *real* or *virtual*.

Definitions. (1) *When a pencil of rays diverging from a point is made by reflexion or refraction to converge to a second point, that second point is called a Real Image of the first point.*

(2) *When a pencil of rays diverging from a point is made by reflexion or refraction to appear to diverge from a second point, that second point is called a Virtual Image of the first point.*

In the case of a real image of a point the rays which form it actually pass through it; in the case of a virtual image the rays which form it would, if produced backwards, pass through it, but do not actually do so.

The image of any *object* is made up of the images of the various *points* which form the object. Pencils of rays diverging from each of these points are made to converge to or to diverge from a series of images of those points, and this series of images constitutes the image of the object.

When rays diverging from an image fall upon the eye they produce vision of that image in the same way as if it were actually a source of light; if rays converging to a real image be allowed to fall on the eye before they reach the image, there will in most cases be no distinct vision produced, but only a general impression of luminosity; if on the other hand they be allowed to fall on the eye after they have converged to and when diverging from a real image they will produce vision of that image. Moreover, if a white screen be placed in the position of the real image the screen will scatter or diffuse the incident light in all directions, and the image will become visible from all points from which the screen can be seen, instead of merely from positions in which the light diverging from the image can reach the observer's eye.

The pins seen by reflexion in the last experiment are virtual images. Many other examples of both real and virtual images will be given later.

EXPERIMENT (6). *To find by experiment the position of the image of a point seen by reflexion in a plane mirror.*

Set up the plane mirror[1] as before on the drawing-board. Let AB, fig. 19, be its trace.

Place an upright pin in the board at L, and a series of pins M_1, M_2, etc. at intervals of about a centimetre against the front face of the glass. The figure and all such figures should be constructed on a much larger scale than can be shewn here; the point L being some 20 cm. from the glass.

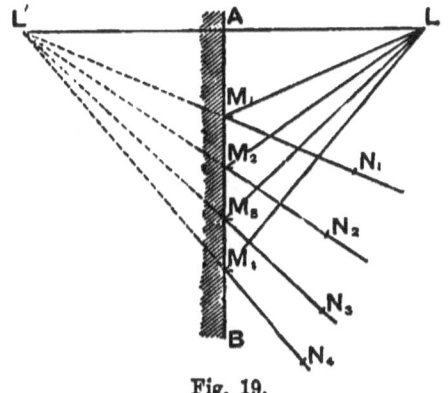

Fig. 19.

Join LM_1, LM_2, etc., thus drawing a series of incident rays. Look obliquely at the glass, moving the head until the reflexion of the pin L is seen in a straight line behind M_1, and place another pin N_1 in the board to cover these two, so that N_1, M_1 and the reflexion of L are in one line, then M_1N_1 is the reflected ray corresponding to the incident ray LM_1. Proceed thus for the various incident rays LM_2, LM_3, etc., placing in pins N_2, N_3 etc. so that M_2N_2, M_3N_3 are the

[1] If a silvered mirror be used for this it should be thin, otherwise error is introduced by the refraction through the glass; it is better to use the reflexion from the *front* surface of a thick rectangular block of glass, a block such as is used for a letter-weight will be found convenient. Care must be taken to avoid confusion with the images formed at the back. These may be avoided by covering the back face with a piece of black velvet or of moist blotting-paper.

reflected rays. Remove the mirror and draw the reflected rays by joining N_2M_2, N_3M_3, etc. Produce the rays backwards, it will be found that they meet at a point such as L'. Join LL' cutting the front of the mirror AB, or the front produced, in A suppose. Thus rays of light diverging from L appear after reflexion to diverge from L', hence L' is a virtual image of L. Moreover it will be found from the figure by direct measurement that LL' is perpendicular to the mirror and that $L'A$ is equal to LA.

Thus the image of a point formed by a plane mirror is virtual and its position is obtained by drawing a normal from the point to the mirror, and producing it as far behind the mirror as the point is in front of it. This result may be verified in the following way.

EXPERIMENT (7). *To verify the position of the image of a point formed by a plane mirror.*

Take two pins which are rather longer than the height of the mirror. Stick them upright into the board, one some way in front of, and the other behind, the mirror. On looking obliquely at the mirror, if the pins be suitably placed, it will be possible to see simultaneously the one pin reflected in the mirror and the second pin over the mirror. Now the second pin may be placed so that it appears from all positions from which it is visible to be a continuation of the image of the first which is terminated by the upper edge of the mirror. When this position is found, as the observer's eye is moved about, the two, the real pin and the image, do not separate, but remain continuous. Find by experiment this position, then it is clear that the second pin coincides with the image of the first. Draw on the paper, as in the previous experiment, the trace of the mirror and mark the positions L, L' of the two pins. Join LL' cutting the mirror in A. Then measurement will shew that LA is equal to $L'A$ and is perpendicular to the mirror. Thus the statement which we wished to prove is verified.

The last two experiments may be performed before a class by using apparatus on a large scale. Knitting needles held in suitable stands serve for the pins, or in the case of Experiment 7 two luminous objects such as two gas burners of the same height may be used. Two jucandescent lamps mounted on suitable stands serve very well. In this case a large sheet of plate glass should be used for the reflecting surface. One lamp is placed in front of the sheet, the other behind it, and the latter is adjusted until as viewed through the glass it coincides with the luminous image of the first. A slight error is introduced by the refraction through the glass, but it is very small if the glass be not too thick.

26. Geometrical construction to find the image, of a point, formed by reflexion at a plane surface.

Let AB (fig. 20) be the trace of the surface, P the luminous point. Draw PM perpendicular to the surface and produce it to P', making MP' equal to PM. Let PR be any incident ray. Join $P'R$ producing it to Q, then RQ shall be the reflected ray. Draw RN normal to the surface at R.

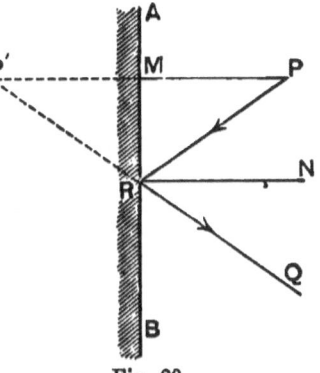

Fig. 20.

Then from the construction PR, RQ and RN are in one plane.

Also in the triangles RPM, $RP'M$, the side $PM = MP'$ and MR is common.

Moreover
the angle PMR = the angle $P'MR$,
both being right angles.

Thus the triangles are equal in all respects and
the angle RPM = the angle $RP'M$.

But since RN and MP are parallel,
the angle NRP = the angle RPM,
and the angle NRQ = the angle $RP'M$.

Therefore the angle NRQ = the angle NRP.

Hence RQ is in the same plane as the incident ray and the normal, and makes with the normal an angle equal to the angle of incidence.

Thus RQ is the reflected ray.

Now PR is any incident ray, hence the reflected ray corresponding to any incident ray passes through P'. Thus all the reflected rays pass through P'; hence P' is the image of P.

27. To trace the rays by which an eye sees a luminous point reflected in a mirror. Let AB, fig. 21, be the mirror, P the luminous point, E the eye. Draw PM perpendicular to the mirror and produce it to P', making MP' equal to MP. P' is the image of P. The light after reflexion appears to come from P'. Join the centre of the eye to P' cutting the mirror in R. A small cone of rays with $P'RE$ as axis, appearing to diverge from P' enters the eye and produces vision, the direction of the rays behind the mirror is shewn in the figure by dotted lines. The rays however really come from P; their directions then before incidence are found by joining to the source P the points where each ray respectively cuts the mirror. Thus join PR, then PR is the axis of the incident small pencil by which vision is produced, and the other rays of the pencil travel as shewn. The image is virtual.

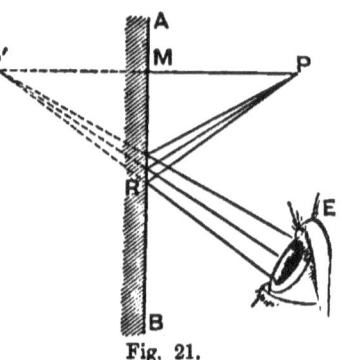

Fig. 21.

28. To trace the rays by which a luminous object placed in front of a mirror is seen. For this purpose we have merely to make a construction similar to that of the last section for each point of the object. Thus let the object be the arrow PQ, fig. 22.

Draw PP', QQ' perpendicular to the mirror, taking points P', Q' as far behind as P, Q are in front. P', Q' are the images of P and Q. Small pencils of rays, appearing to diverge from P', Q' respectively, reach the eye. The rays in these pencils really diverge from P and Q. Thus join to P, Q respectively the points where the lines joining the eye to P' and Q' cut the mirror. These lines give the path of the incident light.

The figure shews that in this case the image $P'Q'$ is of the same size as the object PQ, and is virtual.

A plane mirror produces a virtual image of an object of the same size as the object.

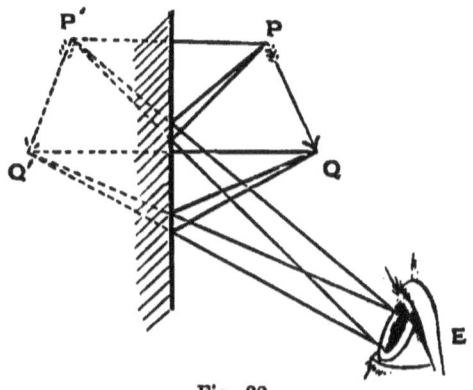

Fig. 22.

29. Lateral inversion due to reflexion. There is however a difference between the object and the image which must be noted. If an observer looks from E at the object the point P is towards his left hand side, Q towards his right hand; on the other hand in the image P' is to the right, Q' to the left. The image is inverted right to left. This is always the case.

The inversion may be illustrated by various observations. Thus draw the letter D on a sheet of paper and hold it near a vertical mirror with the straight side vertical and the convex side towards the mirror (fig. 23), looking at it from a position such that the mirror is on your left. The image seen is also the letter D with its convexity towards the mirror, that is towards the left hand of the observer.

Or again, hold up your right hand before a mirror with the palm facing the mirror, the image seen is a left hand. Note this by holding the left hand against the mirror with its palm towards your face.

Write your name in ink on a sheet of paper and while the

ink is wet press a sheet of clean blotting-paper on it, the writing on the blotting-paper is inverted. Hold up the blotting-paper with the writing towards the mirror; it is re-inverted and becomes legible.

Fig. 23.

30. Reflexion at two or more plane surfaces. If a ray of light after reflexion at a plane mirror falls on a second plane mirror it is again reflected according to the same laws. In finding the position of the image formed by this second mirror it must be remembered that the light when incident is travelling as though it came from the image formed in the first mirror. For the second reflexion then this first image must be treated as the source and the position of the second image found from it in the usual way.

(1) **Two parallel mirrors.** This case is sometimes exemplified in a room having two mirrors fixed on opposite walls. If a lamp or gas-light be placed between the two an observer looking into either mirror will see a long string of images.

(a) *To find the positions of the images formed by reflexion at two parallel mirrors and to trace the path of a ray reflected at the two.*

Let KL, MN (fig. 24) be the two parallel mirrors, P the source of light. Draw APB perpendicular to the mirrors and produce it in both directions. A ray PQ falling on the first mirror at Q is there reflected and appears to come from the image of P.

Take a point P_1 on PA produced making AP_1 equal to AP, P_1 is the image. Join P_1Q producing it to meet the second mirror in R; QR is the first reflected ray. After reflexion at R the ray comes from the image of P_1 in the second mirror MN.

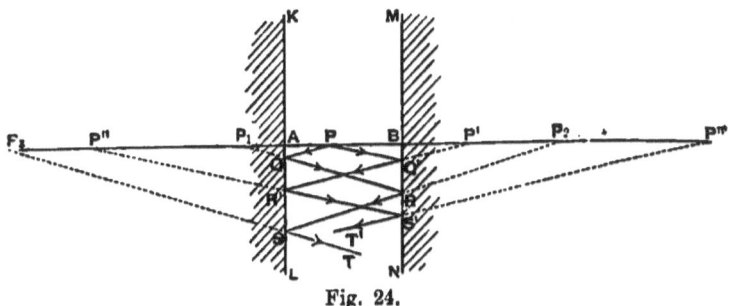

Fig. 24.

Take P_2 in PB produced such that $P_2B = P_1B$, then P_2 is the image of P_1 in the second mirror. Join P_2R, producing it to meet KL in S. RS is the ray reflected once at the second mirror. The ray is now again reflected in KL and comes from P_3 the image of P_2 in the first mirror, P_3 being a point on AB produced such that $P_3A = AP_2$. Join P_3S and produce it to T. Then ST is the reflected ray. We thus get an infinite series of images lying on the line AB, of these the eye only sees a limited number because light is lost after each reflexion and after a time the intensity of the reflected light becomes too small to cause vision. But we have started with a ray which was reflected first in the mirror KL. Some of the light may fall directly on the mirror MN, be reflected there and then reach KL. There will thus be a second series of images P', P'', P''' etc. such that P' is the image of P in MN, so that $BP' = BP$, P'' is the image of P' in KL, so that $AP'' = AP'$, and so on and there will be another series of reflected rays such as $PQ'R'S'T'$.

When the mirrors are parallel an infinite number of images can be formed; the light however is weakened at each reflexion and so the number visible is limited.

(b) *To trace the path of the rays by which the eye sees an object by reflexion in two parallel mirrors.* In this and similar cases it must be remembered that a small pencil of rays is always needed to produce vision. For the sake of clearness in the diagram however only the axis of the pencil is drawn.

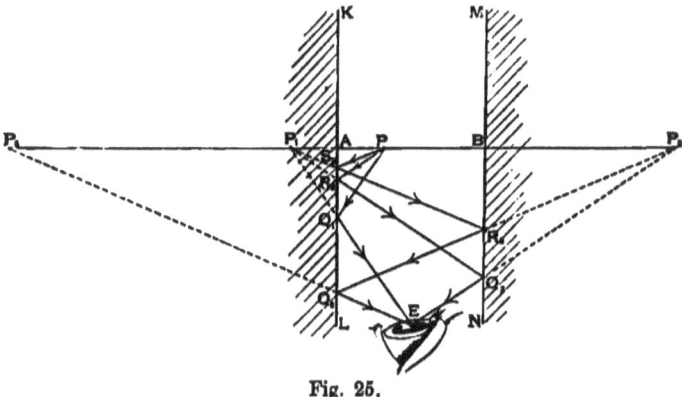

Fig. 25.

Determine the position of the images P_1, P_2, P_3 etc. as above.

In order to trace the rays by which P_3 is seen by an eye E, join E to P_3 cutting the mirror KL in Q_3. Q_3E is the axis of the pencil, P_3 is an image of P_2 and the ray Q_3E before reflexion was coming from P_2. Join P_2 to Q_3 cutting the mirror MN in R_3. P_2 is an image of P_1 and R_3Q_3 before reflexion was coming from P_1. Join P_1 to R_3 cutting KL in S_3. P_1 is the image of P and S_3R_3 before reflexion came from P. Thus the axis of the pencil by which the third image P_3 is seen is $PS_3R_3Q_3E$. In a similar manner the axes of the pencils by which any other images are visible can be determined. Thus for P_2 the path of the ray is PR_2Q_2E and for P_1 it is PQ_1E.

In all such cases the path is best traced by joining the eye to the image seen, joining the point where this line cuts the mirror to the previous image, and so on.

(2) **Two mirrors inclined at any angle.**

(c) *To find the position of the images formed by reflexion at two plane mirrors inclined at any angle.*

Let AO, BO (fig. 26) represent the mirrors meeting at O. Let P be the luminous point. Draw PM perpendicular to AO meeting AO in M and produce it to P_1 so that $P_1 M = PM$. Then P_1 is the image of P.

Now, in the triangles MOP and MOP_1, PM is equal to $P_1 M$ and MO is common, while the angles at M are right angles. Thus the triangles are equal and OP is equal to OP_1. Thus P and P_1 both lie on a circle with O as centre. Describe this circle with radius OP cutting the mirrors in A and B. Then we see that the arcs AP and AP_1 are equal. Now find P_2 the image of P_1 in the mirror B. We can shew in the same

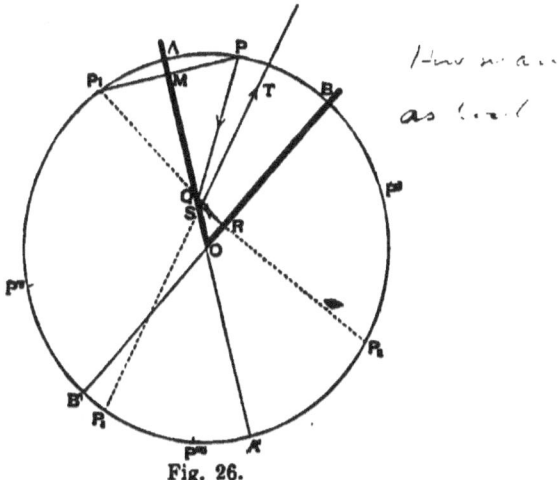

Fig. 26.

way that P_2 is on this circle and that the arc BP_2 is equal to the arc BP_1. Thus the images lie on the circle $APBA'B'$, $A'B'$ being the points in which AO and BO produced cut it—its circumference takes the place of the straight line in the first case—and their position is found by drawing the circle centre O radius OP and taking points P_1, P_2 etc. such that $AP_1 = AP$, $BP_2 = BP_1$, $AP_3 = AP_2$ etc.

The path of a ray is given by a similar construction to that already used.

Let PQ (fig. 26) be any ray cutting the mirror OA in Q. Join P_1Q cutting the second mirror OB in R. Join P_2R cutting OA in S. Join P_3S and produce it to T. Now suppose as in the figure that P_3 is the first image which falls between A' and B'. Then it is clear from the figure that P_3S must cut the mirror OB produced between O and B'. No ray therefore proceeding from P_3 can fall on the second mirror OB. There can therefore be no image of P_3 formed by reflexion in the second mirror and the number of images is limited. The limiting number depends on the angle between the mirrors, in Figure 26 as drawn it is three. In addition we have the images P', P'', P''' formed by rays which are first reflected in the mirror OB, making six altogether.

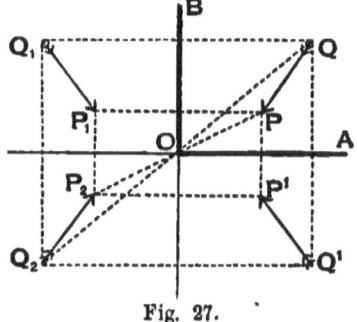

Fig. 27.

If the two mirrors were at right angles as in Figure 27 each series would contain two images but the second images of each series would coincide; this is shewn in Figure 27 at P_2Q_2.

(d) *To trace the rays by which the various images formed by two plane mirrors are seen by an eye looking into the angle between the mirrors.*

The method of doing this is exactly the same as that given above in (b) and the description applies using fig. 28 instead of fig. 25.

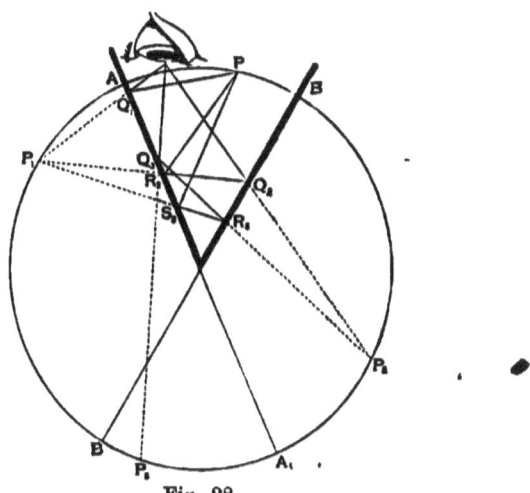

Fig. 28.

In fig. 28 P_1, P_2, P_3 are the images, and the axes of the pencils by which they are seen are respectively $PS_3R_3Q_3E$, PR_2Q_2E and PQ_1E.

31. Experiments on multiple reflexions. The results obtained by geometrical construction may be verified by various experiments. Thus:

(a) EXPERIMENT (8). *To shew that the images formed by reflexions from two plane mirrors lie on a circle.*

Fix to the table two sheets of glass with their planes vertical and inclined at any angle to each other, an angle of 50° or 60° will be convenient. Place a source of light in the angle between the two sheets. An incandescent lamp may be conveniently used for demonstration purposes. On looking into the angle between the mirrors a number of images are seen. Place a second similar object behind the glass and move it about until it coincides in turn with each of the images seen by reflexion. Measure in each case the distance of this object from the vertical line of intersection of the mirrors. These distances will all be found to be equal, and the same as the distance of the source from this vertical line of intersection. Thus the source and its images lie on a circle. The arrangement of the apparatus is shewn in fig. 29.

(b) **The Kaleidoscope.** If the angle between the glass plates be 60° five images will be seen, and these with the object will be arranged symmetrically with respect to the mirrors. This is made use of in the kaleidoscope; in its simplest form the instrument consists of two long narrow mirrors enclosed in a tube and inclined to each other at 60°. One end of the tube is formed by a piece of metal or cardboard with a hole at its centre, the other end of the tube is closed with a piece of ground glass. An observer looking

Fig. 29.

through the hole along the axis of the tube at any object on the glass would see a symmetrical six-fold pattern formed by the object and its five images in the mirrors. A number of pieces of coloured glass rest on the ground glass and can be shifted about by moving the tube. As this is done the pattern seen changes its arrangement.

In this case when the angle is 60° there are three images in each of the series such as $P_1 P_2 \ldots\ldots P'P''P'''$ etc., as shewn in fig. 26, but the third images of each series overlap, thus reducing the number seen to five, one of the five being really formed by two coincident images.

(c) Multiple images formed by a thick mirror.

Place a candle or lighted taper close in front of a mirror of thick glass and look somewhat obliquely at the mirror. A number of reflexions will be seen as shewn in fig. 30, of these the image nearest to the candle is fainter than the succeeding one which is the brightest of the series, the others gradually decrease in brightness. This first image is formed by light which is reflected from the front surface of the mirror; most of the incident light penetrates the glass being refracted at the first surface.

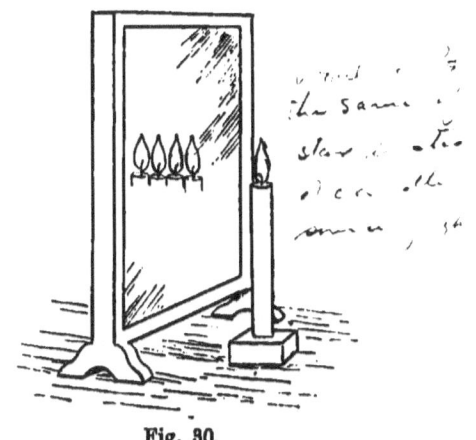

Fig. 30.

On reaching the silver at the back it is all reflected and most of it is again refracted out at the front, appearing to come

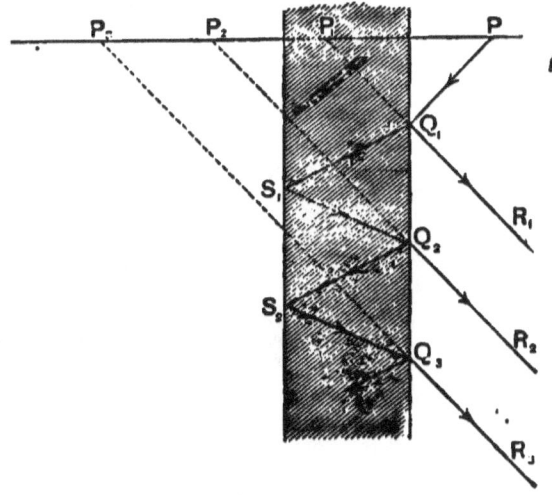

Fig. 31.

from the second and brightest image, some however is reflected back from the front surface of the glass and emerges after two or more reflexions at the silver.

The path of the ray and the approximate positions of the successive images are shewn in fig. 31. To obtain their true position a knowledge of the law of refraction is requisite.

EXAMPLES.

REFLEXION (PLANE MIRRORS).

1. Given the law of reflexion, prove that the image of an object in a plane mirror is on the perpendicular to the mirror and as far behind as the object is in front.

2. When a horizontal beam of light falls on a vertical plane mirror which revolves about a vertical axis in its plane, shew that the reflected beam revolves at twice the rate of the mirror.

3. A candle is placed in front of a thick mirror. On looking obliquely at the mirror several images are seen. Explain this and indicate in a figure the positions of the images.

4. Two mirrors are inclined to each other at right angles. Shew that three images of an object placed in the angle between the mirrors are formed, and draw the pencil of rays by which the second image can be seen by an eye looking at one mirror.

5. Two mirrors are placed parallel to one another at opposite ends of a room. Explain, with a diagram, the formation of the long series of images of an object between them seen on looking into either mirror.

6. Apply the laws of the reflexion of light to explain the series of images formed when an object is placed between two plane mirrors inclined at an angle to each other.

A ray of light is incident on the first mirror in a direction parallel to the second and after reflexion at the second retraces its own course: find the angle between the mirrors.

7. Find the angle between two mirrors in order that a ray incident on the first parallel to the second may after reflexion at the two be parallel to the first. Illustrate your answer by a figure.

8. Illustrate the laws of reflexion by the action of the kaleidoscope.

CHAPTER IV.

REFRACTION AT PLANE SURFACES.

32. Simple Experiments on Refraction. When a ray of light travelling in any medium falls obliquely on the surface of that medium part of the ray in general passes out into the medium beyond, but in so doing it is bent or refracted and the new direction of the ray differs from the old.

If the second medium is denser than the first the refraction takes place in such a way that the ray in the second medium lies nearer to the normal to the bounding surface than in the first, while, conversely, if the second medium is the less dense the ray in it is further from the normal than in the first.

The angle between the ray and the normal to the surface is less in the denser medium than in the less dense. This is illustrated in fig. 32, where AB represents the bounding surface, MRN the normal, and PRQ a ray passing from the upper medium, such as *air*, to a denser medium below, such as *water* or *glass*. The angle PRM between the ray and the normal in air is greater than the angle QRN between the ray and the normal in the glass.

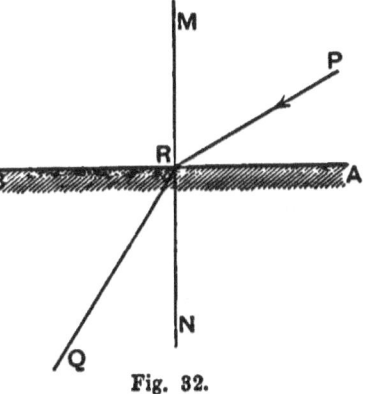

Fig. 32.

G. L.

EXPERIMENT (9). *To shew the refraction of light.*

(a) Take a bowl or vessel with opaque sides. Place some small object such as a coin at the bottom and move back from the vessel until the coin is just hidden below the upper edge of the side. Pour some water into the vessel; the coin is

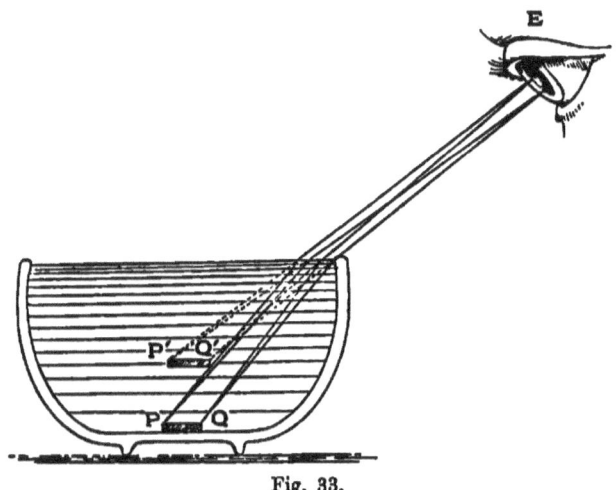

Fig. 33.

now visible. A pencil of rays from any point such as P, fig. 33, on the coin could not, before the water was poured in, reach the eye; when the vessel is filled the rays are bent down and enter the eye, appearing to diverge from a point such as P' nearer the surface than P. The whole coin is apparently raised and becomes visible.

(b) Arrange the lantern so as to produce a horizontal beam of parallel rays. Fill a rectangular glass tank with water and mix with the water a few drops of eosine or some other fluorescent substance. Reflect the rays from the lantern by means of a mirror downwards on to the surface. The path of the beam before entering the water will probably be easily visible through the motes in the air; if not it can be made visible by blowing some smoke above the surface of the water. The fluorescence of the eosine marks its path in the water and the refraction on entrance is clearly seen.

By arranging a graduated circle on one face of the tank in such a way that the beam is incident on the water along a line which passes through the centre of the circle, while the face of the tank carrying the circle is parallel to the direction of the rays, the angles of incidence and refraction can be measured.

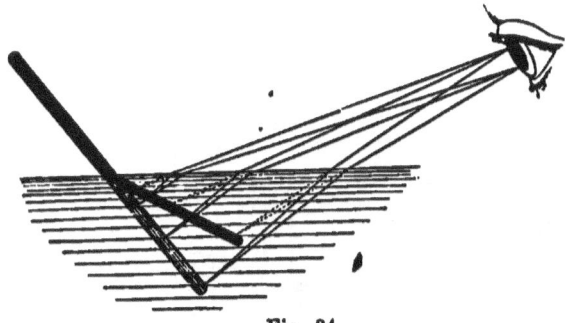

Fig. 34.

(c) Place a stick or pencil obliquely in a vessel of water and look at it sideways. The stick appears bent where it enters the water. The rays diverging from any point on the stick are refracted downwards where they meet the water and enter the eye appearing to diverge from a point nearer the surface. The part of the stick in the water is apparently raised, as shewn in fig. 34.

(d) In fig. 35, ABC is a semicircular trough of ground glass with vertical sides. The diametral side AB is opaque, but at the centre there is a narrow vertical slit S. The semi-circular side is graduated in degrees, starting from a zero division at C exactly opposite to the slit, and reading either way to 90 at A and B. Arrange the lantern to produce a narrow horizontal beam of light and allow this to fall obliquely on the slit. The light falls on the ground glass and a narrow vertical patch is produced as at P.

The angle which the ray makes with the normal to the

glass surface at S is given by reading the position of this patch P on the scale.

Pour some water or other liquid into the tank filling it about half full.

Two patches of light are now seen on the ground glass. The one Q, fig. 35, is formed by light which has traversed the liquid so that the arc CQ gives the angle of refraction, the other P is produced by rays which pass through the air above the liquid, so that CP measures the angle of incidence on the liquid[1].

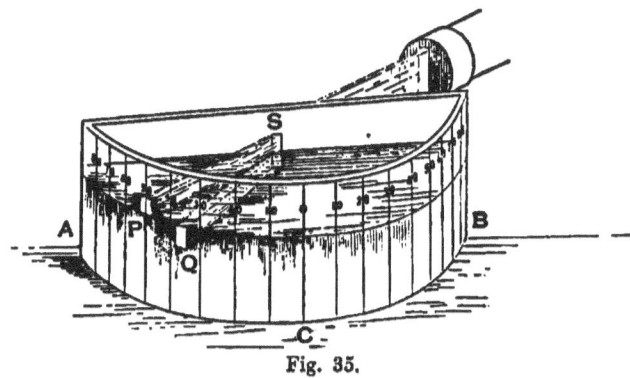

Fig. 35.

By varying the inclination of the tank to the beam of light we vary the angle of incidence and can thus obtain a series of values of the angle of incidence which we will denote by ϕ and the angle of refraction which we will call ϕ'. Such a series is given in the Table on page 53.

Such a series of observations will enable us to verify by means of some Trigonometrical Tables the law connecting ϕ and ϕ'. This law[2] was first stated by Snell, who shewed that

[1] It will be seen below §§ 41, 45 that provided the faces of the glass of the tank at S are parallel, the fact that the light has traversed this plate of glass does not modify the direction in which it travels in the liquid.

[2] The student who is not acquainted with Trigonometry will find the law stated in a geometrical form in Section 35. A knowledge, even though very slight, of a few Trigonometrical terms will be found useful. This may be obtained from the Introductory Chapters of any Elementary Trigonometry such as Hobson and Jessop's Treatise, *Pitt Press Math. Series.*

32–33]   REFRACTION AT PLANE SURFACES.   53

for two given media the value of the ratio $\sin\phi/\sin\phi'$, i.e. the ratio of the sine of the angle of incidence to the sine of the angle of refraction was constant for all angles of incidence.

In Table I. are tabulated in the first two columns the values of ϕ and ϕ', then the values of $\sin\phi$ and $\sin\phi'$, and in the fifth column the ratio $\sin\phi/\sin\phi'$ which is seen to be within the limits of the experiment the same for all the angles observed.

TABLE I.

ϕ	ϕ'	$\sin\phi$	$\sin\phi'$	$\dfrac{\sin\phi}{\sin\phi'}$
°	°			
30	22	·500	·375	1·33
45	32·30	·707	·537	1·32
60	40·30	·866	·649	1·33
75	46	·966	·719	1·34

Thus the experiments illustrate the refraction of light and have enabled us to deduce the law connecting the positions of the incident and refracted rays.

33. Laws of Refraction. Refractive Index.

The laws of refraction may be stated in a form resembling that adopted for the laws of reflexion.

(1) *The incident ray, the normal to the surface at the point of incidence, and the refracted ray lie in one plane.*

(2) *The sine of the angle between the incident ray and the normal at the point of incidence bears to the sine of the angle between the refracted ray and the normal a ratio which depends only on the two media and on the nature of the light*[1].

Let us denote by ϕ the angle of incidence, i.e. the angle between the incident ray and the normal, and by ϕ' the angle of refraction, i.e. the angle between the refracted ray and the

---

[1] The exact importance of these last words will appear later; see Section 107.

normal; then the law states that $\sin\phi/\sin\phi'$ is constant. Let us put this constant equal to μ, so that

$$\frac{\sin\phi}{\sin\phi'}=\mu.$$

Then μ is called the *Refractive Index* of the medium. To find the refractive index, then, we require to know the ratio of the sine of the angle of incidence to the sine of the angle of refraction.

If the medium from which the light is incident be air, then for all transparent bodies except some few gases μ is a quantity greater than unity.

VALUES OF THE REFRACTIVE INDEX.

Diamond	2·42	Fluor spar	1·43
Ruby	1·71	Carbon disulphide	1·63
Rocksalt	1·54	Turpentine	1·46
Crown Glass	1·50	Water	1·33

We shall see later (§ 107) that the values of the refractive index depend on the colour of the light. The above values are for yellow light.

According to the undulatory theory of light, the refractive index of a medium is inversely proportional to the velocity of light in that medium. Experiment shews this result to be true. Thus

$$\text{Refractive index from air to glass} = \frac{\text{velocity of light in air}}{\text{velocity of light in glass}}.$$

If we consider light travelling from glass to air, ϕ' being the angle of incidence in the glass, ϕ the angle of refraction in the air; then $\sin\phi = \mu \sin\phi'$ or $\sin\phi' = \frac{1}{\mu}\sin\phi$, and we may look upon $\frac{1}{\mu}$ as the refractive index from glass to air.

It may be noted that if we suppose that for reflexion the refractive index is -1, the law of reflexion is included in that of refraction; for we have

$$\sin\phi = \mu\sin\phi' = -\sin\phi' \text{ if } \mu = -1,$$
$$\therefore \phi' = 180 - \phi,$$

that is, the refracted ray is turned back into the first medium and the acute angle it makes with the normal in that medium is equal to the angle of incidence.

34. Geometrical Representation of the Law of Refraction. We can find the direction of the refracted ray geometrically in various ways. Thus

(1) Let PR, fig. 36, be an incident ray incident at R on a refracting surface ARB, and let MRN be the normal at R.

Let μ be the refractive index. With R as centre and any radius describe a circle $APBQ$.

Let the incident ray PR cut the circle in P. Draw PK perpendicular to the surface. Express μ the refractive index as a fraction, a/b suppose. Divide RK into a parts, a being the numerator of the value of μ. In RB take RL equal to b

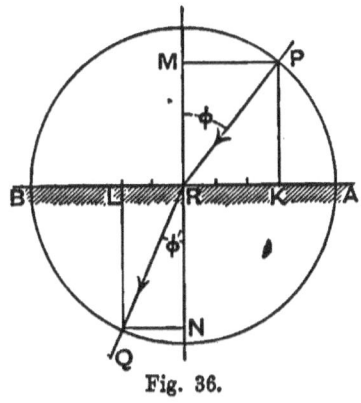

Fig. 36.

of the same parts, b being the denominator of the value of μ. Draw LQ in the second medium normal to the surface to meet the circle in Q. Join RQ; then RQ is the refracted ray.

The figure has been drawn to represent the case of light going from air to glass, for which $\mu = 1\cdot 5 = 3/2$, so that $a = 3$ and $b = 2$.

Thus RK is divided into three parts and RL contains two of these. The general construction just given may be described more briefly by saying that L is a point in RB such that $RL = RK/\mu$.

To verify this construction we may have recourse to a direct experiment, such as that described in Experiment 10, Section 35. We shall there see that if PR and RQ be an incident and refracted ray, P and Q being the points in which they cut respectively a circle with R as centre, and if

PM and QN be drawn perpendicular to the normal at R, then the ratio of PM to QN is constant for all directions of the incident ray.

Hence the ratio of the two perpendiculars PM, QN drawn to the normal from two points P, Q equidistant from R on the incident and refracted rays respectively, is a constant if the law of refraction is true; our experiment shews that this ratio is constant.

Now $PM = RK$, $QN = RL$. Hence
$$\frac{RK}{RL} = \frac{PM}{QN} = \mu = \text{a constant.}$$

Thus if the law be true $RL = RK/\mu$ which is what we assumed.

We may however also deduce the construction as a direct consequence of the law given in § 33. For from the above figure
$$\angle RPK = \angle PRM = \phi,$$
$$\angle LQR = \angle QRN,$$
$$\frac{\sin QRN}{\sin \phi} = \frac{\sin LQR}{\sin RPK} = \frac{LR}{RQ} \cdot \frac{RP}{RK} = \frac{LR}{RK} = \frac{1}{\mu},$$
for $RP = RQ$,
$$\therefore \sin QRN = \frac{\sin \phi}{\mu}.$$

But if ϕ' is the angle of refraction, then
$$\sin \phi' = \frac{\sin \phi}{\mu},$$
$$\therefore QRN = \phi',$$
the angle of refraction, that is RQ is the refracted ray. Clearly also a ray in the glass travelling along QR will emerge along RP.

(2) The following is a second construction.

Let PR, fig. 37, be an incident ray. Draw PL normal to the surface ARB. Produce RP to P', so that $RP' = \mu RP$. With R as centre and RP' as radius describe a circle cutting LP produced in Q'. Join $Q'R$ producing it to Q, then RQ is the refracted ray. To prove this make $RQ = RP$, and draw PM, QN perpendicular to MRN the normal at R; let $Q'M'$ also perpendicular to the normal meet it in M'. Then $RP = RQ$, $Q'M' = PM$, and the triangles QRN and $Q'RM'$ are similar.

Therefore

$$\frac{QN}{RP} = \frac{QN}{RQ} = \frac{Q'M'}{RQ'} = \frac{PM}{RP'},$$

$$\therefore \frac{PM}{QN} = \frac{RP'}{RP} = \mu \text{ by construction.}$$

Hence the perpendiculars on the normal at R from P and Q, two points equidistant from R, bear to each other a constant ratio, and this is one form of the law of refraction.

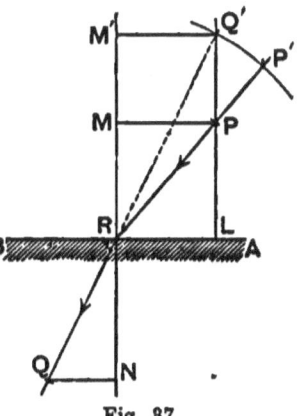

Fig. 37.

The trigonometrical proof is as follows:

$$\frac{\sin QRN}{\sin \phi} = \frac{\sin Q'RM}{\sin PRM} = \frac{\sin RQ'L}{\sin RPL}$$

$$= \frac{RL}{RQ'} \cdot \frac{RP}{RL} = \frac{RP}{RP'} = \frac{1}{\mu},$$

$$\therefore \sin QRN = \frac{\sin \phi}{\mu},$$

or $QRN = \phi'$, the angle of refraction.

*(3) The following construction is sometimes useful. With R the point of incidence as centre and radii RA, RB such that $RB = \mu RA$, describe two circles, fig. 38. Draw the incident ray PR cutting the circle with radius RA in P. Through P draw LPQ' normal to the surface to meet the second circle in Q'. Join $Q'R$ and produce it to Q, then RQ is the refracted ray. This construction it is clear is practically the same as that given in (2) above.

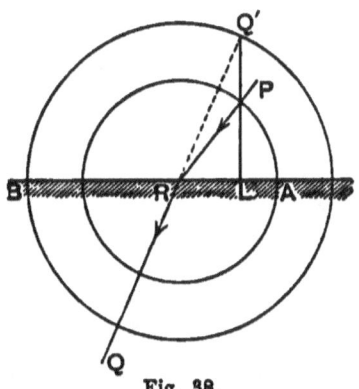

Fig. 38.

(4) The following is a mechanical arrangement devised by Sir George Airy to illustrate the law. In fig. 39, RN is

58   LIGHT.   [CH. IV

a straight rod representing the normal to the refracting surface. A rectangular bar of thin brass is convenient. To this a sliding piece R' is attached which can move up and down the rod. At R a rod PRQ' is pivoted and R' Q' are joined by a third rod pivoted at R' and Q'. The lengths RQ', $R'Q$ are such that $R'Q'/RQ' = \mu$ the refractive index. $R'Q$, RQ are two other rods pivoted at R, Q and R', such that $RQ = R'Q'$, $R'Q = RQ'$.

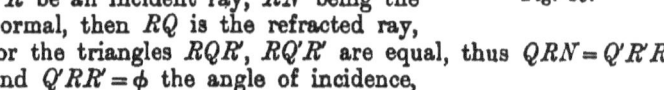

The various rods may be thin strips of brass or tin, and the pivots consist of loosely fitting rivets fastening them together.

If R' be put in any position and PR be an incident ray, RN being the normal, then RQ is the refracted ray, for the triangles RQR', $RQ'R'$ are equal, thus $QRN = Q'R'R$ and $Q'RR' = \phi$ the angle of incidence,

Fig. 39.

$$\therefore \frac{\sin QRR'}{\sin \phi} = \frac{\sin Q'R'R}{\sin Q'RR'} = \frac{Q'R}{Q'R'} = \frac{1}{\mu},$$

$\therefore \sin QRR' = \dfrac{\sin \phi}{\mu}$ or RQ is the refracted ray.

35. Experiments on the Law of Refraction.

EXPERIMENT (10). *To verify the law of refraction.*

Fix a sheet of paper to a drawing-board as in Experiment (5). Take a rectangular slab of glass, such as is sometimes used for a letter-weight, its dimensions may conveniently be 10 × 7·5 × 2·5 c.cm., though these are not important if the slab is large enough. Place it flat on the board and rule or scratch a vertical line on one of the vertical faces. This and the opposite face should be polished. Mark on the paper with a pencil the positions of the foot of this line and of the front surface of the glass. Look at the line obliquely through the front surface of the glass and mark with a vertical pin the point on the front surface of the glass through which you are looking. Stick another pin vertically in the board so that it, the first pin and the line on the back surface as seen through the glass may appear to be in the same straight line. Then a ray in the glass which passes from the foot of the vertical line to the foot of the first pin will after refraction into the air pass through the foot of the second pin. Remove the glass.

Let $ABCD$, fig. 40, represent the trace of the glass on the paper, Q the foot of the vertical line, R the foot of the first pin and P that of the second. Then QR is a ray in the glass which after refraction into the air travels along RP and conversely PR on refraction becomes RQ. Draw NRM the normal to the surface at R. Notice that the refracted ray is bent from the normal in passing from glass to air.

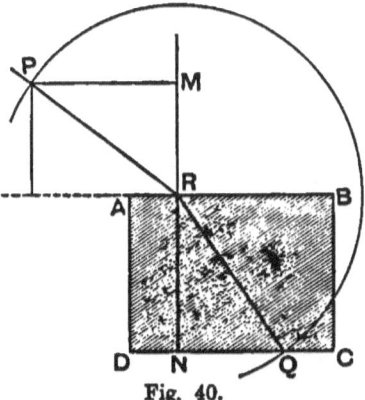

Fig. 40.

With R as centre and RQ as radius[1] describe a circle cutting RP in P. Draw PM perpendicular to the normal MN.

Measure PM and QN and take their ratio. This, if the law of refraction holds, measures the refractive index and should be the same for all angles of incidence, i.e. for all positions of R on the front face. To verify this repeat the experiment, placing the pin against a different point of the front face. It will be found that the ratio of the perpendiculars corresponding to PM, QN respectively is always constant. This ratio measures the refractive index for glass, it will be about 1·5. Hence we may enunciate the law of refraction thus.

LAW OF REFRACTION. *Let P, Q be two points, on an incident*

[1] If the block is not of some thickness so that RQ may be of considerable length such as 10 cm., it is better to produce it backwards and describe a circle of larger radius, the construction can then proceed in a similar way.

and refracted ray respectively, equidistant from R the point of incidence, PM, QN perpendiculars on the normal at R. Then the ratio PM/QN is invariable for all directions of the incident ray[1].

36. Deviation caused by refraction. Whenever a ray of light falls obliquely on a refracting surface and is bent out of its course it is said to be deviated. The deviation is measured by the angle between the directions of the ray before and after refraction. Thus, let PR, fig. 41, be a ray incident at R and refracted along RQ. Produce PR to P'. The ray was travelling before refraction in the direction RP'; after refraction it is moving in the direction RQ. Thus it has been deviated from RP' to RQ, the deviation is $P'RQ$. Draw the normal MRN. Then if ϕ, ϕ' are the angles of incidence and refraction

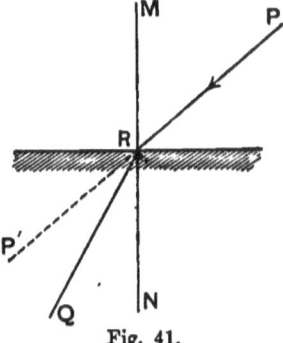

Fig. 41.

$$P'RN = PRM = \phi.$$
$$QRN = \phi'.$$
Deviation $= P'RQ = P'RN - QRN$
$$= \phi - \phi'.$$

37. Total reflexion. We have been dealing mainly, up to the present, with the refraction of light from a medium such as air into one which is optically denser such as glass or water. The geometrical constructions and the results will apply in general to the case of light travelling from glass or water to air. Under certain circumstances however, there is in this case a peculiarity to be noted. Consider first a ray of light entering glass from air; as the angle of incidence is increased, the angle of refraction also becomes greater. Now let PR, fig. 42, be a ray in air which almost grazes the surface ARB of the glass and let RQ be the corresponding refracted ray. Let MRN be the normal at R. A ray travelling in the

---

[1] Various other experiments illustrating the law of refraction can be performed in a similar manner. For an account of some of these see Glazebrook and Shaw, Practical Physics, Section O.

glass along QR will be refracted out into the air along RP. And any ray in the glass such as Q_1R falling between QR and NR will also emerge as RP_1 between RP and RM.

But consider now a ray such as Q_2R between QR and the surface of the glass. Since the angle which this ray Q_2R in the glass makes with the normal is greater than that made by QR, the angle which the emergent ray corresponding to Q_2R

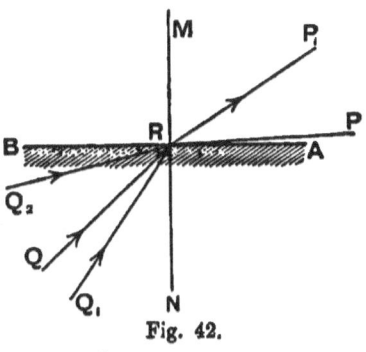

Fig. 42.

should make with the normal must be greater than that made by RP, the emergent ray corresponding to QR. Now this ray RP just grazes the glass and is at right angles to the normal NR. It is impossible therefore to have a ray making with the normal an angle greater than that made by RP; it is impossible, that is, to find a refracted ray corresponding to Q_2R. Some of the light falling on the glass along such a ray as QR or Q_1R is reflected at the surface of the glass, *some* of it is refracted out; *all* the light travelling along a ray such as Q_2R is reflected, *none* is refracted.

This phenomenon, which only occurs when light is travelling from a denser to a rarer medium, is known as Total Reflexion.

Definition of the Critical Angle. *If a ray is travelling in any medium in such a direction that the emergent ray just grazes the surface of the medium, the angle which it makes with the normal is called the critical angle.*

If a ray makes with the normal an angle less than the critical angle it can emerge from the denser medium; if it makes with the normal an angle greater than the critical angle it can not emerge; all the light travelling in the direction of the ray is totally reflected.

38. Experiments on Total Reflexion. (a) Fill the rectangular tank used in Experiment 9 with water containing a little eosine. Arrange the lantern to throw a horizontal beam of light on to a mirror from which it can be reflected upwards as in fig. 43, so as to fall obliquely on one of the vertical faces of the tank. When the angle of incidence on this face is considerable, the angle between the refracted ray and the normal to the horizontal surface of the water is not greater than the critical angle, the light can emerge and casts a bright patch on a screen placed to receive it. Tilt the mirror so as to decrease the angle of incidence on the first face.

Fig. 43.

The angle which the refracted ray makes with the normal to the horizontal surface is increased and can be made greater than the critical angle. The light ceases to emerge at the top of the water and is all totally reflected and its path can be seen in the water.

(b) Look at a small gas flame or other object at some distance through a tank or vessel with flat parallel sides containing water. Make a second small flat glass vessel with parallel faces[1]. Immerse this in the water with its glass faces vertical and parallel to those of the tank, arranging it so that it can be turned about a vertical axis. The light can be seen through the glass vessel. Turn it round its axis so that the angle at which the light falls on the air enclosed in the vessel is increased. On reaching a certain inclination the transmitted light disappears and the gas flame ceases to be visible. The angle of incidence on the air film has just reached the

[1] This may be done by cutting four pieces of wood about 7·5 × 1 × 1 cm., arranging them to form a rectangle, and cementing with red lead a piece of glass on both faces.

critical angle; turn the vessel back again, the light reappears and vanishes again as the rotation is continued and the critical angle on the other side of the normal is reached. If a graduated circle be attached to the apparatus so that the position of the glass vessel can be noted, the angle through which the vessel must be turned from the first position at which the light vanishes to the second can be measured. Half this angle will be the critical angle for light travelling from water[1] into air.

(c) Place a test-tube in a vessel of water with the closed end downwards; hold it obliquely and allow the light to fall on it in a horizontal direction. On looking downwards on to it the surface of the tube is as bright as a mirror; the light cannot pass from the glass into the air in the tube but is totally reflected up. Pour water into the tube, the reflexion ceases, the part filled with water looks dark by the side of the bright belt between the water in the tube and that in the vessel.

39. Conditions for total Reflexion. Refer again to the construction by which in Section 34 (1) the path of the

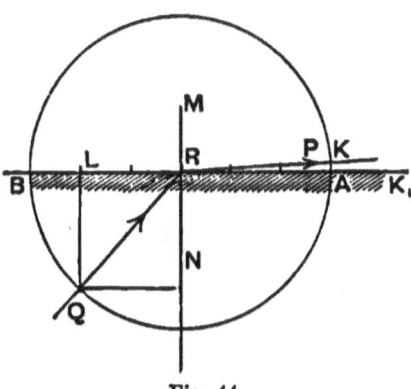

Fig. 44.

[1] It is true that the light has not travelled directly from water to air but has traversed the glass. If the faces of this are parallel however, the refraction through the glass plate makes no difference in the result. See Section 41.

refracted ray corresponding to a given incident ray is found, and let us apply it to the case of a ray going from a more dense to a less dense medium. We should, as in fig. 44, take QR as the incident ray and draw QL perpendicular to the surface, then make $RK = \mu RL$ and draw KP to meet the circle through Q in P. RP would then give us the refracted ray.

Now in fig. 36 the point P can be found, but since μ is greater than unity RK is greater than RL. Thus RK may be equal to or greater than RA. If RK is just equal to RA the point P will just coincide with A and the emergent ray will, as in fig. 44, just graze the surface. In this case the angle of incidence at R from the glass is the critical angle, and we have

$$RQ = RA = RK = \mu RL = \mu QN$$

and if $\overline{\phi}$ is the critical angle, then

$$\overline{\phi} = QRN, \quad \sin \overline{\phi} = \frac{QN}{RQ} = \frac{1}{\mu}.$$

Thus the critical angle is the angle whose sine is $1/\mu$; hence if the refractive index is known the critical angle can be found; and conversely if the critical angle be observed the refractive index can be calculated.

Suppose now it happens that L is so near to B that RK or μRL is greater than RA, then K will be to the right of A as at K_1, fig. 44, and a perpendicular to the surface at K_1 will not meet the circle. No point such as P can be found; there will be no refracted ray. For instance, in the case of glass let (fig. 44) $RL = \frac{2}{3} RA$. Then since for glass

$$\mu = 3/2 \quad RK = \mu RL = RA, \text{ and } \sin \overline{\phi} = \frac{1}{\mu} = 2/3 = \cdot 666.$$

Whence $\overline{\phi} = 41°.\ 45'$.

Thus the critical angle for glass is 41°. 45', so that if light be incident on glass at a greater angle than this it is totally reflected, none is refracted.

The relation between the critical angle and the refractive index is given directly thus. We have $\sin \phi = \mu \sin \phi'$, thus ϕ' is greatest when ϕ is greatest.

Now the greatest possible value of $\sin \phi$ is when $\phi = 90°$, and then $\sin \phi = 1$. Thus the critical angle $\overline{\phi}$ which is the greatest value of ϕ' is given by

$$\mu \sin \overline{\phi} = 1$$

or

$$\sin \overline{\phi} = \frac{1}{\mu}.$$

TABLE OF CRITICAL ANGLES.

Diamond	24°.25	Fluor spar	44°.20
Ruby	35°.50	Carbon disulphide	37°.50
Rock salt	40°.30	Turpentine	43°.15
Crown glass	41°.45	Water	48°.45

The brilliance of a diamond or ruby is partly explained by these figures. In consequence of the small value of the critical angle, there is inside a diamond a great amount of total reflexion, and as a result the directions in which light incident on any given face can emerge are few, and a large quantity of light is condensed into any one of these directions.

40. Consequences of total reflexion. (a) To an eye placed under water, all external objects appear concentrated into a certain conical space, the vertical angle of the cone being twice the critical angle. For let E, fig. 45, be the eye, P an object which is visible just above the surface, a ray from P which can reach the eye grazes the surface of the water and is refracted as at R along RE.

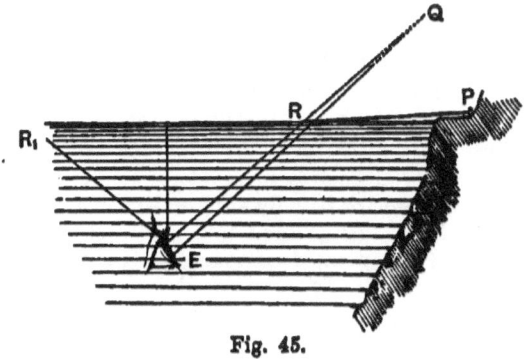

Fig. 45.

Now the angle which RE makes with the vertical at E is the same as the angle of refraction at R, and since PR is grazing the surface this angle is the critical angle. The object P will appear raised, being visible as at Q in the direction ER. Any object above P will be raised above Q, and the apparent directions in which all external objects can be seen will be included between ER and a line ER_1, equally inclined to the vertical at E, but on the other side of it, the same will occur in any other vertical plane through E and all the lines such as ER will form a cone whose vertical angle RER_1 is twice the critical angle; the only light which can reach the eye from points outside this cone is light which has entered the water, been reflected from objects below the surface and again reflected to the eye from the under side of the surface. Since for water the critical angle is 48°.45' we see that to an eye under water all external objects will be crowded into a conical space having this for its semi-vertical angle.

(b) The critical angle for crown glass is, we have seen, 41°.45'. If light travelling in glass fall on the surface at a larger angle than this it is totally reflected. This is made use of in a total reflexion prism. For let ABC, fig. 46, be a section of a prism of glass, the angles at A and B being each 45°. Consider a ray falling normally on the face AC, it enters the glass and is incident on AB at an angle of 45°, which is greater than the critical angle. All the light therefore is totally reflected and emerges in a direction perpendicular to the face BC. In this case the reflected ray is at right angles to the incident, but total reflexion prisms can be made having equal angles at A and B, differing from 45°. All that is necessary is that they should be greater than 41°.45'.

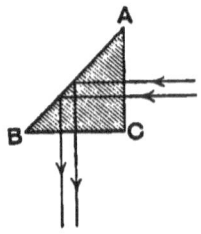

Fig. 46.

The advantage of such a surface over a plane mirror lies in the fact that a mirror usually has two surfaces, the silvering being on the back. Some light is reflected from both these surfaces and in many cases confusion is caused by the two images thus formed. To obviate this, good mirrors are necessarily silvered in front but then the surface tarnishes easily. By means of a total reflexion prism complete reflexion of the light is secured without any trouble from either of these causes.

(c) The luminous cascade affords an example of total reflexion.

A glass vessel such as a two-necked receiver is fitted with a tube or nozzle which should be at least a centimetre in diameter. The vessel is placed with this in a horizontal direction, and by means of a supply tube from a tap it is kept filled with water. The water escapes in a curved jet from the nozzle. The lantern is arranged so as to project a narrow beam along the axis of the nozzle tube. The light falls everywhere on the surface of the water at an angle greater than the critical angle, none of it therefore is regularly refracted out of the jet but the whole is reflected down the jet which appears brilliantly luminous.

41. Refraction through a plate of a transparent medium. By a *plate* of a medium is meant a portion of the medium bounded by two parallel planes. Light falling on such a plate is refracted on entering and again on emerging. By the first refraction it is deviated or bent from its course; by the second refraction it is again deviated, but this second deviation is equal in amount to the first and is in the opposite direction to it. The consequence is that the ray emerges from the plate in a direction parallel to that of the incident ray. There is on the whole no deviation; the ray is displaced laterally but not bent out of its course. This is shewn in fig. 47. $ABCD$ is the plate. A ray PR incident at R is refracted along RQ and

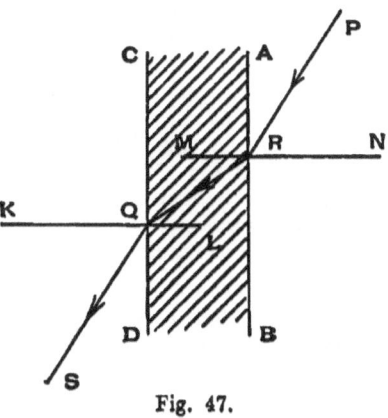

Fig. 47.

meets the second surface at Q, and being again refracted there, it emerges along QS. Then QS will be parallel to PR. For, draw the normals MRN, KQL, the angle of incidence RQL at Q is equal to the angle of refraction QRM at R. Hence the angle of emergence SQK must be equal to the original angle of incidence PRN. Now RN and QK are parallel, hence PR and QS are parallel.

42. Refraction through a prism. If a portion of a medium have two plane faces which are inclined to each other at an angle, it is called a *prism*. A plane at right angles to these faces is the principal plane of the prism.

A book standing upright on the table on its edge and closed is a plate; if it be open so that the two covers are vertical, but inclined to each other, it is a prism. The table which is at right angles to the covers is a principal plane. When dealing with the passage of light through a prism we shall suppose the rays to lie in a principal plane.

The angle between the two plane faces is spoken of as the angle of the prism.

Let BAC, fig. 48, be a prism. A ray of light PQ falling on it at Q is refracted along QR and emerges after refraction at R. We can find the path of the ray by determining, as in Section 35, the path of the refracted ray QR, refracted at Q and then the path of RS refracted out at R. In this case PQ produced and RS are

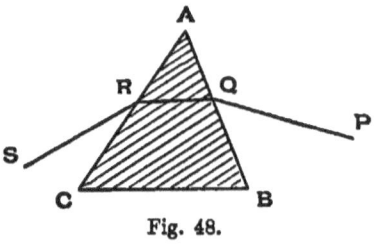

Fig. 48.

not parallel but inclined, the ray is deviated by traversing the prism and we notice that in the figure the ray is turned from the edge to the base or thicker part of the prism.

We can shew by calculation or by carefully drawn figures as well as by direct experiment that whenever light is refracted through a prism denser than the surrounding medium the deviation is from the edge towards the thick end.

43. Observations on refraction through plates or prisms.

(a) Open the window; place an upright stick near it and a second some distance within the room in such a position that the two sticks and some well-defined mark outside are in one straight line, i.e. so that an observer looking from behind the second stick sees the first stick just in front of the mark. Close the window and observe again; unless the glass is bad, the two sticks and the mark are still in a line; the light now passes through the window glass which is a plate, but it emerges from it in the same direction as it entered it.

(b) Arrange a narrow vertical slit in the slide holder of the lantern and form an image of this on the screen. Place a plate obliquely in the path of the light, arranging it so that some of the rays can pass over the top of the plate. The image of the slit will appear broken, the light which passes through the plate being displaced laterally. Move the screen further away, the distance between the images does not change; the rays which traverse the glass travel after emergence parallel to those which pass over it.

Replace the plate by a prism, selecting one of a small angle, i.e. one in which the two faces are nearly parallel—the reason for this will appear in Section 107. Two images are again seen but they are considerably separated—the one formed by light passing through the prism will also be slightly coloured. Moreover as the screen is moved further away the separation between the two images increases; the light forming the two is not travelling parallel to the incident light which passes over the top. Turn the prism round a vertical axis, the refracted image moves on the screen, approaching the image formed by the direct light but never coinciding with it; then as the rotation continues, moving away again in the opposite direction. When the two are as close together as possible the deviation is the least possible, the prism is said to be in a position of minimum deviation. Notice that in all cases the light is turned towards the thick end and away from the edge of the prism.

(c) Repeat the observations by looking directly at a source of light, which may be a small gas jet, or preferably a slit cut in a sheet of tin or other metal and placed in front of a gas-burner. With a plate the slit will appear in the same direction as before, but by arranging to look at the slit partly through the plate and partly above it, the slight lateral displacement will be observed. Replace the plate by a prism. On looking in the same direction as before, the slit is no longer visible. If the prism be close in front of the observer's eye with its edge on his left hand he must look to the left to see the slit, and conversely if the edge be to the right the observer must look to the right. For the first case the emergent light is bent towards the right, i.e. away from the edge; it appears therefore to come to the observer from the left (fig. 49 a); in the second case the converse is true, the light is bent towards the left, appearing to come from the right (fig. 49 b).

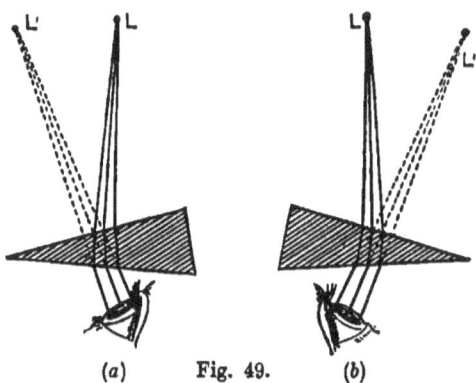

(a)　　Fig. 49.　　(b)

In each case L is the true position, L' the apparent position of the light.

44. Experiments on refraction through plates and through prisms.

EXPERIMENT (11). *To trace the path of a ray through a plate and to shew that there is no deviation.*

Lay the plate used in Experiment (10) flat on a sheet of paper fastened to the drawing-board and mark its outline $ABCD$ (fig. 50) on the paper.

Put two pins P, P' into the board in such a position that the line joining their feet may meet the glass obliquely as at R. Look at the pins through the opposite face CD of the plate and stick two other pins S, S' into the board so that the four pins may appear to be in the same straight line. Join SS' and produce it to meet the face of the glass in Q. Then

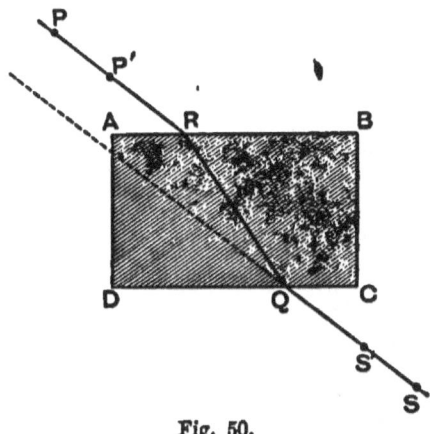

Fig. 50.

a ray incident along PR is refracted through the glass along RQ and emerges along QS. Remove the glass and join RQ. The path of a ray through the glass is thus traced. Produce SS' backwards. It will be found that SS' and PP' are parallel. The ray emerges parallel to its direction before incidence; there is no deviation; it is only displaced laterally.

EXPERIMENT (12). *To trace the path of a ray through a prism and to find the deviation.*

Repeat the last experiment, using a prism in place of the plate. The path of the ray will be as shewn in fig. 51. Produce PR to T. Produce SQ cutting RT in O. Then it will be found that however the ray is incident, provided

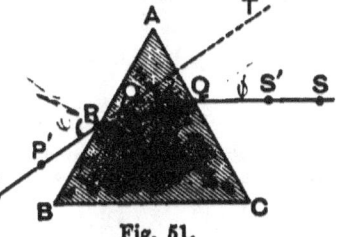

Fig. 51.

that it can emerge from the glass and is not totally reflected at the face AC, it is turned as in the figure from the edge A.

The ray is deviated through the angle TOS. Measure this with a protractor[1], let it be D. Measure also i the angle of the prism, and ϕ and ψ the angles which the incident and emergent rays make with the normals at R and Q. Then it will be found that $D + i = \phi + \psi$. Moreover if the normals at R and Q be drawn, the angles ϕ', ψ' between the ray in the prism and these normals can be measured and it will be found that they satisfy the relation

$$\phi' + \psi' = i.$$

These formulae can also be obtained from the figure by geometry.

*EXPERIMENT (13). *To measure the refractive index of the prism.*

Turn the prism so as to alter the angle of incidence at R. It will be found in general that the direction of the emergent ray is altered; the eye will have to be moved in order to see the pins in line. Suppose that the deviation is such that the eye, with the rays as in fig. 51, would need to be moved to the right so that S in the new position comes nearer to T. The change has made the deviation less than before. Continue to turn the prism in the same direction. S continues at first to move towards T, but after a time this motion ceases and S now recedes from T. Determine the position of the prism for which S is as close as possible to T and trace a ray through the prism in this position. The deviation now has its minimum value, D_1 suppose, and it will be found by measurement that in this position ϕ and ψ the angles of incidence and emergence are equal, so that we have

$$\phi = \tfrac{1}{2}(D_1 + i).$$

Moreover ϕ' and ψ' are also equal. Thus

$$\phi' = \tfrac{1}{2}i.$$

Now if μ be the refractive index

$$\mu = \frac{\sin \phi}{\sin \phi'} = \frac{\sin \tfrac{1}{2}(D_1 + i)}{\sin \tfrac{1}{2} i}.$$

---

[1] Graduated circles printed on cardboard divided to degrees can now be had in various sizes. One of these cut in two along a diameter makes a useful protractor for measuring angles.

Thus we can calculate the refractive index by observing the angle of the prism and the minimum deviation even when we cannot trace the path of the ray graphically.

*EXPERIMENT (14). *To measure the angle of a prism optically.*

Place the prism on the paper and draw its trace. Stick a pin P (fig. 52) into the board at a distance of about 30 cm. from the edge of the prism in such a position that the line PA joining it to the vertex is approximately equally inclined to either face. Look at the face AB and obtain an image of

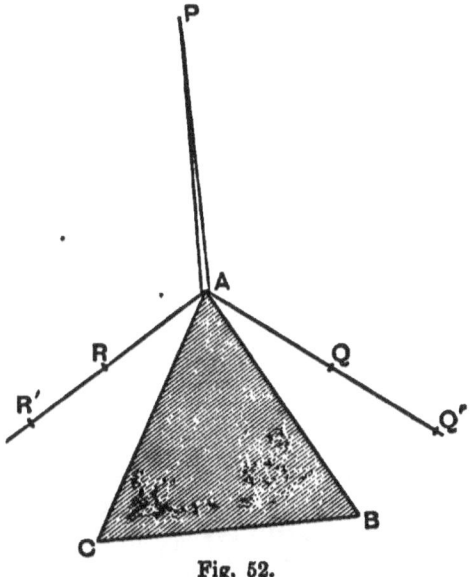

Fig. 52.

the pin by reflexion in it, placing the eye so that the image coincides as nearly as possible with the edge A of the prism. Stick two pins Q, Q' into the board, so that these two pins and the image are in a line. Join QQ' cutting the face of the prism close to A. Join PA; the ray PA is reflected along AQ. Proceed in the same way with the ray AR reflected from the other face of the prism. Measure with the protractor the angle QAR, it will be found to be twice the angle of the prism. Now it is often possible by various means to measure accurately the angle between two rays reflected respectively like AQ and AR from the two faces of a prism when the angle between the faces themselves cannot be measured. In such a case the angle between the faces can be found by halving that between the rays.

The formulae which have been used in the last Sections may be proved mathematically as follows.

In fig. 53 let PA be an incident ray falling just at the edge of the face AC. Produce PA to S, then by the law of reflexion

$$CAS = CAQ, \therefore QAS = 2CAS.$$
Similarly $RAS = 2BAS, \therefore QAR = 2BAC.$

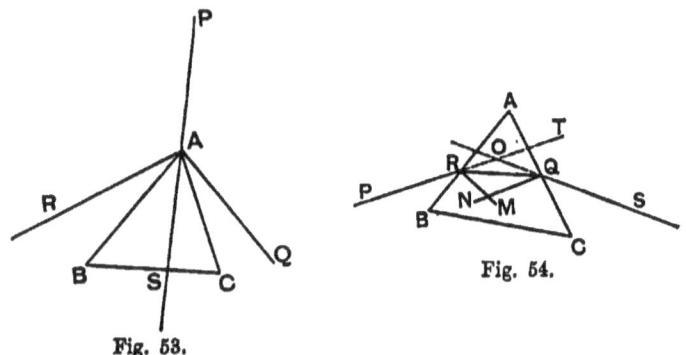

Fig. 53.

Fig. 54.

Again in fig. 54 draw RM, QN normals at R and Q meeting at M.
Then $RMQ + RAQ =$ two right angles
and $RMQ + RMN =$ two right angles.
Hence $RAQ = RMN = MRQ + MQR,$
$$\therefore i = \phi' + \psi'.$$
Also $D = QOT = ORQ + OQR$
$$= ORM - QRM + OQM - RQM$$
$$= \phi - \phi' + \psi - \psi' = \phi + \psi - (\phi' + \psi')$$
$$= \phi + \psi - i.$$

45. To find the image of a point formed by direct refraction at a plane surface. We have seen that in the case of reflexion from a plane surface rays which diverged from a point before incidence diverge also after reflexion from a second point the image of the first. We proceed to enquire whether a similar result is true for refraction.

Let P (fig. 55) be a point from which rays diverge and fall on a plane refracting surface. Let PA normal to the surface be one of these rays. This ray falls on the surface normally and is transmitted in the same straight line, PA produced will be the direction of the refracted ray. Take a ray PR incident obliquely at R. Determine as in Section 35 the direction of the refracted ray. For this purpose produce RP to P' making $RP' = \mu RP$, where μ is the refractive index, and with R as centre, RP' as radius, describe a circle, cutting AP produced in Q'; then $Q'R$ produced is the refracted ray.

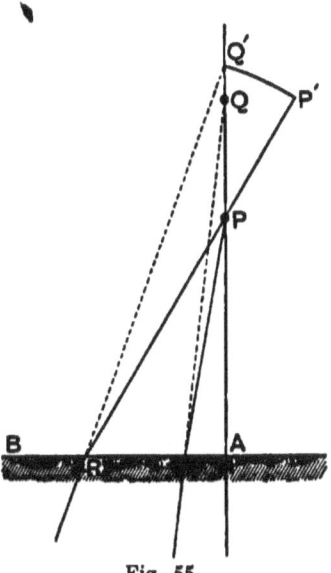

Fig. 55.

Now if this construction be made carefully for a number of incident rays diverging from P and falling at various angles on different points of the surface, it will be found that the refracted rays do not all pass through the same point but that they intersect the line APQ' in a series of points; there is strictly speaking no geometrical image of the point P. If however we confine ourselves to a small pencil of rays falling almost normally on the surface in the neighbourhood of the point A, the foot of the normal from P, we shall find that the corresponding refracted rays all pass very nearly through one point Q on AP produced; there is in this case a point which we may call the geometrical image of P. To find its position we have always $RQ' = \mu RP$, PR being any incident ray; now Q is the position of Q' when R is very close to A, and then RP is very nearly equal to AP and RQ to AQ so that we have approximately $AQ = \mu AP$. Thus a small pencil of rays from P, the axis of which is incident normally at A, diverge after refraction from Q, a point on AP produced, such that $AQ = \mu AP$. In this case Q is called the geometrical image of P. Thus if u be the distance of a point from the surface, v the distance of its image formed by direct refraction;

we have $\qquad v = \mu u.$

An eye situated in the second medium receiving the light from P would see Q; the rays would enter it as though they diverged from Q, not from P. The image would in this case be further away than the object; the object would appear more distant than it is. On the other hand if the object P were in the more dense medium, the rays on emergence would be refracted away from the normal. The point Q will be above P, if μ

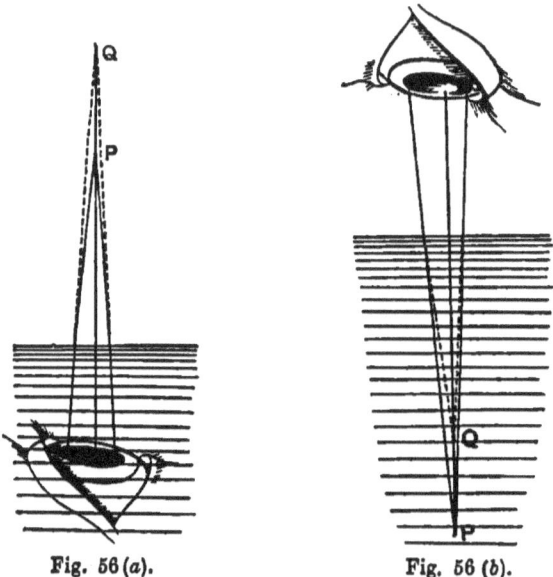

Fig. 56 (a).   Fig. 56 (b).

be the refractive index from air into the denser medium, we have

$$AP = \mu AQ \text{ or } AQ = \frac{1}{\mu} AP.$$

The two cases are shewn in figure 56 (a) and (b). It is in consequence of this, that a pool of water looks less deep than it is really.

The conclusions just stated are it must be remembered only true for a *small* pencil of rays incident nearly normally. This can be seen readily by drawing a figure carefully on a large scale. The pupil of the eye is small compared with the distance of a point which we can see distinctly, and the rays which enter it are all very close together. There are however many cases in which the rays do not fall normally on the refracting surface, but strike it obliquely as in fig. 57. In this case the rays from any point of the object after refraction pass less nearly through a point than they do when the incidence is direct. It can be shewn that when we are dealing with a small pencil such as can enter the eye, the rays pass

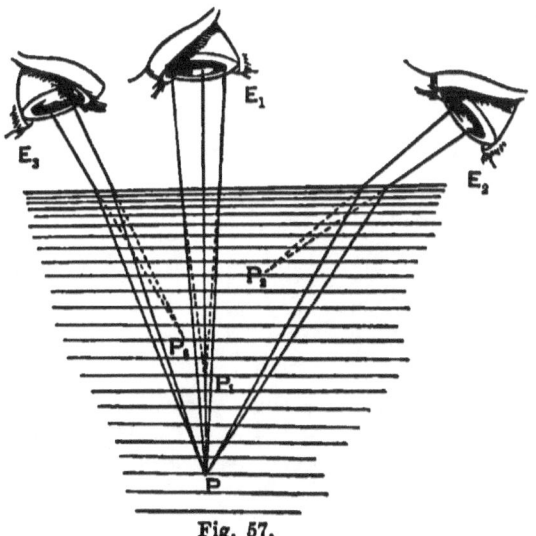

Fig. 57.

very nearly through a small circle called the circle of least confusion. The image of an object seen by oblique refraction is thus made up of a series of small circles of least confusion corresponding to the various points of the object and is less perfect than when the incidence is direct.

Moreover as the eye moves, the pencil of rays by which any point is seen changes, and the position of the image is correspondingly altered. Thus the apparent positions of a point P under water seen by an eye in the positions E_1, E_2, E_3 respectively will be P_1, P_2, P_3.

EXPERIMENT (15). *To verify the position of the image formed by refraction at a plane surface and to find the refractive index of a plate.*

(a) Let $ABCD$ (fig. 58) be a vertical section of the glass block already used in EXPERIMENTS 10, 11. Make a mark P at the back of the glass. This can be done by sticking a bit of gummed paper on to the glass or by means of a little sealing-wax. Stick a pin into the board, the head of the pin being at the same height above the board as the mark. Look at the front face of the glass directly, from behind the pin, with the eye placed at a slightly higher level than the top of the pin. The mark will be seen through the glass, and also the image of the pin reflected in the front face. Move the glass backward or forward until the apparent position of the mark and the reflected image coincide.

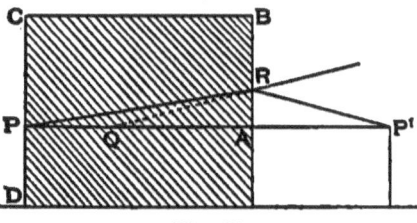

Fig. 58.

Test the coincidence by slightly shifting the eye about. Let P' be the top of the pin and let Q be the image of the pin and of the mark P. Then PQP' is a straight line normal to the front of the glass, let it cut it in A. Then since Q is a reflected image of P', $AQ = AP'$, and since Q is an image of P formed by direct refraction, if the formula established at the beginning of this Section be true, $AP = \mu AQ$.

$$\therefore AP = \mu AP',$$

and $\mu = AP/AP'$.

Measure the distances AP, AP', their ratio will give the refractive index; if this be known, the experiment affords a verification of the formula; if the formula be assumed, the experiment enables us to find the refractive index.

*(b) The experiment can be arranged rather differently thus[1].

A magnifying-glass or microscope, which can be adjusted vertically and the height of which above the table can be measured, is needed. An object can be seen distinctly through such a glass only when it is at a definite distance, depending on the lens, from the microscope; see Section 101.

Place a piece of paper with a cross on it on the table and focus the microscope on the cross. Place a plate of glass on the paper between the mark and the lens of the microscope; the cross is no longer visible but on raising the microscope it comes into view. Measure the distance the microscope is raised, let it be a. Place a bit of paper on the upper surface of the glass. Raise the microscope again until this is seen and measure the distance the microscope is moved in this second operation, let it be b.

In fig. 59 let P be the cross, P_1 the image of P in the upper surface, as seen through the glass and A the point in which PP_1 cuts the surface, L_1, L_2, L_3 the three positions of the lens. Then

$$L_1L_2 = a, \quad L_2L_3 = b.$$

Since the points P, P_1, A are all seen in turn we know that the distances

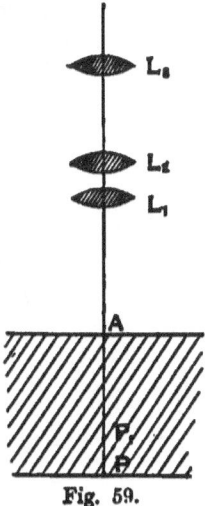

Fig. 59.

[1] See Glazebrook and Shaw, *Practical Physics*, Section 21, p. 383.

80   LIGHT.   [CH. IV

of these points from the respective positions of the lens are equal.

Thus $\qquad L_3A = L_2P_1 = L_1P.$

Hence $\qquad PP_1 = a, \quad P_1A = b, \quad AP = a + b.$

But since P_1 is the image of P we have
$$AP = \mu AP_1,$$
$$\therefore \mu = \frac{AP}{AP_1} = \frac{a+b}{b} = 1 + \frac{a}{b}.$$

Thus the refractive index is found by observing a and b.

*46. To determine the geometrical image of a point seen by direct refraction through a plate.

Let P (fig. 60) be the point, $ABSR$ the plate. Draw PAB normal to the plate. Let q be the geometrical image of P formed by refraction at the upper surface, then
$$Aq = \mu AP.$$
The rays in the plate are diverging from q and fall on the second surface; they then diverge from Q the geometrical image of q in this second surface and we have
$$BQ = \frac{1}{\mu} Bq,$$
or $\qquad Bq = \mu BQ.$

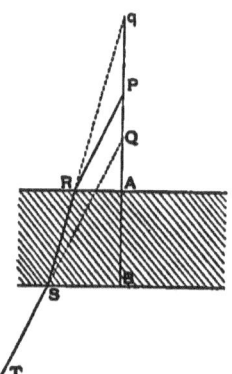

Also if the thickness of the plate AB be a, then
$$Bq = Aq + a,$$
$$\therefore \mu BQ = \mu AP + a,$$
or $\qquad BQ = AP + \frac{a}{\mu}.$

Fig. 60.

$$AQ = BQ - a = AP + \frac{a}{\mu} - a.$$
$$= AP - a\frac{(\mu - 1)}{\mu}.$$

REFRACTION AT PLANE SURFACES.

Thus the virtual image Q seen through the plate is nearer to the plate than the object P, the distance between the object and image being $a(\mu - 1)/\mu$.

This can be verified experimentally thus: Place a block of glass on the drawing-board and fix behind it a pin or needle rather taller than the glass. Place another pin in a clip in a vertical position and at such a height that its lower end is just above the level of the upper surface of the glass. View the first pin directly through the glass and adjust the second so that it may be exactly above the image of the first seen through the glass. The first pin is in the position P, the second in the position Q of figure 60. Measure the distance between the pins, let it be b and the thickness of the glass a. Then we have seen that

$$b = a\frac{(\mu - 1)}{\mu},$$

or
$$\frac{1}{\mu} = 1 - \frac{b}{a}.$$

For glass μ is about $3/2$; hence b/a is about $1/3$ or the distance between the pins about a third of the thickness of the plate.

Thus an object seen through a plate is apparently brought nearer by an amount which depends on the thickness and on the refractive index of the plate.

*EXPERIMENT (16). *To trace a ray through a series of plates in contact.*

Obtain two plates of different materials, such as ordinary crown glass and some very dense flint glass. Place one of them on the drawing-board and trace a ray through it as in Section 35.

Let $ABCD$, fig. 61, be the plate, $PQRS$ the path of the ray. Place the second plate as shewn in the figure at $CDEF$ so that the emergent ray may traverse it and trace its path as before, let it be RTU. Trace a second ray $P'Q'$, parallel to PQ, through the second block only. Let its path be $P'Q'R'S'$. Then it will be found that the three emergent rays RS, TU, $R'S'$ are all parallel, and that the two rays RT, $Q'R'$, in the second plate one of which has entered it from the first medium the other from air, are also parallel. It follows from this that the path of a ray in any medium is the same in direction whether the ray has entered the medium (1) directly from air, or (2) after traversing a plate of some other medium. Thus in experiment (*b*) of Section 38 in which light traverses water, then a glass plate and then a layer of air, the direction in the air is the same as it would be if the glass plate were removed. The experiment therefore gives the critical angle between water and air, the refraction through the glass does not affect the result.

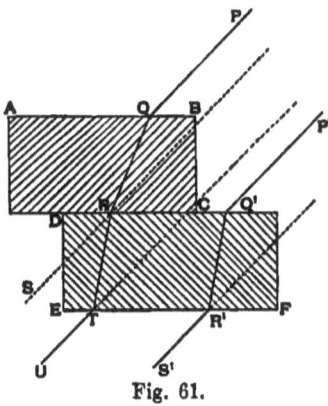

Fig. 61.

This result also enables us to calculate the refractive index between two media, say water and glass, if we know the indices between some third medium, such as air and the other two respectively. For in fig. 61 let ϕ be the angle of incidence at Q or Q', ϕ_1 the angle of refraction at Q, ϕ_1 is also the angle of incidence at R. Let ϕ_2 be the angle of refraction into the second medium at R, then since $Q'R'$ and RT are parallel ϕ_2 is the angle of refraction at Q'.

Let $_a\mu_\beta$ be the refractive index from air to the first medium at Q, $_a\mu_\gamma$ the refractive index from air to the second medium as at Q', $_\beta\mu_\gamma$ the refractive index from the second to the third medium as at R.

Then from the definition

$$\frac{\sin \phi}{\sin \phi_1} = {_a\mu_\beta}, \qquad \frac{\sin \phi_1}{\sin \phi_2} = {_\beta\mu_\gamma},$$

$$\frac{\sin \phi}{\sin \phi_2} = {_a\mu_\gamma}.$$

Hence multiplying the first two together,

$$_a\mu_\beta \cdot {_\beta\mu_\gamma} = \frac{\sin \phi}{\sin \phi_1} \times \frac{\sin \phi_1}{\sin \phi_2} = \frac{\sin \phi}{\sin \phi_2} = {_a\mu_\gamma}.$$

Hence
$$_\beta\mu_\gamma = \frac{_a\mu_\gamma}{_a\mu_\beta},$$

or, putting this in words,

If A, B, C denote the three media, then the refractive index from B to C is equal to the refractive index from A to C divided by the refractive index from A to B. Thus the refractive indices of water and glass from air are respectively 4/3 and 3/2. Hence the refractive index from water to glass is equal to $(3/2) \div (4/3)$ or 9/8.

The above result is obvious if we assume that the refractive index measures the reciprocal of the ratio of the velocities of light in the two media.

For
$$_B\mu_\gamma = \frac{\text{velocity of light in } B}{\text{velocity of light in } C}$$
$$= \frac{\text{velocity of light in } A}{\text{velocity of light in } C} \times \frac{\text{velocity of light in } B}{\text{velocity of light in } A} = \frac{_a\mu_\gamma}{_a\mu_\beta}.$$

EXAMPLES.

REFRACTION AT PLANE SURFACES.

1. Explain the apparent raising of a picture stuck on the bottom of a cube of glass, so that it appears to an eye looking down as if it were in the glass. If the index of refraction is 1·6, how much does the picture appear raised to perpendicular vision?

2. Explain why a thick plate of glass produces an appreciable displacement in the apparent position of a near object viewed through the plate, but an unappreciable displacement for distant objects.

3. Explain how to measure the refracting angle of a prism, and the refractive index of the material of the prism.

4. What effect is produced by interposing a plate of glass between an object and the eye?

5. State with reasons, whether the image formed by the plate will be (a) real or virtual, (b) erect or inverted, (c) magnified or diminished.

6. A ray of light is incident perpendicularly upon one of the two faces of a right-angled isosceles glass prism which bound the right-angle. Draw a picture shewing the subsequent path of the ray, and give reasons for your figure.

7. Explain under what circumstances a ray of light undergoes total reflexion at the boundary of two media.

8. What is meant by total internal reflexion?

9. A piece of plate glass 10 cm. in thickness is placed between a source of light and the observer's eye; find the change which takes place in the apparent position of the source when viewed directly through the plate.

10. Describe some method of finding the refractive index of a liquid.

11. Shew how the refractive index may be determined if the critical angle can be found.

CHAPTER V.

REFLEXION AT SPHERICAL SURFACES.

47. Reflexion at a surface of any form. Up to the present in dealing with reflexion and refraction we have supposed the surfaces between the two media under consideration to be plane.

Mirrors and lenses which are used in optical apparatus, however, have not plane surfaces and we must consider more general cases. We deal now with reflexion at a spherical surface. Many mirrors are spherical in shape, others are so nearly spherical that we may treat them as such without serious error.

The laws of reflexion at any surface are stated above in Section 23. These are true whatever be the form of the surface. If the surface however be not plane the direction of its normal is different at each point, and the determination of the position of the image formed by reflexion is more complicated than in the case of a plane surface.

Spherical mirrors are either concave or convex.

Let $ABCD$, fig. 62, be a sphere, O its centre. Suppose that the inner side of the surface ABC is polished, the

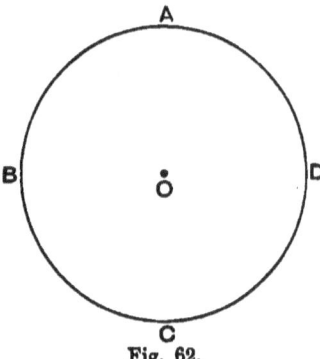

Fig. 62.

portion ADC being removed and that light travelling from right to left falls on ABC. Then ABC is a concave mirror. If on the other hand the outer surface ADC is polished, the light still travelling from right to left, we have a convex mirror; the concave mirror is concave or hollow towards the light, the convex mirror is convex towards the light.

48. Experiments with mirrors. (a) Obtain a concave mirror and place a lighted gas-burner close to it. On looking into the mirror a magnified image of the flame is seen; draw the burner gradually away, the image grows larger, until at last it appears to fill the whole mirror, and if the distance be still further increased the image ceases to be visible. Place a screen at some distance away beyond the gas flame, but on the same side of the mirror; a luminous patch of light is visible, and by adjusting the distance of the flame from the mirror a distinct inverted image of the flame can be formed on the screen. Move the flame somewhat further from the mirror, the picture on the screen becomes indistinct, but by moving the screen nearer to the mirror a distinct image can be again formed. The image will be larger than the flame in this case. Interchange the position of the flame and the screen, placing the screen slightly to one side so that it does not intercept the rays from the flame to the mirror. By slightly turning the mirror an image of the flame can again be seen on the screen. This time the image is smaller than the object but it is still inverted. In both these last cases the images formed are real, they can be seen on a screen, the rays which form them actually pass through them. Move the flame which is now more distant from the mirror than the screen, nearer to the mirror; the screen must be moved away from the mirror, i.e. nearer to the flame in order that a clear image may still be formed on it. This can be continued until the flame and the mirror are at the same distance from the screen. If, when the flame is more distant from the mirror than the screen, it be moved away from the mirror, the image moves towards the mirror; when the flame is at some distance away it may be moved considerably without causing much alteration in the position of the image, which moves very slowly towards the mirror and tends to come to a position which it only reaches when the source of light is very distant indeed. This point at which the image of a very distant object is formed, is called the principal focus of the mirror.

Thus observation shews that a concave mirror produces a magnified virtual image of an object which is close to it; as the object is moved further from the mirror the image becomes real, magnified and inverted. As the distance between the mirror and the object is increased, the image moves nearer to the mirror; in one position the image and object coincide, and as the object is moved further away the image continues to approach the mirror, is real and inverted, but is diminished in size.

(*b*). Take a convex mirror and repeat the observations with it. For all positions of the flame it will be found that the image is erect, virtual, and less than the object. Observation shews that a convex mirror produces a virtual, erect, diminished image of any object.

49. Definitions of terms used in connexion with spherical mirrors.

Centre of curvature of the mirror. *The centre of the sphere of which the mirror forms part is called the centre of curvature of the mirror or sometimes the centre of the mirror.*

This must be distinguished from the centre of the surface of the mirror which is the middle point of that portion of the surface of the sphere of which the mirror is formed.

Fig. 63.

Axis of a mirror. *The line joining the centre of the sphere to the middle point of the surface of the mirror is the axis of the mirror.*

The axis of the mirror is perpendicular to its surface. In fig. 63, the point O is the centre of the sphere or the centre of curvature, A is the centre of the surface of the mirror BAC, and OA is the axis of the mirror.

In most of the problems with which we deal we shall suppose that the source of light Q is not far from the axis of the mirror, and that the axis of the pencil of rays from Q with which we are dealing falls on the mirror near A. In such a case the axis of the pencil is inclined at only a small angle to the axis of the mirror, the incidence is very nearly *direct*. If the incidence becomes oblique the question is more complicated, for the present we treat only of the case of a small pencil incident directly.

Principal Focus. *If a small pencil of parallel rays, parallel to the axis of the mirror, is incident directly on a concave mirror, these rays after reflexion are found to converge to a point on the axis of the mirror. This point is called the principal focus of the mirror.*

If the mirror be convex the rays after reflexion appear to diverge from a point on the axis behind the mirror, this point is the principal focus of the convex mirror.

Focal length. *The distance from the mirror of the point to which a pencil of rays, incident parallel to the axis of the mirror, converge after reflexion, or from which they appear to diverge, is called the focal length of the mirror.*

It will appear from Section 50 that the focal length of a mirror is equal to half the radius.

Geometrical Image of a Point. *A pencil of rays diverging from a point on the axis of a mirror and incident directly on the mirror, after reflexion either converges to or appears to diverge from a second point, on the axis. This second point is called the geometrical image of the first point.*

A point and its geometrical image are spoken of as *conjugate foci*, for if an object be placed in the position originally occupied by the image, an image will be formed in the original

88   LIGHT.   [CH. V

position of the object, the two foci are therefore interchangeable.

50. Principal Focus. To shew that each ray of a small pencil of parallel rays falling directly on a mirror parallel to its axis intersects the axis in a definite point; and to find the position of that point[1].

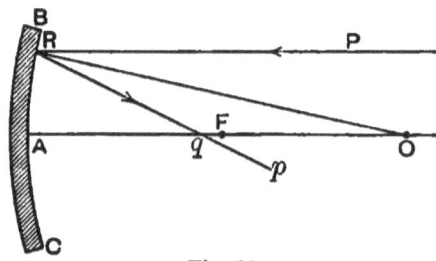

Fig. 64.

Let OA, fig. 64, be the axis of a concave mirror BAC, and let PR be a ray parallel to the axis falling on the mirror at R. Join OR, then since the mirror is spherical and O is its centre, OR is a normal to its surface. Make the angle ORp equal to the angle ORP and let Rp cut the axis OA in q. Then by the law of reflexion Rp is the reflected ray which corresponds to the incident ray PR.

Now the angle qRO = the angle PRO = the angle qOR, since PR is parallel to OA; hence, in the triangle OqR, the angles qRO and qOR are equal, therefore $qR = qO$.

But if R is very close to A, and the incidence in consequence direct, qR is very nearly equal to qA. Thus qA is very nearly equal to qO, and in this case q is midway between A and O. Again PR is any ray of the incident pencil, provided only that it is sufficiently close to OA. Thus if the incident pencil be very small, all the reflected rays pass very approximately through a point in the axis midway between the mirror and its centre. This point is the principal focus of the mirror and its distance from

---

[1] In other words, to determine the position of the principal focus of a mirror.

the surface, i.e. the focal length, is one half of the radius. We shall denote the point by F and the focal length by f.

A similar proof will apply to the case of a convex mirror, the principal focus will however be, as shewn in fig. 65, behind the mirror and at a distance from the mirror equal to half the radius.

51. Convention as to signs. If we compare figs. 64 and 65, we see that in the first case q and O are to the right of A, while in the other they are to the left—the incident light is supposed as usual to travel from right to left. We

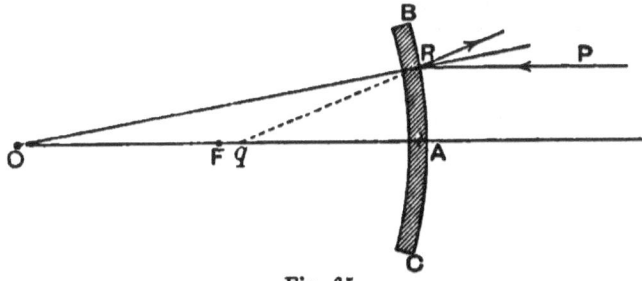

Fig. 65.

can express this distinction between the two cases if we agree to distinguish lines drawn from A in opposite directions by opposite signs. The usual convention is that lines drawn to the right from A are called positive, those drawn to the left negative; if then f and r are the numerical values of the focal length and radius of the mirror, we have for the concave mirror, fig. 64,

$$AO = r,$$
$$AF = f = \frac{r}{2},$$

and for the convex mirror, fig. 65,

$$AO = -r,$$
$$AF = -f = -\frac{r}{2}.$$

We shall find that formulae which are established for a concave mirror will hold for a convex mirror, and vice versa, if we make these changes in sign.

52. Graphical Solutions. Many problems in reflexion can be solved graphically. Thus draw on a large scale a section of a mirror of considerable radius such as 50 or 60 cm. Suppose the breadth of the mirror to be 10 cm., 5 cm. on either side of the axis. Draw a series of rays parallel to the axis at distances of half a centimetre apart incident on the mirror, join the centre to the respective points of incidences, the lines so drawn will be normal to the mirror; draw in each case the reflected ray, making the angle of reflexion equal to that of incidence; it will be found that these reflected rays intersect the axis very approximately in the same point which is the principal focus of the mirror[1].

A similar construction will enable us to find the image of any point formed by reflexion, it would however be a cumbersome course to follow in all cases and may be much simplified by noting the following principles.

(a) *In order to determine the position of the image, if it is formed, we need only trace two reflected rays.* The two rays will in general intersect, but the point of intersection of all the reflected rays is the image, hence the point thus found must therefore be the image required and all the other reflected rays must pass through it.

(b) *It is always possible to draw easily and without the necessity of measuring any angles the paths of two reflected rays, and hence to find the image required.* A ray which falls on the mirror parallel to the axis will after reflexion pass through the principal focus; while an incident ray which passes through the centre falls on the mirror normally and is reflected back along its own course. The point then in which these rays intersect will be the image of the source from which they start; if the pencil be not too large all the reflected rays

[1] In making such graphical constructions it is convenient to use squared paper on which two sets of fine lines at known distances such as a millimetre apart have been ruled at right angles, a figure can be drawn to scale on this paper more readily than on plane paper.

will pass through this image; if the pencil be large there will be no point through which *all* the reflected rays pass, in this case a point source of light will not have a point image.

53. To determine graphically the image of a point formed by reflexion in a concave mirror. There are various cases of this problem to consider, these are shewn in figs. 66–68, but the method of treatment is the same in all.

Let A be the centre of the surface of the mirror, F the prin-

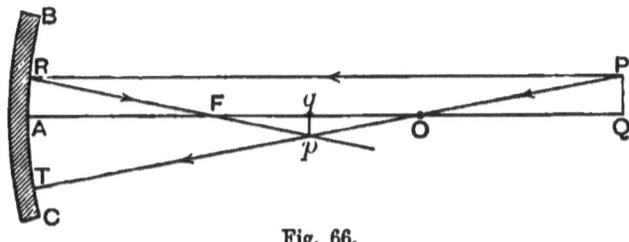

Fig. 66.

cipal focus, O the centre of the sphere, OFA the axis. Let P be a luminous point not far off the axis, and let PQ be perpendicular to the axis; we may treat PQ as a small object, the image of which, formed by reflexion, is required. Draw a ray PR parallel to the axis meeting the mirror in R. This ray is reflected through the principal focus. Join RF, then RF is the reflected ray. Draw a ray PO through the centre O. This ray falls on the mirror normally, at T say, and is reflected directly back. Let p be the point of intersection of the two reflected rays RF and TO. Then p is the image of P. Draw pq perpendicular to the axis. Then the image of any point on PQ will lie on pq, thus pq is the image of the object PQ.

Figures 66 to 68 give the cases which occur for different positions of the object. In fig. 66, the object PQ is some distance from the mirror, further away than O, the centre of the sphere. The image pq is real, inverted and diminished. As PQ is moved to the left towards O, pq moves to the right and the two coincide at O. When PQ is still further to the left between O and F, then pq is to the right as shewn in fig. 67, and is real, inverted and magnified. When the object is at F, the principal focus, the reflected rays proceeding from

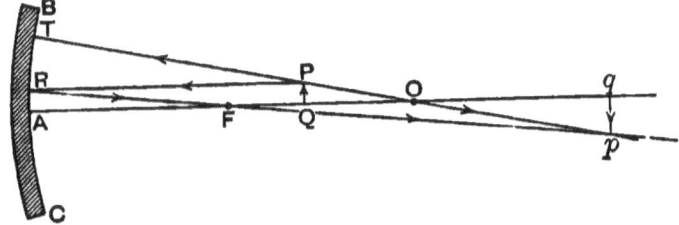

Fig. 67.

any one point of the object are parallel after reflexion. When the object is placed between the mirror and its principal focus as in fig. 68, the reflected rays produced backwards, meet behind the mirror. The image is virtual, erect and magnified.

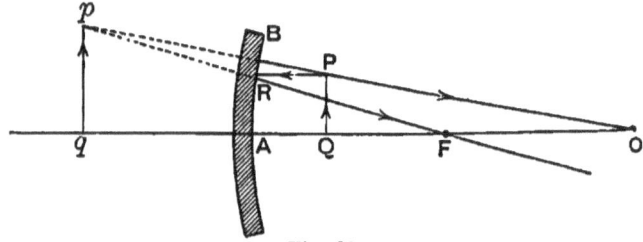

Fig. 68.

54. To determine graphically the position of the image of a point formed by reflexion in a convex mirror. The construction is exactly the same as

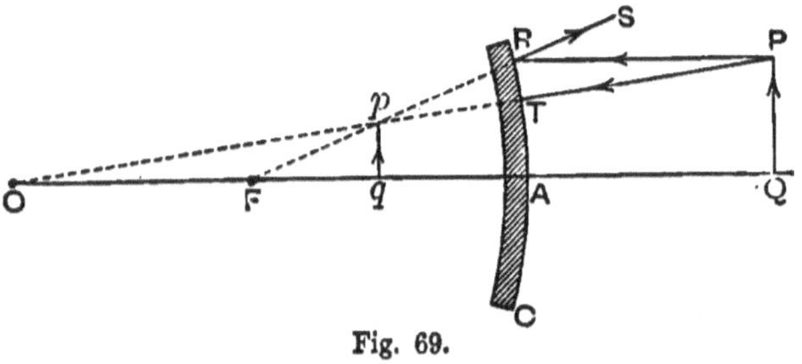

Fig. 69.

for the concave mirror, only the points F and O are to the left of A behind the mirror. Thus in fig. 69, draw PR parallel to the axis. Join FR and produce it to S, then RS is the reflected ray. Join OP meeting the mirror in T and FR in p. An incident ray PT is reflected along TP; the two reflected rays produced backwards meet at p and pq is the image of PQ. It is virtual, erect, and smaller than the object.

55. To obtain a formula connecting together the position of a point Q and its image q formed by direct reflexion in a concave mirror. Determine the position of the image pq by a graphical construction as in

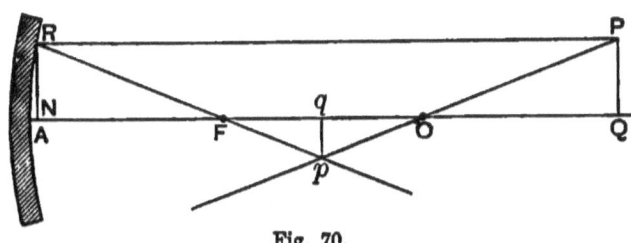

Fig. 70.

Section 53. Draw RN, fig. 70, perpendicular to the axis. Then since we are dealing only with rays which are incident very close to A, the point R is near to A and N is very close indeed to A. We may without sensible error measure the distances of Q and q either from A or from N.

Let us put $AQ = u$, $Aq = v$, $AO = r$.

Thus $AF = \dfrac{r}{2}$.

Now the triangles POQ and poq are similar. Hence

$$\frac{pq}{PQ} = \frac{Oq}{OQ}.$$

Also the triangles RNF and pqF are similar. Thus

$$\frac{pq}{RN} = \frac{Fq}{NF}.$$

But $RN = PQ$,

thus $\dfrac{Fq}{NF} = \dfrac{pq}{PQ} = \dfrac{Oq}{OQ}.$

Now $Fq = v - \dfrac{r}{2},\ NF = \dfrac{r}{2},$

$Oq = r - v,\ OQ = u - r.$

Hence $\dfrac{v - \dfrac{r}{2}}{\dfrac{r}{2}} = \dfrac{r - v}{u - r},$

$\therefore uv = \dfrac{r}{2}(u + v),$

or $\dfrac{1}{v} + \dfrac{1}{u} = \dfrac{2}{r}.$

If we write f for the focal length $\dfrac{r}{2}$, this becomes

$$\dfrac{1}{v} + \dfrac{1}{u} = \dfrac{1}{f}.$$

We could have deduced the same formula from either of the two other figures in Section 53; had we employed fig. 68 it would have been necessary to remember the rule of signs, since q is to the left of A we know that Aq or v is negative, we must therefore put $Aq = -v$.

56. To obtain the formula for a convex mirror. The same formula holds also for a convex mirror if we adhere to the proper signs. Thus let us denote by $u_1,\ v_1,\ r_1$ the

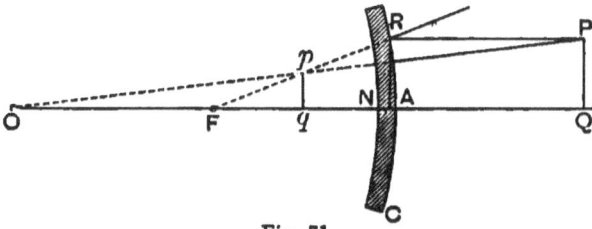

Fig. 71.

numerical values of AQ, Aq and AO without reference to the sign.

Then in fig. 71
$$\frac{pq}{PQ} = \frac{Oq}{OQ}.$$

Also, since $RN = PQ$,
$$\frac{pq}{PQ} = \frac{pq}{RN} = \frac{Fq}{FN}.$$

Therefore
$$\frac{Fq}{FN} = \frac{Oq}{OQ},$$

$$\frac{\frac{r_1}{2} - v_1}{\frac{r_1}{2}} = \frac{r_1 - v_1}{r_1 + u_1}.$$

Whence
$$-\frac{1}{v_1} + \frac{1}{u_1} = -\frac{2}{r_1}.$$

Thus may be written
$$\frac{1}{-v_1} + \frac{1}{u_1} = \frac{2}{-r_1}.$$

Now from this figure AQ is positive, while Aq and AD are negative. We therefore have
$$u = AQ = +u_1$$
$$v = -Aq = -v_1$$
$$r = -AO = -r_1.$$

Hence, on substituting, the formula becomes
$$\frac{1}{v} + \frac{1}{u} = \frac{2}{r}.$$

This one formula therefore is applicable to all cases of direct reflexion at a spherical mirror. We have thus the result.

If **u** *and* **v** *be the distances from the surface of an object and of its image, formed by direct reflexion, in a spherical mirror of radius* **r** *and focal length* **f***, then*

$$\frac{1}{\mathbf{v}} + \frac{1}{\mathbf{u}} = \frac{2}{\mathbf{r}} = \frac{1}{\mathbf{f}}.$$

57. Definition of the magnifying power of a mirror. Let pq be the image of a small object PQ formed by reflexion at a spherical mirror and suppose PQ is at right angles to the axis of the mirror. Then the ratio of the length pq to the length PQ is called the magnifying power of the mirror.

We may put this more briefly by saying that the magnifying power is the ratio of the size of the image to the size of the object, but in this statement it must be remembered that size refers to linear dimensions, not to area.

58. To determine the magnifying power of a mirror. Let PR be a ray incident parallel to the axis, RFp

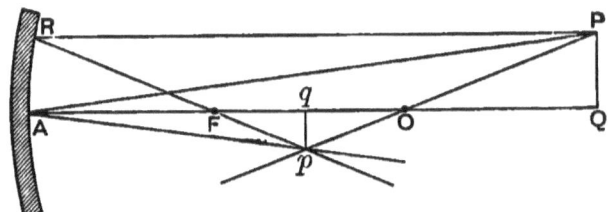

Fig. 72.

the reflected ray, PO a ray incident through the centre of the sphere, and reflected along itself so as to meet RF in p, then, as we have seen, p is the image of P. Join AP and Ap. Since p is the image of P an incident ray PA is reflected along Ap. Therefore the angle PAQ is equal to the angle pAq and the triangles APQ, Apq are similar. Hence if m be the magnifying power or linear magnification

$$m = \frac{pq}{PQ} = \frac{Aq}{AQ} = \frac{v}{u}.$$

Hence the magnification is the ratio of the distance from the mirror of the image to the distance of the object.

The figure will give us another expression for m, for the triangles POQ, pOq are similar, hence

$$m = \frac{pq}{PQ} = \frac{Oq}{OQ} = \frac{\text{distance of image from centre}}{\text{distance of object from centre}}.$$

Again, we have
$$\frac{1}{u} = \frac{2}{r} - \frac{1}{v}.$$

Thus
$$\frac{v}{u} = \frac{2v}{r} - 1 = \frac{2v-r}{r} = \frac{v-f}{f},$$

writing f for $r/2$ and this gives us the magnifying power if we know the position of the image and the radius of the mirror.

Or again
$$\frac{1}{v} = \frac{2}{r} - \frac{1}{u},$$

$$\frac{u}{v} = \frac{2u}{r} - 1 = \frac{2u-r}{r}.$$

Hence
$$\frac{v}{u} = \frac{r}{2u-r} = \frac{f}{u-f}.$$

And this gives the magnifying power if we know u, the distance of the object from the mirror, and r the radius of the mirror.

From these two expressions for the magnifying power we deduce that
$$(v-f)(u-f) = f^2.$$

Now $v-f$ is the distance of the image from the principal focus while $u-f$ is the distance of the object from the same point. Thus the formula expresses the fact that the product of the distances of the object and of the image from the principal focus is equal to the square of the focal length.

In the above formulae for the magnifying power no notice has been taken of the fact that in the figure the image is inverted. PQ is above the axis while pq is below it; we can allow for this by giving different signs to lines drawn above and below the axis. If PQ is to be treated as positive we ought to call pq negative and then
$$m = \frac{-pq}{PQ} = -\frac{v}{u}.$$

The result can be obtained from figure 72 and the formula
$$\frac{1}{v} + \frac{1}{u} = \frac{2}{r},$$

for we have
$$\frac{pq}{PQ} = \frac{Oq}{OQ} = \frac{r-v}{u-r}.$$

Now
$$\frac{1}{v} - \frac{1}{r} = \frac{1}{r} - \frac{1}{u},$$

$$\therefore \frac{r-v}{vr} = \frac{u-r}{ru},$$

$$\therefore \frac{r-v}{u-r} = \frac{v}{u},$$

Thus $$m = \frac{v}{u}.$$

The formulae for direct reflexion from a spherical mirror can all be found somewhat more directly thus.

Let Q (fig. 73) be a point on the axis, O the centre of the sphere, QR an incident ray, Rq the reflected ray, then OR is normal at R and bisects

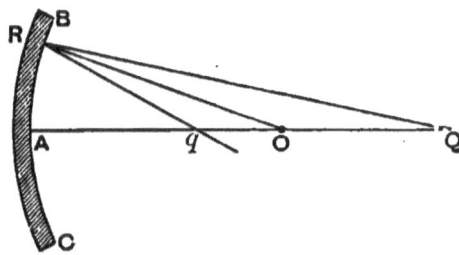

Fig. 73.

the angle QRq. Therefore by Euclid vi. 3, the segments of the base of the triangle RqQ are proportional to the sides.

Hence $$\frac{OQ}{Oq} = \frac{QR}{qR}.$$

But when the incidence is direct R is very close to A, QR is very nearly equal to QA and qR to qA.

Hence in this case we have
$$\frac{OQ}{Oq} = \frac{QA}{qA}.$$

Thus $$\frac{u-r}{r-v} = \frac{u}{v}.$$

Whence $$\frac{1}{v} + \frac{1}{u} = \frac{2}{r}.$$

Again, when the incident pencil consists of parallel rays, we must consider that Q is infinitely distant so that u is infinite and $1/u$ zero.

We then get $1/v = 2/r$ and hence $v = r/2$. Thus a pencil of parallel rays converges after reflexion to a point on the axis at a distance $r/2$ from the mirror. We have thus another proof of the fact that the principal focus is midway between the centre of the sphere and the centre of the surface of the mirror.

59. Methods of Calculation.

In working examples on mirrors and lenses, and in calculating the results of experiments we have often to deal with formulae such as those of the preceding sections, involving the reciprocals of known numbers. It is therefore convenient to have a table of reciprocals and to simplify the arithmetic by its use. Such a Table is here given.

TABLE OF RECIPROCALS OF NUMBERS FROM 1 TO 99.

Number.	Reciprocal.	Number.	Reciprocal.	Number.	Reciprocal.
1	1	34	·0294	67	·0149
2	·5000	35	·0286	68	·0147
3	·3333	36	·0278	69	·0145
4	·2500	37	·0270	70	·0143
5	·2000	38	·0263	71	·0141
6	·1667	39	·0256	72	·0139
7	·1429	40	·0250	73	·0137
8	·1250	41	·0244	74	·0135
9	·1111	42	·0238	75	·0133
10	·1000	43	·0233	76	·0132
11	·0909	44	·0227	77	·0130
12	·0833	45	·0222	78	·0128
13	·0769	46	·0217	79	·0127
14	·0714	47	·0213	80	·0125
15	·0667	48	·0208	81	·0123
16	·0625	49	·0204	82	·0122
17	·0588	50	·0200	83	·0120
18	·0556	51	·0196	84	·0119
19	·0526	52	·0192	85	·0118
20	·0500	53	·0189	86	·0116
21	·0476	54	·0185	87	·0115
22	·0455	55	·0182	88	·0114
23	·0435	56	·0179	89	·0112
24	·0417	57	·0175	90	·0111
25	·0400	58	·0172	91	·0110
26	·0385	59	·0169	92	·0109
27	·0370	60	·0167	93	·0108
28	·0357	61	·0164	94	·0106
29	·0345	62	·0161	95	·0105
30	·0333	63	·0159	96	·0104
31	·0323	64	·0156	97	·0103
32	·0313	65	·0154	98	·0102
33	·0303	66	·0152	99	·0101

Example. *An object is placed at a distance of* 18 *inches from a concave mirror* 1 *foot in radius, find the position of the image and the magnifying power.*

Let v be the distance of the image from the mirror.

Then since
$$\frac{1}{v} = \frac{2}{r} - \frac{1}{u},$$

$$\frac{1}{v} = \frac{2}{12} - \frac{1}{18} = \frac{1}{6} - \frac{1}{18},$$

$$= \cdot 1667 - \cdot 0556 = \cdot 1111,$$

$$\therefore v = 9 \text{ inches.}$$

$$\text{Magnifying power} = \frac{v}{u} = \frac{9}{18} = \frac{1}{2}.$$

Almost any problem, such as the above, can be solved graphically in the manner of Section 52 by a large scale diagram carefully drawn. The position of the image is thus obtained and its distance and size can be measured.

60. Experimental Verifications. The various formulae can all be verified by direct experiment. For demonstration to a class the optical bench shewn in fig. 11 will be found convenient, the mirror is placed at one end over the zero division, the luminous object may conveniently be an incandescent lamp, or when this is not available, a gas burner, in front of which is placed a sheet of zinc with a hole in it; for some purposes a sheet of perforated zinc or of wire-gauze is useful.

In performing the experiment a little adjustment is necessary to allow the rays of light to reach the mirror without being intercepted by the screen.

For practical work in a class the bench is not necessary; the mirror may rest on the table in a suitable stand and a luminous object, such as a small gas jet, or an illuminated piece of wire gauze, be placed in front of it; a vertical sheet of white paper or card forms a screen on which real images can be formed, and the distances of the object and image from the screen can be measured, either directly with a rule or more exactly by means of a pair of compasses applied to a rule. For some experiments two stout pins mounted so as to be

59–60] REFLEXION AT SPHERICAL SURFACES. 101

vertical, and have their points at the same height as the centre of the mirror are useful, or the vertical knitting needle used in Experiment (7) may be employed.

When using the pins or knitting needles, one of them is placed in front of the mirror as the object. On looking into the mirror from a suitable position the reflected image can usually be seen, and the second pin can be placed so as to coincide with this image; by measuring the distances of the pins from the mirror, the values of u and v in the formulae are found, and hence the formulae can be verified. If the image formed is virtual it will be behind the mirror, the second pin when placed to coincide with it cannot be seen. To avoid this difficulty a narrow horizontal strip of the silvering is scraped off the centre of the mirror, thus forming a small transparent portion through which the pin can be seen.

The mirrors which are frequently used for decorative purposes by shop fitters are, if selected with care, sufficiently good to enable the measurements to be made and can be obtained at a small cost.

With this apparatus, shewn in figure 74, the following experiments may be made.

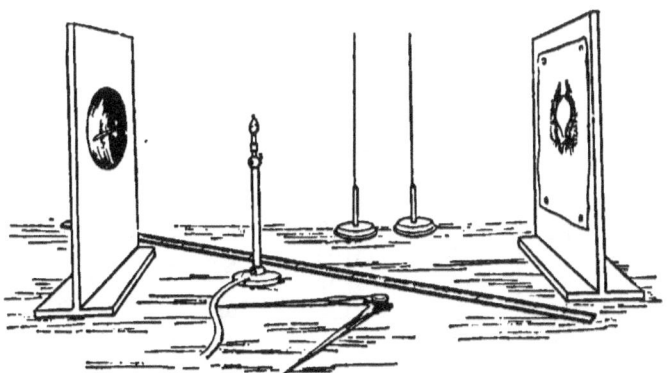

Fig. 74.

61. Measurement of the radius of a mirror.

EXPERIMENT (17). *To verify the formula* $\frac{1}{v} + \frac{1}{u} = \frac{2}{r}$ *connecting the positions of an object and its image formed by reflexion in a mirror, and to find the radius of the mirror.*

(a) *Case of a concave mirror producing a real image.* Place the object at some little distance from the mirror, taking care that it shall be at the same height as the centre of the mirror. Adjust the screen so that the image formed on it may be as distinctly focussed as possible. Measure with the scale the distances u between the object and mirror, and v between the image and mirror. Move the object further away from the mirror, again adjust the screen and measure v and u. Proceed thus to find a series of corresponding values of u and v. A position can be found in which the object and image are at the same distance from the mirror; in this case it is clear that they are at the centre of curvature of the mirror, for then all the rays fall on the mirror normally and are reflected directly back. Form a Table as below, of the values of u, v, $1/u$, $1/v$, these last being taken from the Table of Reciprocals, and also of $1/u + 1/v$. The Table, which gives the results of a series of experiments with the optical bench, shews that the quantity $\frac{1}{u} + \frac{1}{v}$ is constant, and if we remember that when u is equal to v as in the sixth line each is equal to r, we see that the value of the constant is $2/r$. We thus verify for this case the formula $\frac{1}{v} + \frac{1}{u} = \frac{2}{r}$.

u	v	$\frac{1}{u}$	$\frac{1}{v}$	$\frac{1}{v} + \frac{1}{u}$
250	60·9	·0040	·0164	·0204
200	65·2	·0050	·0154	·0204
150	73·2	·0067	·0137	·0204
120	84	·0083	·0119	·0202
100	96·5	·0100	·0104	·0204
98	98	·0102	·0102	·0204
80	127·5	·0125	·0078	·0203
70	166·5	·0143	·0060	·0203

The experiment also gives us the radius of the mirror, for we see, taking the mean of the observations in the last column as being more accurate than the single measurement of the sixth line that $2/r$ is ·02035, and hence

$$r/2 = 49{\cdot}1 \text{ and } r = 98{\cdot}2 \text{ cm.}$$

(b) *Case of a concave mirror producing a virtual image.* Place one of the knitting needles or pins close to the mirror, from which a strip of silvering has been scraped; and place the other behind the mirror so that it can be seen through the clear glass. It can be made more readily visible by placing the white paper behind it. Adjust it as in Experiment (7) until it coincides with the virtual image formed by reflexion; this will be the case when the needle and the image do not appear to separate as the eye is moved about. Then measure the distance from the mirror of the one needle in front, and that of the other behind. In using the observations to verify the formula, remember that the distance of the image is to have a negative sign. We shall therefore have to calculate the difference of the two reciprocals $1/u$ and $1/v$, and shall find that this difference has the same value as the sum had in the former case. Thus for this case also if we give v the proper sign the formula $\dfrac{1}{u} + \dfrac{1}{v} = \dfrac{2}{r}$ is verified.

(c) *Case of a convex mirror.* The image formed in this case is always virtual. Proceed exactly as in (b), and substitute in the formula, remembering that v is negative. We shall again find that $1/u + 1/v$, v having its proper sign, is constant, but in this case the constant value will be negative, for r the radius of the convex mirror is negative.

*62. Measurement of Magnification. EXPERIMENT (18). *To find the magnifying power of a mirror.*

In the case of a real image take an object which can be measured. A circular hole, about 1 cm. in diameter, cut in a piece of zinc plate will serve, a transparent scale of millimetres engraved on glass is better. Obtain on a screen a real image of this object and measure its size, if the glass scale is used as an object a similar scale, backed by a piece of ground glass or white paper, forms a convenient screen, for by means of it the ratio of the size of the image to the size of the object can be found immediately. It is only necessary to count the number of divisions on the screen which coincide with some convenient number, such as 10 of the image. If for example we find this number to be 25, the magnifying power is 25/10 or 2·5. Measure at the same time u and v, the distances of the object and image from the mirror, and thus verify that $m = v/u$.

In the case of a virtual image proceed in a similar way. Take some object, such as a circular hole, whose size can be measured, and place a scale behind the mirror; for this purpose a sheet of squared paper divided into millimetres will be useful, adjust this until the virtual image of the object appears to be distinctly focussed on the squared paper, and read off the number of millimetre divisions covered by the diameter of the hole. Divide this number by the diameter in millimetres, and thus find the magnifying power.

63. To find the image formed by a convergent pencil of rays. In some cases a convergent pencil of rays converging to a point P falls on a concave mirror and is reflected. We can find the position of the image by the method already used. For consider an incident ray parallel to the axis, it is reflected so as to pass through the principal focus, while a ray which passes through the centre O is reflected back along its former course. The point p where these two rays intersect is the image of P. This is shewn in

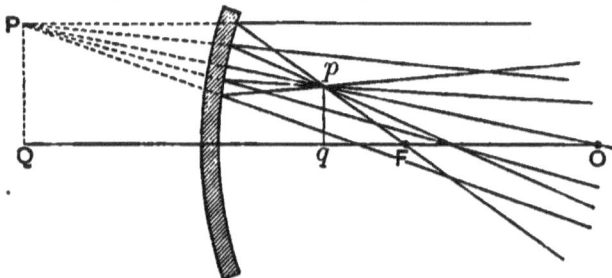

Fig. 75.

fig. 75. It is clear that pq is the real image of an image PQ which would be formed by the rays if they were not intercepted by the mirror before reaching PQ.

64. To draw the rays by which an eye sees the image of an object formed by reflexion in a spherical mirror. Let pq, fig. 76, be the image of an object PQ formed by reflexion in a mirror, and let E be an eye which can see pq. If the incidence is to be direct, E must not be far from the axis

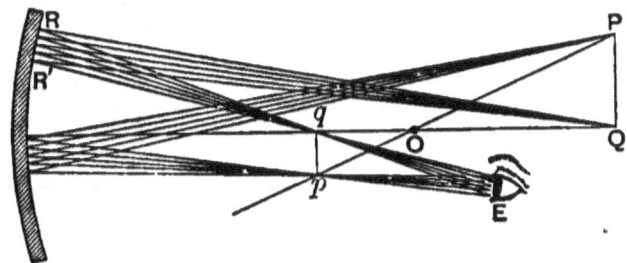

Fig. 76.

of the mirror; in the figure, for the sake of clearness, this distance is somewhat exaggerated. Draw a pencil of rays diverging from q and falling on the pupil of the eye. Produce these rays back to meet the mirror in R, R'. Join RQ and $R'Q$, then the pencil QR, QR' is reflected so as to converge to q, and after diverging from q reaches the eye, producing distinct vision of q, the geometrical image of Q. In a similar way the pencil by which p any other point on the image is seen can be drawn.

A similar construction gives, as shewn in fig. 77, the rays

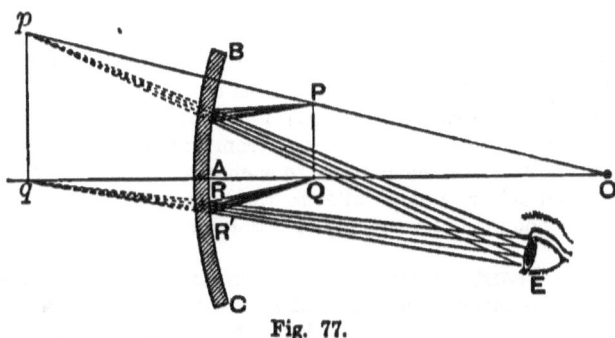

Fig. 77.

by which a virtual image is seen.

106   LIGHT.   [CH. V

If the incidence be oblique, the image is not formed at the geometrical focus, but a discussion of its position would carry us beyond our limits.

65. To use a mirror to produce a pencil of parallel rays. A pencil of rays falling on a mirror parallel to its axis is brought to a focus at the principal focus, hence conversely, if a luminous point be placed at the principal focus the reflected rays will all be parallel to the axis. It should be noticed however that to secure this we must have at the focus merely a point of light. For let FF' be an object perpendicular to the axis at the principal focus F of a mirror, fig. 78. The rays from F are all reflected parallel to the axis,

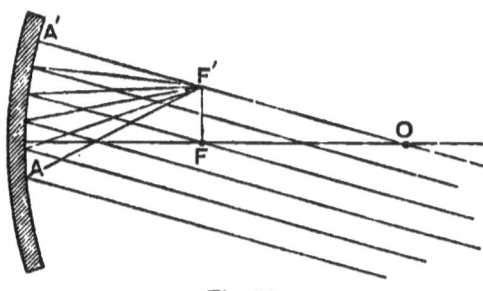

Fig. 78.

but rays diverging from F' will not, after reflexion, be parallel to OF but to OF'. For join OF' meeting the mirror in A', a ray from F' in the direction $F'A$ is reflected back along itself, moreover F' is very approximately half way between O and A', it is practically the principal focus of a mirror having OA' for its axis, thus rays diverging from F' will, after reflexion, be all parallel to OF'. All the rays from any one point in FF' will after reflexion be parallel to each other, but the reflected rays from F' are not parallel to those from F; the reflected pencil is not made up entirely of parallel rays.

66. Caustics formed by reflexion. If a careful drawing be made of a pencil of rays diverging from a point and reflected from a spherical mirror it will be found that the consecutive rays intersect each other and the points of intersection form a curve. Near this curve the rays are more closely packed together than elsewhere, in other words more light will fall on a given area when placed near the curve than in other positions. Such a curve is known as a caustic curve, it is seen when a glass nearly filled with water stands in the sunshine. A bright curve can be traced on the surface of the water. It may be shewn again by taking a concave mirror of some size, reflecting the light from a luminous source from the mirror, which should be tilted slightly forwards so as to throw the reflected rays downwards and receiving them on a horizontal sheet of paper. The caustic will be seen on the paper.

What is equation of caustic curve?

EXAMPLES.

SPHERICAL MIRRORS.

1. Prove that the principal focus of a concave mirror is midway between the centre of curvature and the mirror; and draw careful diagrams shewing the position of the image of a given object formed by such a mirror, (a) when the object is more distant from the mirror than its centre of curvature, (b) when it is between the centre and the principal focus, (c) when it is between the principal focus and the mirror.

2. An object is moved from a distance along the axis of a concave spherical mirror close up to the mirror. Draw figures shewing the alterations which take place in the position and size of the image.

3. How would you determine whether a mirror, which you cannot touch but in which you can see objects reflected, be plane, concave or convex?

4. When a concave mirror is looked at, inverted images of objects in front of the mirror are often seen. Explain the production of these images, and draw diagrams illustrating your remarks.

5. Find the position of the object for a given position of the image in a spherical concave mirror.

6. Draw a figure shewing the paths of the rays by which an eye placed near the axis of a spherical mirror sees an object directly reflected in the mirror.

7. State the laws of the reflexion of light, and draw a diagram shewing under what circumstances a virtual image of an object can be formed by a concave mirror. The radius of such a mirror is 6 feet, and a circular disk one inch in diameter is placed on the axis of the mirror at a distance of 2 feet from it. Determine the size and position of the image.

108   LIGHT.   [CH. V

8. Define the focal length of a spherical reflecting surface. How far from a concave mirror of radius 3 feet, would you place an object to give an image magnified three times? Would the image be real or virtual?

9. A bright object, 4 inches high, is placed on the principal axis of a concave spherical mirror, at a distance of 15 inches from the mirror. Determine the position and size of its image, the focal length of the mirror being 6 inches.

10. Describe an experiment to verify the laws of reflexion of light, and draw a series of careful figures to shew the changes which take place in the position of the image as an object is moved from a long distance close up to a concave mirror.

11. Prove the formula $\frac{1}{v} + \frac{1}{u} = \frac{2}{r}$ connecting the position of the object and image formed by reflexion at a concave spherical mirror.

Trace the changes in the position of the image and in its magnification as the object moves from a considerable distance close up to the mirror.

12. Determine (a) by the formula, (b) by a graphical construction, the size and position of the image of an object 1 inch high placed respectively at distances of 6 inches, 9 inches, 1 ft. and 18 inches from a concave mirror 9 inches in radius.

13. Determine the size and position of the image of an object 1 inch high placed 10 inches from a convex mirror 20 inches in radius.

14. A concave and a convex mirror each 20 cm. in radius are placed opposite to each other and at 40 cm. apart in the same axis. An object 5 cm. in height is placed midway between them. Find the position and size of the image formed by reflexion, first at the convex, then at the concave mirror. Trace carefully a ray from a point on the object to its image.

15. An object is placed at a distance of 8 inches from a concave mirror 1 ft. in radius. A plane mirror inclined at 45° to the axis of the concave mirror, passes through its centre of curvature, find the position of the image formed by the reflexion, first at the concave, then at the plane mirror.

16. The sun subtends an angle of half a degree at the centre of the surface of a concave mirror 36 feet in radius. Find the size of the image of the sun formed by the mirror.

17. Trace in the different cases which may arise the rays by which an eye near the axis (a) of a convex, (b) of a concave mirror sees the image of an object reflected by the mirror.

CHAPTER VI.

LENSES.

67. Refraction at spherical surfaces. By applying the laws of refraction to the case of a pencil of rays directly incident on a spherical refracting surface, we can determine the position of the image of a point formed by refraction at such a surface, and investigate the problem in a similar manner to that employed in the last chapter for reflexion.

Many of the terms, such as Principal Focus, Focal Length, Conjugate Foci, and others, apply equally to the case of refraction. Thus we can prove that if a pencil of rays parallel to the axis fall directly on the surface, they will after refraction diverge from a point at a distance $\mu r/(\mu - 1)$ from the surface, μ being the refractive index and r the radius of curvature of the surface[1].

Thus denoting the focal length by f, we find

$$f = \frac{\mu r}{\mu - 1}.$$

If we assume this result we can obtain by a graphical construction the position of the image of a point. For let A (fig. 79) be the centre of the surface, O the centre of the sphere, F the principal focus, so that FOA is the axis, and let

$$AO = r, \quad AF = f = \frac{\mu r}{\mu - 1}.$$

Let PQ be a small object. Draw PR parallel to the axis and join FR. After refraction the path of the ray PR will be FR produced. Join PO and let it meet the surface in T.

---

[1] A proof of this formula will be found in Section 84.

The ray POT is incident directly and therefore is not deviated by the refraction. Let the directions FR and PT of the two refracted rays meet at p, then p is a virtual image of P

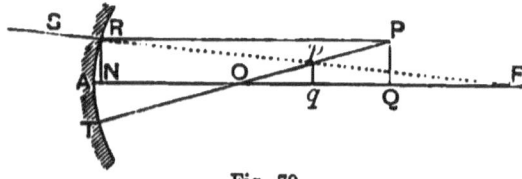

Fig. 79.

formed by refraction, and if pq be perpendicular to the axis, Q and q are conjugate foci and pq is the image of PQ. We can discuss the various cases which arise for different positions of the object in a manner similar to that employed in Section 53. The discussion however is not of very great importance, for in practice we have usually, except in the case of the eye, to deal with problems in which the light again emerges from the refracting medium into air, and in which therefore there are two refractions to consider; such cases can best be treated in a different manner.

We may however obtain in the following way a formula connecting together the positions q, Q, and F.

Let $AF=f$, $AQ=u$, $Aq=v$. Draw RN perpendicular to AO. Then when the incidence is direct, N is very close indeed to A, and we may measure u and v indiscriminately from A or N.

Now we have
$$\frac{Oq}{OQ} = \frac{pq}{PQ} = \frac{pq}{RN} = \frac{Fq}{FN}.$$

Therefore
$$\frac{v-r}{u-r} = \frac{f-v}{f},$$

or
$$f(u-v) = v(u-r),$$

whence
$$\frac{1}{v} - \frac{1}{u}\left(1 - \frac{r}{f}\right) = \frac{1}{f}.$$

But
$$f = \frac{\mu r}{\mu - 1}.$$

Therefore
$$\frac{1}{v} - \frac{1}{u}\left(1 - \frac{\mu-1}{\mu}\right) = \frac{\mu-1}{\mu r}.$$

Hence
$$\frac{\mu}{v} - \frac{1}{u} = \frac{\mu-1}{r}.$$

By the aid of this formula or by construction we can shew that for a concave surface, for which r is positive, v is always positive and the image is virtual, while for a convex surface for which r is negative we have

$$\frac{\mu}{v} = \frac{1}{u} - \frac{\mu-1}{r},$$

and v may be either positive or negative; thus the image formed by refraction at a convex spherical surface may be either virtual or real.

68. Refraction at two spherical surfaces. We have already dealt with the refraction of light through a plate and through a prism, and have seen that (1) a ray transmitted through a plate is not deviated, but emerges parallel to its path before incidence, (2) that a ray transmitted through a prism is deviated towards the thick end and away from the edge. We proceed now to consider refraction through a portion of a transparent medium bounded by two spherical surfaces.

Suppose we have a plate of some transparent material, such as glass, and a number of truncated prisms with different refracting angles.

Arrange these in order as shewn in fig. 80, which represents a section of the whole by a plane perpendicular to their faces. In this figure $ABCD$ is the plate, $ADFE$, $EFGH$ etc. the successive prisms. The edges of all the prisms are turned away from the centre, their thick ends being in all cases nearest to the axis of the whole figure.

A ray such as QP falling on any prism, as we have seen in Section 42, is bent by refraction through the prism away from the edge, i.e. toward the axis of the whole system, the refracting angles of the various prisms increase the further from the axis they are situated, and therefore the rays which fall on a prism at a distance from the centre are more refracted than those which pass through near the centre; it is possible therefore that a pencil of rays diverging from a point such as Q may be refracted so as to converge to a point q, and the combination of prisms may thus form an image of Q at q.

Again since the central portion $ABCD$ is a plate, a ray which traverses it is not deviated by refraction, but emerges in the same direction as that before incidence.

112   LIGHT.   [CH. VI

If now we suppose the prisms to become extremely numerous, the size of each being correspondingly diminished,

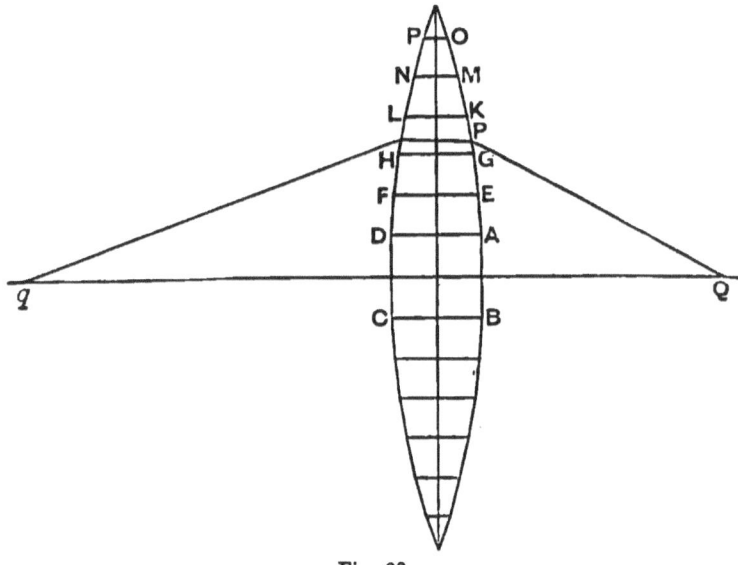

Fig. 80.

the lengths of the lines AE EG etc. become extremely small, and the surfaces of the prisms may be treated as a continuous curve instead of a number of small plane facets. In many cases the curves are portions of circular arcs.

69. Lenses. A portion of any transparent medium bounded by two circular arcs will refract rays of light like the assemblage of prisms described in the last section. Let BAC, $BA'C$, fig. 81, be two such circular arcs. Let the line AA' pass through the centres of the two circles so that it is perpendicular at A and A' to the two arcs respectively, and consider the solid formed by causing the arcs to rotate about AA', the two arcs will generate portions of two spheres which will intersect. If we suppose the space common

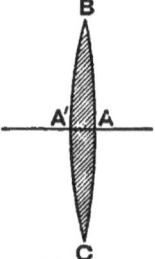

Fig. 81.

to the two spheres to be composed of some transparent material differing from the surrounding medium, light traversing it will be refracted similarly to the light which passes through the assemblage of prisms just described. A ray incident at any point except A, will on emergence be bent towards the line AA'. Such a portion of a transparent medium constitutes a lens. The line AA' is the axis of the lens.

When as in fig. 80 the edges of the prisms are all turned outwards from the axis so that the lens is thickest at its middle part, it is said to be a convex or converging lens; if on the other hand the edges of the prisms be turned towards the axis so that the lens formed is thinnest at the centre, as in fig. 82, the rays which traverse it are bent away from the axis and the lens is said to be concave or diverging.

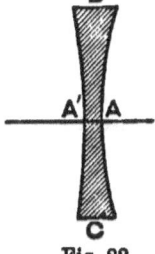

Fig. 82.

Definition of a lens. *A lens is a portion of a transparent refracting medium bounded by two surfaces*[1], *usually spherical.*

The line joining the centres of the two spheres which bound the lens is called *the axis of the lens*.

A convex lens is thickest at its axis and refracts rays which traverse it towards its axis.

A concave lens is thinnest at its axis and refracts rays which traverse it from the axis.

At the points at which they are cut by the axis the surfaces of a lens are parallel; in the neighbourhood therefore of the axis the lens behaves like a plate; rays which fall on it near these points are undeviated by refraction through the lens. The path of such a ray is given in fig. 83, PR incident at R very close to the axis is refracted along RS in the lens, again refracted in the opposite direction at S, and since the surfaces at R and S

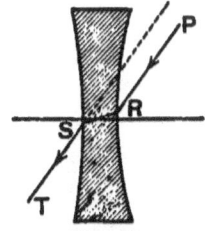

Fig. 83.

[1] In some lenses one of the surfaces is plane; such a lens may, if necessary, be treated as a special case of one having two spherical surfaces, if we suppose the radius of one of these to become infinitely large, for a plane may be looked upon as part of a sphere of very large radius.

are practically parallel to each other, it emerges along ST parallel to PR and is undeviated.

Principal Focus. If a pencil of parallel rays fall on a convex lens in a direction parallel to its axis they are made to converge by the lens and meet very approximately in a point on the axis. This point is called the *principal focus* of the convex lens.

If a pencil of parallel rays fall on a concave lens in a direction parallel to its axis they are made to diverge by the lens and appear after refraction to proceed very approximately from a point on the axis. This point is the *principal focus* of the concave lens.

Focal length. The distance between the lens and its principal focus is called the *focal length* of the lens.

Optical Centre of a lens. Consider two points at which the bounding surfaces on opposite sides of a lens are parallel. Join these two points and let the line joining them cut the axis in a point C. Then this point is found to be fixed on the axis and is called the *Optical Centre of the lens.*

The position of the Optical Centre may be found thus.

Let R, S, fig. 84, be two points on the lens at which the faces are parallel. Draw RO and SO' normals at R and S passing through O and

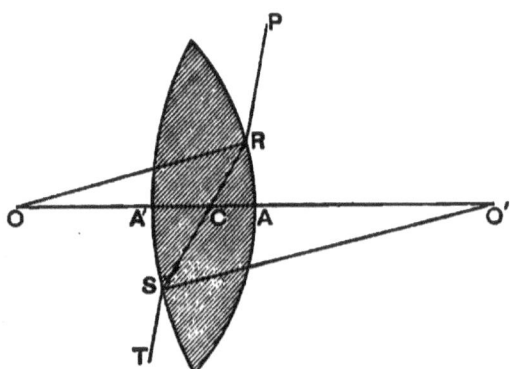

Fig. 84.

O' the centres of curvature of the faces. Then RO and SO' are parallel. Let RS cut AA' in C. Then the triangles ORC, $O'SC$ are similar.

Therefore
$$\frac{OC}{O'C} = \frac{OR}{O'S} = \frac{OA}{O'A'}.$$

Hence
$$\frac{AC}{A'C} = \frac{OA}{O'A'}.$$

Hence the point C divides AA' in the ratio of the radii of the surfaces and is therefore the same for all positions of R and S, provided only that the normals at R and S are parallel. This point is the optical centre and is fixed in position. In the case of some lenses the point C lies outside the lens dividing AA' externally in the ratio of the radii.

Now let PR be a ray which, when traversing the lens, passes through the optical centre C and let ST be the emergent ray. Since the angles between RS and the normals at R and S are equal, the angles between these same normals and the incident and emergent rays at R and S are also equal, but the normals at R and S are parallel, therefore the incident and emergent rays at R and S are parallel. Hence we arrive at the conclusion that if a ray be incident on a lens in such a direction that the refracted ray in the lens passes through the optical centre, the emergent ray is parallel to the incident ray. We may thus give the following definition of the optical centre of a lens.

If a ray of light traverses a lens in such a way that the incident and emergent rays are parallel, the path of the ray in the lens intersects the axis in a fixed point which is called the optical centre of the lens.

Thus when the ray in the lens passes through the optical centre the emergent ray is parallel to the incident ray, but is displaced laterally through an amount depending on the thickness of the lens and the angle of incidence.

70. Thin lenses. In most of the lenses with which we have to deal, the thickness of the lens is very small compared with its focal length. The points A and A' of figure 84 are very close together and the optical centre C is very close to either of them. When this is the case the lens is called *a thin lens*. In treating of a thin lens we neglect the thickness and consider the points A, A' and C as coincident. Either of them may be spoken of as the centre or optical centre of the lens.

In this case then a ray incident at A is neither deviated nor laterally displaced by refraction. The emergent and incident rays are in the same straight line. If we neglect the thickness of a lens near the axis we must neglect it elsewhere and treat the points of incidence and emergence of any ray as coincident.

71. Experiments with lenses. *To shew the refraction of light by a lens.*

(a) Arrange the lantern to produce a parallel pencil of horizontal rays and allow them to fall directly on a trough containing water mixed with a little fluorescent material. The path of the parallel beam through the water is clearly visible. Place a convex lens in the path of the beam before it enters the water. The emergent rays are convergent and are brought to a focus beyond the lens. Replace the convex lens by a concave one, the emergent rays are seen to be divergent.

(b) Light a gas flame and allow the light to fall on a convex lens at some distance away, place a screen beyond the lens; a luminous patch is seen on the screen, and by adjusting the screen a distinct inverted image of the flame can generally be seen. Move the gas flame nearer to the lens; the image ceases to be distinct, but on moving the screen further away it can again be brought into focus. If however the flame be brought fairly near up to the lens, it will be found impossible to obtain a real image on the screen: when this is the case, on looking through the lens at the flame, an erect magnified virtual image is visible.

(c) Replace the convex lens by a concave one; a real image can not now be obtained, but, on looking at the flame, an erect diminished virtual image is seen.

72. Positive and negative focal lengths. In numerical problems on lenses the various distances involved are usually measured from the centre of the lens, and the same convention with regard to signs as was explained in Section 51 is adopted. Lines drawn from the lens in a direction opposite to that in which the incident light travels are called positive, lines drawn from the lens in the same direction as that in which the incident light is travelling are negative.

Consider now a concave lens on which a parallel pencil is incident, the rays are made to appear to diverge by refraction from a point F, fig. 85, on the same side of the lens as the distant source. Thus the principal focus is virtual. The focal length AF is drawn from the lens in a direction meeting the incident light and is therefore positive.

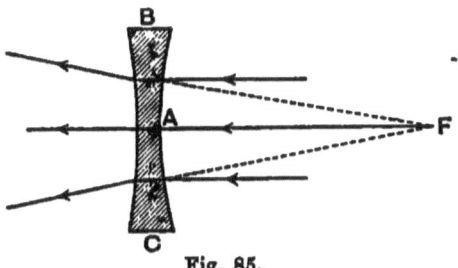

Fig. 85.

In the case of a convex lens, fig. 86, the parallel rays are made to converge by the lens. The point F is on the opposite

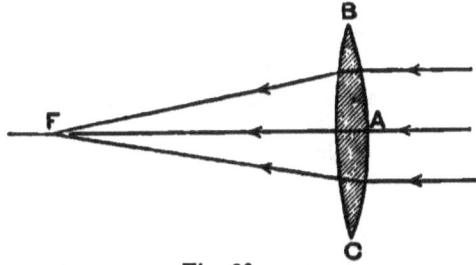

Fig. 86.

side of the lens to the distant source. The principal focus is real and the focal length AF is negative. Hence

The focal length of a concave lens is positive, that of a convex lens is negative.

The relation between the focal length of a lens, the form of its surfaces and its refractive index is discussed in § 84. It is there shewn that, if r and s are the radii of its first and second surfaces, μ the refractive index and f the focal length, then

$$\frac{1}{f} = (\mu - 1)\left(\frac{1}{r} - \frac{1}{s}\right).$$

In this formula r and s are subject to the usual convention as to signs. In the various forms of concave lens described in the next section it will be seen that s is either negative or, if positive, it is greater than r, so that in either case $\frac{1}{r} - \frac{1}{s}$ is positive and the focal length is positive; for a convex lens either r is negative, or s is less than r, thus the focal length is negative.

73. Forms of lenses. In fig. 87, are shewn three sections through the axis of various forms of concave lens. (a) is a *double concave* lens, both faces having their concavities turned outwards, (b) is a *plano-concave* lens, one face being

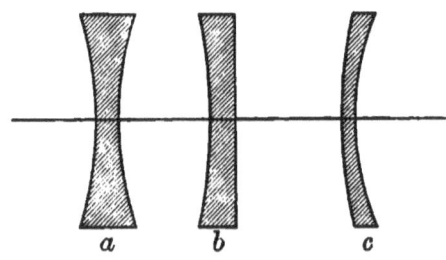

Fig. 87.

plane, while (c) is a *concave meniscus*, the second face is convex outwards but its radius is greater than that of the first face, so that the lens is thinnest at the centre. In all cases the principal focus is virtual and the focal length positive.

In fig. 88, are given three sections of convex lenses, (a) is a *double convex lens*, (b) a *plano-convex* lens, and (c) a *convex meniscus*; one face of (c) is concave outwards, but the radius of this face is greater than that of the second face, and the lens is thickest at the centre.

In all cases the principal focus is real and the focal length is negative.

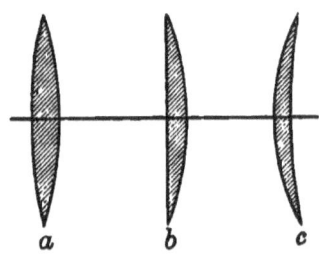

Fig. 88.

In most problems it is sufficient for us to know the position of the principal focus of a lens in order to obtain a solution. The forms of the surfaces do not affect the solution unless we are attempting to go to a higher order of approximation than is allowed by the limits of this book. Provided the focal lengths of the three lenses in fig. 88 be the same, any one of them produces, so far as our present purpose is concerned, the same effect on an incident pencil. It is only when we come to deal with more complex problems than are now before us that the form of the surface has to be considered.

74. Images formed by a lens. In determining the position of the image formed by a lens we make use of two principles, practically the same as those enunciated in Section 52 when dealing with reflexion.

(1) *A ray falling on a lens in a direction parallel to its axis passes on emergence through the principal focus.*

(2) *A ray incident at the optical centre passes through the lens with its direction unchanged.*

The point where these two emergent rays meet is the image of the source of light.

In applying these two principles to a graphical construction, a small practical difficulty arises from the fact that a lens, as drawn, usually has an appreciable thickness. Thus let CAB, fig. 89, be a lens, PR a ray incident parallel to the axis $F'AF$, A the optical centre, F the principal focus, and F' a point on the axis to the right of A such that AF' is equal to AF. Then PR is refracted at R along RS say, and after a second refraction at S emerges along SF. The points R and S are distinct. To find S we ought to apply the construction given in Section 67 for a

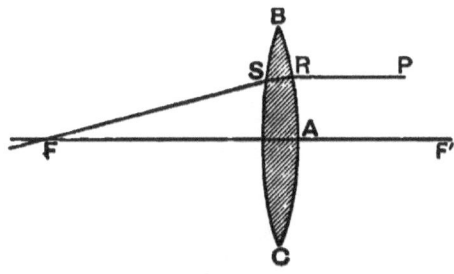

Fig. 89.

single refraction. But since the lens is to be treated as very thin, R and S are very close together, we may without serious error suppose them coincident, and treat RF as the emergent ray, the two lines RF and SF

are so near together that no appreciable error is introduced by this. The following method will give a slightly better result in the important case of a double convex lens. Join CB and let A, fig. 90, be the point in

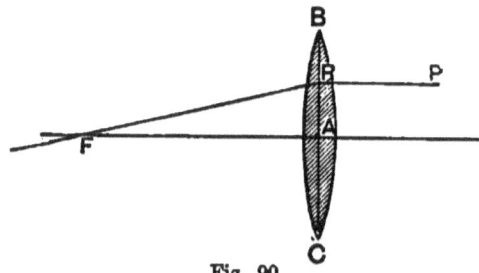

Fig. 90.

which CB cuts the axis. Produce the incident ray to meet CB in R. Join RF, then RF is the refracted ray. For a double concave lens take a plane BAC perpendicular to the axis and passing through the optical centre and proceed in the same way.

75. To find the image of a point formed by direct refraction through a thin concave lens. Let F be the principal focus, A the centre of a concave lens BAC, P a point on the object near the axis of the lens. Join PA and produce it

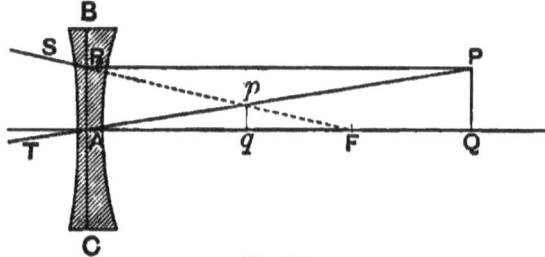

Fig. 91.

to T. A ray incident along PA emerges in the same straight line along AT. Draw PR parallel to the axis to meet the line BAC through the optical centre in R. Join FR and produce it to S. A ray incident along PR is refracted along RS; let FR and PA meet in p. The two emergent rays AT and RS appear to diverge from p, thus p is a virtual image of P. Draw PQ and pq perpendicular to the axis. Then pq is a virtual, erect and diminished image of PQ.

76. To obtain a formula connecting together the positions of an object and its image formed by direct refraction through a concave lens and to determine the magnifying power. Determine as in the last section the position of the image pq of an object PQ. Let $AQ = u$, $Aq = v$, $AF = f$. Then $RA = PQ$.

And we have

$$\frac{u}{v} = \frac{AQ}{Aq} = \frac{PQ}{pq} = \frac{RA}{pq} = \frac{AF}{Fq} = \frac{f}{f-v}.$$

$$\therefore f(u-v) = uv,$$

$$\therefore \frac{1}{v} - \frac{1}{u} = \frac{1}{f}.$$

Again, the magnifying power is equal to the ratio of pq to PQ, and we have

$$\frac{pq}{PQ} = \frac{v}{u} = \frac{\text{distance of image from lens}}{\text{distance of object from lens}}.$$

We can express the magnifying power in different ways for, from the figure, we find

$$m = \frac{pq}{PQ} = \frac{pq}{RA} = \frac{f-v}{f}.$$

Also from the formula

$$\frac{1}{v} - \frac{1}{u} = \frac{1}{f},$$

we have

$$\frac{u}{v} = 1 + \frac{u}{f} = \frac{f+u}{f},$$

$$\therefore m = \frac{v}{u} = \frac{f}{f+u}.$$

Moreover the formula shews us that v is always positive, so that the image is always virtual, and since $1/v$ is greater than $1/u$, v is less than u, and the magnifying power less than unity. We have also

$$\frac{f-v}{f} = m = \frac{f}{f+u}.$$

Thus $(f-v)(f+u) = f^2.$

Produce FA to F' making AF' equal to AF, then qF is equal to $f-v$, and QF' to $f+u$, hence we see that

$$QF' \cdot qF = f^2.$$

These results may be compared with those given for a mirror in Section 58.

77. To find the image of a point formed by direct refraction through a thin convex lens. The construction is the same as that in Section 75 but various cases arise. In the case of a convex lens, assuming the light to come from the right, the principal focus is to the left of the lens and f the focal length is negative.

Let F be the principal focus of the lens BAC, fig. 92. Take a point F' on the axis to the right of the lens and at a distance from the lens equal to its focal length f, so that AF' is equal to AF.

Case (1). *The object is at a distance less than f.*

Let PQ be an object nearer to the lens than F', fig. 92. Draw PAT through the centre, the ray PA emerges without deviation. Draw PR parallel to the axis meeting the line BAC in R. Join RF, the ray PR emerges along RF and it

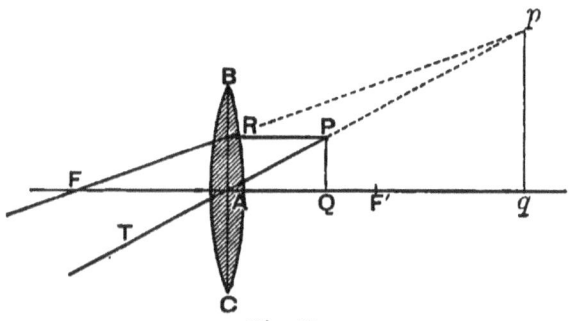

Fig. 92.

will be found that FR and TA can be produced backwards to meet; let them meet at p. Then p is a virtual image of P. Draw pq perpendicular to the axis; pq is the image of PQ and it is virtual, erect and magnified. This will be found to be the case whenever PQ lies between A and F'.

Case (2). *The object is at a distance greater than f, less than $2f$.*

Let PQ, fig. 93, be an object, further from the lens than F' but at a less distance than $2f$. Construct the figure in the same manner as previously. Draw PR parallel to the axis meeting BAC in R, join RF. Draw PA through the

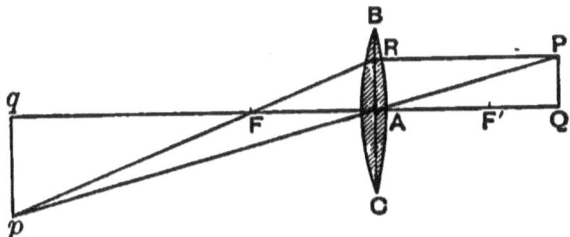

Fig. 93.

centre and produce it to p. It will be found that RF produced intersects Ap, let them meet at p. Draw pq perpendicular to the axis. Then pq is an image of PQ. In this case the image is real, inverted and magnified.

Case (3). *The object is at a distance from the lens greater than $2f$.*

Let PQ, fig. 94, be the object and suppose the distance AQ is greater than $2f$. Construct the figure exactly as for Case (2).

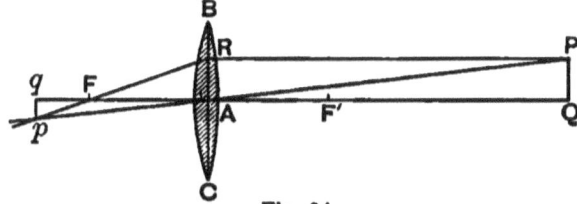

Fig. 94.

An image pq is formed, and it will be found that the image pq is in this case real, inverted and diminished.

Hence we may sum up our results for convex lenses thus: *A convex lens produces a virtual, magnified and erect image of an object which is nearer to it than its own focal length.*

When an object is placed at a distance from a convex lens greater than the focal length of the lens, the image formed by the lens is real and inverted. If the distance between the object and the lens is greater than the focal length but less than twice the focal length, the image is magnified, if the distance between the object and the lens is greater than twice the focal length the image is diminished.

78. To obtain a formula connecting together the positions of an object and its image formed by direct refraction through a convex lens and to determine the magnifying power. The formula and the method of proof given in Section 76 apply, if we remember that for a convex lens f is negative. We must therefore change the sign of f in the expressions there given and write

$$\frac{1}{v} - \frac{1}{u} = -\frac{1}{f}.$$

We can readily obtain the formula in this form from the figure thus.

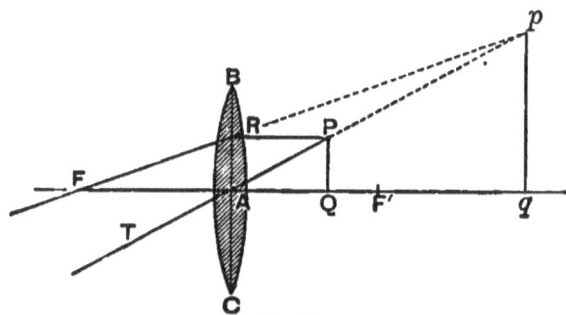

Fig. 95.

Determine as in the last Section (Case 1) the position of pq, a virtual image of an object PQ formed by a convex lens. Let

$$AQ = u, \quad Aq = v, \quad AF = f.$$

Then $RA = PQ$,

and we have

$$\frac{u}{v} = \frac{AQ}{Aq} = \frac{PQ}{pq} = \frac{RA}{pq} = \frac{AF}{Fq} = \frac{f}{f+v}.$$

Whence $f(u - v) = -uv$,

or $$\frac{1}{v} - \frac{1}{u} = -\frac{1}{f}.$$

In this formula f stands merely for the numerical value of

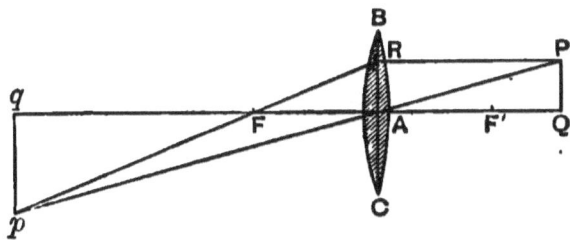

Fig. 96.

the focal length.

Again, if the image formed be real (Cases (2) and (3)), we have from fig. 96, in which

$$Aq = v, \quad AQ = u, \quad AF = f,$$

$$\frac{u}{v} = \frac{AQ}{Aq} = \frac{PQ}{pq} = \frac{RA}{pq} = \frac{AF}{Fq} = \frac{f}{v-f},$$

whence
$$f(u+v) = uv$$

or
$$\frac{1}{v} + \frac{1}{u} = \frac{1}{f}.$$

This formula only applies to the case of a convex lens forming a real image; it may be obtained from the standard form $\dfrac{1}{v} - \dfrac{1}{u} = \dfrac{1}{f}$ if we remember that v and f are both negative. We thus have

$$\frac{1}{-v} - \frac{1}{u} = \frac{1}{-f},$$

or
$$\frac{1}{v} + \frac{1}{u} = \frac{1}{f}.$$

Again, the magnifying power m is equal to the ratio of pq to PQ and we have

$$m = \frac{pq}{PQ} = \frac{v}{u} = \frac{\text{distance of image from lens}}{\text{distance of object from lens}}.$$

79. Measurements with convex lenses.

EXPERIMENT 19. *To verify the relation between the positions of an object and its image formed by a convex lens; to determine the focal length of the lens and to find its magnifying power.*

In making the observations we may use the optical bench shewn in fig. 11, the lens will take the place of the Bunsen disc and the screen that of one of the sources of light. Apparatus similar to that shewn in fig. 74 may also be employed. A convenient form of mounting for the lens is given in fig. 97.

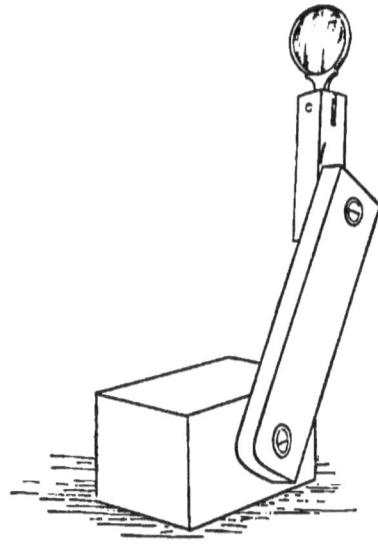

Fig. 97.

A substantial wooden block rests on the table and carries an arm which can rotate about a screw through one end. The lens, held in a metal or ebonite frame, is secured to a second arm attached to this by another screw, and is thus capable of various adjustments. The lens will come between the screen and source of light and the distances required can be measured by the scale and compasses.

(a) If the object be not too near the lens a real image will be formed on the side of the lens remote from the object.

Take as object a small gas flame, or preferably a flame in front of which a metal screen pierced with a hole some 5 mm. in diameter is placed. Arrange a white screen on the side of the lens remote from the light, and adjust it until the image is in focus on the screen. Measure the distance u of the object from the lens, and also the distance $-v$ of the image; the sign of v is negative because the image and object are on opposite sides.

Obtain in this way a series of corresponding values of u and $-v$, arrange them as in Table III. and calculate the value of $\frac{1}{v} - \frac{1}{u}$, for the different values of v and u. This value will, within the limits of error of the measurements, be found to be a constant negative quantity, if we denote it by $-\frac{1}{f}$ then f is the focal length of the lens. We thus find the focal length of a convex lens.

TABLE III.

u	$-v$	$\frac{1}{-v}$	$\frac{1}{u}$	$\frac{1}{v} - \frac{1}{u}$
60	138	·0072	·0167	− ·0239
70	103	·0097	·0143	− ·0240
80	87	·0115	·0125	− ·0240
90	77	·0130	·0111	− ·0241
100	71	·0141	·0100	− ·0241
120	63·5	·0158	·0083	− ·0241
140	59	·0169	·0071	− ·0240
160	56	·0178	·0063	− ·0241
180	54	·0185	·0056	− ·0241
83	83	·01204	·01204	− ·02408

The mean of the values in the last column is ·02405, and none of the values found differ much from this value. The reciprocal of − ·02405 is − 41·58, and this then is the focal length of the lens. Thus the formula is verified and the focal length is determined.

(b) If the object be near the lens a virtual magnified image is seen. Use a lens which has been cut in two along a diameter and mount it so that this diameter is vertical. It is then possible to see at the same time, by looking through the lens, the image of a horizontal pin or knitting needle formed by light refracted through the lens, and, by looking to one side, a second pin or needle which can be made to coincide with the image of the first.

By measuring the distance from the lens of the two pins we have the values of u and v, these we can substitute in the expression $\dfrac{1}{v} - \dfrac{1}{u}$, and thus again verify that the expression is constant for the various values of u and v.

This can be best done by tabulating the values as in (a). If the same lens be used in the two experiments the resulting values of f will be the same.

(c) To determine the magnifying power we need to measure the size of the object and the size of the image. This is done as in Section 62, using as object either, a circular hole of measured diameter or a translucent scale lighted from behind, and as screen a piece of squared paper or a second scale on which the image of the first may be cast.

(d) The following is a simple approximate method of finding the focal length of a convex lens. Hold the lens so as to throw on the wall or on a screen the real inverted image of some distant object; the bars of a window at a distance of 10 or 12 feet will serve, then if the focal length be about 1 foot or under, the window is practically an object at an infinite distance, and the distance between the lens and the wall is the focal length. Measure this with a scale.

80. Measurements with concave lenses.

EXPERIMENT 20. *To verify the relation between the positions of an object and its image formed by a concave lens; to determine the focal length of the lens, and to find its magnifying power.*

Use a lens cut in two across a diameter as in Experiment 19 (*b*). Look at one pin through the lens and adjust a second so that the image of the first seen through the lens may coincide with it. The distances of the pins from the lens give

79—81]   LENSES.   129

u and v. Tabulate these and calculate the values of $\frac{1}{v} - \frac{1}{u}$; they will be found to be constant and their reciprocal will be the focal length. To find the magnifying power, measure as in Section 62 (c) the size of the object and the image, and verify that their dimensions are in the ratio of their respective distances from the lens.

81. Vision through a lens. *To trace the pencil of rays by which an eye sees the image of an object formed by refraction through a lens.*

If an eye be placed at a suitable distance from a lens and in such a position that a pencil of rays diverging from a point on the image may enter it, the image formed will be seen by the eye. The course of the rays by which vision is produced in various cases is shewn in figs. 98-100.

Figure 98 shews a convex lens forming a real image. The eye E, is placed at some distance behind the image pq. To trace the rays, find the position, pq, of the image of an object PQ.

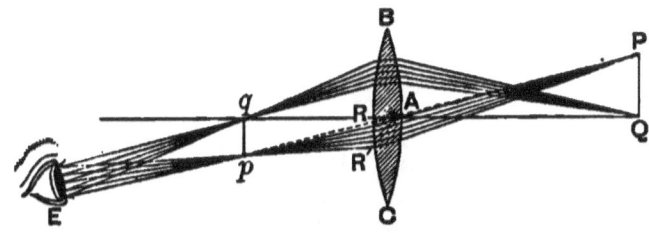

Fig. 98.

Draw the conical pencil of rays proceeding from p to fill the pupil of the eye and produce the rays back to meet the lens in RR'. Join RR' to P. Then a conical pencil diverging from P is made by the lens to converge to p, and on diverging thence enters the eye and produces vision; the eye sees pq, the image of PQ formed by the lens.

Figs. 99, 100, constructed in a similar manner, give the path of the rays in the case of a virtual image formed by a convex lens and concave lens respectively.

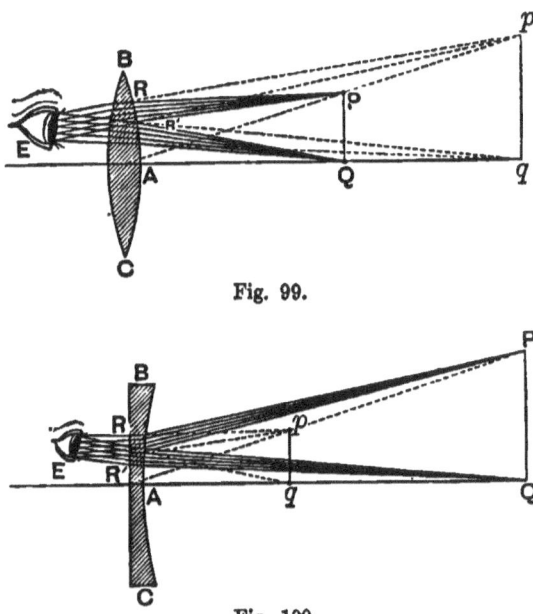

Fig. 99.

Fig. 100.

Examples. Many examples on lenses can be solved by aid of a graphical construction; if the drawings are done carefully and to scale numerical results may be readily obtained.

In working examples by the aid of the formula, it is much the best plan to adhere to the standard form $\dfrac{1}{v} - \dfrac{1}{u} = \dfrac{1}{f}$. If the lens be convex, f is negative, if, on substituting the values of f and u, v turns out to be negative, then the image and object are on opposite sides of the lens and the image is real. For example,

(a) *An object is placed at a distance of 15 inches from a concave lens 10 inches in focal length; find the position of the image and magnification.*

We may solve this graphically, constructing as in fig. 91, making

$AF = 10$, $AQ = 15$, or thus, in the formula, $u = 15$, $f = 10$,

$$\frac{1}{v} = \frac{1}{f} + \frac{1}{u} = \frac{1}{10} + \frac{1}{15} = \frac{3+2}{30} = \frac{1}{6},$$

$v = 6$ inches.

Magnification $= v/u = 6/15 = 2/5$.

(b) *Determine the position of the image under the same circumstances if the lens be convex.*

In this case

$$\frac{1}{v} = -\frac{1}{f} + \frac{1}{u} = -\frac{1}{10} + \frac{1}{15} = \frac{-3+2}{30} = -\frac{1}{30},$$

$v = -30$ inches.

Also $\qquad m = v/u = -30/15 = -2.$

Thus the image is real, at a distance of 30 inches from the lens on the side remote from the object and of twice the size of the object. Since the magnification is negative we infer that the image is inverted.

(c) *An object is placed at 5 inches from the same convex lens; find the position of the image and the magnification.*

We have $\qquad \dfrac{1}{v} = -\dfrac{1}{f} + \dfrac{1}{u} = -\dfrac{1}{10} + \dfrac{1}{5} = \dfrac{1}{10},$

$v = 10$ inches,

$m = v/u = 2.$

Thus the image is 10 inches from the lens and is virtual, the magnification is 2.

*82. Formulae connected with a lens. (a) *To shew that in a concave lens the image of a real object is always virtual.* This may be done by experiment or by constructing graphically for the position of the image corresponding to a series of positions of the object. It follows at once from the formula for

$$\frac{1}{v} = \frac{1}{u} + \frac{1}{f}.$$

Thus since u and f are positive v is positive, and the image is virtual. Moreover $1/v$ is greater than $1/u$; thus v is less than u and the image is diminished.

(b) *To shew that in a convex lens the image of a real object may be virtual or real.* We have for this case

$$\frac{1}{v} = \frac{1}{u} - \frac{1}{f}.$$

If u is less than f, $1/u$ is greater than $1/f$ and $1/v$ is positive. The image is virtual. If u is equal to f, $1/v$ is zero and v is infinite.

If however u is greater than f, $1/u$ is less than $1/f$, thus $1/v$ is negative and the image is real.

(c) *To trace the changes in the position of the image as the object is moved from a distance up to the lens.*

Take the case of a convex lens for which the formula gives

$$\frac{1}{v} = \frac{1}{u} - \frac{1}{f}.$$

When u is infinite, $v = -f$, the image is formed at the principal focus and is real and inverted; as u decreases, the object moving nearer to the lens, v increases, remaining negative.

Again, v is less than u until $u = 2f$ when $v = -2f$, and the object and image are of the same size. As u decreases further, v is still negative and increases until the value $u = f$ is reached, when v becomes infinite. Throughout these changes the image is real and inverted.

When u is less than f, $1/u$ is greater than $1/f$, thus v is positive and greater than u; hence, when the object is nearer to the lens than its principal focus, the image is virtual and magnified.

*83. **Special problems with Lenses.** We require in some experiments to consider the path of a pencil of rays which are converging to a point, but which before actually reaching it fall on a lens. In finding this the same principles apply. Let us suppose that an image of some distant object is formed by a convex lens or concave mirror and that the rays which go to form it are intercepted by a lens, which may be either concave or convex.

(a) Let P, fig. 101, be a point to which a pencil of rays is converging, and let the pencil fall on a *concave lens*. Two cases occur depending on the position of the lens.

(i) Suppose P be at a greater distance from the lens than its focal length. Consider a ray $P'RP$ travelling parallel to the axis, let F be the principal focus, join F to R and produce it to R', then the ray $P'R$ is refracted along RR'. Consider another incident ray pAP passing through the centre

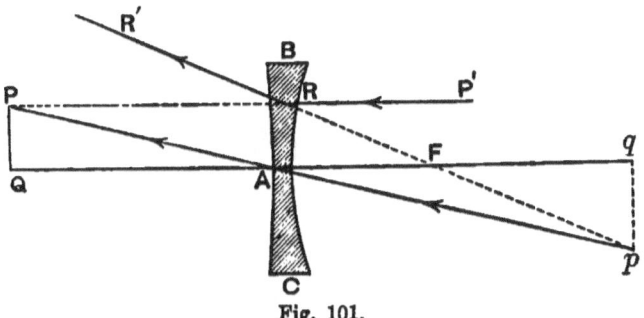

Fig. 101.

of the lens. This ray travels on without deviation. Let $R'R$ produced backwards meet it in p. Then rays converging to P appear after refraction to diverge from p and a virtual image pq is formed of PQ.

(ii) Suppose P to be nearer the lens than its principal focus. The same construction will apply, but it will be found that p is to the left of P. A real magnified image is formed.

(b) Let the convergent pencil fall on a *convex* lens. Then the incident pencil is made more convergent by refraction, the construction is the same and it will be found that a real diminished image of P is always formed nearer the lens than the point P itself.

*84. Formulae connected with direct refraction at a spherical surface.

Let QR, fig. 102, be an incident ray making an angle ORQ equal to ϕ with the normal at R; let the refracted ray produced backwards meet the axis in q. Draw RN perpendicular to the axis. Then $ORq = \phi'$, let

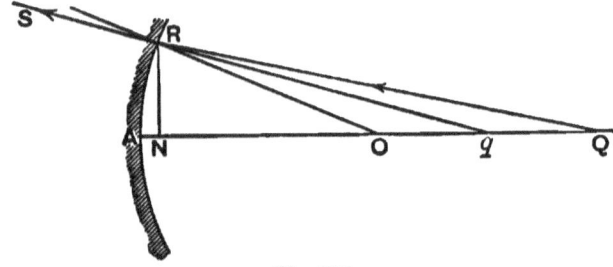

Fig. 102.

$AOR = \theta$. Then $RQO = \theta - \phi$, $RqO = \theta - \phi'$. When R is very near to A, RQ becomes equal to u, Rq to v. Put RN equal to a.

Then from the figure when R is near A, i.e. when the incidence is direct,

$$\sin \theta = \frac{a}{r} \quad \sin(\theta - \phi) = \frac{a}{u} \quad \sin(\theta - \phi') = \frac{a}{v},$$

and since when an angle is small it may be put equal to its sine, we have ultimately

$$\theta = \frac{a}{r}, \quad \theta - \phi = \frac{a}{u}, \quad \theta - \phi' = \frac{a}{v},$$

$$\therefore \phi = \frac{a}{r} - \frac{a}{u}, \quad \phi' = \frac{a}{r} - \frac{a}{v}.$$

Also $\sin \phi = \mu \sin \phi'$, or if ϕ and ϕ' are small, $\phi = \mu \phi'$.

Therefore
$$\frac{a}{r} - \frac{a}{u} = \mu \left(\frac{a}{r} - \frac{a}{v} \right),$$

or
$$\frac{\mu}{v} - \frac{1}{u} = \frac{\mu - 1}{r}.$$

When u is infinite and $1/u$ zero, v is equal to f the focal length. Hence

$$f = \frac{\mu r}{\mu - 1}.$$

Refraction through a lens. Let AB, fig. 103, be the axis of the lens. Let r be the radius of the first, s that of the second surface, and suppose that both surfaces turn their concavities towards the light so that r and s are positive. If the lens is thin we may measure distances indiscriminately from either A or B. Let Q be a source of light on the axis. Let Q' be the geometrical image of Q formed by the first refraction, and let

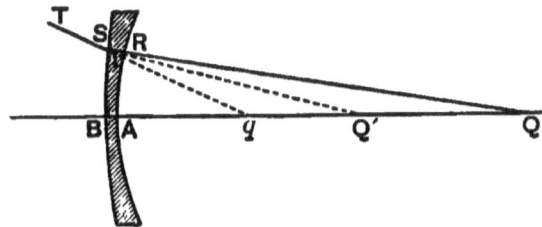

Fig. 103.

q be the image of Q' formed by refraction at the second surface. Let
$$AQ = u, \quad Aq = v.$$
Then the formula just proved gives
$$\frac{\mu}{AQ'} - \frac{1}{u} = \frac{\mu - 1}{r} \quad\dots\dots\dots\dots\dots\dots(1).$$

For the second refraction from glass to air the refractive index is $1/\mu$, and since A and B are, if the thickness be neglected, coincident, we have
$$\frac{\frac{1}{\mu}}{v} - \frac{1}{AQ'} = \frac{\frac{1}{\mu} - 1}{s}.$$
or
$$\frac{1}{v} - \frac{\mu}{AQ'} = -\frac{\mu - 1}{s} \quad\dots\dots\dots\dots\dots\dots(2).$$

Hence adding (1) and (2) we eliminate μ/AQ', and find
$$\frac{1}{v} - \frac{1}{u} = (\mu - 1)\left(\frac{1}{r} - \frac{1}{s}\right).$$

If u is infinite $v = f$. Thus
$$\frac{1}{f} = (\mu - 1)\left(\frac{1}{r} - \frac{1}{s}\right) \quad\dots\dots\dots\dots\dots\dots(3).$$

Therefore
$$\frac{1}{v} - \frac{1}{u} = \frac{1}{f} \quad\dots\dots\dots\dots\dots\dots(4).$$

The formula (3) gives us the value of the focal length in terms of the radii of curvature of the surfaces of the lens.

For a double convex lens r is negative, for a plano-convex r is infinite, and for a convex meniscus r is positive but greater than s. Thus in all these cases f is negative.

EXAMPLES.

LENSES.

1. A small object 1 inch in length is placed at a distance of 3 feet from a convex lens of focal length 1 foot. Where and of what size is the image? Illustrate your answer by a figure.

2. Explain with figures the action of a convex lens, (1) when used as a magnifying glass, (2) when forming a real image of an object.

A circular disc 1 inch in diameter is placed at a distance of 2 feet from a convex lens of 1 foot focal length. Where and of what size will the image be?

3. Draw accurately the paths of four rays, two proceeding from each end of an object 2 inches high, placed symmetrically on the axis of a concave lens of 4 inches focal length at a distance of 6 inches from it; and thus obtain the height and position of the image.

4. Determine the positions of the images formed when an object is placed at a distance (a) of 3 feet, (b) of 1 foot, in front of a convex lens of 2 feet focal length.

5. A convex lens of 6 inches focal length is used to read the graduations of a scale and is placed so as to magnify them three times; shew how to find at what distance from the scale it is held, the eye being close up to the lens.

6. An object is placed at a distance $2f$ from a convex lens of focal length f. The rays after traversing the lens are reflected from a convex mirror and again refracted by the lens, forming a real inverted image coincident with the object: if the distance between the lens and the mirror is a shew that the radius of the mirror is $2f-a$.

7. A circular disc 1 inch in diameter is placed at a distance of 2 feet from a concave lens of 1 foot focal length. Where and of what size will the image be?

8. Two convex lenses are placed on the same axis at a distance apart slightly less than the sum of their focal lengths. Shew how to trace a pencil of rays from a distant object through such a combination. Determine the magnification produced by the lenses.

9. Shew how to determine, either graphically or arithmetically, the position and magnitude of the image of an object placed in front of a convex lens. An arrow 1 inch long is placed 8 inches away from a convex lens whose focal length is 8 inches. Find the position and length of the image.

10. You are provided with a lens of 6 in. focal length and a screen 15 ft. square, and are required to form an image of a lantern slide 3 in. square so as to just fill the screen. Where must the lens and slide be placed?

LENSES.

11. Explain how to determine the focal length of a double convex lens without the aid of sun light.

12. A person looks at an object through a concave lens of 1 foot focal length, the object being 5 feet beyond the lens. Draw a figure shewing the paths of the rays by which he sees the image formed, and determine its position.

13. A convex lens of focal length f is placed at a distance $4f$ in front of a concave mirror of radius f and an object is placed half way between the two. Compare the sizes of the images formed by refraction through the lens (1) directly, and (2) after one reflexion at the mirror.

14. A convex and a concave lens each of 10 in. focal length are held coaxially at a distance of 5 in. apart. Find the position of the image if the object is at a distance of 15 in. beyond (a) the convex lens, (b) the concave lens.

15. If an observer's eye be held up close to a convex lens of 3 cm. focal length to view an object at a distance of 2·5 cm. from the lens shew that the magnifying power is 6.

16. Light from a luminous object passes through a concave lens and after reflexion from a concave mirror forms a real inverted image of the object between the lens and the mirror. Trace the path of the rays; and shew how to find the focal length of the lens from a knowledge of the radius of the mirror, the distance between the lens and mirror and the positions of the object and image.

17. A circular disc 1 inch in diameter is placed at a distance of two feet from a convex lens; a virtual image 1 foot in diameter is formed. Find the focal length of the lens.

18. Describe a method of finding the focal length of a concave lens by experiment, giving diagrams showing the course of the rays of light.

19. Give drawings to scale shewing the formation of a real image by a concave mirror and a convex lens respectively.

20. An object is placed at a distance f from a concave lens of focal length f. The rays after traversing the lens are reflected from a concave mirror and again refracted by the lens, forming a real inverted image coincident with the object: if the distance between the lens and the mirror is a shew that the radius of the mirror is $a + \tfrac{1}{2}f$.

21. A small air-bubble in a sphere of glass 4 inches in diameter appears when looked at so that the bubble and the centre of the sphere are in a line with the eye, to be 1 inch from the surface. What is its true distance? ($\mu = 1\cdot 5$.)

22. An object 3 inches in height is placed at a distance of 6 feet from a lens, and a real image is formed at a distance of 3 feet from the lens. The object is then placed 1 foot from the lens. Where, and of what height, will the image be?

138   LIGHT.

23. A convergent pencil of light falls upon a concave lens. Trace the position of the image as the point of convergence of the pencil moves from an infinite distance up to the lens.

24. What is meant by the statement—the focal length of a given convex lens is 2 feet? Draw a figure, approximately to scale, indicating the paths of the rays of light and the positions of the images formed, when an object is placed (a) at a distance of 6 feet, (b) at a distance of 1 foot from such a lens.

25. Explain the action of a convex lens when used as a simple microscope and shew by a figure the mode of determining the magnitude and position of the image when the focal length of the lens and the position of the object are given.

26. If the focal length of a concave lens be 4 in. and the object 6 in. away from it, where will the image be?

CHAPTER VII.

OPTICAL INSTRUMENTS. THE EYE. VISION.

85. The Optical Lantern. This piece of apparatus has been referred to in several of the preceding sections. It is usually employed as in the Magic Lantern to produce on a screen a magnified image of an object, such as a photographic transparency. This can be done by the aid of a convex lens which, as we have seen, produces a real magnified image of an object placed at a rather greater distance from the lens than its principal focus.

When the image is much magnified, the light proceeding from the object is diffused over a large area; its intensity therefore at each point of the area is diminished, and unless the object is brilliantly illuminated the image is faint. In the optical lantern a brilliant source is used to illuminate the object. The rays diverging from this source traverse a large convex lens or pair of lenses called the condenser, and are caused by this to converge on to the object in such a way as to illuminate it all over, and afterwards to traverse the convex lens or combination of lenses by which the image is formed on the screen; when a lamp is used as the source a concave mirror is placed behind it so as to reflect on to the condenser the rays which proceed backwards from the source, and thus increase the illumination. The arrangement of the apparatus is shewn diagrammatically in fig. 104.

The position of the convex lens can be adjusted so as to

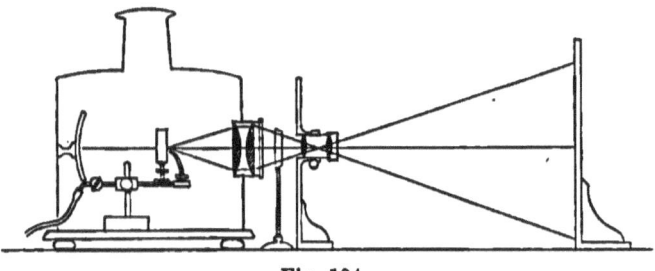

Fig. 104.

focus the image distinctly on the screen.

86. The Camera Obscura. The principle of this is shewn in fig. 105. AB represents a plane mirror or a large right-angled prism with its reflecting face at 45° to the vertical. Light, from a distant object, falling on this is reflected vertically on to a convex lens appearing to come from the virtual image of the object which is formed by the mirror.

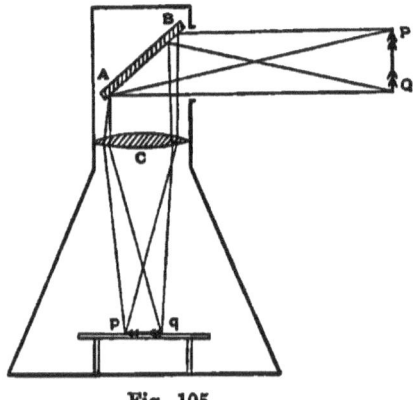

Fig. 105.

The mirror and lens are placed in the roof of a darkened chamber, and the focal length of the lens is such that a real image of the object is produced on a white table placed below.

85–87] OPTICAL INSTRUMENTS. THE EYE; VISION. 141

The mirror can be turned round the vertical and, as this is done, images of objects in various directions are formed on the table below.

87. The Photographic Camera. The optical part of this consists of a convex lens, by aid of which a real diminished image of an object at some little distance can be formed on a screen. This screen forms one end of a box of adjustable length, the lens or combination of lenses being placed in the centre of the opposite end. The sides of the box are everywhere opaque to light, which can thus reach the screen only by traversing the lens.

The image formed by the lens is at first received on a screen of ground glass, so that it is visible to an eye placed behind the glass, and the distance between the screen and the lens is adjusted until the focussing is distinct. When this is secured, the ground glass is replaced by a plate coated with a film of collodion or of gelatine containing a salt of silver which is sensitive to light and the image formed on this. Chemical changes take place in the film, depending on the intensity of the light and the time of exposure, and the impression thus formed is rendered visible and made permanent by the action of developing and fixing solutions. So far as the optical action is concerned, the essential part of the camera is a convex lens arranged to form on a sensitive plate a real image of an object.

The above three instruments are based on the action of a convex lens in forming a real image of a distant object. This end can be attained by the use of either a single lens or a combination of lenses. A more complete study of the action of a lens would reveal various defects; thus the images which have been hitherto considered are formed by rays which traverse the lens directly; in a photographic camera much of the light falls very obliquely on the lens and the image produced by a single lens would be far from perfect. Moreover, as is explained in Chapter IX., owing to dispersion the images formed would be coloured at their edges. These and other defects are more or less completely remedied by the use of a combination of lenses, and the optical parts, of the Camera or the Magic Lantern are therefore less simple than those shewn in the figures.

88. The eye. The eye is practically a photographic camera. A combination of lenses forms an inverted image of external objects on the retina, a network of nerves at the back of the eye. These nerves convey the sensation of sight to the brain.

The eye is nearly spherical in form and is surrounded, except in front, by an opaque horny coat called the *sclerotica*. In front the outer coat is transparent and protrudes somewhat beyond the spherical surface of the rest. This protuberant

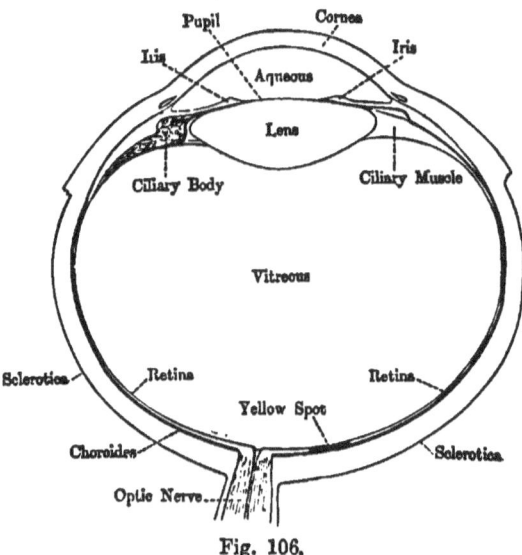

Fig. 106.

portion, fig. 106, is called the *cornea* and has a radius of about 8 mm. The axis of the eye is a line through its centre and the centre of the cornea; the eye is nearly symmetrical about this line.

Within the sclerotic coat is a second opaque coat called the *choroides*, which has a circular aperture, called the *pupil*, behind the cornea. The size of this aperture can be varied so as to change the amount of light admitted to the interior of the eye. The portion of the choroides which is visible through the cornea is variously coloured in different eyes, and is called the *iris*. The back of the eye is covered with a black substance called the *pigmentum nigrum*. Behind the pupil is the *crystalline lens*, a double convex lens with its axis coincident with that of the eye. The radii of its first and second surfaces are about 10 mm. and 6 mm. respectively. The lens is attached to the choroid coat by the *ciliary processes* and the *ciliary muscle*, and by their aid the curvature of the surfaces of the lens can be varied, thus making it more or less convex at will.

The interior of the eye within the choroid coat is covered by a semi-transparent membrane of nerve-fibres resulting from the spreading out of the terminal fibres of the optic nerve. This is the *retina*. In the centre of the retina is a round yellowish spot known as the *yellow spot*, or "macula lutea." Vision is most distinct when the image of an object looked at is formed on the yellow spot. About 2·5 mm. to the inner side of the yellow spot is the *blind spot*, from which the fibres of the optic nerve diverge to form the retina. This portion is so named because it is insensitive to light; an image formed on it does not produce vision. The space between the crystalline lens and the cornea is filled with a watery fluid called the *aqueous humour*, between the crystalline lens and the retina is another fluid called the *vitreous humour*. The refractive indices of these fluids differ little from that of water; Listing gives them as about 1·34. The crystalline lens has a refractive index rather greater than that of water, its value is about 1·45.

According to Listing the axis of the normal eye has a length of 21 mm., the distance between the cornea and the front surface of the lens being 4 mm., the thickness of the lens 4 mm., and the distance between the posterior surface of the lens, and the retina 13 mm.

In such an eye the first principal focus lies 12·8 mm. in front of the cornea; rays diverging from this point will be parallel when they reach the retina. The second principal focus lies 14·6 mm. behind the posterior surface of the lens; parallel rays, falling on the cornea, converge after entering the vitreous humour to this point, which it will be observed is very slightly behind the retina.

The normal eye acts very much as though it were a convex lens, having its centre about ·5 mm. in front of the posterior surface of the crystalline lens, with a focal length of 14·6 mm.

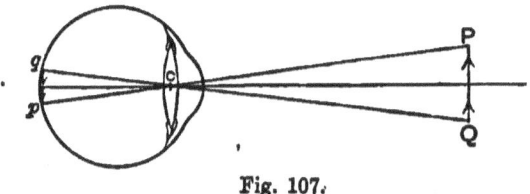

Fig. 107.

When an object at some little distance is viewed an inverted image is formed on the retina. This is shewn in a diagrammatic manner in fig. 107.

Thus, in the case of such an eye, an object at a considerable distance would be focussed as a sharp inverted image on the retina, and the impression of vision conveyed to the brain would be distinct.

It is generally supposed, in explaining the optics of vision, that, for a normal eye at rest, the principal focus is on the retina, so that an infinitely distant object could be seen distinctly. If the surfaces of the refracting media of which the eye is composed were rigid, distinct vision would only be possible for this one position of the object; as the object moved nearer to the eye the image would move further from the lens, i.e. behind the retina and the impression on the retina would be blurred and indistinct. But experience shews that there is a wide range of distance through which distinct vision is possible. This is secured by changes in the curvature of the refracting surfaces of the eye. These changes are known under the term *accommodation*. Thus the normal eye becomes accommodated for near objects, through the crystalline lens being made more convex. Both surfaces of the lens become more curved, but the change is greatest in the anterior surface, whose radius alters from some 10 mm. to about 6 mm. when the eye is adjusted to view a near object, while the radius of the posterior surface may change from 6 mm. to 5·5 mm. An experiment shewing these changes is described in Section 89, Experiment (23).

These various curvatures are measured by an instrument called an Ophthalmometer. This depends for its action on the fact that, if light from an object of known size at a given distance from a surface be reflected from the surface, and if the size of the image can be measured, the curvature of the surface can be calculated. The ophthalmometer enables us to measure the size of any inaccessible small object, and in particular of the images of a distant object formed by the surfaces of the eye.

Its action is illustrated by the following experiment. Focus a small telescope on an object at a little distance. Cover half the object glass of the telescope with a plate of thick glass; so long as the glass is perpendicular to the axis of the telescope a single image is seen; tilt the glass a little from this normal position, a second image of the same size as the first appears. The rays from the object fall obliquely on the glass, and emerge parallel to their original directions, but displaced slightly to one side. The amount of this displacement can be calculated if the thickness and refractive index of the glass plate and the angle of incidence on the glass be known.

Rotate the glass until the image is displaced through its own length, so that opposite ends of the two images coincide. By measuring the angle through which the glass is rotated, the lateral displacement can be found, and this lateral displacement is the size of the image. From this the curvature of the reflecting surface can be calculated. In the ophthalmometer two glass plates are used, covering the two halves of the telescope lens. These are turned in opposite directions, and the observed lateral displacement is thus half due to each glass.

89. Experiments on the eye and vision. For these a long rectangular glass trough is useful; one end of the trough is convex outwards. It may consist of a large glass capsule such as is sometimes used in chemical laboratories, cemented into a suitable frame and forming the end. This convex glass represents the cornea in the eye. Within the trough is a ground glass screen which can be made to slide backwards and forwards, and represents the retina. In front of the screen hangs a convex lens of glass which can also slide backwards and forwards; this represents the crystalline lens. The trough is filled with water containing a little eosine, to represent the aqueous and vitreous humours. Place at some little distance in front of the artificial eye a sharply defined luminous object such as an illuminated hole in a metal sheet. The rays are refracted on entering the convex glass surface, and again when traversing the lens. By suitably adjusting the lens and screen, an image of the source can be formed on the latter, which represents the retina; the eye is then focussed for the luminous object, and the path of the rays can be traced through the fluorescent liquid.

It can be shewn in various ways that the image is inverted. Thus use as the object a triangular hole with its vertex downwards: the image is a triangle with its vertex upwards.

Now move the source further from the eye; the image is formed nearer to the lens than previously; on the screen there is only a blurred patch. The distinct image may be brought on to the screen again, either (1) by moving the screen nearer to the lens, thus shortening the eye, or (2) by moving the lens nearer to the screen, or (3) by modifying the shape of the lens, making it thinner and therefore less convex. Observation tells us (see Experiment 23) that it is this last plan which is adopted in Nature. In our experiment we can imitate it by changing the lens for a thinner one.

If we had moved the light from its original position nearer to the eye, we should have found the opposite effects to those just described. The image would be formed behind the screen, the eye needs lengthening or the lens must be replaced by a more convex one. Thus the process of accommodation is illustrated. In the normal eye the lens is adapted for vision of a point at infinity; accommodation is attained by thickening the lens.

The following experiments illustrate the same points.

EXPERIMENT (21). *To prove that images formed on the retina are inverted.*

Take a piece of cardboard with three pinholes bored in it so as to make an equilateral triangle smaller than the pupil of the eye. Hold the cardboard so that the triangle shall have its vertex uppermost and shall be as near as possible to and opposite the pupil. Let light fall on these holes through a pinhole in another piece of cardboard held just in front of them at a distance of about an inch. It is clear that in this case there will be three patches of light on the retina forming a triangle of which the vertex is uppermost. The impression received however is that of such a triangle with the vertex undermost. This proves that the brain considers as the lowest part of any object that part which gives rise to the highest part of the image on the retina. The inverted image formed by the lens on the retina is reinverted by the brain.

EXPERIMENT (22). *To prove the existence of the blind spot.*

A piece of paper is taken with a cross and a black circle marked upon it about 10 cm. apart. It is held with the line joining these marks horizontal so that the cross is opposite to the right eye and the circle is to the left of the cross.

The right eye is then closed and the paper moved backwards and forwards, the left eye being kept fixed on the cross. It will then be found that in a particular position of the paper the circle becomes invisible, but that it reappears if the paper is brought nearer or taken further off. In the particular position found that part of the left retina upon which the image is formed cannot be sensitive to light and is called the blind spot. It is the point at which the optic nerve enters the eye.

The experiment may also be performed with the right eye open, the cross in this case being held opposite to the closed left eye.

EXPERIMENT (23). *To illustrate the process of accommodation in the eye.*

A convex lens is placed in a holder, a luminous object, such as a candle, is placed in front of it and at a considerable distance, and a white screen is placed behind so that the image of the candle falls upon it. The lens and screen may be taken to represent the crystalline lens and retina of the eye, and we then have an illustration of the manner in which a distant object is seen. Now if the candle is moved up nearer to the lens, say to a distance of a foot from it, a distinct image will no longer appear on the screen, but in order to obtain it a lens with more curved surfaces must be substituted.

This is exactly what takes place in the eye, the crystalline lens becomes more convex as the object looked at moves nearer, and so within certain limits of distance a distinct image is always formed on the retina.

If the lenses used in this experiment be put up side by side and a candle be placed some little distance in front of them we can by looking at them from the front see in each case two images of the candle formed by reflexion at the two surfaces of the lens respectively. Since the front surface forms a convex and the back a concave mirror, and the object is beyond the centre of the latter, both images will be diminished, that formed at the front surface will be erect, and that formed at the back surface will be inverted. The images formed by the more curved surfaces will be the smaller, as they should be from the theory of spherical mirrors.

If a taper is held in front of an eye which is looking at a distant object an image of the taper formed by reflexion at the cornea will be seen, and also a pair of images formed by reflexion at the surfaces of the crystalline lens as in the above experiment. If the eye be now employed to view a near object the images formed by the cornea and the back surface of the lens do not change appreciably, shewing that these surfaces do not change in curvature, but the image formed by the front surface of the lens gets smaller, shewing that this surface becomes more curved.

90. Defects of Vision. The most prominent defects of vision are (a) *Short-Sight*, (b) *Long-Sight*, (c) *Astigmatism*.

(a) **Short-Sight** or *Myopia*. An eye which is short-sighted cannot see distant objects distinctly. The eye-ball is too long for the lens, having usually become elongated from one or other of various causes. When the lens is in its normal state, i.e. as thin as possible, the rays from a distant object are brought to a focus *in front* of the retina. The eye, since the ball cannot be shortened, needs a less powerful lens. As the object is moved nearer to the eye, the image moves further from the lens, approaching the retina until a position is reached in which it is formed on the retina; for this distance vision will be distinct. As the object approaches still nearer, accommodation is needed and the lens is thickened; thus for some way within this distance vision is distinct.

Since in short-sight the crystalline lens is too thick for the length of the eye, the defect can be remedied by placing before the eye a concave lens of suitable focal length; such a lens counteracts the excessive refraction of the eye itself and renders vision at greater distances possible.

(b) **Long-Sight** or *Hypermetropia*. An eye which is long-sighted cannot see near objects distinctly. The eye-ball is too short, so that with the accommodation relaxed the focus is beyond the retina. The eye described in Section 88 is slightly long-sighted, the focus is 1·6 mm. behind the retina. More or less accommodation is needed to see distant objects distinctly. Convergent rays would be required to produce vision when the eye is in its normal state. As the object approaches the eye, the accommodation required for vision increases, and in a long-sighted eye even at a considerable distance, the necessary accommodation is more than the eye admits of. The lens cannot be made sufficiently thick to focus near objects on the retina: for this purpose the assistance of a convex lens is needed.

Thus Long-Sight is remedied by the use of convex spectacles.

(c) **Astigmatism.** In the preceding explanation it has been assumed that the eye is symmetrical about its axis, so that any section through the axis is equally curved, thus the focal lengths of all such sections are the same. Hence, if the eye is adjusted to see distinctly a horizontal line, a vertical or oblique line at the same distance will be equally distinct. In some eyes this is not the case; on looking at a sheet of paper on which a number of vertical and horizontal lines are drawn, the vertical lines may appear distinct, while the horizontal are blurred, and vice versa. This defect is called Astigmatism. It arises from an inequality of curvature of the vertical and horizontal sections of the eye; in general the cornea is the principal seat of this want of symmetry, a vertical section in an astigmatic eye being usually more curved than a horizontal one. The defect, if in other respects the sight is normal, may be remedied by the use of a cylindrical lens; if such a lens be employed, its axis being vertical, the curvature of a horizontal section of the lens makes up for the defective curvature of the horizontal section of the cornea, and the foci for the vertical and horizontal portions of the object coincide.

91. Experiments to illustrate defects of vision and their remedies.

(a) *Short-Sight.* The rectangular trough already described in Section 89 will be of use for these experiments. Arrange the trough as for the experiments in that section, but place the screen—the retina—at a greater distance from the lens than the image of the luminous source. This corresponds to the short-sighted eye; the lens is too powerful for the length of the eye, or the eye is too long for the lens. Place in front of the convex transparent end of the trough—the cornea—a concave lens; the image is thrown back towards the screen and may by a suitable choice of a lens be accurately focussed on to the screen. Short-sight is corrected by the aid of a concave lens. Short-sighted individuals wear concave spectacles.

(b) *Long-Sight.* Arrange the trough as before, but adjust it so that the image formed by the lens is behind the screen. The eye is long-sighted; its length is too short for the lens, which is not sufficiently convex. Place before the cornea a convex lens; the image is brought nearer to the crystalline lens, and by a suitable choice may be made to fall on the screen. Long-sight is corrected by the aid of a convex lens. Long-sighted individuals wear convex spectacles.

(c) *Astigmatism.* This can be imitated by introducing behind the cornea a cylindrical lens of long focus, the axis of the cylinder being horizontal. Refraction through it combined with refraction at the cornea will produce the same effect as though the cornea were not spherical, but of rather greater curvature in a vertical plane than in a horizontal. Take as source of light a slit in a sheet of card or metal in the form of a cross and place it with one arm horizontal and the other vertical. Adjust the screen so that the horizontal arm may be in focus. It will be found that the vertical arm of the image appears blurred; to focus it the screen must be moved further back, and when it is in focus the horizontal arm is not.

To correct the defect place a cylindrical lens, the axis of the cylinder being vertical, before the cornea; by a proper choice of this lens it will be possible to bring both arms into focus together.

The following experiments illustrate the same points.

EXPERIMENT (24). *To illustrate the action of lenses in remedying short or long sight.*

(a) Take the more convex of the two lenses used in Experiment 23. Place a candle at some little distance, say 30 cm. from it, and arrange a screen so that an image of the candle may be formed on it. Move the candle considerably further away from the lens, the image is no longer distinct. The lens and screen represent a short-sighted eye which brings the rays from the distant candle to a focus in front of the retina. Place a concave lens in front of the powerful convex lens; if the lens be suitably chosen, the image can be focussed on the screen; distinct vision becomes possible.

(b) Take the less powerful of the two convex lenses, and arrange it to form on the screen an image of the distant candle. Bring the candle near; the image is no longer distinct. It would, did not the screen intercept it, be formed behind the retina. The eye is long-sighted. Introduce a suitably chosen second convex lens between the candle and the eye, the image can then be focussed on to the retina. Convex spectacles remedy long-sight.

For the first of these experiments a convex lens of 10 cm. and a concave one of 30 cm. will be found useful. The candle with these lenses should in the first case be at 30 cm. from the lens, and afterwards be moved to a considerable distance.

For the second experiment use a convex lens 20 cm. in focal length. If the candle be moved from a long distance to one of about 60 cm. from this lens, it will be found that a second convex lens 30 cm. in length will produce the necessary compensation.

*92. **Binocular Vision.** When both eyes are used for vision, an image of the object looked at is formed on the retina of each. The axes of both eyes are directed towards the object so that the images fall on corresponding parts of either retina. The impressions received from these two images are combined by the brain and a single object is seen. If the images do not fall on corresponding portions of the retina, the object is seen double. Thus look towards a window with a vertical bar Q (fig. 108) at some little distance,

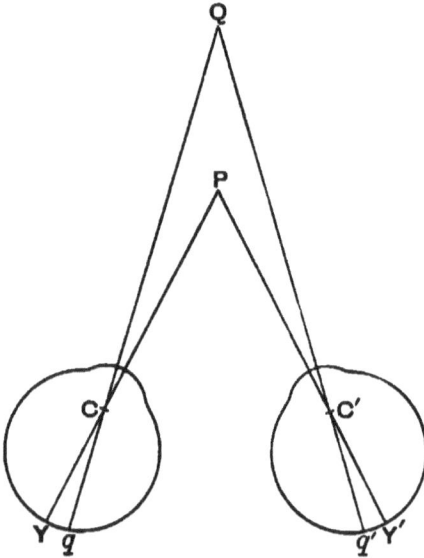

Fig. 108.

and hold up an object P such as a pen-holder or pencil at some 30 or 40 cm. from the face. Focus the eyes on the pencil, the axes CP, $C'P$ respectively of both eyes point to it; the window bar will appear double, because the two images are not formed on corresponding parts of the retina; the image q' seen by the right eye is to the left of the yellow spot Y', that q seen by the left eye is to the right of the yellow spot Y; thus a double impression is conveyed to the brain.

But the images of a solid object as formed on the retinas of the two eyes are not identical. Owing to the slight difference of position of the two eyes, the right eye can see rather more of the right hand side of an object viewed than is visible to the left eye, and vice versa. It is by this means that the impression of solidity is conveyed to the brain. This action is imitated in the stereoscope. The two pictures on a stereoscopic slide are not identical, they are taken from two positions differing very slightly. On the right hand side is a picture of the object as seen by the right eye, on the left a picture of the object as seen by the left eye. The lenses of the stereoscope are arranged so that the virtual magnified images of these two pictures are superposed; the right eye sees the image as it would appear to a right eye placed at the centre of the lens of the camera when the photograph was taken; the left eye sees, superposed on this, the picture as it presented itself to the left eye at the camera in the second position. The brain combines the two impressions and obtains from them the solid appearance wanting in either view separately. This is illustrated in fig. 109. If we look down on a truncated pyramid placed symmetrically with regard to the two eyes, the image formed by the right eye is as represented by R, that formed by the left eye is represented by L. The two combined give us the impression of the solid object shewn at C and we realize that the object is solid.

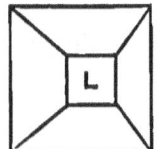 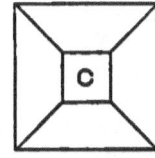 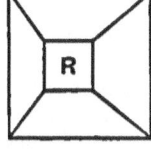

Fig. 109.

93. Least distance of distinct vision. A normal eye we have seen is one which can see distinctly objects at a considerable distance. As the object is brought nearer to the eye the lens thickens and the image is still focussed on the retina, the size of the image increases and detail in the object previously unnoticed becomes visible. This continues until the limit of accommodation is reached; if the object be brought still nearer, the lens can no longer focus it, the image is blurred. The least distance from the eye at which distinct vision can be obtained is known as *the least distance of distinct* *vision*. For persons with normal vision this distance is from 25 to 30 cm. For persons with short-sight the distance may be much less than this; for long-sighted persons it is much greater.

*94. Spectacles. We have seen that a short-sighted person requires a concave lens to produce distinct vision; the focal length of the most suitable lens is obtained thus. Determine first by experiment the greatest distance from the eye at which distinct vision is possible, the position of the "far point" as it is called. Let it be d cm. Then, if concave spectacles of d cm. focal length be used close to the eye, the image of an object at a great distance will be d cm. from the eye and will therefore just be distinctly visible, the image of a less distant object will be nearer to the eye than the principal focus of the spectacles and therefore also will be within the range of vision. Thus a lens having the distance of the far-point for its focal length will just correct the defect, one with a focal length slightly less than this will probably be best suited to the observer.

The calculation of the focal length of the lens required for a long-sighted eye is rather more complex. For such an eye there is a point—the "near point"—at some distance, d say, within which vision is impossible. The virtual image formed by the convex spectacles must be further away than this point. Now suppose we require to find a lens which will permit of vision up to a distance D say—comparable with the least distance of distinct vision for a normal eye—then the image of this object must be at a distance d from the lens, assuming the lens held close to the eye and the full accommodation used; hence if its focal length be f we have

$$\frac{1}{d} - \frac{1}{D} = -\frac{1}{f}$$

or

$$\frac{1}{f} = \frac{1}{D} - \frac{1}{d}.$$

If the object be at a somewhat greater distance from the eye than D the image formed will be further away than the "near point," and vision will be possible; if the object be at a considerably greater distance than D the lens may be too strong; the object may be outside its principal focus and the rays in consequence be convergent instead of only slightly divergent when reaching the eye. A person with long-sight would use different glasses for reading and for looking at pictures at some moderate distance from his eyes.

Thus suppose the "near point" be at a distance of 2 metres, and that a lens is required which will produce distinct vision of an object at a distance of 25 cm., we have

$$\frac{1}{f} = \frac{1}{25} - \frac{1}{200} = \frac{7}{200},$$

$$\therefore f = 28\cdot 5 \text{ cm.}$$

Such a lens however would need that the observer should use his whole accommodation. The range within which it would be useful would depend on the state of the eye when the accommodation was entirely relaxed; it might be that vision for long distances was nearly normal and that no accommodation was needed, the long-sight being due to defective accommodation at short distances, or it might be that even at the longest distances accommodation was required, so that with the lens entirely relaxed a convergent pencil would be needed to produce vision. This point would require further investigation for its elucidation; the simplest test is to try if the vision of a distant object is improved by weak convex glasses; if this is so, the latter alternative is the true one.

CHAPTER VIII.

AIDS TO VISION.

95. The Simple Microscope. We have seen already in Section 77 that a convex lens produces a virtual enlarged image of an object placed closer to it than its principal focus

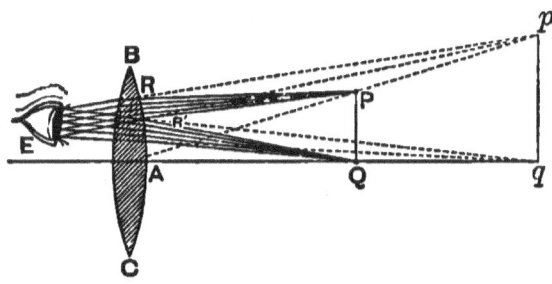

Fig. 110.

and that an eye placed behind the lens sees this image. The lens so used constitutes a simple microscope or magnifying glass and the path of the light through it is shewn in fig. 110.

The *apparent size* of an object depends on the angle which it subtends at the eye; as the object is brought nearer to the eye this angle increases and with it the apparent size of the object. The nearer an object is, the larger it will appear; but this method of securing magnification, by bringing the object near to the eye, can only be employed up to a certain limiting distance; if the object be nearer the eye than its least distance of distinct vision, the eye cannot focus it; the impression on the retina is large but too indistinct to be seen clearly.

When an object is viewed through a magnifying glass held close to the eye the image and the object subtend practically equal angles at the eye; if it were possible to see the object in its actual position without the glass it would appear of the same size as when viewed through the glass, but at this small distance it cannot be seen clearly; it is within the least distance of distinct vision. The effect of the glass, practically, is to remove it to beyond the least distance of distinct vision and at the same time to retain undiminished the angle it subtends at the eye, or what amounts to the same, the actual size of the image formed on the retina. *Thus in determining the magnifying power of a microscope, we must compare the angle which the image seen subtends at the eye with the angle which the object would subtend at the eye if it were placed at the least distance of distinct vision.* This last angle is the largest which the object could subtend under the condition of distinct vision.

In calculating the magnifying power it is usual to suppose that the image formed by the lens is at the least distance of distinct vision from the eye, so that Aq in fig. 110 is equal to D.

We have thus to compare the angle subtended by pq with that which would be subtended by PQ if it were at the distance D, that is if it were at the same distance as pq. These angles, supposing both to be small, are in the ratio of pq to PQ.

Hence the magnification, as thus defined, is measured as before by the ratio of the size of the image to that of the object, when the image is at the least distance of distinct vision.

Let AQ the distance of the object be u, and let the focal length of the convex lens be f, then

$$\frac{1}{D} - \frac{1}{u} = -\frac{1}{f}.$$

Hence
$$\frac{1}{u} = \frac{1}{D} + \frac{1}{f} = \frac{D+f}{Df},$$

and the magnification $= \dfrac{pq}{PQ} = \dfrac{D}{u} = \dfrac{D+f}{f} = 1 + \dfrac{D}{f}.$

The above considerations enable us to solve various problems relating to vision through a lens.

Examples. (1) *The least distance of distinct vision is 25 cm., find the magnification when using a lens of 2·5 cm. focal length.*

Here $\qquad D = 25, \quad f = 2·5.$

Thus $\qquad m = 1 + \dfrac{25}{2·5} = 11.$

(2) *What must be the focal length of a lens which will produce a magnification of 5, when used by an eye for which $D = 25$ cm.?*

We have $\qquad 5 = 1 + \dfrac{25}{f}.$

Thus $\qquad f = \tfrac{25}{4} = 6·25$ cm.

The above considerations only apply when the lens is held close to the eye, if it be held at some distance from it a figure will shew that the object and image subtend different angles at the eye; the calculations become a little more complex. Thus

(3) *Find the magnification produced by a lens of focal length f, when held at a distance a from the eye.*

The angle subtended by the image is $pq/(a+v)$, that subtended by the object when at the least distance of distinct vision is PQ/D.

Hence
$$m = \frac{pq}{PQ}\frac{D}{a+v} = \frac{v}{u}\frac{D}{a+v},$$
$$= \frac{v+f}{f} \cdot \frac{D}{a+v} = \frac{D}{f}\left(\frac{v+f}{v+a}\right).$$

If as above we suppose the image to be at the least distance of distinct vision, then
$$v + a = D, \quad v = D - a,$$
$$m = \frac{D+f-a}{f} = 1 + \frac{D-a}{f}.$$

Again suppose the object is at a given distance b from the eye, find the magnification produced by a lens of focal length f at a distance a from the eye. As above
$$m = \frac{v}{u}\frac{D}{a+v} = \frac{D}{u}\frac{1}{1+\dfrac{a}{v}},$$

$$\frac{1}{v} = \frac{1}{u} - \frac{1}{f} = \frac{f-u}{uf},$$

$$m = \frac{D}{u} \cdot \frac{1}{1 + \frac{a(f-u)}{uf}} = \frac{Df}{f(a+u) - au}.$$

But $a + u = b$.

$$\therefore m = \frac{Df}{bf - a(b-a)}.$$

96. Simple Microscope Lenses. The simple microscope has been described as though it consisted of a single convex lens; in some cases combinations of two convex lenses are employed, the deviation of the rays necessary to give the magnification is divided between the two. Wollaston's doublet is arranged thus.

A sphere of glass or other refracting substance may also be used. In this case it is desirable to restrict the pencils to those which pass approximately through the centre of the sphere. This can be done by cutting a deep groove in the sphere, and filling it up with some opaque material. Coddington's lens is an arrangement of this kind.

97. Telescopes. We have seen how a magnified image of a *near* object may be obtained by the aid of a convex lens of short focus; the method is clearly inapplicable to *distant* objects. There are, however, various arrangements of apparatus by which magnified images of distant objects can be produced. These may be classed together as telescopes.

Thus take a convex lens of somewhat long focal length and arrange it to produce on a translucent screen a real image of a distant object. The image will be a diminished one, that is, its actual size will be less than that of the object. Its apparent size as viewed by the eye will depend on the focal length of the lens; the size of the image formed on the retina may be greater or less than that formed by the object when viewed directly, the ratio of the two being that of the focal length of the lens to the least distance of distinct vision. Thus if the image of the moon be formed by a lens 100 cm. in focal length, and viewed from a distance of say 25 cm., the linear dimensions of the image on the retina will be four times as great as those of the image formed when the moon is looked at directly.

160   LIGHT.   [CH. VIII

But the image formed on the screen may by the aid of a second convex lens of short focus be again magnified.

Place such a lens behind the screen so that the light after traversing the translucent screen may fall on it, and adjust the lens to give a distinct virtual magnified image of the image on the screen. The convex lens will for a normal eye be at a distance from the screen rather less than its focal length, and the virtual image formed will be at a considerable distance from the lens. Suppose this lens magnifies the apparent size of the image 5 fold; the image on the screen already appears to the eye 4 times as great as the object. Thus when viewed through the second convex lens the object is magnified 5 × 4 or 20 times. But the screen is not essential, the real image is formed by the lens whether it be there or not; the screen only obstructs some of the light; remove it, on looking through the convex lens we see a virtual inverted and magnified image of the distant object; we have an Astronomical Telescope.

The same end can be attained by various other methods. Thus in a reflecting telescope we obtain, by means of a concave mirror, a real image of a distant object and then magnify that image with a convex lens or combination of lenses.

In describing the action of a telescope, it is usually supposed that the object viewed is infinitely distant, and that the apparatus is in adjustment for a normal eye. Thus the real image formed by the first lens or mirror is formed at its principal focus, while the second lens is adjusted so that this image is at its principal focus; thus the rays from any point of this image emerge from the second lens as a parallel pencil capable of giving distinct vision to a normal eye. In reality most people will push the second lens—the eye-piece—rather nearer to the image than this involves, so that the light may emerge from it as a slightly divergent pencil.

98. To describe the Astronomical Telescope and to trace a pencil of rays through it from a distant object to a normal eye. The astronomical telescope consists of two convex lenses mounted so as to have a common axis. The first lens, called the object glass, is of considerable focal length and forms at its principal focus a real inverted image of the distant object, the second lens or eyepiece magnifies this image and for a normal eye is placed at the distance of its own focal length away from the image. Thus in fig. 111 let BAC be the object glass, bac the eyepiece.

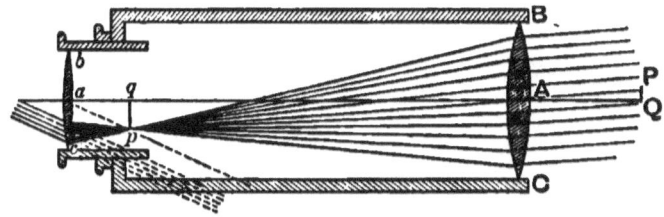

Fig. 111.

Consider a pencil of rays coming from a point P on a distant object PQ. The object is so distant that the rays from P falling on the object glass may be treated as parallel to the line PA. The object glass forms an image of P at p on the line PA produced, and pq a real image of the object PQ is thus produced. Moreover since Q is infinitely distant from A, q will be at the principal focus of the object glass and Aq will be its focal length (F say). The rays diverging from p now fall on the eyepiece bac and since q is the principal focus of the eyepiece they emerge from it as a parallel pencil. Join ap and let $aq = f$. The emergent rays will be parallel to ap, and an eye situated close to the eyepiece will see in the direction ap produced a magnified image of P. Rays from any other point of PQ are similarly refracted and a virtual magnified image is seen[1]. Since pq is an inverted image, this virtual image is inverted.

The angle which the image viewed subtends at the eye is paq, the angle which the object would subtend at the eye is practically the same as that which it subtends at the centre of the object glass or PAQ. But PAQ is equal to pAq, thus the magnifying power is paq/pAq. Now when an angle is not large, it is measured approximately by its tangent; thus

$$paq = pq/aq, \quad pAq = pq/Aq.$$

[1] In this figure and those which follow, the size of the eyepiece is greatly exaggerated in proportion to that of the object glass. This is necessary in order to secure clearness in the figure.

Hence $$m = \frac{paq}{pAq} = \frac{pq}{aq} \times \frac{Aq}{pq} = \frac{Aq}{aq} = \frac{F}{f}.$$

Since the rays which emerge from the eyepiece have all to enter the pupil of the eye it is clearly unnecessary for the eyepiece lens to be large; if its aperture be a little greater than that of the pupil, say some 8 mm., it will be sufficient.

The size of the object glass affects the amount of light concentrated into the image and hence its brightness when magnified. It is clear that if we block out a portion of the object glass in figure 111, the remaining portion will form an image at pq all the same, this image will however be less bright; we might without affecting the magnification substitute for the object glass a smaller lens of the same focal length. It can be shewn however that the power which the telescope has of separating two small objects which are close together at a great distance is increased by increasing the size of the object glass.

In an actual telescope the object glass consists of two lenses, one a convex lens of crown glass, the other a concave lens of flint glass, placed close together and equivalent to a convex lens of considerable focal length. By this means chromatic aberration (see § 114) is corrected. The eyepiece also usually contains two lenses, since by this means a more perfect magnified image can be produced[1].

The image formed in the Astronomical Telescope is inverted; by means of suitable lenses placed in the eyepiece it can be reinverted. The eyepiece then is an erecting eyepiece.

99. Galileo's Telescope. We have already seen that if a converging pencil of rays falls on a concave lens, a virtual image may be formed by the lens and distinct vision may be obtained by an eye placed behind it.

This is made use of in Galileo's Telescope (Fig. 112). This consists of a convex lens of long focal length forming an object glass and a concave lens of small focal length on the same axis

---

[1] For an account of these see Glazebrook, *Physical Optics*, Text-book of Science Series, Chapter IV.

as eyepiece. The rays from any point P of the distant object PQ fall as a parallel pencil on the object glass BAC and are refracted by it towards a point p on PA produced, at a distance

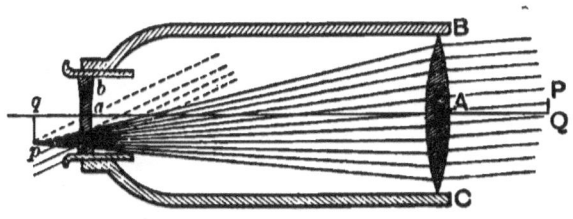

Fig. 112.

from the object glass equal to its focal length. But before reaching p they are intercepted by the concave lens bac, which forms the eyepiece, placed in such a position that aq is its focal length. The rays therefore emerge from the lens as a parallel pencil parallel to ap and capable of producing normal vision in an eye placed to receive them. The image seen is magnified and erect. This arrangement of lenses is used in opera and field glasses, which consist of two such telescopes, one for each eye. Its magnification is, it may be shewn, measured by the ratio of the focal length of the object glass to that of the eyepiece. Since the distance between the lenses is the difference between their focal lengths instead of as in the Astronomical telescope their sum, the length of a Galilean telescope is shorter than that of an Astronomical telescope of the same magnifying power and having a lens of the same focal length for its object glass.

*100. Reflecting Telescopes. Two forms of reflecting telescopes are shewn in figs. 113 and 114. In both an image is formed by a concave mirror and magnified by a convex eyepiece. The eyepiece has to be arranged in such a manner that the observer's head when looking through it does not intercept any of the incident light.

In figure 113 which represents a Newtonian telescope, a small plane mirror DE or total reflexion prism is placed

11—2

between the concave mirror *BAC* and its principal focus.

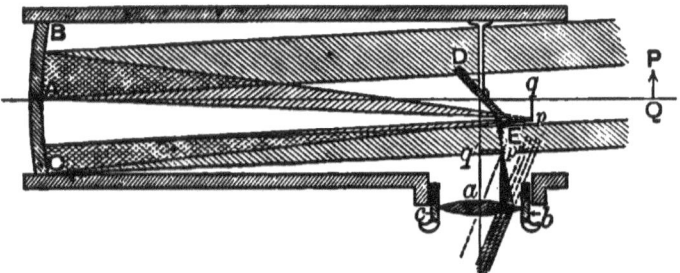

Fig. 113.

This mirror is inclined at 45° to the axis of the large mirror.

Parallel rays from a point P at a considerable distance are reflected by the concave mirror to form an image p at its principal focus. Before reaching p they fall on the plane mirror and are reflected by it to form a real image $p'q'$, the image in the plane mirror of pq. This image $p'q'$ is at the principal focus of a convex lens *bac*. After traversing this lens the rays emerge as a parallel pencil, parallel to ap, and a normal eye, on which they fall, sees a magnified image of P in the direction ap.

Fig. 114 represents Herschel's telescope. In it the axis of

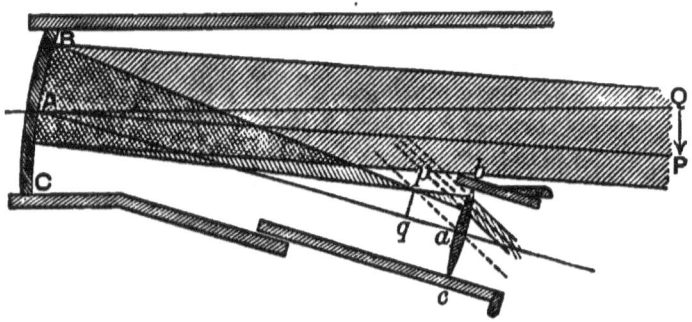

Fig. 114.

the convex mirror is slightly oblique to that of the tube in which it is placed. Thus rays incident parallel to the axis of the tube are reflected somewhat obliquely. A real image of P is thus formed at p and an eyepiece can be placed to view this image without interfering with the incident light.

101. The Compound Microscope. This is an arrangement of lenses for magnifying a small object very considerably. It is practically an astronomical telescope adapted to view near objects. An object glass BAC, Fig. 115,

Fig. 115.

forms at pq a real inverted and magnified image of an object PQ, placed at a rather greater distance from the object glass than its focal length. The focal length of the object glass is small.

The rays diverging from p fall on a convex eyepiece bac, placed at the distance of its own focal length f from pq; they thus emerge parallel to ap, and an eye placed behind the eyepiece sees a greatly magnified virtual image of PQ.

The simple theory of lenses given in the preceding pages is not sufficient to explain completely the action of a modern microscope; the object viewed is at a very short distance from the lens, hence the angle it subtends at the lens is considerable and the pencils are not by any means *directly* incident, moreover the thickness of the lens is comparable with its focal length, there is also chromatic aberration to be considered. Thus the object glass consists of a number of achromatic lenses, sometimes three, each composed of a convex lens of crown glass and a concave one of flint glass, placed in order and adjusted to give a well-defined magnified real image of the object. This is viewed with an eyepiece consisting usually of two lenses.

166   LIGHT.   [CH. VIII

Fig. 116 shews an object AB, in front of such an object glass consisting of three pairs of lenses 1, 2, 3.

A_1B_1 is a virtual image of AB formed by the lens 1, A_2B_2 a virtual image of A_1B_1 formed by the lens 2, $A'B'$ is a real

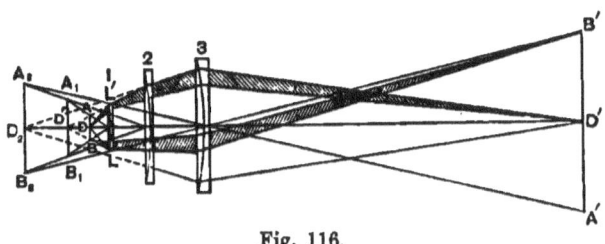

Fig. 116.

image of A_2B_2 formed by the lens 3. It is this real image which is viewed by the eyepiece.

*102. The Camera Lucida. This instrument shewn in section in fig. 117 consists of a four-sided prism, $ABCD$, of

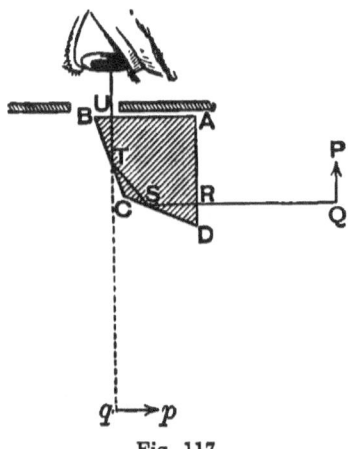

Fig. 117.

glass. The angle at A is a right angle and when in use the sides AB, AD are generally horizontal and vertical respectively, the angles at B and D are 67° 30', so that the angle at C is 135°. When in use a ray from an object PQ at some little distance, travelling approximately in a horizontal direction, falls upon the vertical face AD at R. The ray is totally reflected from the two oblique faces at S and T and emerges in a vertical direction from U on the horizontal face AB. An eye looking vertically down on this face sees a virtual image pq of the object PQ. The distance of this image from the prism is approximately the same as that of the object. A sheet of paper can be placed on the table below the camera and the height of the instrument can be adjusted until this virtual image appears to coincide with the paper. A stop is placed above the prism as in the figure, in such a position that its aperture is just bisected by the edge at B. The observer looks through the aperture of this stop and sees with one half of his eye the paper, and with the other half the image of the object PQ projected on the paper. He is thus able to draw on the paper with a pencil an exact representation of the object. The distance between the paper and the observer's eye should, for normal vision, be about 25 cm.; if it be not possible to place the object at about this distance, so as to project its image on to the paper, the same end may be attained by the use of a lens.

If the object be very distant, a concave lens of about 25 cm. focal length may be placed in front of the vertical face of the prism, a virtual image of the object is formed then at 25 cm. from the prism and thus can be focussed along with the paper. In some cases it is preferable to put a convex lens of about the same focal length between the paper and the prism; the paper is viewed through this lens and a virtual image at a great distance is thus seen.

*103. **The Sextant.** This is used for measuring the angular distance between two inaccessible points.

In figure 118, BC is an arc of a circle of about 60° with A for its centre. This arc is graduated into degrees etc. Each single degree is marked as two, so that the 60 degrees are marked as 120. AD is a moveable arm with an index and vernier. At A is a mirror which turns with the arm; the plane of the mirror is parallel to the arm, so that the reading of the index gives the position of the mirror. At E is a second piece of plane glass, only one half of which is silvered. The plane of this glass is parallel to AB, so that when the arm D is at B and the circle reads zero, the two mirrors are parallel. A small telescope T is fixed to the arm AB and points towards the mirror E, being so adjusted that its object glass is apparently half covered by the silvered portion of E and half by the unsilvered. The direction of this telescope is such that the

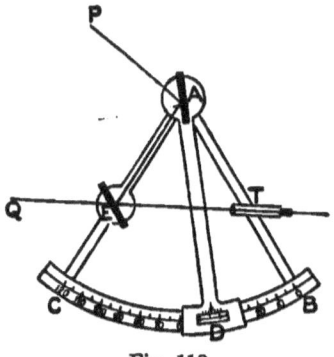

Fig. 118.

line AE and its axis ET are equally inclined to the mirror E. Hence light incident along AE is reflected into the telescope. To use the instrument it is held in the left hand so that its plane is parallel to that through the two objects Q and P, and the telescope is pointed so as to view Q directly through the unsilvered portion of the flat glass. Light from P is reflected from the mirror A. By turning the arm AD, this reflected light can be made to fall on the mirror E and after a second reflexion there to enter the telescope, the observer can thus see both objects simultaneously, the one directly, the other by two reflexions at A and E, and the two images can thus be brought into coincidence. By the two reflexions the light has been deviated from the direction PA to the direction QE. Now when a ray is deviated by reflexion at two mirrors the angle between the directions of the ray before and after the two reflexions is twice that between the mirrors. But the angle between the mirrors is given by the arc BD. Twice this arc then gives the angle between PA and QE, i.e. since the objects are a long way off the angle which they subtend at the eye is twice the angle BAD. But the circle BDC is graduated so that each degree reads as two. Hence the reading on the circle gives the angle which the objects subtend at the eye.

*104. The Spectrometer. This instrument shewn in fig. 119 is used for the measurement of the angle and refractive index of a prism as described in Section 44. ABC is a graduated circle supported on a suitable vertical stand. An arm moving round this circle carries a telescope DE which points to the centre of the circle. The position of this arm can be read by a vernier attached to it. The weight of the telescope is balanced by a counterpoise hung on the other end of the arm and shewn at F. GH is a collimating telescope, this consists of a convex lens G mounted in a tube. The length of the tube is the focal length of the lens and at H there is a narrow vertical slit. This is illuminated from

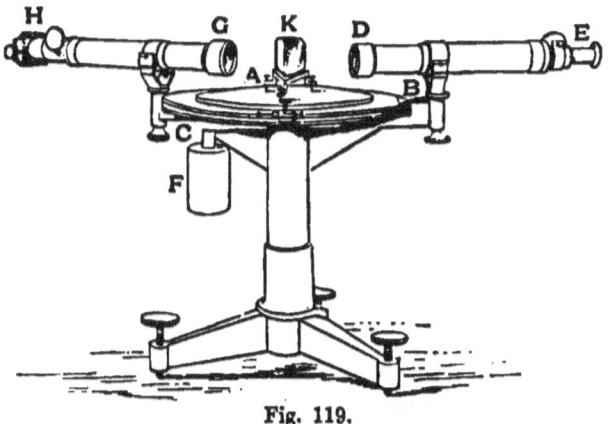

Fig. 119.

behind by a light and the rays diverging from the slit fall on the lens G. Since the slit is at the principal focus of the lens the rays emerging from the lens are parallel. These parallel rays fall on the prism K, placed at the centre of the circle. To find the angle of the prism it is placed with its edge facing G so that the light falls on both faces. The telescope is then turned to receive the reflected beam, and adjusted until the image of the slit is seen coincident with a cross wire fixed in the centre of the field of view. The position of the telescope is read and it is then turned to view the image reflected from the second face, and the vernier again read. We know (§ 44) that the angle of the prism is half that turned through by the telescope.

The prism is then turned so that the light falls on one face and is refracted through. The position of minimum deviation is found as in § 44, and the angle of minimum deviation obtained by viewing first the refracted image and then the direct image seen when the prism is removed and the telescope pointed directly to the collimator. The angle between these two positions is D, and if i be the angle of the prism we have

$$\mu = \frac{\sin \frac{1}{2}(D+i)}{\sin \frac{1}{2} i}.$$

To obtain accurate results with the sextant or the spectrometer a number of adjustments and precautions are necessary. For these see Glazebrook and Shaw, *Practical Physics*, Chapter XIV.

*105. The Ophthalmoscope. Since in the case of a normal eye parallel rays are brought to a focus on the retina, it follows that rays emanating from a point on the retina will emerge parallel. They will therefore be in a condition to give distinct vision to another eye, if it be in a position to receive them, or, if they be allowed to fall on a convex lens, they will form at the principal focus of the lens an image of the retina. This can be viewed through another convex lens and magnified.

In order, however, that light may emerge from the eye it is necessary to illuminate the retina. Moreover the illumination must be so arranged that the observer does not himself interfere with the incident light.

This can be done with the aid of a mirror. A small circular portion of the silvering is scraped away from the centre and the observer looks through the transparent part thus formed into the patient's eye. The mirror is turned so as to reflect into the eye the light of a lamp with a ground glass globe placed in a convenient position and the retina is thus illuminated, some of the light scattered by the retina emerges as a parallel beam and passing through the transparent patch on the mirror produces vision in the observer's eye. Such an arrangement constitutes an ophthalmoscope. The observer's eye would see a magnified erect image of the retina and choroid coat of the patient's eye.

It is desirable in some cases, however, to form a real image of the back of the patient's eye. This can be done by inserting a convex lens between the mirror and the eye. The parallel pencils emerging from any point on the retina are refracted and an image is formed at the distance of its principal focus from the lens. The observer's eye and therefore the mirror must be at some distance—the least distance of distinct vision—from this image in order that it may be viewed distinctly.

The mirror is used to reflect the light into the patient's eye. It should therefore be of such a shape and size as to illuminate his retina as brilliantly and uniformly as possible. For this purpose it is desirable that the whole of the lens which is of use should be uniformly illuminated. This is secured by arranging the mirror to form on the lens a real image of the globe which surrounds the source of light. Either therefore the mirror must be concave, or if a plane mirror is employed a convex lens must be introduced between the mirror and the source and adjusted to form an image of the globe on the second lens through which the observer looks.

Fig. 120 shews the arrangement when a concave mirror is used. L is the source of light, which may be an Argand burner, this is placed slightly to one side of the patient. The mirror M forms on the lens A an image of the globe surrounding the lamp L. The rays traverse the lens and after

172   LIGHT.   [CH. VIII

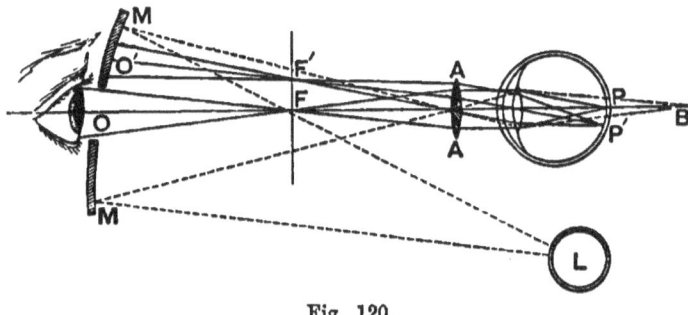

Fig. 120.

refraction at the eye converge to form an image of the lens A at B. This image, if the eye is normal, would be behind the retina. The retina is diffusely illuminated and some of the light scattered from it emerges. The rays from any one point such as P emerge parallel, and after again traversing the lens A form at F an image of the point P. Thus an image of the retina is formed at FF'. This image is at the least distance of distinct vision for an observer placed just behind O, the central aperture in the mirror. Some of the rays from the central part of the image at F traverse the aperture O and the observer can examine the image of the retina. By slightly shifting the position of the patient's eye or of the mirror different parts of his retina can be brought into view.

Thus the image of P' on the retina is formed at F'', and if the mirror were shifted, keeping its centre fixed till the aperture was brought to O', the part of the eye about P' would be visible.

If the patient be short-sighted the rays emerging from his eye will be convergent and the image formed by the lens A will be nearer to the lens than F; if the eye be long-sighted the emergent rays will be divergent and the image formed by the lens will be further from it than F. The image formed can if desirable be further magnified by a convex lens of suitable focus placed between the observer's eye and the aperture O.

In the figure the dotted lines indicate the path of the rays from the lamp to the centre of the lens A. These illuminate the central portion of the retina. Other rays not shewn fall on other parts of the lens and reach other portions of the retina.

Fig. 121 shews the path of the rays when the first method of using the ophthalmoscope is employed. The concave mirror M is used to throw a pencil of convergent rays into the observer's eye. These rays are brought to a focus in front of the retina

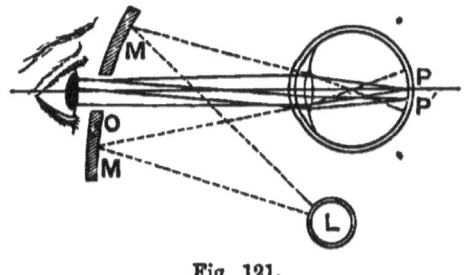

Fig. 121.

and therefore illuminate it diffusely. If the eye be normal, the diffused light from each point of the retina emerges as a parallel pencil, and an eye looking through O, the aperture of the mirror M, sees a magnified and erect image of the retina.

If the patient's eye be short-sighted the emergent rays will be convergent instead of parallel, the observer if of normal vision will require to place a concave lens behind the aperture in order to obtain clear vision, and this concave lens will have the focal length proper to correct the defective vision of the patient.

Similarly, if the patient be long-sighted, the rays will be divergent when they reach the aperture; the observer will need a convex lens which will be of the focal length proper to correct the long-sight of the patient.

106. Experiments on Vision through Lenses.

EXPERIMENT (25). *To arrange two lenses to form a telescope.*

Take a convex lens some 30 or 40 cm. in focal length and set it up in a stand so as to form a real image of a distant object. The bars of a window at the far side of the room or a scale with plainly marked divisions will be suitable. Find the position of the image on a sheet of oiled paper or other translucent material. Take a second convex lens of smaller focal length, such as 5 or 6 centimetres, and arrange it behind the image formed by the first lens in such a way that the axis of the two may be coincident, and the distance between the image and the second lens may be rather less than its own focal length. On looking through the second lens, after removing the paper on which the image was formed, a more or less well-defined inverted image of the scale is seen. Vary the distance between the two lenses until the image is distinctly visible. The two lenses now form an astronomical telescope. To construct a Galileo's telescope remove the convex eyepiece and take a concave lens of about the same focal length. Place it between the large convex lens and the image, at the distance of its own focal length from the image. On looking through it a magnified image of the scale is visible and can be focussed by adjusting the distance between the two lenses. The two lenses constitute a Galileo's telescope. The image seen is erect.

EXPERIMENT (26). *To arrange two lenses to form a microscope.*

Take a convex lens of some 4 or 5 cm. focal length. Place it in front of an object such as a piece of paper or card with some pencil lines or other distinct marks on it. Adjust the distance between the lens and the card so that a real image magnified some 8 or 10 times may be formed on a piece of oiled paper or other translucent material placed to receive it. Place a second convex lens behind this image so as to magnify it, remove the paper on which the image is formed and focus the marks on the paper by adjusting the second lens.

EXPERIMENT (27). *To find the magnifying power of a telescope.*

Turn the telescope to view some well-defined distant object which is divided into a series of equal parts, such as the slates on a distant roof[1].

Look at the roof with one eye directly and with the other through the telescope. Two images will be seen, a small one with the unaided eye and a magnified one through the telescope. It is possible with a little practice to focus the telescope, so that one of these two may appear exactly to cover the other. It will then be clear that the image of a single division as seen through the telescope appears to cover a number of divisions seen directly. Count the number of divisions apparently covered by a single magnified division, or rather, count the number covered by four or five magnified divisions and divide by the 4 or 5 as the case may be, the quotient will be the magnifying power of the telescope.

EXPERIMENT (28). *To find the magnifying power of a lens or microscope.*

The principle of this is the same as that of the last experiment.

Place a finely divided scale at about 25 centimetres from the eye below a lens or simple microscope. Place a second scale so as to be clearly visible through the lens. Look with one eye through the lens at the second scale and with the other at the first scale directly. By adjusting the lens or either of the scales the two images can be made to overlap and will not move relatively to each other on moving the eye about.

Observe those divisions on the two scales which accurately coincide. Let x divisions of the magnified image exactly cover y divisions of the other scale, then by finding the ratio of the length of y divisions of the second scale to that of x of the first, we determine the magnifying power of the lens. In making the observation the eye should be placed close up to the lens.

The magnifying power of a compound microscope can be determined in the same way.

---

[1] In the Laboratory a large clearly marked scale which may stand in a vertical position against the wall is useful for this purpose.

In the case of a lens, measure the distances of the two scales from the lens, and verify the law that the magnifying power is the ratio of these distances.

The determination of the magnifying power can be made more easily with the aid of the Camera Lucida described in § 102. Place the camera over the eyepiece of the microscope in such a way that the eye-lens is half covered by it. On looking through the microscope one half of the eye will receive light which has traversed the microscope, the other half light reflected in the prism of the camera. View one scale through the microscope, and adjust the other in a vertical position so that it can be seen through the camera. The two images are now seen by the same eye and can be made to overlap more readily than when both eyes are used. In performing this experiment attention must be paid to the illumination of the two scales, the magnified scale will need a brighter illumination than the other, it is desirable also to cut off stray light from the reflexion in the camera. This is best done by placing a black background behind the reflected scale.

In some cases a finely divided scale photographed or engraved on glass is placed in the tube of a microscope or telescope and viewed through the eyepiece which magnifies it. We can make use of such a scale for measuring purposes in the following way. View through the microscope a finely divided scale, divided say to tenths of millimetres. The image of this scale will be seen coincident with the micrometer scale. Let the number of divisions of the eyepiece scale which are covered by one division of the object scale be a. Each division of the object scale corresponds to $1/a$ of one-tenth of a millimetre; clearly therefore if an object viewed through the microscope covers b divisions of the eyepiece scale its length is b/a tenths of a millimetre[1].

---

[1] For further details see Glazebrook and Shaw, *Practical Physics*, Chapter XIII.

EXAMPLES.

THE EYE AND OPTICAL INSTRUMENTS.

1. Describe the human eye considered as an optical instrument and shew how the defects of short and long sight can be remedied by the use of lenses. What sort of a lens would you use for a short-sighted person who cannot see distinctly objects at a distance greater than 2 feet from his eye?

2. If the focal length of a convex lens be 2 inches, and the minimum distance of distinct vision for the eye looking through it be 10 inches, what is the magnifying power?

3. Of two equally far-sighted persons, one has the habit of wearing his spectacles low down on his nose, the other wears them close to his eyes. Which should have the stronger spectacles, the object being held at the same distance from the eye by both persons.

4. Why ought a person totally immersed in water to wear convex spectacles in order to see distinctly?

5. Explain the action of a lens when used as an eye-glass. A man who can see most distinctly at a distance of 5 inches from his eye wishes to read a notice at a distance of 15 feet off, what sort of spectacles must he use, and what must be their focal length?

6. A pair of spectacles is made of two similar lenses, each having two convex surfaces of ten and twenty inches radius respectively, and a refractive index 1·5. A person looking through them finds that the nearest point to which he can focus is one foot away from the glasses. What is his nearest point of distinct vision without spectacles?

7. A man who can see distinctly at a distance of 1 foot finds that a certain lens when held close to his eye magnifies small objects 6 times, determine the focal length of the lens.

8. Trace a pencil of rays from an object to the eye of an observer—(a) through a lens adapted for a short-sighted person; (b) through a simple microscope.

9. Shew that a convex lens may be used to produce either a real image of a distant object or a virtual image of a near object. How are the two combined in the compound microscope?

The focal length of the object glass of a microscope is $\frac{1}{2}$ an inch, that of the eye piece is 1 inch. Taking the least distance of distinct vision as 12 inches, find the distance between the object glass and the eye piece when the object viewed is $\frac{3}{4}$ of an inch from the object glass.

10. Explain with the aid of a diagram the principle of the compound microscope. From what data and how would you calculate its magnifying power?

11. The focal length of the object glass of a telescope is 2 feet and of the eye lens $\frac{1}{4}$ an inch. Find the magnifying power when used to view an object at a distance of 10 feet from the object glass.

12. Explain the action of that kind of telescope which is constructed with one concave and one convex lens.

If in such a telescope the focal lengths of the two lenses are equal, what will be the effect of putting them quite close together?

CHAPTER IX.

THE SPECTRUM. COLOUR.

107. Experiments with a prism. We have already seen that when a pencil of rays is refracted through a prism it is refracted or deviated from the edge towards the thicker portion of the prism.

EXPERIMENT (29). *To examine the dispersion of light produced by a prism.*

(*a*) Look through a prism at the flame of a lamp or of an ordinary gas burner some two or three metres away, placing the flame so that it is turned edgeways to the eye. If the prism be placed before the right eye with its edge inwards, it will be necessary to look to the left to see the image of the flame, which will appear coloured. This coloured image of the flame is called a spectrum. The left side of the spectrum with the prism held as described will appear violet and the colours will pass in order through indigo, blue, green, yellow and orange to red.

(*b*) Cut a narrow vertical slit 1 to 2 cm. long and 1 or 2 mm. in width in an opaque screen and place it in front of a lamp or gas flame in a darkened room. Turn the flame edgeways to the slit. Allow the light passing through the slit to fall on a white screen at some little distance. Place a prism in the path of the beam with its edge parallel to the slit. The light is deviated towards the thick end of the prism and on shifting the screen in this direction the narrow white patch which before was visible is seen to be drawn out into a long coloured band. Move the prism round so as to vary the angle of incidence, it will be found that the spectrum moves on the screen. Turn the prism in such a direction that the red end of the spectrum may move towards the position formerly occupied by the white patch of light. As the prism is turned continuously in the same direction, the red end of the spectrum at first moves towards the white patch; then the motion ceases, and, if the prism be still turned, the spectrum begins to move away from the patch. When the prism is in such a position that the spectrum is as near as possible to the position occupied by the unrefracted beam the deviation is the least possible, and the prism is said to be in the position of minimum deviation. In many experiments with a prism it is desirable for various reasons to place the prism in this position and we shall usually suppose this done.

These two experiments shew us that the light of the lamp consists of rays differently refrangible; moreover these rays of different refrangibility are differently coloured, the most refrangible being violet, the least refrangible red.

(c) Interpose in the path of the light before it falls on the prism pieces of variously coloured glass, red, blue, or green. In each case only the corresponding part of the spectrum will get through and be visible on the screen. With the red glass there will be a red patch, on the screen with the blue glass a blue patch in a different position to that occupied by the red[1].

The red and blue rays are clearly both present in the white light and are differently refracted by the prism. This dispersion of the light due to the different refrangibility of different rays was first investigated by Newton and the two experiments just given were performed by him and are described in his Opticks published in 1704. They had previously been described in a paper read at the Royal Society in 1676. Fig. 122 shews in

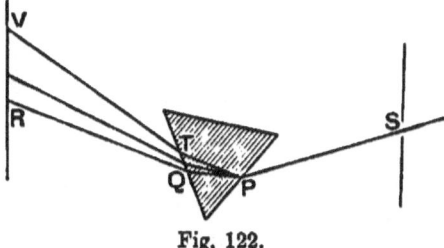

Fig. 122.

[1] The blue glass may let a little red through as well as blue, but the green and yellow will be stopped.

a general way the path of the rays corresponding to a single incident ray. Robert Hooke describes in his Micrographia, published in 1664, an experiment practically identical with the second of the above, but he was unable to follow out its consequences.

108. Further Experiments on Dispersion.

EXPERIMENT (30). *To illustrate the different refrangibility of the variously coloured rays.*

(a) Form a spectrum as already described, but allow it to fall on a second prism placed close behind the first in the position of minimum deviation and in such a position that the edges of the two are parallel. The deviation of the light is much increased, so also is the length of the spectrum, the angle between the extreme red and violet rays is now, if the two prisms be alike, about twice as great as before; this angle measures the dispersion produced by the prism. Move the second prism some distance from the first, and then turn it so that its edge may be at right angles to that of the first—if the slit and edge of the first prism be vertical, the edge of the second must be horizontal—so that the length of the spectrum, which is formed on the second prism, is parallel to the edge of that prism.

Each coloured pencil as it passes through the second prism is deviated, thus the whole spectrum is raised—assuming the vertex of the second prism to be downwards—but each colour is refracted through its own proper amount, the red less than the green, the green less than the violet. Thus the spectrum is no longer a horizontal band. Its direction is oblique to the horizontal the violet end being raised above the red. The appearance on the screen is shewn in fig. 123, in which the lower spectrum $CD...G$ is that cast by the first prism alone, while $C'D'...G'$ is the spectrum after the rays have traversed the second prism.

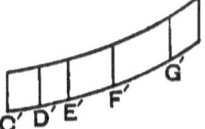

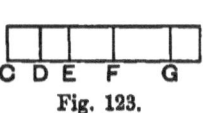

Fig. 123.

(b) The same result may be obtained by looking through a second prism at a spectrum on a screen, placing the edge of this prism parallel to the spectrum.

109. The Recombination of Colours to form white light.

EXPERIMENT (31). *To shew the combination of coloured rays to form white light.*

(a) Take a second prism similar to the first and having the same refracting angle. Place it with its axis also vertical so that the light from the first prism may fall on it; turn the edges of the two in opposite directions and their faces parallel as shewn in fig. 124. The light on the screen will now be white, the two prisms behave as a plate, the second undoes the effect of dispersion produced by the first by causing dispersion in the opposite direction. Interpose an opaque obstacle between the two prisms so as to obstruct some of the light. The image is again coloured.

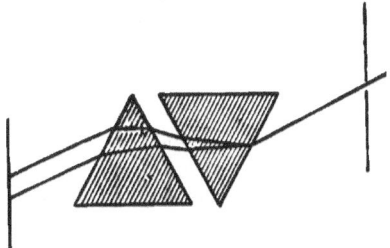

FIG. 124.

(b) Form a spectrum on a screen and look at it through a second prism similar to the first from a distance equal to that between the first prism and the screen, keeping the edges of the two prisms parallel. If the refracting angles of the two be turned in the same direction, the length of the spectrum is doubled; if the refracting angles be turned in opposite directions the spectrum, when viewed through the second prism, appears white and is reduced in length to a narrow patch. The violet rays which are most refracted by the first prism are also most refracted, but in the opposite direction, by the second and the two dispersions annul each other.

(c) Obtain two prisms, lamps and slits. Place the prisms parallel and at some distance apart adjusting them so that the two spectra formed overlap, the violet end of one being coincident with the red end of the other and vice versâ, and the colours being mixed throughout. Now view this patch through a third prism with its edge parallel to the spectrum. The image seen is refracted by the prism from its true position, but the violet in each is refracted more than the red. In consequence the two spectra are separated again and appear to cross each other, forming a X.

(d) A cardboard disc, some 25 or 30 cm. in diameter, is mounted on an axis through its centre, in such a way that it can be made to rotate rapidly by means of a handle and multiplying gear. The disc is divided into four quadrants and each quadrant is divided into seven sectors. These sectors are coloured in order with the seven colours of the spectrum, the breadth of each sector being proportional to the length occupied by the corresponding colour in a spectrum formed by a glass prism. Place the disc in a good light and rotate it rapidly; it will appear to be of a greyish white colour. The impression produced on the retina by any bright object lasts for an appreciable time after the exciting cause is removed. As the disc rotates each point on the retina has impressed on it in turn images of all the colours of the spectrum in rapid succession, and the eye sees the combined effect of all, thus producing the impression of white or grey. The disc will look grey compared with a white card illuminated to the same extent, for much less light reaches the eye from the disc than from the card—most of the incident light being absorbed by the colours —and a white surface imperfectly illuminated appears grey.

We thus, by a repetition of Newton's own experiments, can illustrate the analysis and composition of white light.

Newton used the Sun as his source and with this or with an Electric Arc, the experiments can be shewn on a large scale. For class work it will suffice to employ a good lamp or burner with a narrow slit in a metal plate. The prism should be of considerable size. A bottle prism filled with carbon disulphide gives considerable dispersion, but for most purposes prisms of crown glass having refracting angles of 60° will do. For the above experiments it is not necessary that the glass should be perfect or the faces accurately plane, and the glass lustres used for decorative purposes on chandelier and gas fittings serve well. These can be obtained at a moderate cost from any firm of shop-fitters. Concave and convex mirrors which will give sufficiently good images for the Experiments on mirrors may usually be selected from a shop-fitter's or decorator's stock. Cheap Lenses may be had from a wholesale optician.

110. To trace the path of the rays through a prism. We have explained in Section 45 how this may be done with the aid of a drawing board and pins and have seen.

Section 43, that the refracted beam is coloured. Newton's experiments have shewn in a general way the cause of the colour, it remains to trace more accurately the path of a beam of white light through a prism. Now a white beam is an aggregate of variously coloured beams and each of these has its own index of refraction. Each ray of white light is dispersed on refrac-

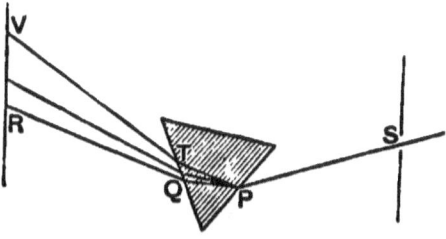

Fig. 125.

tion into the glass into its coloured components; this dispersion is still further increased by the refraction at emergence, and thus the emergent beam is coloured. If we could isolate a single ray its path would be as shewn in fig. 125. Each of its various components would be deviated from the edge of the prism by the two refractions, but the deviation of the violet would be greater than that of the red.

In fig. 126 is shewn the path of a single ray through a plate. Dispersion is produced, in this case also, by the refraction both at incidence and at emergence, the dispersion at emergence however takes place in the opposite direction to that at incidence, and the red and violet rays emerge slightly separated but parallel. Two parallel rays affect the eye as though they were coincident, being brought to a focus at the same spot on the retina and so no sensation of colour is produced.

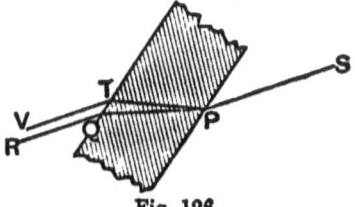

Fig. 126.

But we cannot thus isolate a single ray, we have in all cases to deal with a small pencil and we must consider what happens to it. Each ray of the pencil will be dispersed in the same manner as the single isolated ray and each will produce its own spectrum on the screen. These spectra will overlap but will not exactly coincide. Thus in fig. 127 let *ABC* be

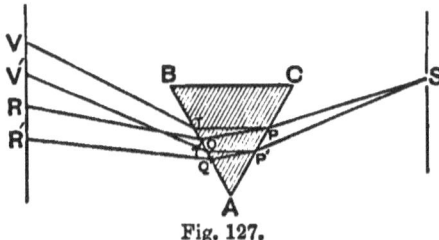

Fig. 127.

the prism, *S* the slit, *SP*, *SP′* the extreme rays of the incident pencil. The ray *SP* will be dispersed into a red ray *PQR* and a violet ray *PTV* with the other colours between them, and will form a spectrum *RV* on the screen. The incident ray *SP′* will be dispersed into its red ray *P′Q′R′* and its violet ray *P′T″V′* with the other colours between, and the spectrum will be *R′V′*. This spectrum will be lower down on the screen than *RV*, the distance between *R* and *R′* and *V* and *V′* respectively will depend on the breadth of the incident beam. Thus at any point on the screen the colour will be somewhat mixed. Between *R* and *R′* the red of one spectrum will overlap some other colour, orange or yellow say of another. The spectrum produced in this way is said to be impure, the spectra thrown on the screen in Experiments (29), (30) are impure spectra.

In the case in which the prism is placed in a position of minimum deviation, it is possible to draw more accurately the path of the rays. We have seen (Section 46) that in general a geometrical image is not formed by oblique refraction. A pencil of rays diverging from a point does not in general after refraction appear to diverge from a second point. In general therefore even if the incident light were homogeneous and consisted, let us say, entirely of red rays, a red *image* of the slit would not be formed. But both experiment and a mathematical investigation shew that there is one position of the prism for which a geometrical image is formed. If a pencil, diverging from a point, fall on a prism in such a way that its axis undergoes minimum deviation, it can be shewn that the emergent pencil diverges very approximately from a point. This point is situated as far from the edge of the prism as the slit; the incident and emergent rays are (Section 45, Exp. 13) equally inclined to the faces of incidence and emergence respectively. In this case a geometrical image is formed.

To verify this, illuminate the slit with homogeneous light either by the use of a piece of ruby glass, or better by taking as the source a Bunsen flame in which a small spoon of platinum gauze filled with common salt is placed. The heat vapourizes the sodium in the salt—chloride of sodium—and the flame assumes an intense yellow hue. Look at the slit from a distance, two metres or so, through a prism held parallel to the slit and turn it round to vary the deviation. It will be found that the image seen is best defined when the deviation is a minimum; in this position a sharp clear image of the slit is formed. An object, such as one of the upright rods used in Experiment (17), can be viewed with half the eye by holding the prism so as to cover only half the pupil, and can be placed, by a second observer, so as to coincide with the position of the yellow virtual image. It will then be found that this image is at the same distance from the prism as the slit. Now if white light be used, since its various components are differently refrangible, there will be a series[1] of these

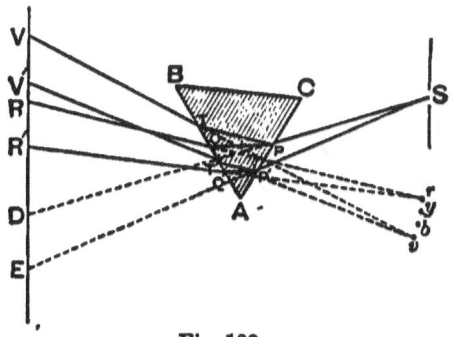

Fig. 128.

[1] Strictly speaking, the prism is not accurately in a position of minimum deviation for all the colours at the same time, but it is very nearly so.

virtual images, each differently coloured, arranged side by side in a line.

In fig. 128 ABC is the prism, S the slit, SP, SP' the extreme rays of the pencil diverging from the slit, v, b, y, r, the virtual images of the slit formed by the variously coloured rays. Let PQ, PT be the red and violet rays in the prism corresponding to SP, $P'Q'$ and $P'T'$ those corresponding to SP'. The emergent beam consists of a violet pencil vT', vT' diverging from v and meeting the screen in VV', and a red pencil rQ, rQ' which meets the screen in RR', with the various other pencils between.

If the prism were removed the incident rays would form a broad white patch on the screen as at DE; corresponding to this we have the red patch RR' and the violet patch VV', each of about the same width as DE, with the patches of other colours in between overlapping each other.

If an eye be placed behind the prism so as to receive the emergent rays it will see the virtual spectrum vr. Now this spectrum differs from that on the screen in that all the red rays are concentrated at one point, all the violet at another and so on for the various colours. If the eye be adjusted so as to view this virtual spectrum distinctly, the image formed on the retina will resemble vr, in that all the colours will be distinct. The spectrum in this case is said to be pure. Thus a pure spectrum is one in which all the colours of various refrangibilities are distinctly separated.

In order to obtain a pure spectrum it is necessary that the slit should be narrow, for otherwise the virtual images formed at v, y, r will not be narrow but will 'overlap and cause impurity. If such a slit be illuminated by white light and be looked at through a prism placed in the position of minimum deviation, the spectrum seen is a pure one.

Thus Newton, when looking at his narrow slit through a prism, saw a pure spectrum, but in those experiments hitherto described in which he formed the spectrum on a screen, the spectrum was not pure.

111. To explain how to produce a pure spectrum on a screen. The method by which we can attain this will be clear if we consider the cause of the impurity. The incident rays are divergent and if not intercepted would form a broad patch on the screen as at DE, fig. 128. The breadth of the corresponding coloured patches RR', VV' is a consequence of the breadth of DE. If we can reduce DE to a narrow image of the slit, we reduce also VV' and RR' and improve the purity. This may be done, though very imperfectly, if we limit the breadth of the incident beam by a series of diaphragms, but such a device will not help us very far; for one reason, we shall lose too much light.

Newton explained the method to be adopted. We can reduce DE to a narrow image of the slit if, as in fig. 129, we put a convex lens LM between the prism and the slit, and adjust the lens or the position of the screen, so that the lens may form on the screen at S' a real image of the slit S.

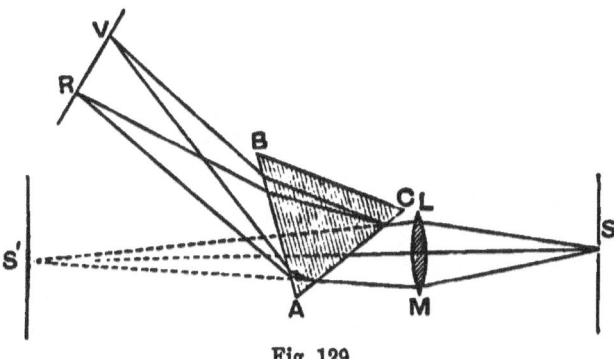

Fig. 129.

Insert the prism in the position of minimum deviation in the path of the rays after they have traversed the lens, they will be refracted, and will converge to form real images V, R, of the slit. These real images will be at the same distance from the prism as S', and on shifting the screen to receive the refracted rays, keeping it at the same distance from the prism as before, a pure spectrum is formed on the screen.

The same end may be attained by forming the spectrum as in fig. 127, and then allowing the rays, after traversing the prism to fall on a convex lens LMN, fig. 130. The rays of any one colour are now diverging from one point of a virtual image of the slit along v, y, r. These rays so diverging will be brought to a focus by the lens which will form a real red image at R, a real violet one at V, and so produce at VR a real pure spectrum. The points V and R in the figure

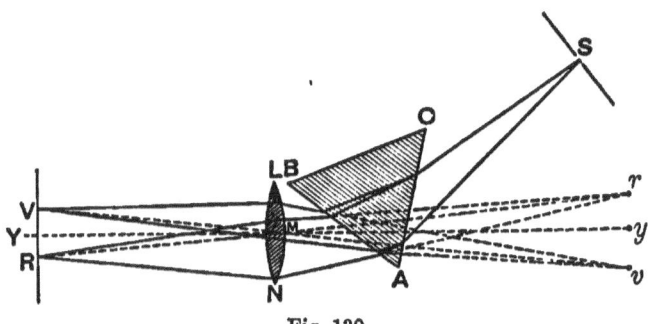

Fig. 130.

are found by joining v and r to the centre M of the lens, as shewn by the dotted lines in the figure, YMy is the axis of the lens. To determine the position of this spectrum, it is best to replace the lamp by the sodium flame, and to adjust the screen, keeping it approximately perpendicular to the rays, until a clear yellow image of the slit is formed. The screen will then be approximately in the right position to receive the real images formed by the rays of other colours, when the slit is again illuminated with white light.

The pure spectrum seen by the eye in Section 109, is formed in this way; the lens of the eye and the retina take the place of the lens and the screen above. By removing the screen and allowing the rays, after forming the pure spectrum, to diverge and enter an eye at some distance, the real pure spectrum formed at VR can be viewed directly. It may also if desired, be magnified, by placing a convex lens between VR and viewing it through this. The original lens LMN and this lens constitute an astronomical telescope, arranged to view the virtual spectrum vr formed by the prism.

112. To trace the path of the rays through a spectroscope or spectrometer. The image formed by refraction through a prism is most perfect when the incident rays form a parallel pencil. It is only when the angle between the extreme rays is very small, that the refracted beam diverges accurately from a point. For accurate work therefore it is desirable that the incident pencil should be as nearly as possible a parallel one. Newton secured this by having a considerable distance, 10 or 12 feet, between the prism and the slit. It may be more readily secured by the use of a collimating lens. The slit is placed at the principal focus of a convex lens. The rays emerging from the lens are parallel, and as such fall on the prism; each ray is then dispersed by the prism to the same extent. Thus, after traversing the prism, the red rays emerge as a parallel pencil in one direction, the violet rays also as a parallel pencil in another. These rays fall on the object glass of the observing telescope, and are brought to a focus by it; the red rays at one point R, the violet at another V. The spectrum thus formed is viewed by the eye-piece and magnified.

The spectrometer by which such an experiment would be carried out, has been described in Section 104, and is shewn in fig. 119. The path of the rays through such an instrument is shewn in fig. 131.

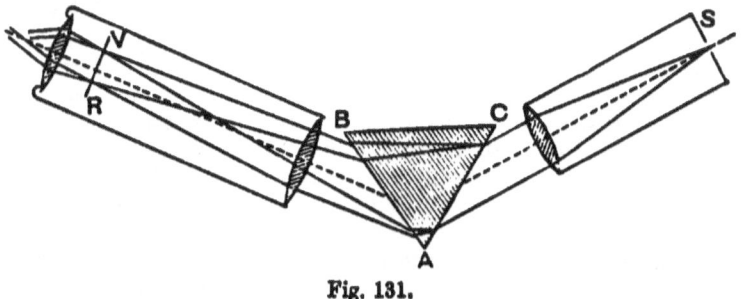

Fig. 131.

113. To produce a pure spectrum on a screen.
EXPERIMENT (31). Illuminate the slit with a Bunsen flame rendered luminous with sodium chloride. Take a convex

lens of about 25 cm. focal length, and place it at about 50 cm. from the slit; an image of the slit will now be formed on a screen placed at about 50 cm. from the lens. Interpose the prism in the path of the light after it has traversed the lens, and move the screen to receive the refracted beam. Turn the prism until the deviation is least, and adjust the screen, keeping it normal to the incident light until a clear yellow image of the slit is again formed on it. Replace the Bunsen flame by a white light. A pure spectrum will be formed on the screen. The lens may, if we wish, be placed so as to receive the light after it has traversed the prism.

If the first method be followed, it is not *necessary* to use the sodium flame, if the distance between the screen and the prism be maintained the same as the screen is shifted and if the other adjustments be accurate, a pure spectrum can be formed without focussing the yellow light of the flame on the screen. It is easier however, to test the adjustments by the aid of the homogeneous light of the sodium flame.

The various experiments with the spectrum described in Sections 107–109 may be repeated, using the pure spectrum in place of that previously employed.

*114. **Dispersion in lenses.** A convex lens is, as we have seen, Section 68, fig. 80 equivalent to a series of prisms one above the other. Consider a pencil of rays of white light falling on such a lens. Each ray at incidence is dispersed into its coloured components and the dispersion is still further increased at emergence. The violet light is at each point more refracted than the red, thus the violet focus will be nearer the lens than the red focus. This can be shewn by placing a somewhat strong convex lens in the path of a beam from a brilliant source of light, and receiving the emergent light on a screen. Thus, take the gas flame as the source of light, hold the lens in such a position as to form an image on the screen, and focus the image as clearly as possible. Move the screen rather nearer to the lens, the image will appear to be tinged with red; move it back beyond the position of most distinct definition, the image appears tinged with violet. The cause of this is seen from fig. 132. The violet rays converge to a point V on the axis, the red to a point R. A violet image is formed at V, and a red one at R. If the screen be held at V there is no violet light in the outer part of the image. It therefore has a red border; if it be held at

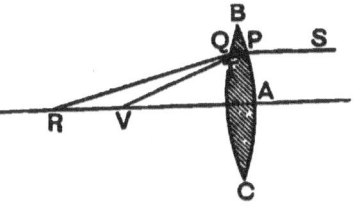

Fig. 132.

R, the red light is concentrated at the centre, the border is violet. The position of most distinct definition is somewhere between these two. This phenomenon is known as chromatic aberration. We can illustrate it by two other experiments due to Newton.

EXPERIMENT (32). *To shew that the focal length of a lens is different for red and violet light.*

(a) Take a piece of card, colour one half blue, the other red; wind a piece of black thread or silk round the card, and place a lamp or candle in front to illuminate it. Form a real image of the card by the aid of a convex lens, and place a screen so that the image may be distinctly defined on it. The position of best definition is found by looking at the images of the black thread. When the edges of the thread are seen clearly, the light on either side of it is forming a sharp image. It will be found that with the screen in one position, the image of the thread is distinctly focussed on the blue part, but is blurred on the red part. On shifting the screen back to a greater distance the red part is in focus, the blue is blurred. In Newton's experiment the distance between the card and the screen was about 12 feet, and the distance between the two positions of the screen about an inch and a half.

(b) Adjust a lens to form a real image of a sheet of print. Illuminate the print with red light by placing a red glass between it and the lamp, and find the position of the image on a screen. Change the red light to blue. The image on the screen will no longer be in focus; the screen must be shifted nearer to the lens to secure definition.

(c) Determine as in Section 79 the focal length of a convex lens using a red glass in front of the source of light. Repeat the experiment with a blue glass. The focal length found will be distinctly shortened. The violet focus is nearer the lens than the red.

*115. To correct a lens for chromatic aberration. These defects of lenses render it impossible to make refracting telescopes or microscopes of high power with simple lenses. They can however be corrected, though Newton was under the impression that such correction was impossible, and for this reason was led to invent the reflecting telescope.

For consider the dispersion produced by a concave lens, on which a parallel pencil is directly incident. The violet components are more refracted than the red: thus the virtual violet focus is nearer the lens than the red focus. Or again, if a convergent pencil fall on such a lens, the violet is the more refracted; thus the violet focus is further away than the red.

Now let the light after passing through a convex lens fall as a convergent pencil on a concave one. The convex lens tends to bring the violet focus nearer to the lens than the red; the concave lens has the reverse effect. It may be possible so to choose the lenses that these two effects exactly balance, so that after traversing the two lenses the violet and red foci coincide.

This is shewn in fig. 133. The convex lens BAC would

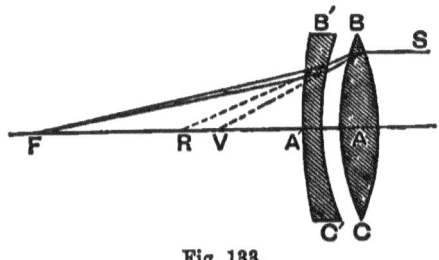

Fig. 133.

bring the violet rays to V, the red to R. The concave lens $B'A'C'$ has an opposite effect, and the two foci coincide at F.

There is one case in which this end can obviously be attained. If the two lenses be of the same material and have the same focal length, the one positive, the other negative, the prisms to which, at any distance from the axis, they are equivalent will be equal, and have their angles in opposite directions, we have at each point of the two lenses the conditions of Section 120; the red and violet rays emerge parallel to their original direction, there is no colour but no image is formed. This is of course useless for our purpose. But by taking two lenses of different materials, such as crown glass and flint glass, it has been shewn that it is possible to correct the chromatic aberration, without at the same time destroying the deviation on which the formation of the image depends. Thus if a spectrum be formed as in Section 109, with a prism of crown glass, we can destroy the colour by the aid of a prism of flint glass, and it will be found that the angle of the prism required is much less than the angle of the crown glass prism, while the deviation produced by the flint glass prism is also less than that caused by the crown glass prism, so that on the whole the rays emerge white but bent in the same direction, though not through as great an angle, as if the crown glass prism alone had been used.

Thus we can correct the chromatic aberration of a convex crown glass lens by the aid of a less powerful concave flint glass lens, and the combination will act as a convex lens of greater focal length than the crown glass lens, but will not produce dispersion. Such a combination is called an achromatic object glass. This discovery was made some time after Newton's death by a Mr Hall. It was rediscovered by Dollond, the optician, and it is in consequence of this that the huge refracting telescopes and the powerful microscopes of the present day have become possible.

116. Spectrum Analysis. It is found that the spectra produced by different sources of light are in many respects very different. Hence, by examining the spectrum of a luminous source, we may in some cases recognize the nature of the source. This method of analysing a substance is called spectrum analysis.

117. Spectrum of an incandescent gas. The spectrum emitted by a glowing vapour consists usually of a number of isolated bright lines. Thus, place a Bunsen flame behind the slit of a spectroscope, and introduce, on a platinum wire coiled into a loop or on a small platinum spoon, the salts of the various metallic elements, the spectra seen will be quite different. Thus if a salt of sodium—such as common salt—be on the spoon, the flame is an intense yellow, and the spectrum observed consists of a single bright line in the yellow—or rather if the spectroscope be a good one, of two bright lines very close together—no other light is visible. Whenever we look at a flame containing sodium we see this line, and so far as we know, it is never produced by anything else but incandescent sodium vapour. If the line be present when some unknown substance is vapourized and examined, we may safely infer that the substance contains sodium.

Again lithium and strontium both colour the flame red, but the spectrum of strontium consists of a number of lines in the red, an orange line rather less refrangible than the sodium line, and a line in the blue; while that of lithium gives a brilliant red line and three fainter lines in the orange, green and greenish blue.

But the Bunsen flame is not at a sufficiently high temperature to volatilize many of the elements. To obtain the spectrum of a metal we cause an electric spark to pass between two pointed pieces of the metal placed close together. The spark tears off from the points small fragments of the metal and volatilizes them. If the spark passes in air, the appearances are complicated by the fact that the gases of which the air is composed are rendered luminous; and we may have as well as the lines due to the metal those due to the incandescent gases.

To obtain the spectrum of a gas it is usually enclosed at very low pressure in a vacuum tube. The central portion of this tube is very narrow. There are terminals sealed through the glass by means of which electric sparks can be made to traverse the tube, which becomes brightly luminous in the capillary portion where it is intensely heated.

118. Spectrum of an incandescent Solid. This

differs from the spectrum of a gas in that it is a continuous band or ribbon of light. It may be seen when the slit of the spectroscope is illuminated by a piece of metal heated white hot. The continuous spectrum of a lamp or gas flame is due to the incandescent particles of solid carbon in the flame. These particles are heated white hot in the process of combustion and emit light of all refrangibilities.

119. Absorption Spectra. Coloured transparent bodies owe their colour to the fact that they absorb and do not transmit certain definite rays of a pencil of white light which may fall on them.

This is easily seen by the following experiments. Form a spectrum of a source of white light such as a gas flame either in the spectroscope or on a screen. Interpose between the light and the slit a piece of ruby glass; only the red light is transmitted, the blue, green and other colours are wanting in the spectrum; similarly a piece of cobalt blue glass transmits only the red and the blue rays, while a solution of bichromate of potash cuts out all but the red and orange. In these cases the substances examined stop all the rays belonging to a considerable portion of the spectrum and appear coloured in consequence. There are other substances which stop certain definite rays, but allow the major portion to pass. If white light be allowed to traverse a thin layer of such a substance and then examined in the spectroscope, the spectrum will be crossed by certain definite dark bands or lines. Thus if a very dilute solution of permanganate of potash be placed in a test tube or small glass cell and interposed between the source of light and the slit, the spectrum is seen to be crossed by five dark bands in the green. A piece of glass coloured with oxide of uranium and interposed, gives a similar but quite distinct spectrum. A dilute solution of blood gives a spectrum which is crossed by two dark bands in the orange and in the yellow green respectively, while the violet portion is wanting altogether; if the blood be deoxidised by a suitable agent the spectrum changes. All these are examples of absorption spectra. Thus, any substance which has a characteristic absorption spectrum can be recognized if it exist in a solution through which light is allowed to pass.

Many gases also have absorption spectra. Put some iodine in a test tube and vapourize it by holding it over a lamp for a short time. Place the tube between the light and the slit of the spectroscope, and a large number of narrow dark bands become visible in the spectrum.

120. Reversal of the spectrum. Obtain a continuous spectrum from a very hot source of white light such as the electric arc. Place a Bunsen burner between the source and the slit, and vapourize some sodium in the flame of the burner so that the white light may traverse the incandescent sodium vapour. A dark absorption band appears in the spectrum and, as was first shewn by Kirchhoff in 1859, this dark band coincides with the yellow line which we have already seen is characteristic of the presence of sodium vapour.

The white light is coming from a source at a higher temperature than that of the glowing yellow vapour of the sodium flame, just that constituent which the sodium flame itself emits is absorbed, and from the beam, the yellow light of the flame is substituted for this, but, being much less bright than the rays on either side from the white source, the line looks black by contrast. If lithium, thallium or other salts be introduced in turn into the flame, black bands appear which coincide in position with the bright bands characteristic of the vapours of these various substances when they are glowing themselves at a higher temperature.

A gas absorbs from the incident light just the rays which it itself emits. If then we allow white light to traverse a mass of unknown gas, and find that there are in the spectrum black absorption bands which coincide with the bright lines emitted by some known substance, we may infer that this substance exists in the gaseous form in the mass of unknown gas. This is the fundamental principle of spectroscopy as it is applied to the sun.

121. The Solar Spectrum. The Solar Spectrum, as described by Newton, is a continuous band of colours. Fraunhofer was the first to notice that when a pure solar spectrum is formed it is crossed by a number of dark absorption bands. These he denoted by the letters of the alphabet $ABCDEFG$, A and B are in the extreme red, C is in the brightest part of the red, D in the yellow orange, E in the yellow green, the brightest part of the spectrum, F in the green, G on the blue violet. He noticed moreover that the dark line D coincided with the bright line of sodium.

Since his time many other dark lines in the solar spectrum have been found to coincide with the bright lines due to various incandescent gases. Thus C, F and G all coincide with lines due to hydrogen, H coincides with a calcium line, A and B with oxygen lines. There are many coincidences with iron lines, magnesium lines, and those of numerous other substances.

Kirchhoff's experiments on the reversal of the lines give the explanation. Light, from a white hot nucleus at the centre of the sun, passes on its way to the earth through various gases and vapours, and the rays which those gases and vapours would themselves emit, if at a high temperature are absorbed. Part of the absorption may be due to the earth's atmosphere, indeed the A and B lines are known to come from that; they vary in appearance with the position of the sun, and the thickness of the atmosphere which the rays have to traverse. The other substances mentioned do not exist in the atmosphere, they must therefore be present in the sun, and hence we infer that there exist in the sun hydrogen, sodium, iron, magnesium and a host of other substances known to us on earth.

122. Colours of bodies. The natural colours of bodies are due in the main to the fact that they only return to the observer certain definite colours out of those which are combined in a beam of white light. Thus a white lily is white because it can return to the eye all the colours in the same proportions as they exist in white light, a red rose only returns red, a blue hyacinth blue. Project a fairly pure spectrum on a screen. Hold a piece of white paper in the spectrum, the paper will appear to be of the same colour as the part of the spectrum which falls on it. Repeat the experiment with a piece of scarlet ribbon or flannel. When in the red part of the spectrum it appears a more vivid red than when seen in white light, when in the green or blue it looks black and colourless. A green leaf shines out brightly in the green, but is quite dark in the red or blue, a blue flower appears black at the red end of the spectrum, but is of a bright blue when the blue rays fall on it.

The object owes its definite colour to the fact that it allows light of that colour to reach the eye and stops the rest.

123. Natural colours due to absorption. Take a glass cell and fill it with a clear solution of copper sulphate. On looking through it at the light the solution appears blue. This we have seen is because it absorbs the red and yellow rays. Place it against a black background and look at it obliquely it appears black, a certain amount of light is reflected from the surface and we may see objects reflected there of their own proper colour, but the solution seen by reflected light is colourless. Drop into the liquid a small quantity of finely powdered chalk, the solution now appears to be of a bright blue colour. Light is reflected from the surfaces of the chalk particles and reaches the observer's eye, but to do so it has traversed a layer of the liquid of greater or less thickness, and, by this passage, the incident white light has been deprived of all its constituents but the blue. The solution derives its colour from light which has lost all rays but the blue by its passage through the liquid to the chalk and back.

It is to this cause that the natural colours of bodies are mostly due. A leaf is green because chlorophyll—the colouring matter it contains—absorbs all but the green rays. Light penetrates a little way into the leaf and reaches our eyes after being scattered from some of the particles in the interior. This light is robbed of all colours but the green by the absorption of the chlorophyll. The colour of the leaf is due to this green light diluted more or less by light reaching us after reflexion at the surface. In the red part of the spectrum the leaf looks black because the red light is at once absorbed by the chlorophyll; there is none reflected from the particles in the interior to the eye.

124. Sensation of Colour—Colour matches. Experiment shews that there are various ways in which we can excite in the eye the sensation of most given colours. Thus, take two circular discs of red and green paper, slit each along a radius up to the centre and place them both on the colour top, described in Section 109 (*d*), slipping one disc partly above and partly beneath the other through the slits, so that part of the disc is green, the other red. Let there be about twice as much red exposed as green. Rotate the top rapidly, the sensations due to the two colours are superposed in the eye and a yellow impression is the result. Hence the sensation of yellow may be produced by a mixture of green and red.

In this way the effect of mixing together different colour impressions may be studied; we can shew, for example, by using three discs that the effect of mixing together red, green, and blue in the proportions of 4, 3, and 3 is to produce a dull grey. If we have two tops or two sets of discs of different sizes, one large, the other small, which fit on to the same top we can make a series of matches; thus a combination of red and green when diluted with a certain amount of white will match a mixture of yellow and blue. Again, two colours are complementary when their mixture produces white; if we divide the rays of the spectrum into any two arbitrary groups and then combine the rays in each group, the two resulting colours will be complementary.

By experiments with the colour top and the like, Maxwell shewed that any colour could be matched to the eye by taking in proper proportion quantities of three principal or primary colours. These principal colours he proved to be red, green and violet. The eye alone cannot tell whether any given colour, such as yellow, is a pure spectral colour or a mixture of two or more of the above.

125. Mixtures of pigments. It must be noted that in the above we are dealing with the effects of mixing colour impressions in the eye, not pigments painted on card. Thus green paint is produced by mixing blue and yellow. This is because the blue paint allows not only the blue to pass, but also a little of the adjacent green, the yellow paint allows yellow light to pass and also some green, but it stops the blue; when blue and yellow are mixed, it is only the green light which can get through, the paint looks green. Ammoniated sulphate of copper transmits the green and all the blue, it looks blue itself. Picric acid is a yellow solution which allows some green to pass. Pass a beam of white light first through the ammoniated copper sulphate, it emerges blue, then through picric acid, it emerges green, the green is the only colour which can pass both, so with the green pigment which arises from a mixture of indigo and gamboge.

126. Theories of colour sensation. It was suggested, first by Young, and afterwards by Helmholtz, that the three principal colours correspond to three primary colour sensations in the eye. The apparent colour of a body will, according to this theory, depend on the proportion in which it excites these sensations. An object looks yellow because it excites the red and the green in the proportion of 2 to 1. It looks blue because it excites the violet sensation and more or less of the green. To produce white the sensations of red, green and violet are excited in the proportions of 2, 3, and 3 approximately. We must distinguish between this theory and the experiments on which it is based. White can be matched by mixing the impressions of red, green and violet in the proportion of 2, 3 and 3, but we do not know that each of these colours corresponds to a single primary stimulus given to the optic nerve.

Other theories as to the cause of colour sensations have been proposed; for an account of these see Foster's *Text-book of Physiology*.

127. Colour Blindness. There are some eyes on which certain colours make no impression; such are called colour-blind. The most common defect consists in a confusion between red, yellow and green. These colours all appear to a colour-blind person as shades of yellow; blue-green tints appear as grey, the blue and violet are called blue. A red object is either black or brown, orange is a light brown verging towards yellow, while green is called a greyish yellow. To such an eye some shades of green can be matched by reds. According to the Young-Helmholtz theory one of the primary sensations—the red—is wanting. If an observer with such an eye were to match a yellow by a mixture of red and green, the best match possible to him would appear a brilliant red to a normal eye. The ordinary colour-blind eye confuses red with green and various shades of grey. To such an eye any colour can be matched by a mixture of two colours with black and white.

A colour-blind person calls the two principal colours yellow and blue, and to him all other colours are more or less saturated compounds of these. According to the Young-Helmholtz theory each of the primary colours excites in the main the one definite set of nerves to which they correspond, but each also stimulates though in a very limited degree the nerves corresponding to the other primary colours. Thus a red colour excites chiefly the red nerves, but to a limited extent also the green and violet; yellow light excites both the green and red nerves and to a limited extent the violet, while green excites chiefly the green nerves, but to a limited degree the red and violet. If then the red nerves are absent, the extreme red of the spectrum will look black, a bright scarlet will excite to a limited extent the green and will be described as a shade of green or greenish grey, yellow will appear as a brighter shade of green, while purple will appear much the same as blue, for the red of the purple produces no impression. Moreover since the yellow green is the brightest part of this spectrum and persons are told by their friends with normal vision that, when they are looking at that colour they are looking at yellow, they call the colour sensation produced in their own eyes yellow, not green, although it is in the main the green nerves which are being stimulated.

The violet sensation is called blue by such persons for a similar reason. Indigo is a brighter colour than violet; a colour-blind person while able to recognize a difference between blue and violet prefers to call it a difference of brightness, not of hue. Violet, owing to the absence of the red nerves, appears as a dark blue, and he gives to his primary sensation of violet the name of blue.

There is another form of colour-blindness, but it is much less common than the above, in which, as we have said, the red sensation is apparently wanting.

The usual method of testing for colour blindness is to ask the person whose eyes are under examination to make a series of matches with variously coloured skeins of wool. The colour-blind eye will make mistakes between grey, greens and some shades of reddish yellow.

128. The Colour box. More accurate tests can be made by means of the colour top with variously coloured discs or by the aid of the colour box by which the spectral colours are themselves mixed.

The principle of this apparatus will be clear on referring to figure 134. VR is a pure spectrum of light coming from a

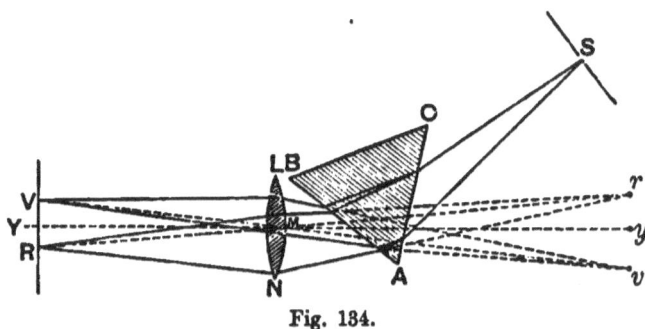

Fig. 134.

slit S; the red rays from S are all brought to a focus at R, suppose now that a slit were placed at R and illuminated with white light, a spectrum would be formed by the prism and the red of that spectrum would be focussed at S. Place a second slit at V; the light from this slit will be dispersed to form a pure spectrum, and since violet rays from S are focussed at V, the violet rays from V will be focussed at S.

Thus if there be two slits at R and V respectively, and these two slits be illuminated with white light, an eye looking through the slit S will receive red light from R, violet light from V, and the two sensations are combined. Similarly by placing a slit in another part of the spectrum VR, and illuminating it with white light, the colour corresponding to this part is brought to a focus at S. The amount of light of any given colour admitted is varied by varying the breadth of the slits, the colours of the lights mixed can be altered by shifting the positions of the slits.

Maxwell's colour box consists of a box in one end of which there is a slit, while an arrangement of prisms and lenses inside form a pure spectrum at the other end. A number of movable adjustable slits are placed at this end, which is turned towards a source of light; by this means the red from one slit, the green from a second and the violet from a third are superposed at the first slit and the effect of mixing these or any other colours can be examined[1].

EXAMPLES.

DISPERSION AND COLOUR.

1. Explain carefully (illustrating your answer by means of a drawing) how you would prove that white light is a mixture of light of various colours, and that the constituents of the light can be recombined to produce the sensation of white light.

2. Describe briefly the constitution of white light. Why does the object glass of a telescope generally consist of a convex and a concave lens of different kinds of glass?

3. An observer places a prism close to his eye in a darkened room and looks at a slit which is illuminated by a lamp, the edge of the prism being parallel to the slit. Describe what he sees, and illustrate your answer by a figure.

4. Explain why a cube of glass can never shew any prismatic separation of the rays. What ought to be the refractive index of a substance that such a separation should just be possible?

5. How would you arrange a lamp, slit, lens, and prism to form a pure spectrum on a screen?

Draw a diagram carefully shewing the path of the light.

6. Sunlight is entering a darkened room through a very narrow vertical crack in the shutter. An observer who can see the crack distinctly looks at it through a prism with its edge vertical. Describe

[1] For further details, see Glazebrook and Shaw, *Practical Physics*, § 68.

what he sees and indicate in a figure the path of the rays to his eyes. How could he produce on the opposite wall a real image corresponding to the one which he sees?

7. Trace a pencil of rays from a slit through a lens and prism arranged to form a pure spectrum on a screen. How would you shew that the light having thus been decomposed by the prism is incapable of further analysis?

8. What changes would be produced in the appearance of the moon at rising and setting if dispersion of light existed in the space between it and the earth?

9. Describe and explain the arrangement of the apparatus required for the production of a pure spectrum of an electric spark. How would you arrange the apparatus so as to examine in detail the light from each portion of the spark, *e.g.*, to compare the spectra from the parts near the two poles respectively?

10. Describe the construction of the spectrometer and the way in which it is used to determine the refractive index of a substance.

Why is it important to arrange the collimator so that the rays proceeding from a point on the slit should be rendered parallel?

11. Describe the optical parts of a spectroscope and shew how a pure spectrum is formed in the focal plane of the eyepiece.

12. The presence of Carbonic Oxide in the blood is indicated in its spectrum by certain dark bands; what apparatus should you require to test for the presence of Carbonic Oxide in a specimen of blood? Draw a figure to indicate how you would set it up.

13. Explain the origin of colour when white light passes through a solution of copper sulphate, and trace the effect of varying the thickness traversed.

14. What are the differences between the spectra (*a*) of an incandescent gas, (*b*) an incandescent solid, (*c*) of the sun? How do you account for these differences?

EXAMINATION QUESTIONS.

I.

1. Give a proof of the statement that light travels in straight lines, and explain how the penumbra in a shadow is formed. The sun shines through a small triangular hole in the window shutter of a darkened room; what is the shape of the patch of light seen on the opposite wall?

2. Distinguish between the "illuminating power of a source of light" and "the intensity of the illumination at a point due to a given light," explaining how they are measured; shew that the latter is inversely proportional to the square of the distance of the point from the source.

3. Describe Bunsen's Photometer and Rumford's Photometer, and explain how to find the candle power of a gas flame by one of them.

4. State the laws of reflexion of light and describe experiments to prove them.

5. What is meant by the image of a luminous point? Distinguish between real and virtual images. Two mirrors are placed at right angles and an object is placed between them; draw a figure giving the position of the images seen with the paths of the rays by which they are each visible.

6. State the laws of refraction, defining carefully the term index of refraction, and give a geometrical construction to determine the path of the refracted ray corresponding to a given incident one. Explain why a stick placed obliquely in water appears bent at the point where it enters the water.

7. Draw figures shewing how light is refracted when passing through (a) a plate, (b) a prism of a transparent substance such as glass.

II.

1. What is meant by the terms, a pencil of rays, direct incidence, principal focus, conjugate foci, axis of a mirror? Shew that the principal focus of a spherical reflecting surface is halfway between the centre of curvature and the surface.

2. Shew how to find the image of a luminous point formed by reflexion at a concave spherical surface.

3. An object is placed in front (1) of a concave, (2) of a convex spherical reflector. Trace the changes in the position of its image as the object is moved from some distance away up to the surface. In case (1) under what circumstances is the image virtual?

4. What is a lens? Shew how to find the image of a luminous point placed near a lens. How would you determine if a given lens were (1) convex, (2) concave?

5. Prove the formula $\frac{1}{v} + \frac{1}{u} = \frac{1}{f}$ for refraction through a convex lens. How would you find the focal length of a convex lens?

6. Describe the eye as an optical instrument, stating what its principal defects are and how they may be remedied.

7. How are lenses combined (1) in a telescope, (2) in a microscope?

8. What is a spectrum? What apparatus do you require, and how would you arrange it to produce a pure spectrum from a gas flame? Give a figure shewing the path of the rays.

III.

1. Prove the formula $\frac{1}{v}+\frac{1}{u}=\frac{2}{r}$ for reflexion at a concave mirror and describe how to find the focal length of such a mirror.

2. Describe the methods of finding the focal length of a convex lens.

3. Trace the rays by which an eye sees the image of an object at a little distance formed (a) by a concave lens, (b) by a convex lens.

4. Describe experiments to illustrate the defects of (a) short-sight, (b) long-sight, (c) astigmatism.

5. What is meant by chromatic aberration? Describe experiments to shew its existence in a convex lens of ordinary glass and to illustrate the method of correcting for it.

6. Describe some methods of combining the colours of the spectrum to produce white light.

7. Explain the cause of the natural colours of bodies.

8. How would you examine the spectrum of blood?

9. Describe an experiment to illustrate the production of the dark lines in the solar spectrum.

ANSWERS TO EXAMPLES IN HEAT.

CHAPTER III. (Page 27.)

4. $11°\frac{1}{4}$ C., $166°·66$ C.   **6.** $37°·7$ C., $4°·4$ C., $-17°·7$ C., $36°·6$ C.
9. $30°$ C., $-17°·7$ C., $-30°$ C., $212°$ F., $14°$ F., $-22°$ F., $160°$ C.   **11.** 144.

CHAPTER IV. (Page 49.)

1. 25·65, ·064, 449°·6 Fah.   **2.** 171·37.   **3.** 99°·42 C.
4. 95, 118·7 grms.   **6.** 20° C.   **7.** 6°·8 C.
8. ·639.   **9.** 48°·9 C.   **10.** 80.
11. 71°·5 C.   **12.** ·0869.   **14.** ·446 lbs.
15. ·0096.   **16.** 83·3.   **17.** 52°. No.   **20.** ·427.
21. (a) $\frac{4.5}{5}$ lbs. are melted, (b) ice is melted and raised to 24° C.
22. 919·5 C.   **23.** 540.   **24.** 80·9.   **25.** 12·38.
27. ·3.   **28.** ·056.   **29.** 1358° C.   **31.** 60° C.
32. ·095.   **33.** 5690.

CHAPTER V. (Page 72.)

1. ·9995 c. ft, 1·0045 c. ft.   **2.** 2·000534 litres.   **3.** 7·733.
4. ·0000167.   **5.** ·2047 ft.   **6.** 79°·8 C.
7. ·181 cm.   **8.** ·928 metre.   **9.** 19°·8 C.
10. ·04212 inch.   **11.** 50·058 sq. cm.   **12.** ·0306 yd.
13. ·991 grm.   **15.** ·184 inch.   **16.** ·0000185.
17. (i) 2·000351 metres, (ii) 2·00234 metres, (iii) 2·0117 metres.
18. ·0000121.   **20.** 12·36 c. inches.   **21** 200117 sq. feet.

ii ANSWERS TO EXAMPLES IN HEAT.

CHAPTER VI. (Page 94.)

1. ·000188.
2. 5·35 grms.
5. ·000150, ·000013.
6. 752·65 mm.
7. 753·25 mm.
8. ·0000076.
9. ·0000095.
10. 29·42 inches.
11. (i) 10·027 c. in. (ii) 10·18 c. in. (iii) 10·9 c. in.
12. 30° C.

CHAPTER VII. (Page 114.)

2. 1330 mm.
3. 345·2 c. in., 577·4 c. in.
5. 19·43 c. ft.
6. 10 c. ft.
9. 41·25 c.cm.
10. $\frac{3}{4}$ c.cm.
11. 131°·8 C.
12. ·878 grm. per litre.
13. 32·74 c.cm.
14. ·00368.
15. 50° C.
16. (i) ·968 litre, (ii) 1·26 litres.
17. (i) 1·366 litres, (ii) ·6336 litre.
18. (i) 1·322 litres, (ii) ·8026 litre.
19. 153 c. in.
20. 29·45 in.
21. 273°·24 C.

CHAPTER VIII. (Page 121.)

8. 200160 ft. lbs.
9. 20 hrs. 5 min.
10. 4·158.
11. (i) 142, (ii) 965.
12. 7·67 grms.

CHAPTER IX. (Page 157.)

1. 90·7 c.cm.
9. ·0958 grm.
10. ·0492 grm.
12. ·559 atmo.
14. (1) lowered nearly $\frac{1}{4}$° C., (2) changed in ratio of 283 to 288.
15. 12·7 mm.
16. ·101 grm.
17. 1318 grms.
18. 99°·43 C.

CHAPTER XI. (Page 176.)

2. 537000 grms.
5. 249200000.
6. 105°·39 C.
8. 1080000.
11. 15.

CHAPTER XIII. (Page 220.)

4. $\frac{1}{3}$ of 1° C.
5. 146 grms.
7. 1402 ft.
8. 0°·1177 C.
9. 2·38 × 10^{14}.
10. 0·237 lb.
11. 0°·033 Fah.
12. 985 ft. lbs.
13. 0·225 lb.
14. 3·138 ft. lbs.

INDEX TO HEAT.

The references are to the pages.

Absolute dilatation, 76; of a liquid, 82; of mercury, 85
Absolute temperature, 103
Absorption of radiation, 197; definition of, 198
Adiathermanous substances, 183
Air-thermometer, 22, 23; construction of, 23; differential, 24; graduation of, 103; forms of, 112
Apparent loss of Energy, 2, 3

Balance wheel of a watch, 69
Barometer readings, corrections to, for expansion, 92
Boiling, or ebullition, 136; under diminished pressure, 139; under increased pressure, 142
Boiling-point, of a liquid, 141; definition of, 141, 142
Boyle's law, 96—98; deductions from, 98; variations from, 100
Bunsen's calorimeter, 45, 46

Calorimeters, 30; ice, 43, 44; of Lavoisier and Laplace, 44, 45; of Bunsen, 45, 46; steam, 47; other forms of, 47, 48
Calorimetry, 29—36
Capacity of a body for heat, 34
Centigrade scale, the, 12
Charles' law, 100, 101
Change of dimensions due to heat, 7
„ of internal stress due to heat, 7

Change of volume, on melting, 117
Chemical change, development of heat by, 120
Chemical effects due to heat, 14
„ action in production of heat, 15
Coefficient of dilatation, definition of, 74; values of, 86, 94
Coefficient of emission, 206
Coefficients of expansion, 62; relation between, 63; density and, 66
Conduction of heat, 160; definition of, 160; experiments on, 161; variable and steady state in, 166; practical effects of, 169; in liquids, 171; in gases, 172
Conductivity, thermal, definition of, 163; rise of temperature and, 164; comparison of, 167; measurement of, 168
Conservation of Energy, 4, 5; historical account of, 6
Constant volume, change of pressure at, 109
Convection of heat, 160; definition of, 160
Convection currents, 173
„ in air, 174
Cooling, law of, 204, 205
Critical temperature, 134; definition of, 135
Cryophorus, the, 144
Cubical expansion, 62; dilatation, 75

Currents, convection, 173

Daniell's Hygrometer, 151
Davy, Sir Humphry, 6; safety-lamp of, 170
Density and coefficients of expansion, 66
Density of water, maximum, 88—90; Hope's experiment, 90
  ,, of ice, 92
Development of heat, by chemical change, 120; by solidification, 120
Dew, formation of, 146
Dew-point, the, 149; definition of, 149; determination of, 150
Diathermanous substances, 183
Dilatation, coefficient of, definition of, 74; and cubical expansion, 75; absolute and relative, 76; of a liquid, 82; of mercury, 85; of a solid, 86; at different temperatures, 86; of water, 88; of gases, 100
Dines' Hygrometer, 151

Ebullition, or boiling, 136; under diminished pressure, 139; under increased pressure, 142
Effects of expansion, 71
Electrical effects due to heat, 14
Electricity and Heat, 15
Emission, coefficient of, 206
  ,, of radiation, 196
Energy, 1, 2; apparent loss of, 2, 3; conservation of, 4, 5
  ,, Kinetic, 2
  ,, Potential, 2
  ,, transformation of, 2
Evaporation, 123; heat required for, 144
Expansion, experiments on, 53, 54; linear, 54, 55; measurement of, 56, 57; micrometer method of measuring, 60, 61; coefficients of, 62; superficial and cubical, 62; linear and cubical, 65; practical consequences of, 67; effects of, 70, 71; of solids, 72; of liquids, 78; of water, 92; of a gas, 215, 219

Experiments, of Joule, 4, 211—214
on vapour pressure, 125—128

Fahrenheit Scale, the, 11, 12
Favre and Silbermann's calorimeter, 49
Fusion, latent heat of, 38; of ice, 39, 40; of a solid, 116; laws of, 121
Freezing mixtures, 120
  ,, machines, 145

Galileo, inventor of thermometer, 16
Gas, work done by expansion of, 215, 219
Gases, dilatation of by heat, 100; laws connecting pressure, volume and temperature of, 107, 108; conduction of heat in, 172
Graduation of air-thermometer, 103
Graham's mercurial pendulum, 68

Harrison's gridiron pendulum, 68
Heat, nature of, 1; effects of, 7; electrical and chemical effects of, 14; sources of, 14; chemical action in production of, 15; electricity and, 15; a physical quantity, 29; unit quantity, 29, 30; measurement of a quantity of, 31; specific, 32; definition of, 34; capacity of a body for, 34; relation between specific and capacity, 34; dilatation of gases by, 100; development of by chemical change and solidification, 120; conduction of, 160; convection of, 160; radiation of, 160; rate of loss of, 206
Heat and Work, 3
Heat-energy, nature of, 4
Hope's experiment, 90
Hot-water apparatus, 174
Humidity, relative, 149; definition of, 150
Hygrometer, Daniell's, 151; Regnault's, 152; Dines', 153; simple, 156

Hygrometry, 146
Hypsometry, 142, 143

Ice, latent heat of fusion of, 39, 40; density of, 92
Ice calorimeters, 43, 44; of Lavoisier and Laplace, 44, 45; of Bunsen, 45, 46
Intensity of radiation, 190; definition of, 191
Inverse square, law of the, 192; experimental evidence of, 194

J, determination of by friction, 214, 215; Mayer's method, 217
Joule's experiments, 4, 211–214

Kinetic Energy, 2

Laplace's calorimeter, 44, 45
Latent heat, of fusion, 38; of vaporization, 40, 41
Lavoisier's calorimeter, 44, 45
" method, 58
Law, Boyle's, 96—98; deductions from, 98; variations from, 100; of the inverse square, 192; experimental evidence for, 194
Law of cooling, 204, 205
Laws of fusion, 121
" Dalton's, 131
Linear expansion, 54, 55
Linear and cubical expansion, 65
Liquids, expansion of, 78; absolute dilatation of, 82; definition of boiling-point of, 141, 142; conduction of heat in, 171
Loss of Energy, apparent, 2, 3

Maximum density of water, 88
Mayer's method, 217
Measurement, of heat, 31; of expansion, 56, 57
Mechanical Work, 5
Melting-point, 116
" " and pressure, relation between, 118
Mercury, absolute dilatation of, 85
Mercury thermometer, construction of, 17, 18; graduation of, 21; compared with other thermometers, 21
Mercurial pendulum, Graham's, 68
Metallic thermometers, 70
Metals, specific heat of, 35
Method of cooling, 207
Micrometer method of measuring expansion, 60, 61
Mixtures, freezing, 120
Molecules, 6

Nature of heat-energy, 4
Novum Organum, the, 6

Pendulum, Graham's mercurial, 68; Harrison's gridiron, 68
Potential Energy, 2
Pressure, of a gas, 107; change of at constant volume, 109; relation between melting point and, 118; of vapours, 123, 124; of water vapour, 128
Prevost's theory, 207—209
Propagation, rectilinear, 192

Quantity of Heat, 29; measurement of, 31

Radiant energy, 178; transmission of, 182; reflection of, 186; refraction of, 189
Radiating power, 191; definition of, 192
Radiation, 178; means of measuring, 180; intensity of, 190; emission of, 196; absorption of, 197; reflection of, 202, 203
Radiation of heat, 160; definition of, 161
Rate of loss of heat, 206
Réaumur's Scale, 12
Rectilinear propagation, 192
Reflection of radiant energy, 186
" " radiation, 202, 203
Refraction of radiant energy, 189
Regelation, 119
Regnault's Hygrometer, 152
Relative dilatation, 76
" humidity, 149

Safety-lamp, the Davy, 170
Scale, the Fahrenheit, 11, 12; Réaumur's, 12
Scales of temperature, 11, 12; comparison of, 12
Simple hygrometers, 12
Solidification, development of heat by, 120
Solids, expansion of, 72; dilatation of, 86; fusion of, 116
Sources, of Heat, 14, 15; of error, 61, 84, 85
Specific Heat, 32, 207; of metals, 35
Steam calorimeter, the, 47
Substances, diathermanous and adiathermanous, 183
Superficial and cubical expansion, 62

Temperature, change of, 8; definition of, 8, 9; scales of, 11; of a gas, 107
Temperatures, comparison of, 9
Thermometer, description of, 10; fixed points of, 10, 11, 19, 20; history of, 16; boiling point of, 19, 20; special form of, 25—27
,, the Mercury, construction of, 17, 18; graduation of, 21; comparison with other thermometers, 21
,, the Air, 22, 23; construction of, 23; the differential, 24; graduation of, 103
,, Rutherford's maximum and minimum, 25

Thermometer, the clinical, 26
,, Six's, 26; metallic, 70; weight, 81
,, wet and dry bulb, 154
Thermal conductivity, definition of, 163; rise of temperature and, 164; measurement of, 168
Trade Winds, the, 175
Transformation of Energy, 2
Transmission, of Heat, 160; of radiant energy, 182

Unit quantity of Heat, 29, 30
Unsaturated vapours, 131

Values of coefficients of dilatation, 94
Vapours, pressure of, 123, 124; experiments on, 125—128; Dalton's laws for, 131; unsaturated, 131; and gases, 134
Ventilation, 175
Volume, relation between pressure and, of a gas, 107; change of, on melting, 117

Water, dilatation of, 88; maximum density of, 88; expansion of, 92
,, equivalent of a body, 34
,, vapour, pressure of, 128
Watch, balance wheel of, 69
Weight thermometer, the, 81
Winds, the Trade, 175
Work and Energy, 1
,, and Heat, 3

ANSWERS TO EXAMPLES IN LIGHT.

CHAPTER I. (Page 20.)

6. Approximately 10 to 1.

CHAPTER III. (Page 48.)

6. 45°.   7. 60°.

CHAPTER IV. (Page 83.)

1. $\frac{2}{3}$ of the thickness.   9. $3\frac{1}{3}$ cm.

CHAPTER V. (Page 107.)

7. 8 in. diameter; 6 ft. behind the mirror.
8. 2 ft. Real.   9. $3\frac{3}{4}$ in.; 1 in.
12. Sizes, 3 in., 1 in., $\frac{3}{7}$ in., $\frac{1}{3}$ in.; distances, 18 in., 9 in., $7\frac{1}{5}$ in., 6 in.
13. $\frac{1}{2}$ in., 5 in.
14. $12\frac{1}{11}$ cm. from the concave mirror, $\frac{1}{11}$ cm. high.
15. On a line perpendicular to axis and 1 ft. from centre.
16. ·157 feet.

CHAPTER VI. (Page 136.)

1. 18 in. behind the lens; $\frac{1}{2}$ in. long.
2. 2 ft. behind the lens; 1 in. diameter.
4. (a) 6 ft. behind the lens, (b) 2 ft. in front of the lens.
5. 4 in.   7. 8 in. in front of the lens, $\frac{1}{3}$ in. diameter.

ANSWERS TO EXAMPLES IN LIGHT.

9. $2\frac{1}{4}$ in. behind the lens, $\frac{3}{16}$ in.
10. Lens 30·5 ft. from screen, slide 6·1 in. from lens.
12. 10 in. from lens.   13. As 1 to 7.
14. (a) $16\frac{2}{3}$ in. in front of the concave lens, (b) 110 in. behind the convex lens.
17. $2\frac{2}{11}$ ft.   21. 1·2 in. from the surface.
22. 2 ft. in front of the lens; 6 in. high.
26. $2\frac{2}{3}$ in. in front of the lens.

CHAPTER VIII. (Page 177.)

1. A concave lens 2 ft. in focal length.   2. 6.
3. The second.   5. Concave, $5\frac{1}{2}$ in.   6. 10 ft.
7. $2\frac{3}{4}$ in.   9. $2\frac{11}{14}$ in.   11. 5.

INDEX TO LIGHT.

The references are to the pages.

Aberration, chromatic, 192
" of the stars, 24
Absorption spectra, 195
Analysis, spectrum, 193
Angle, critical, definition of, 61
Astigmatism, 149
Astronomical Telescope, the, 160
Axis of a mirror, 87

Bench, the optical, 17—19
Blindness, colour, 200, 201
Bodies, luminous and non-luminous, 3; colours of, 197
Bunsen's Photometer, 17

Calculations, methods of, 99
Camera Lucida, the, 166, 167
" Obscura, the, 140
" the Photographic, 141
Candle power, 15
Caustics formed by reflexion, 106
Centre of curvature of a mirror, 86
" (optical) of a lens, 114
Chromatic aberration, 192
Colour blindness, 200, 201
" box, the, 202, 203
" matches, 198, 199
" sensation of, 198, 199
" -sensation, theories of, 200
Colours, re-combination of, 181; of bodies, 197; due to absorption, 198
Compound Microscope, the, 165
Concave lenses, 113, 120, 121; measurements with, 128

Concave mirror, 91, 92
Convergent rays, image formed by, 104
Convex lenses, 113, 122; measurements with, 126
" mirror, 92; formula for, 94
Critical angle, definition of, 61

Defects of vision, 148, 149; experiments on, 150
Deviation caused by refraction, 60
Dispersion, experiments on, 180; in lenses, 190
Distinct vision, least distance of, 153

Eclipses, 10
Experimental verifications of formulæ, 100, 101, 127
Experiments, with mirrors, 85; with lenses, 116; on the eye, 145—148; on defects of vision, 150; on vision through lenses, 174—176; with a prism, 178, 179; on dispersion, 180
Eye, description of, 142—144; experiments on, 145—148

Fizeau's method, velocity of light, 25, 26
Focal length of a mirror, 87; positive and negative, 116
" " of a lens, 114
Focus, principal, of a mirror, 87, 89

INDEX TO LIGHT.

Focus, principal, of a lens, 114
Formation of shadows, 8, 9
Forms of lenses, 118
Formula for a concave mirror, 93
  ,,   for a convex mirror, 94
Formulae, connected with a lens, 131; with direct refraction at a spherical surface, 133
Foucault's method, velocity of light, 27, 28

Galileo's telescope, 162
Geometrical construction, applied to optical problems, 37
  ,,   image of a point, 80, 87
  ,,   representation of the law of refraction, 55
Graphical methods of solution, 29, 90

Illuminating power of a source of light, 10; definition of, 11
Illumination, intensity of, 11; definition of, 12
Image of a point formed by direct refraction, 75, 120; formed by reflection in a concave mirror, 91
  ,,   formed by convergent rays, 104
Images, 33; definitions of, 34—36; multiple, 47, 48; formed by a lens, 119
Intensity of illumination, 11; definition of, 12
Inverse square, law of the, 13, 14; experimental verification of, 19

Kaleidoscope, the, 46

Lantern, the optical, 139
Lateral inversion, 39
Law of the inverse square, 13, 14; experimental verification of, 19
Laws of reflexion, verification of, 31, 32
  ,,   of refraction, 53; geometrical representation of, 55; experiments on, 58
Lenses, 112; definition of, 113; thin, 115; experiments with, 116; forms of, 118; images formed by, 119; concave, 113, 120, 121; convex, 113, 122; vision through, 129; formulæ connected with, 131; special problems with, 132; simple microscope, 159; experiments on vision through, 174, 175; dispersion in, 190
Light, nature of, 3, 28; terms used in connection with, 4; rays of, 5; rectilinear propagation of, 6, 7; velocity of, 21—24; reflexion of, 30; at plane surfaces, 40—44
Long-sight, or *hypermetropia*, 149
Luminous bodies, 3
  ,,   points, 38

Magnification, measurement of, 103
Magnifying power of a mirror, 96; definition of, 96
Measurement, of the radius of a mirror, 102; of magnification, 103; with convex lenses, 126; with concave lenses, 128
Methods of calculation, 99
Microscope, the simple, 156; the compound, 165
Microscope lenses, simple, 159
Mirror, luminous points reflected in, 38; experiments with, 85; centre of curvature of, 86; spherical, 86; axis of, 87; concave, 91, 93; convex, 92; formula for, 94; magnifying power of, 96
Mixtures of pigments, 199
Multiple images, 47, 48
  ,,   reflexions, experiments on, 45

Natural colours due to absorption, 198
Nature of Light, 3, 28
Non-luminous bodies, 3

Observations on refraction, 69, 70
Ophthalmoscope, the, description of, 170, 171
Optical bench, the, 17—19
  ,,   lantern, the, 139
  ,,   medium, 4

Parallel rays, 88, 106
Photographic Camera, the, 141
Photometer, Rumford's, 16; Bunsen's, 17
Photometry, 15
Pigments, mixtures of, 199
Point, image of a, formed by direct refraction, 75; geometrical image of, 80, 87; formed by reflexion in a concave mirror, 91
Principal focus, 87, 88, 114
Prism, refraction through, 68; experiments with, 178, 179; path of rays through, 182
Problems with lenses, 132
Propagation of light, rectilinear, 6, 7

Radius of a mirror, measurement of, 102
Rays, of light, 5; parallel, 88; convergent, 104; parallel, 106
Re-combination of colours, 181
Rectilinear propagation of light, 6, 7
Reflecting telescopes, 163
Reflexion, laws of, verification of, 31, 32; caustics formed by, 106
Reflexion of light, 30; definition of, 30; at plane surfaces, 40—44, 84; total, 60
Refraction, simple experiments on, 49—52, 70—74; laws of, 53; geometrical representation of, 55; experiments on, 58; deviaticn caused by, 60; through a plate of a transparent medium, 67; through a prism, 68; observations on, 69, 70; at spherical surfaces, 109, 111
Refractive Index, 53
Reversal of the Spectrum, 196
Rumford's Photometer, 16

Sensation of colour, 198, 199; theories of, 200

Sextant, the, description of, 167, 168
Shadows, formation of, 8, 9
Short-sight, or *myopia*, 148, 149
Signs, convention as to, 89
Solar spectrum, the, 196, 197
Solutions, graphical, 90
Source of light, illuminating power of, 10
Spectacles, 154, 155
Spectrometer, description of, 169; path of rays through, 189
Spectrum, production of, 186, 187, 189; of an incandescent gas, 194; of an incandescent solid, 194; absorption, 195; reversal of, 196; the Solar, 196, 197
Spectrum analysis, 193
Spherical mirrors, 86, 107
„ surfaces, refraction at, 109—111
Stars, aberration of, 24

Telescope, 159; the astronomical, 160; Galileo's, 162; reflecting, 163
Terms used in connection with light, 4
Theories of colour sensation, 200
Total reflexion, 60; experiments on, 61—63; conditions for, 63; consequences of, 65, 66

Velocity of light, 21—24; Fizeau's method, 25, 26; Foucault's method, 27, 28; graphical methods of solution, 29
Verification of the laws of reflexion, 31, 32
Verifications, experimental, 100, 101
Vision, defects of, 148, 149; experiments on, 150; binocular, 151; experiments on—through lenses, 174—176
Vision through a lens, 129

www.ingramcontent.com/pod-product-compliance
Lightning Source LLC
Chambersburg PA
CBHW032008300426
44117CB00008B/939